A
PLACE
AT THE
TABLE

A
PLACE
AT THE
TABLE

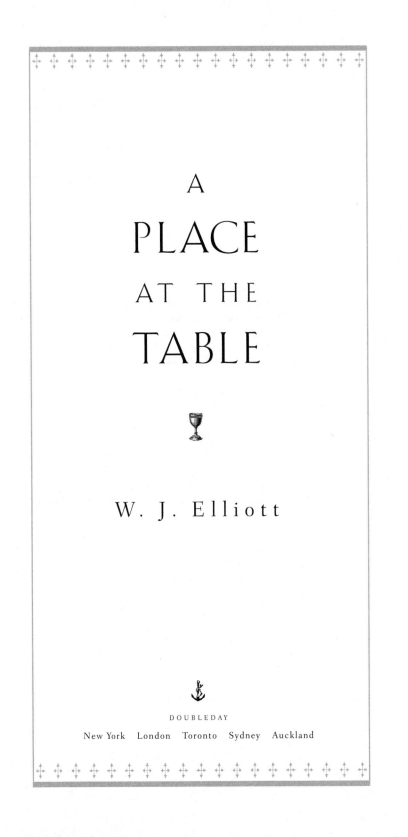

W. J. Elliott

DOUBLEDAY

New York   London   Toronto   Sydney   Auckland

PUBLISHED BY DOUBLEDAY
a division of Random House, Inc.
1540 Broadway, New York, New York 10036

DOUBLEDAY and the portrayal of an anchor with a dolphin are trademarks of
Doubleday, a division of Random House, Inc.

Book design by Donna Sinisgalli

The Library of Congress Cataloging in Publication Data
Elliott, W. J.
A Place at the Table / W.J. Elliott.—1st ed.
p. cm.
Includes bibliographical references and index.
1. Jesus Christ—Person and offices. 2. Religious leaders—United States—
Interviews. I. Title.
BT203.E55 2002
232—dc21   2002019254

ISBN 0-385-50234-6

PRINTED IN THE UNITED STATES OF AMERICA

February 2003

First Edition

1   3   5   7   9   10   8   6   4   2

ACKNOWLEDGMENTS

This book is as much of a love story as anything. As I say in my introduction "writing for me is soul work" and "It's attrition. It's war. It's love." In many ways, this book (and even myself) is a product of those close to me. At this moment I am reminded of Jesus, who stumbled while carrying his cross. That is why I write these acknowledgments. I, too, have stumbled while bearing my cross (as we all do), and often there was a friend to help steady me.

My soul rejoices at the thought of my dearest friend, Elizabeth Bonnie Milgrim, who loved and supported me through this wonderful-crazy time of etching my heart upon these and other pages.

I am indebted to Mort Mortenson, whose assistance, friendship, and great faith gave me the support I needed while I worked on this book. And also Tellurian UCAN and Mike Florek for their support.

I am grateful to Jane Alden, whose sensitive and kind heart welcomed me into her life and the life of her friends Gigi, Jane Alden, Sr., Charlotte, Calvin, Tommy, and Claire.

My sisters Mary and Liz, who supported me in many ways during the writing of this book because I am their brother and they love me. My sister Diane (who did a good job of raising me after my parents died); my brother Jim the (ex) Chicago cop, who taught me that stories are works of art, and that simple, direct questions cut through presumptuous self-deception. And our big brother, Ed, whose presence is always among us.

Trace Murphy, a great editor and friend. Thanks Siobhan Dunn, Frances Jones for the copyediting, and my agent, Claudia Cross.

Pat McBride, who gave the kind of feedback I needed from a friend—he took this work to heart, and was critical yet loving. Mark Sweet, Mark Hottman, and Angela Smith, who read my book and encouraged me when I wasn't sure it was any good. Mike Bernarde, Andy Moore, Henry Brockman, Rich Beilfuss, Bones, Michael Blatnick, and Jim Kramlinger. Roger

Peasley and Julie Alexander, who did the transcriptions. Don Shmauz, who has helped me in special ways throughout the years. And J.

To each of you who have touched my life in many different ways: Sue Joy, Fran, Janice DuRose, Dave DuRose, Dr. "Kak" Dorgan, Ursula Hermacinski, Jeff, Alison and Eli, Robin Daley, Dooley, Dan Doden, Karin Elstad, Roget, Lex, Nurunisa and Bill, Mickey and Marv, Jared, Derrick, Marge Rolfing, Judith Estrin, Michelle Prentice, Phil Hopkins, Betsy and Len, and Bill, Bob Schwartz, Teri Page, Ed Anderson, John and Teri, Steve Stein, Dave Phillips, Pam White, Pat Esch, Ernie of E&S Auto, Jeff and Karen, Cindy, Kevin and Amy. The Tuesday morning group: Skip, Doug, Bill Y., Bill, Bob and Dee and Brad.

To the gang at Ground Zero Coffee Shop (Lindsey, the owner; Amanda, Jill, Susan, Elle, Sigrid, Sara, Jeremy, Connor, Drew Griffin, Matt, Eric) who always made me feel welcome as I spent hours which turned into years sitting in the corner chair. And by the way, I've also had numerous exquisite triple espressos (over ice) at Mother Fools, Ancora, the Coffee Gallery and Victor Allen's Coffee shops.

My friends Atum O'Kane, and Martin Zahir of the Zenith Institute, whose tour to Israel showed me the spiritual places within as well as without.

To Chokyi Nyima (Chokling Tersar Foundation) and Matt Flickstein (The Forest Way Retreat Center) whose spiritual friendship helped me remember who I am.

St. Benedict's Monastery: Brother Bill, Theophane the monk, Father Keating, Father Joseph, Sara and your mom, Pat Johnson. Anna Marie (you owe me spaghetti and meatballs), Peter and Cindy.

Past and future indebtedness to all the people who I hope will be in Book 2 like the Pope, the Dalai Lama, and Margaret Starbird. Thanks to Quickverse for their wonderful Bible software. And of course my nieces and nephews: Ed, Laura, Barb, Rebecca, Jeff, Keith, Pat, Jen, Shannon, Chris, Jimmy, Jack, Jill, Jessie, and Ty.

I am grateful to the founding fathers and mothers of this country who set the table of freedom, allowing for the free exchange of ideas and expression contained in this book.

And finally, to my mother, who manifested Jesus' heart and showed me how to rest in God's Presence; and my father, who instilled in me the ruthless pursuit of truth and the ability to sniff out the BS.

CONTENTS

For Jesus and those who seek Truth

1
THE BEGINNING

Do you remember the day your parents' world died in you, and the day you began making your own life?

I do.

For me, it was twenty-seven years ago, I was twelve years old and three things stand out in my mind. I remember the quiet, I remember my breathing, and I remember my praying hands upon her head as she died.

We had been watching television when my mother passed out. I ran into the kitchen and grabbed the phone.

"Billy," her weak voice called out, "come here."

I dropped the phone and ran back to her.

"Help me into the living room," she said softly.

I helped her stand up, and supported her as we walked into the living room.

"There . . ." she said, pointing to the couch.

We almost didn't make it because with each step, she got weaker and her body got heavier. My arms held her as she slumped onto the couch and I cushioned her fall. I laid her head gently on the pillow and stood back. Above her, a painting of *The Last Supper* hung on the wall. It was huge, four feet across, and three feet high with a frame that was thick, carved, and painted gold. My mother's favorite painting was looking down at us and bearing witness.

In the painting, Jesus stood in the center of the twelve apostles. He held a chalice high above his head.

He was praying.

I looked down at my mother and realized she was dying. I placed my hands on her head.

I started praying.

I remembered the miracles of Jesus. I believed in miracles. I actually thought I had a good shot at one because my father had died six months before, my mother was a good Christian, and I was an altar boy. If I wasn't due a miracle, who was?

I put every ounce of soul I had into bringing her back to life.

My mother died.

I was just a kid then and home alone with my mother. When my father died, I came through it okay because I never talked to him much anyway. The only thing I remembered about him was that he spent the evenings in front of the fireplace with one foot up on the ledge, poking and prodding the glowing embers with a blackened, ashen poker.

I didn't live in his world—instead, I lived in the world of my mother. She was a Christian who went to church every morning, and often took me with her. She taught me that God was my friend, and like I said, that world died twenty-seven years ago under a painting of *The Last Supper.*

A few days later, when I asked the parish priest why my parents had to die, he replied, "It was God's will."

The day we buried my mother, my family gave the picture of *The Last Supper* to my mother's best friend.

Twenty-seven years later, I met with my editor at Doubleday. We went for a walk in the park and I handed him my first novel. I was excited and eagerly awaited his reaction, but without looking at it, he suggested a different book, a book about Jesus. He didn't look at me when he made that suggestion, instead he looked at the scenery while we walked. I'm glad he didn't see my face, because he would have seen my "crazy Elliott face." My brother, a Chicago cop like my father, was on the force for thirty-six years. He's been punched, shot, and stabbed. Whenever I tell my brother something he doesn't like, his jaw tightens, his eyes bulge and then roll around in their sockets. I call it "the crazy Elliott face."

If my editor had looked at me when he suggested the Jesus book, he would have seen my eyes roll around in my head just like my brother's. For a moment, I was angry, perhaps a little crazy. But then I thought about Jesus, and remembered how he had turned over the tables in the Temple. He was angry that day, a little crazy, and the world was never the same. Who knows, maybe his eyes even bulged out a little, and I'm sure his disciples probably knew that look and got out of his way whenever they saw it. I took a deep breath and thought about it. A book about Jesus? *Wouldn't that be a book about Christianity?*

I tossed the idea into the well of my soul and waited. Not a sound. Not a splash. Not a single ripple. That told me that my soul had no interest in writing a book about Christianity. Because for me, *writing is soul work.* It comes from the heart, and more than the heart, it comes from the guts. It takes everything I've got and more to write a book. It's attrition. It's war. It's love. It's an endeavor that I can only finish if I have soul on my side and passion in my heart.

You see, Christianity had become irrelevant in my life. It had failed me twenty-seven years ago when my parents died. And now, when my editor suggested I write a book about Jesus, something in me felt like the way that fire must have felt when my father poked and prodded it. Irritated. Enraged. Glowing.

Yet, at the same time, I felt nothing. I felt like the ashes my father had swept aside. Spent. Burnt up. Lifeless.

No, I thought. I wanted nothing to do with this book.

When I was a kid, I got up early on Saturday mornings to watch cartoons. I always made two stops on my way to the television.

First, I stopped in the kitchen and grabbed a turkey baster. Then I went to the back door and grabbed a quart of chocolate milk, which was delivered every Saturday morning by the milkman. I spent the rest of the morning happily rocking in my chair and watching cartoons. Every ten rocks or so, I'd squirt a turkey baster full of chocolate milk into my mouth. That was heaven—*rocking, squirting,* and *watching.*

The fireplace was next to the television, and one morning, I got up even before the sun came up. In the morning's darkness, I was surprised to see that a single ember still burned in the center of the fireplace.

Twenty-seven years later, I awoke before dawn with images from a dream still in my head: a dream about different blocks that moved and switched places with each other. On each block was a phrase about Jesus, and they were trying to fit together. Daybreak slowly revealed to me what I already knew. *I had to write the Jesus book.*

"You Elliotts are all the same," my sister-in-law had once said. "You get an idea in your head and you can't let it go."

Now, she's not always right about everything but she was right about this. I realized I was compelled, as though something or someone poked and prodded at me from within until I agreed. On that day, I caught a glimpse of my torturer—a single, smoldering ember from some long ago fire. As I breathed life into it—it glowed ever brighter until the anger came, and as the anger grew it threatened to destroy everything in its path. For a moment, and longer than a moment I might add, I wanted to destroy every-thing about Christianity because twenty-seven years ago it had failed me so badly that I had to stop being a kid like other kids and instead go on a long and painfully confusing journey that brought me to the brink of suicide and death.

Eighteen years ago, at the age of twenty-one I had had enough of life. I now realize that I didn't really want to die, it's just that I didn't want to live the way I was living. I didn't know why I hated and loathed myself so much—but I did, and after months of trying to erase the self-hate through smoking pot, watching television, and trying on every other distraction I could find—the answer became obvious. *It was time to die.*

Each night, over a period of months, I prayed for God to kill me. As soon as my head hit the pillow, my prayer began.

"Please, God . . ." I pleaded, "I know I'm only twenty-one years old—but I'm tired. I've had and seen enough of this life. Please let me die. Please!"

But no matter how much I prayed, no matter how much I cried out during my nightly torture and no matter how much I begged God to kill me—my prayers were never answered. What kind of God was this? When I prayed for a happy life—I was denied. Now when I prayed for death—I was denied again. What did God want from me? Why was I left in this hell—this place that was neither alive, nor dead?

Since God wasn't killing me fast enough, I decided to kill myself. I had discovered that there was something in me that felt tight as though it were grasping on to life. Maybe if I could just let go of this holding that would be enough to sever the cord that kept me attached to life? Thus my nightly attempts at ending my life began.

I would start by lying in bed and imagining myself as a corpse. Then I would let go of my connection to my life systematically by letting go of my body, my emotions, and my thoughts. I thought that if I could just disconnect from those three things, then perhaps my breathing would simply stop and I would die. This detachment was made even easier when I saw how I had suffered because of possessing those three things.

I had that fantasy many times, and then one night I went deeper—actually "I" shouldn't say I did it—*it just happened*. I went deeper than my body, my emotions, my thoughts, and I found myself in a place where I was immersed in God. Immediately, I realized that God had always been with me, though I hadn't been aware of it. My experience was like one of those comic strips where the characters are playing hide-and-go seek. In the first picture there's someone hiding in a dark closet and the person thinks he or she is alone and all you see is one set of eyes in the dark. Then in the next picture you see another set of eyes in the dark with the individual and the person realizes he or she is not alone in the dark. That's how it felt when I realized I wasn't alone—and *actually had never been alone*. I was filled with the knowledge that without a doubt, God had loved me, and had loved all of us, since the beginning—and even before the beginning, and throughout our lives. Since I was faced with—and experienced—the all-encompassing love of God, I just had to ask the most natural of questions.

"Why the hell are you screwing me over in life?"

The answer came back to me—not in words but in a conveyed feeling—"If you sincerely try, we will show you."

After that experience of God's presence, my whole life changed. Looking back on it—the term "born again" could have applied *because I was starting over from a place of spirit*. I still had all the same fears, thoughts, emotions, and depression that I'd had before, but now whenever I encountered them—I would take a deep breath and remember God's presence and that I was loved. Then I'd walk through the fear and realize that that fear had been *a creation of my own mind*.

Most important, I had experienced that I, along with all human beings are born from a place of love—and we are born into a world accompanied by love—not abandoned. I now understood the meaning of the Gospel of

John's words that the true Light had "lighteth every man that cometh into the world" (John 1:9, King James Version).

Whereas before I had been living my life from a place of feeling forsaken (and thus I had experienced Jesus' words *"Eloi, Eloi, lama sabachthani?"*—which means, "My God, my God, why have you forsaken me?" [Mark 15:34, NIV]), I could now start anew, knowing I had been conceived and always lived in the midst of love, not fear. In meaning, not meaninglessness. In the presence of Spirit, and not abandoned or forsaken.

I spent many years after that traveling and trying to understand what I had experienced. Gradually I found a deeper peace, wisdom, and relationship with God—but not through Christianity—through other religions like Buddhism, Hinduism, and Sufism, and also through psychology and psychotherapy.

So when my soul finally decided to pick up a pen and begin this book, my first inclination was to use the pen as a knife, cutting and ripping away all the faded and dusty fabric Christianity had at one time tried to comfort me with. But as I threw off the robes of my religion, I saw Jesus watching me off in the distance and his manner seemed to ask, *"What have those robes to do with me?"*

It was then that I realized that twenty-seven years ago, when my world died under a picture of *The Last Supper*, it was my understanding of Christianity that failed me—not Jesus—and between he and I stood a labyrinth of interpretation and teaching that was two thousand years in the making.

I had been told my whole life that Jesus was the ideal human being, and if this was true, then I wanted to know all of who he was, and not just what *they* wanted to tell me. Without being too paranoid, who were *they* anyway? Who were *they* who had interpreted Jesus' life for me? What mistakes had they made in their interpretations? What did they leave out? And what did they put in? Who was he? And what was his relationship to me?

In hindsight, I realized that Jesus had always been too much a part of me to ignore. I grew up with Jesus, and our lives were intertwined in the same way that a vine grows around a trellis. While I had often tried to ignore and reject my Christian roots as many people do, I couldn't really separate Jesus from who I am without injuring myself. That kind of rejection only leads to a resentment and anger that never die.

Thus, there was only one way to be free.

Forgiveness.

I am on a search to find the real Jesus, so that I can accept myself and forgive others. Jesus said, "I no longer call you servants, because a servant does not know his master's business. Instead, I have called you friends, for everything that I learned from my Father I have made known to you."[1]

In my search for Jesus, I'm looking for my friend, not my master.

I want to meet a Jesus I can wrestle with. Someone to argue and fight with. Someone I can play with. A man I can love.

I want to meet a Jesus I can lie down at night in the desert with, and looking up, see the same stars together. I want to scoop up handfuls of earth with him and watch it trickle through our fingers. I want to see the fear in his eyes as he felt his life slip away, and see the love and excitement he had for life in those very same eyes. I want to see the joy and profound awe in his face that came from witnessing the birth of a child. I want to be there to see the bitter disappointment in his tightened jaw after the death of his friend Lazarus. I want to cry with him, laugh with him, and live like him. I want to use my anger like him. I want to turn over the tables of ignorance and lies that I had been told and have told myself. I want to turn them over in the house of God: to reveal the false prophets, their empty teachings, and the fear that underlies all ignorance and deceit. Most of all, I want to ruthlessly pursue him, and experience what he experienced, and thereby make it *my experience—and our experience.*

Why?

Because Jesus was my brother, and *The Last Supper Is Always Now.*

2
SETTING THE TABLE

How do I start looking for a man who died over two thousand years ago? I didn't know where to start. Then I remembered something my brother, the Chicago police detective, had said.

---

1. John 2:15.

"At the scene of a crime," my brother told me, "a detective shows up. They interview everybody. Usually somebody knows who did it. If not, you got to hit the road. You got to stay on the road, and if one guy won't tell you what you need to know, then you got to let go and go to the next guy."

I figured that was easy enough. I would just track down those who might have clues—scholars, evangelists, and mystics. In a way, I'd set a table and invite all of Jesus' friends. They would bring whatever Truth they valued most to the supper, and then whoever read this book would par-take—taking whatever food he or she needed.

I decided to hit the road, and go wherever I had to go in order to get at the Truth.

First I took names. I went to libraries and bookstores—*I asked around.* It took me a few months, but I made a list of the people I wanted to inter-view and where they lived. Then I took two small maps out of my desk drawer and with a black felt marker I sketched my way around the world. Afterward, I sat back in my chair and breathed a sigh of relief.

That was easy. In a matter of seconds, or minutes, my mind had imag-ined the project's beginning and its end. *But actually doing it* was going to be a long and tough road. Nobody else was going to do it either—it would be me.

My chest tightened and my stomach swelled with anxiety, while my mind ran itself in circles and I imagined all of the problems I would en-counter. I was immobilized. But then I closed my eyes and remembered the presence of God. That gave me enough strength to get up out of the chair, walk over to the phone, and call my mother's best friend, Teresa. We had given her the painting of *The Last Supper* after my mother died. When I tried to phone her, I found out that she had died a year ago. I was given the phone number of Teresa's daughter, Jody. So I called her.

"Your mother's painting is hanging in my living room—above the couch," Jody said. "But my mother told me that one day you would be com-ing for it—*so it's yours.*"

✥ 3
DRIVING SOUTH

My first wave of requests for interviews had been sent out a month or two before. Since my first book, *Tying Rocks to Clouds,* had some success, I figured it would be easier getting interviews—*it wasn't.*

I had forgotten how much time it took tracking down people. Many of the mystics were in seclusion and they were hard to find, and since their retreats were often silent ones, it was tough communicating with them. The well-known evangelists were busy speaking on television and seemed a bit evasive whenever I tried to contact them—as though they didn't trust my motives.

"We have *Time, Newsweek,* and the *New York Times* calling," I was told. "They're before you."

One famous evangelist said he was too busy to do an interview about Jesus and then that night I saw him on network television debating with a rock star whom he thought was immoral. It was at that moment that I remembered what I had so conveniently forgotten. The rejections! The endless rejections. And after the rejections the despair. At that point I had to be reminded by friends (who remembered what I went through writing my first book) that this was part of the process.

Now the scholars, they were much different than I had imagined. Their willingness and accommodation helped strengthen my otherwise dwindling faith. They didn't have personal assistants who intercepted me; instead they answered the phone themselves and readily agreed.

But suddenly the interviews were the least of my worries because I was almost broke. I had quit my job six months before, bought a motor home (which seemed like the least expensive and most efficient way to travel), and lived in it for the last five months while promoting my first book, writing a second book, and earning enough to get by. But my income had dropped off when all my energy and focus went into the Jesus book, and now that my motor home payment was due I was freaking out a little because I had put my mobile home and car up as collateral when I bought the motor home.

I complained to God that he wasn't helping me out. I mean, I was doing a book about his Son, Jesus, you would think I'd get a break. But I didn't think he heard me, so I punched the door and kicked the chair and then got angrier because now my foot and hand hurt. For a moment, I wondered if Jesus had hurt himself when he angrily turned over the table in the temple? I mean he wore sandals, it would have been easy to stub a toe or get a few splinters. I drank a cup of coffee while I limped around my house trying to figure out what to do. Finally, I swallowed my pride and borrowed $225 from a friend.

Since I wanted the painting of *The Last Supper* with me on my travels, I first needed to stop in Indiana and pick it up. The next day, I drove four hundred miles to a small town outside Gary, Indiana. As I got closer to the house, my breathing quickened because I was finally going to see my mother's painting again. I pulled up in front of a normal-looking, two-story frame house. I had expected something more dramatic—like when I visited a famous writer in California a few years ago. It was nighttime when I arrived and as I got out of my car, a huge owl flew right over my head. It was spooky. The author lived up on a hill and there was a big iron gate surrounding her house. Her yard and walkway were overgrown with vegetation. There must have been seventy steps leading up to her house, and I had to squat the whole time as I walked up the stairs because the bushes and trees had grown over the steps forming a tunnel that was only about four feet high. When I got to the top of the hill, there were a couple of abandoned cars scattered around and all the lights in the house were off but the front door was half-open. I walked in and she was standing over the stove cooking chili in the dark.

I expected something like that, but this was just a regular house, and as I walked up to it, I realized the neighborhood was deserted. There was no one else outside, which was surprising because I half-expected other people to be watching me, that they would somehow know that I was there to pick up the painting my mother had died under.

And then, the anticlimax got even bigger. When I went to the door, I saw a note from Jody saying she was out of town and instructing me to pick up the painting from her neighbors. When I went next door, an older couple answered the door. They pointed to the painting as it leaned on its side against the wall behind them. It was strange, because when I looked at the painting I could see my whole life, and yet to them it was just another painting. I thanked them and carried *The Last Supper* out to the motor home. I placed it on the table and looked at it. Somehow I didn't feel so alone anymore.

As I drove through the night, I often talked to the apostles in the painting.

"So what do you guys think?" I asked. "Am I nuts? Should I do this? Should I drive around and find out who Jesus was?"

Usually, they didn't say anything. But sometimes I'd hear a whisper.

"We're here with you," they said. "All of us are here."

"Even Judas is here," I'd say warmly. "Right, Judas?!"

"Right!" he'd reply, and I'd be surprised because in the painting Judas was shown standing by the doorway, holding a small leather bag and scowling. But in the quiet of the night, I realized that all of the apostles were together because whatever Judas did two thousand years ago, he was forgiven and was still one of them.

Sometimes, during an interview, I could sense the apostles standing behind me, peering over my shoulder, while nodding and smiling in agreement at what had just been said. Other times, I could sense a pain in them that stretched across time—it was the painful recognition that Jesus' words had been misunderstood and that this misunderstanding had been and would continue to be taught to, and misunderstood by, the generations to come. At no time, however, did the apostles try to intercede in what was said; instead, they were just very present with whatever occurred.

It was the middle of summer, and the farther south I drove, the hotter it got. I couldn't use the air conditioning in the motor home because I was already only getting eight mpg and if I used the air conditioner I might get five miles to the gallon and run out of gas money before I reached Georgia. After a few hours, I stripped down to my shorts and drove half-naked, slowly being baptized by my own perspiration. To make matters worse, the refrigerator in the motor home turned itself off and all the food thawed out.

The frozen fish, which was no longer frozen, stank up the whole motor home.

So like I said, I drove down South half-naked, sweating profusely, and smelling like fish.

This is how I began my search for the Real Jesus.

✛ 4
JOHN DOMINIC CROSSAN

CLERMONT, FLORIDA

I stopped at a gas station two blocks from Dominic Crossan's home in Florida, washed up, and did a quick change of clothes in my motor home. There was an old Buick at the pump next to mine. The license plate said JESUS. As the Tibetans would say, it was "auspicious."

"Nice plate," I said to the driver as he started his car.

"It was my momma's," he said with a smile. "I got it after she died."

I could tell right away, by his friendliness, the way he smiled, and the way he said "momma" that she had been a special person. You could see that the good in her still lived in him—and by seeing him, you knew something of her.

After paying at the pump, I drove my motor home down the road to a condominium complex. I parked next to a row of hedges and stepped out onto the sandy Florida soil. The air was humid and hot, which made it that much better when Dominic Crossan opened his front door and I was hit with the full force of a cranked-up air conditioner.

Dominic Crossan is at the forefront of the recent resurgence in Jesus scholarship. His book *Jesus: A Revolutionary Biography* was a best-seller and he is a frequent guest on radio and television. He's a tall thin man with short gray hair and his Irish accent adds a charm to the passionate sensitivity he has about his work. I met with him at his home, where he lived with his wife, Sarah, whom he married three years after his first wife, Margaret, had died. I was immediately struck by the special relationship he had with his wife. The way they looked at each other and worked together—and the way that he talked about her hobbies—not just his interests—told me that his heart and mind truly paid attention to her. Dominic Crossan is focused yet open-minded when studying the scriptures, and he appears to apply these same qualities to relationships. The ability to be present and openhearted, whether with books or people, is a sign of a wise man.

"The real challenge for the next millennium," Dominic Crossan said, "is going to be, how do you hold onto your own particularity; national, ethnic, religious, everything else, with utter integrity, without having to turn round and destroy anyone or everyone else to establish your own validity?"

Dominic Crossan had just described the challenge of being in relationship, and if Jesus taught anything, he taught about relationship—relationship to God, self, and other. When Jesus was asked what was the greatest commandment of all, he replied: "Love the Lord your God with all your heart and with all your soul and with all your mind. This is the first and greatest commandment. And the second is like it: 'Love your neighbor as yourself.' "[1]

While living in Ireland, Dominic Crossan went into the Jesuit order at sixteen. As Dominic recalled, bankers, lawyers, or doctors weren't allowed to recruit at his school—only priests. He was recruited by "missionary priests from Africa with marvelous, fascinating stories." At that time, the celibacy didn't bother him.

"I had spent five years in an Irish boarding school, I was as celibate as they come."

When he left the order nineteen years later it was for two reasons. First of all, he wanted to get married to Margaret Dagenais, a professor at Loyola University. Their marriage, which took place in 1969, lasted until her death in 1983.

"Margaret had a sudden heart attack on May 1, 1983," Dominic Crossan said. I was immediately struck by the fact that he remembered the exact day. I'll bet if I'd asked him, he would have also known the time.

"Nobody said she was dying," he continued, "so I thought it was a small thing. Then on June third she had another heart attack and died."

The second reason he left was because there were several Cardinals and an Archbishop who wanted to get rid of him because of his scholarly research.

---

1. Matthew 22:37–39, NIV (New International Version).

"They trained me to think," Dominic told me, "and then they expected me to think according to their schedule—it didn't work! To me, a scholar is like a scout, whose job is to say what he or she sees. For them scholars are apologists, whose job is to defend the beliefs of their organization; it's an honorable activity—but it wasn't what I wanted."

Dominic Crossan is a member of the Jesus Seminar: a group of scholars who discuss and vote on the authenticity of Jesus' various teachings and actions. Though the members of the seminar disagree on many issues regarding Jesus' ministry, they all agree on the "ethical necessity" of making scholarly findings available to the public.

"For example," Dominic Crossan said, "a huge number of scholars agree that Matthew copied Mark. Ordinary people should know that. What does that mean if you have just seen Matthew change Mark? The conclusions you draw from that may be completely different than the stand the radical right takes. The two extremes of fundamentalism and secularism have failed people and there is an attempt to find redemption in the middle."

Who was/is Jesus?

First of all, Jesus was absolutely and totally human. Under any sort of a microscope nothing would come up funny and there would be no Divine chromosome in there—it's all human. Jesus was born in a perfectly normal way to a man and woman.

But Jesus was not just another guy like Mozart was not just another musician and Michael Jordan is not just another basketball player. Yet, I don't think Jesus has a monopoly on the Kingdom of God. Instead, what he does is to incarnate the kingdom and show us the way to do It—now go do it! He doesn't say "be like me," he says "go do it." In fact, he sends people out to do it.

I find that to be what I call "particularity." It seems to me inalienably human, that we are particular. And what I mean by particular is that if you show me a picture of your son and say, "Isn't this the most beautiful child you've ever seen?" I don't say, "Well, it looks just like another kid to me." Because for you, this is the most beautiful child in the world and the fact

14

that I might have a picture of the most beautiful child in *my* pocket doesn't signify . . . that's not relative, that's "particular." In the same way, falling in love is also particular. I don't say to you, "I don't see what you see in that person."

So, falling in faith is like falling in love—it is absolutely particular. You have an experience and think "How could anyone see God anywhere else?" But you must remember, of course, that others see God somewhere else— in other beliefs and other religions. Our challenge, then, is to hold on to both. And an even greater challenge for the next millennium is going to be how do you hold on to your own particularity; national, ethnic, religious, everything else, with utter integrity, without having to turn around and destroy anyone or everyone else to establish your own validity?

Jesus' religion?

Jesus was utterly and totally Jewish and having said that, I haven't said very much because scholars now know for certain that there were a multiplicity of different types of Jewish options in the first century.

For example, Josephus, who was a Jew and a learned priest in the first century, said that "It is God's will, the will of the Jewish God, that we obey Rome. God has given power to Rome and, therefore, we must be a theocracy under Rome. Do not rebel against Rome, that is rebelling against God," etc. etc.

That's a clear position, that's a Jewish position, and I'm sure he spoke for a lot of people. But down in Qumran the people would have said, "We are praying for God to come and solve this Roman problem because it is evil, it is unjust, we can't do anything about it, do it, God, soon!"

Jesus represents a third option: nonviolent resistance to Rome. He didn't agree with Josephus that Rome was fine, and he didn't agree with those who took to the hills in guerrilla warfare against Rome—violent resistance against Rome.

Christian Jews, Essene Jews, Sadducee Jews, Pharisee Jews, and Qumran Jews—these were all options within Judaism. So, of course, Jesus is Jewish, but which Jew was he? He was a Jew who announced the Kingdom of God as one of divine justice (distributive not retributive) which any could and all should enter here and now upon this earth in nonviolent opposition to the Kingdom of Rome, which was the normalcy of civilization in that time and place.

The crucial question is *What did those first-century writers intend to say?* If they wanted to tell me about the biology of Mary, I don't believe them. I think they wanted to tell me about something else and they are using parables to do it.

Another example of this kind can be found in the writings of the historian Suetonius, who writes that Augustus, the emperor, was conceived when his mother, Atia, was in the Temple of Apollo sleeping and Apollo in the guise of a snake impregnated her. The child born was therefore the son of Apollo and, in fact, her husband had a dream that he saw the sun rising from his wife's womb. I read that and I read the story in Luke and if I were in a court of law today and were asked "Do I believe in the virgin birth?" I would say "Yes." But what I would mean is that these stories are parables. Do I think God intervened in the biology of Mary? No way, not with Atia, and not with Mary.

It would be the same as if you asked me, "Do I believe in Uncle Sam?" Now I would say that you aren't asking me about a character, so you must be asking "Do I think America is the land of the free, the home of the brave, the land of justice?" So I would say, "Yes," I do believe in Uncle Sam because I have chosen to come live in this country—I wasn't born here. But if you were asking me if I thought there was a figure out there, living in Washington, then I would have to say "no."

About "the lost years," first of all, I don't believe the infancy stories are true because only two gospels out of four have infancy stories: Matthew and Luke. Second, those two disagree on everything except the name of Jesus, that he was born to Mary and Joseph, and the virgin birth, based on Isaiah 7:14.

We are seduced into the idea of "the lost years," because Matthew and

Luke tell us something about his infancy, and then don't tell us anything further for twenty years or so. But I think Matthew and Luke decided to write an infancy to act as an overture to the drama. Neither is based on fact. For example, Matthew has Jesus as another Moses and tells a story in which he is almost killed by an evil king, as Moses was by Pharaoh, and Jesus by Herod. You can almost see Matthew making up the infancy story.

*Was Jesus married or
in an intimate relationship?*

Finally, just about every Jewish male with sufficient income was married by age eighteen. But in Galilee in 20 A.D. you had a lot of poor day laborers who never married not because they were observing celibacy or being prophets, but because they just didn't have the opportunity within that society. I think if Jesus was unmarried, it was for that reason and not because he was an ascetic celibate like Paul.

Did Jesus learn things? Was he perfect?

Jesus learned exactly the way anyone else learned. When a person learns, he changes his mind. I have a tangible illustration of Jesus changing his mind. I am completely convinced he was baptized by John and that would mean, for at least that moment, he agreed with John's general program, which announced a sort of an apocalyptic avenging God, who in order to establish justice was going to destroy those who were unjust. It is what I would call revenge. It isn't justice—but I understand it because I'm Irish and there were times in our history we would have liked God to do some nasty things to the British. It is getting rid of all of my enemies, and that is revenge, not justice.

Later I find Jesus with another message, and it is not an apocalyptic message. It is a message of justice. But he was baptized by John who was apocalyptic, so how do I explain those two things?

The only way I can explain it is that he changed his mind. My suspicion is that once he saw that John was put into prison and the avenging God didn't do a single thing, Jesus decided that's not how God works. Jesus changed his mind about God. And since Jesus changed his mind about a vengeful God, he must have learned something that caused him to change his mind.

In regard to the authorship, we don't know a thing about who wrote the gospels, the names Mark, Matthew, Luke, and John are simply put on them. They start appearing on late second-century manuscripts.

They are perfectly accurate as gospels if you are adhering to the definition of a gospel meaning "good news." But the Romans didn't think this was good news, so the news had to be updated in other gospels. I read Mark, which I see updated in Matthew, and then updated in John. Once the gospel is updated four times, the message—the good news—is clear. But the gospel has to be updated all the time.

Now, if you ask me are there discrepancies? I would say "no" because they are not intended to tell us exactly what happened. They are intended to tell us how and what it means for the particular community it was written for.

Again, it is relational. A relationship. Mark is writing an account of Jesus that is laminated together with what his community needs in the seventies, so Jesus was taken straight out of the twenties and updated into the seventies. When I read John who wrote in the nineties, it didn't surprise me that it was totally different from Mark. There is Pilate, Jesus, and the rest, but Jesus is talking differently. And if someone wrote a gospel today, they'd have Jesus talk about the important issues of today, i.e., abortions and separation of church and state. *The point is they are not history, they contain history.* They are not biographies, they contain biography. They are "gospel."

To take them literally would be like saying you weren't going to accept the principle of the story of the Good Samaritan until you checked the records to see if there was a man mugged on the road from Jerusalem to Jericho, and to see if a Good Samaritan helped him. Get a grip!

Suppose you had people today who had read *Aesop's Fables* and insisted that the animals in ancient Greece could talk. You and I would look at them and say, "That's not what he meant!"

"But that's what it says!" And there would be a fight. "Do you think these guys are liars? It says here the fox is talking . . . !"

We would say, "No, that's not what he meant, he was just using animals to make his point." There are no Aesopians who believe the fables are sacred scriptures and that Zeus gave power to them—if there were we couldn't do anything with them—they would be Aesopian fundamentalists.

Is the Bible meant
to be taken literally?

The question for me is *Were the Gospels intended to be taken literally?* I believe there are times when they are being symbolic or making their point through symbolic language, and I will not make them sound like fools by misunderstanding them.

There are things I think they are wrong on now but they made sense in those times. Divorce is totally forbidden because in that world and at that time it destroyed the person. Homosexuality is forbidden because they believed nature was heterosexual, and that if you were a homosexual you were deliberately deciding to go against nature, like a thief might have decided to steal. Nobody in the New Testament could conceive that homosexuality might be an innate and a biological predisposition.

Is the Bible the Word of God and inspired?

"Word of God" I have no problem with. Smart people never say the "Words of God," it's the "Word of God," as in *what's the word from Washington?* It's a quick summary.

As a Christian, the Bible is the Word of God for me. It is not the words of God. It is God in conjunction with human authors and that's why God comes across as rather hateful sometimes. If I hate you and am inspired by God, then God is going to come across as hateful. It's relational—a relationship.

In looking at the gospels we have to face the following fact, *the vast majority of scholars believe that Matthew and Luke used Mark.* Since they added to what they found in Mark, it means that Matthew and Luke didn't like what was in Mark. Matthew read Mark, and as a Christian, Matthew was inspired. He was inspired and said to himself, "This is all right for Mark, but it doesn't work for my people—it is outdated."

Once again I see a relationship—inspiration is a two-way street. You bounce your imagination off God, as it were, and it can come back changed or it can come back with your worst prejudices confirmed. Imagination can be a very dangerous thing.

I believe the gospels were inspired, but do I believe everything in the Bible is right? No—that's not possible. For example, if the Bible is telling me the biology of Mary was changed by God, then I can say two things.

1. I am not interested in a circus. If God wants to play games, then good for God—I have more serious things to think about.
2. If Jesus was born that way, it doesn't matter because I am still not interested until I see how Jesus lived.

If somebody tells me I have to believe in Jesus because Jesus was Divine—I can't do that. But I do believe in Jesus because Jesus lived the way God would if God walked around here with sandals. That's enough, I don't need the pyrotechnics.

*How do you prevent yourself
from projecting yourself onto Jesus and seeing
the Jesus you want to see?*

I don't know if there is any way to beat that. It's an interactive process with any historical figure, not just Jesus. At its best, we get about 50 percent them and 50 percent us. I don't delude myself into thinking I am getting 100 percent straight Jesus. The very best I can do with the past, with anyone in the past, or probably with anyone living and talking to me as you are, is to get about 50 percent.

Who killed Jesus and why?

First of all, from what I understand of Jesus, I would have been waiting for him to get killed, and I would not have been surprised when he was killed. It is a little like when I first heard Martin Luther King had been shot. I didn't immediately think it was an accident—you knew it might be coming.

With Jesus it was a question of *when*. He was threatening the Roman order. But we do know more than that; we know he was crucified in Jerusalem under Pontius Pilate. The fact that he was crucified tells us both that he was lower class, and that he was killed for subverting the Roman order. Josephus was right, the Roman authorities executed Jesus and there was some complicity with the highest Jewish authorities (who also recognized him as a threat). He was not simply in a theological debate with Jewish theologians. He was in a religiopolitical debate.

Why did Jesus disrupt the temple? He must have known that would lead to execution.

That's a big problem. But the bigger problem is this: If Jesus went up regularly to Jerusalem for the feasts, what happened this one time that made it different?

If he did do what happened in the temple, then what happened in the temple is quite clear. The temple at that time was the House of God, the central bank, but it had also become the place of collusion with the Roman authorities because it was questionable whether the high priest Caiaphas was legitimate, as he had been elected by the Romans.

So if you were a pious Jew, you might be totally against the temple because it had become, in your view, impure and tarnished. Consequently, what Jesus did was a symbolic destruction. He attacked the temple's fiscal, sacrificial, and cultic basis. He did exactly the same as somebody who went into the Pentagon during the Vietnam War and poured blood all over the steps.

Jesus was not a fool; he knew this would lead to his death. And if I combine this with what he is doing in Galilee, then the only question I have is *How long* before Herod Antipas gets him?

The reason Herod Antipas doesn't get him sooner is that he may have had to be a little bit careful about taking on another popular prophet after he had just taken out John the Baptist. Jesus had a grace period before Antipas came after him.

In John's gospel it's said that Jesus and Pilate were talking. But I don't believe it would have gone that high up the chain of command because if I were Pilate, I would have anticipated there would be trouble during Passover and I would give standing orders for crowd control: "If anyone causes any trouble, you hang 'em out to dry, don't come back and ask to do it—just do it." You have to remember that it's the most dangerous time of the year because it's Passover (which is a celebration of deliverance from imperial aggression in Egypt), and the Jews are celebrating this deliverance during a Roman occupation. It's a tense time—just as the Fourth of July would be a tense time, if America were occupied by an outside military force.

Second Coming?

As far as I am concerned, Jesus never left, so why does he need to return? The resurrection means that this incarnation of God has never left, and is still in the world as a challenge.

The thing you need is for people to start taking what it means to be a Christian seriously—*that would be the Second Coming.*

And I don't think we should wait for Jesus to do it for us, because that takes the burden off our shoulders. A literal Second Coming, be it Jesus or an apocalyptic advent of God, means that it's hopeless, and we can't do anything about it—but that someday in the future, God will solve it for us. That's the mind-set I think we need to change.

Resurrection?

Once again I have to ask, what were they trying to tell me? Why are they insisting on a bodily resurrection? I don't think they are trying to say his ideas lived on, or his movement lived on, or his sayings lived on. They are insisting on a body because Jesus incarnated the Justice of God and that can only be done in the body. The incarnation of a Just God involves a body—not an idea.

If Gandhi was a philosopher, he could have proposed nonviolent resistance as an idea and we could have read about it. But it was not just an idea—he did it! He embodied it!

Once Gandhi does it, you know it can be done. Once Martin Luther

King does it, it can be done, you can have nonviolent resistance. It takes a lot of courage and maybe martyrdom, however, it can be done. But it always comes back to the body—not only the mind.

If you look at it this way then the gospel writers' insistence that the body of Jesus lived on makes sense. They are insisting not only on a matter of ideas or sayings but on a matter of life—how it can be lived.

Please understand, I don't believe a body came out of the tomb. The best I could hope for was that the body got *into* the tomb because the odds are it may never have gotten off the cross. If it got into the tomb, then that probably meant the soldiers did a fast job, like any soldiers who want to get home as fast as they can. Once the guy is dead, you get him into a tomb. We are talking solid rock around Jerusalem. Shallow grave, mounds of stone, waiting dogs.

So the question becomes why were these people insisting on the body? Why didn't they say, "His spirit lives on"? Because they wanted to say something else and they were groping for language, so they said he appeared and he still had the wounds and that the wounds will never heal, because the wounds are the body that died for justice.

Jesus' spiritual techniques?

For Jesus, prayer would be about union with God and doing the will of God. It bothers Matthew and Luke very much that Mark (who is their source gospel) does not have Jesus praying a lot. He only prays twice, once at the very beginning of his life, once at the very end. But those are the points when there is some danger of not wanting to do the will of God—that's the only time Jesus prays. I think from Mark's point of view, he only has to do it at the points were there might be separation. Otherwise, as far as Mark is concerned, Jesus is totally in union with the will of God. But the crisis points require prayer and that is probably the kind of spirituality we are really talking about. It is only at those points where crisis or separation might occur. So Jesus' spiritual techniques were profoundly "actual."

I suppose the marvelous thing is that anyone did, and what is the Messiah? Many thought the Messiah was supposed to lead them and the armies of God. Maybe the Messiah is a prophet. Maybe there would be a priestly Messiah or a royal Messiah.

To ask the question more broadly, did some Jews consider that God was powerfully at work in Jesus and would solve their oppressive problem? Some did and others said "No way!"

We used to believe either that some Christians said, "Jesus was divine" and no Jews accepted that. Or that Christians said, "Jesus was the Messiah" and no Jew accepted that. But that doesn't work because the early Christians were all Jews. So the question becomes why didn't most of the Jews simply say, "Okay, we are with the Christian Jews rather than with somebody else?"

Most Jews ended their relationship to Christian Jews, not because they didn't believe in Jesus as the Messiah or that he was the Son of God, but because Christian Jews accepted Pagans without demanding the males be circumcised or observe kosher.

✠ 5
RAVI ZACHARIAS

ATLANTA, GEORGIA

"We can have your shirt cleaned and pressed by tomorrow," the lady at the cleaners said.

I had just handed her a pink-striped button-down dress shirt. It was clean, but had gotten wrinkled in my suitcase. I needed to wear it (at least I thought I did) because I was interviewing an evangelist named Ravi Zacharias—and I had noticed that evangelists usually dressed up—never down. I needed to be dressed for the part because as an interviewer, I wanted people to trust me and to feel as though I was one of them.

"I need it in a couple of hours," I said, a little concerned. "I've got an interview."

"Well," she said, looking overworked, "we always wash it and then press it. Tomorrow is the earliest."

"That won't work . . ." I mumbled to myself.

"How about the shirt I have on?" I asked, referring to a gray golf shirt I was wearing. "Do you think this is okay?"

"It's fine," she replied. "Just button another button."

"So you think it's okay?" I asked again.

"Are you the interviewer or being interviewed?" she asked.

"I'm interviewing someone," I replied.

"Don't worry then," she said. "As the interviewer—you're in charge."

"But I'm interviewing someone for a book I'm writing about Jesus," I said. "A man named Ravi Zacharias . . ."

She just looked at me blankly, then looked away and began sorting dirty clothes into a basket. I wanted to tell her that *I really wasn't in charge,* that Ravi Zacharias was doing me a favor, and that I needed my shirt pressed and I was a little worried about the whole thing . . .

But I could tell that as far as she was concerned the conversation was over. Fortunately for me, a few minutes later, I found another cleaners down the street, and the woman said, "Come back in one hour—it will be pressed—no problem." Immediately I felt relieved. Not only because my shirt would be pressed—but because of the way the woman spoke to me. When she told me that it was *"no problem"* I felt that everything would be okay. I have a feeling that's what Jesus conveyed to the people he encountered—that things were going to be okay because no matter what, we are always loved and forgiven.

One hour later and one dollar less—I was wearing a clean, starched shirt.

Ravi Zacharias was born in India, and although he and I differ on some doctrinal issues, we were both brought into a deeper relationship with God through our desperate wish to die. He had a conversion experience in the hospital after making a suicide attempt while in his teens, and

I had an experience of God's presence at the age of twenty-one while praying for God to take my depressed and despairing life.

Ravi Zacharias is a kind man with a keen intellect and a voice that is amazingly soft and comforting while expressing strong conviction. The spiritual strength he derives from his faith is evident in his determination to share and defend the Christianity that literally saved his life.

Ravi Zacharias is the author of *Jesus Among Other Gods, Can Man Live Without God,* and *Cries of the Heart.* He is president of Ravi Zacharias International Ministries and has lectured in over fifty countries.

Who was/is Jesus?

I visited Mother Teresa's home in Calcutta and there was a little sign there that said, "Go out and preach the gospel and only use words if necessary." Her reminder that there is an incarnation aspect to the Christian faith is so wonderful. Jesus is God incarnate, a revelation to us in flesh and blood of what life ultimately is and to the four fundamental questions of life; origin, meaning, morality, and destiny. Christ is the blueprint and the expression of what life is all about; "Nothing was made that was not made through in him, in him was the light of life and he is the Way, the Truth and the Life." So, my origin, my righteousness, my meaning, and my destiny is wrapped up in him.

Jesus is the Christ, he is *the* Son of God who came to seek and to save that which was lost.

Jesus the only Son of God?

The scriptures tell us that there is one God and one mediator between God and man in the person of Christ Jesus. Simon Peter says, "Thou are the Christ, the Son of the Living God" (Matthew 16:16, KJV), and Thomas says, "My Lord and my God" (John 20:28, KJV), which clearly positioned Jesus as one who is the unique one of God and is equal in the Trinity.

We can also be sons and daughters of God, but not in the technical sense in which Jesus is the only begotten of the Father. Paul says, "To as many as received him, to them gave he power to become the Sons of God." In that sense, we are adopted into the relationship with the Heavenly Father and then the life of the Son can be reflected in the sons and daughters of the living God.

How is Jesus different from an avatar?

Dramatically different. The avatar is the manifestation, the representation of God. For Hindus, Krishna, Rama, and Buddha, were avatars. They are not, then, essentially Divine in and of themselves, as much as they have taken on the persona of the Divine or have come in a form that is instrumental rather than essential. Maybe that's the reason avatars are portrayed as sort of a Greek-heroes type, and all kinds of shenanigans are carried on by them, as with Krishna and his carryings-on with milkmaids. That can be encompassed because the avatar concept brings along with it a whole new cosmology and a whole new nature of God himself. Jesus was not an avatar. "In the beginning was the Word and the Word was with God and the Word WAS God" (John 1:1, NIV) and "the Word became flesh and dwelt among us full of grace and truth" (John 1:14, NIV). He was not merely a manifestation in human form, he was God himself and very different from the avatar concept.

Virgin birth?

The virgin birth is a bold and prophetic scriptural fulfillment attested to by those antagonistic to Christianity—the Koran mentions the virgin birth. Fundamental teaching of the virgin birth is bold and prophetic fulfillment. But even greater than that, Jesus was supernaturally conceived for a life that was going to be punctuated by the supernatural.

Jesus is the only way?

Truth by definition is exclusive. Therefore, I believe there is only one way to God in the person of Jesus Christ. And before people jump and say this is exclusivistic and uncaring, they should realize every other religion has its exclusivistic points and each one justifies them. For example, in the East, the law of karma is no less judgmental than the Christian religion. In fact, karma is a law of judgment.

I see what Mahatma Gandhi said and what Martin Luther King, Jr., said contained in the heart of the gospel. But the message in the person of Christ on the cross is so central to the person of Jesus Christ and the gospel that it is without replication or imitation anywhere else. The gospel message of love is very powerful, very clear, and offers grace and forgiveness to those who believe. If the illegality of conversion were removed in Islamic countries, you would see the biggest turning to Christ in recent history. Because when average Muslims (apart from the political framework) hear about the gospel and the love of Christ they are converted in droves.

Truth must stand on its own regardless of the ramifications. You cannot expect a pilot to tell the tower, "I know what you are saying and I know what the instruments are saying but I'm a relativist and I'm going to deal with this the way I want to and go into the side of a mountain if I have to." *The most difficult concept for human beings to come to grips with today is that truth, by definition, is exclusive.* If we do not come to terms with that, all language becomes meaningless.

Jesus' religion?

Augustine used to say, "Where God has closed his holy mouth, let us learn not to open ours." It is very critical that we go only as far as the Word conveys to us. Other thoughts may be great for reflection and meditation, but we have to be careful that they are not extrapolated into dogma.

Christ was raised a first-century Jew, in a Jewish home. He came not to abrogate the law, but to fulfill it. The person of the Christ tried to show Jewish minds of that day how privileged they were and how it was easy to be so close to the truth and yet, when its ceremonialism was allowed to overtake the moral impetus, so far from it. He would have understood the moral law and the ceremonial law of God and always kept them in that order. Because ceremonial law was/is a servant of the moral nature of God, not the other way around.

Sometimes those closest to a claim or Truth will be the hardest to reach. For example, Jesus' own brother James only made his commitment after the resurrection. Culture is a very enshackling thing. Our ways of interpreting and looking at things are enshackled by culture. In Luke chapter 7, Jesus said to the people who were coming to see him and John, "What did you go out into the desert to see, a reed swayed by the wind? If not, what did you go out to see? A man dressed in fine clothes? No, those who wear expensive clothes, clothes which are an indulgent luxury are in palaces. What did you go out to see, a prophet? Yes, I tell you he is more than a prophet, this is the one about whom it is written 'I will send my messenger ahead of you, who will prepare your way before you.' " Then he goes on to talk about John the Baptist and he says these critical and incredible words, "To what then can I compare the people of this generation? What are they like? They are like children sitting in the marketplace and calling out to each other, we played the flute for you and did not dance, we sang a dirge and you say he has a demon. The Son of Man came eating and drinking and you say here is a glutton and a drunkard, a friend of tax collectors and sinners but wisdom has proved right by all her children." What Jesus is saying here is definitive. He is saying that whenever God sends a message to his people, they want to change it. When John the Baptist came with a stern message, they tried to play the flute to get him to dance. When Jesus came with a message of grace and forgiveness, they wanted to sing a dirge so he would mourn. They always seem to raise up a counter-perspective to what God is answering. When God gave them the law, they said, "He is too stern." When he came with forgiveness, they said, "What sort of thing is this? There is no stringency, no parameters here." They rejected him because they were unable to take grace and forgiveness; because the entire edifice of religiosity was built on structure, power, money, sales, commercialism. They rejected him, not because they were worse than us. They rejected him because they were just like us. Too often, when the Son of God comes into our lives, we want to change the terms of engagement.

"The kingdom of God is within you."
Luke 17:20

Many people who quote Jesus as saying, "The kingdom of heaven is within," understand it wrongly. It is now reduced to a personal experience without objectivity. When Jesus said, "The kingdom of God is within you," he meant "the rule of Christ in the heart of men." That's what he meant by the kingdom of God. Today, however, when Deepak Chopra and others quote "The kingdom of God is within you," they mean a spark of Divinity or that you are identical with the divine. But that's not what Jesus was talking about. Jesus was saying, "It's the rule of Christ within your heart." In that sense, it is internal, but it is not internal in that it lacks objectivity—which is the error we make today.

Why are scholars, mystics, and
evangelists all important?

The scholar has to call us to task on the integrity and the coherence of the idea. The mystic has to remind us that it is not all cerebral, that there is a heart, reflective, and contemplative element to it. The evangelist remind us that there is a *gospel,* that the Word became flesh, dwelt among us, the birth—life—death—resurrection of Jesus Christ. That—is—the—gospel!

I've always said philosophy comes at three levels: the theory, the drama, and the kitchen table. The theory is the argument, the drama is the arts, and the kitchen table is the application. To make an effective message, you must argue for it at the theoretical level, you must illustrate it at the artistic level, but you must apply it at the pragmatic level. I believe the Word of God moves from argument to imagination to application. You cannot be righteous until you are redeemed, and you cannot worship until you are redeemed and righteous. If you reverse the sequence, you're in trouble. He took them out of Egypt, gave them the ten commandments, and then gave them the building of the tabernacle of the worship. That sequence always follows as it does in logic or argument, imagination or arts, application or practicality.

The Christian message retains coherence because it pays due credence to the wholeness of the human being, not a fragmented area of it. Mystics who miss the doctrinaire side of it are in danger of constant contradiction. Those who are doctrinaire miss the mystical side of it, making it cerebral and losing the wonder of engagement. You can no more do that and retain integrity than you can have sexuality in a relationship with your spouse and treat it as purely an academic exercise. There is the romance, there is the joining of the bodies and the spirits, because it is a pure form of expression, based on commitment.

Who killed Jesus?

Humanity killed Jesus. Because present at that trial before Pilate was everything in human nature; power, empire, religiosity, greed, conniving, scheming. We mistakenly attribute Jesus' death (historically) to one group. But just as with Adam's fall, we all fell. When Jesus was crucified, we all crucified him. The answer is that when God sent his Son to mankind—all of mankind killed him. That's who crucified Jesus.

Resurrection?

I agree with Paul that "If Jesus Christ be not raised from the dead, we are poor men to be pitied." When you look at the virgin birth and the perfection of his life, which was so magnificently lived, Jesus stands in supreme distinction to anyone else. So much so that friend and foe both say, "There was never a life lived out like this!"

By the way, even the Koran talks about Jesus raising people from the dead, a power it never attributes to Mohammed. Jesus stands supreme through the resurrection of Christ as given in the gospels and expounded on by the apostle Paul.

Second Coming?

Now because of the nature of the kind of work I do, I don't get into the crossing of the t's and the dotting of the i's. I believe he will come and when he comes every knee will bow and every tongue will confess and know that this was indeed the Son of God who has returned. Whether he will come after a time of tribulation on earth or before a time of tribulation, I let eschatologists wrestle with. My point is I know *that* he will return. In the Book of Thessalonians it says that "the Lord himself shall descend with a shout, with the voice of the archangel and the trumpet of God and the dead in Christ will rise . . . we who are alive and remain shall be got up to be with him." To me, all that wonder is swallowed up with the truth of "he is coming," which means that "seal of completion" upon this world is there in his return, for judgment and for the resurrection. That those who have loved him will spend their eternity with him and those who have rejected him will spend their eternity separated from him by their own choice.

The World without Christianity?

Without the Christian message, where would we be today, where would the West be today? Emil Brunner, the German theologian, said, "Hitler should have been given an honorary doctor of divinity degree, because he showed the world what the world would be like without Christianity." Theoretically, Hitler was Christian, but in actual belief he was completely pagan, and the Nazi movement was anything but godly. Although it officially claimed to be Christian, it was based on violence, domination, power, pride.

For me, it is important to always see the strength and the weakness of the Church. I have been in churches where without the Church there would be so many people whose concerns and needs would never have been met. I thank God for the Church as a caring community. I thank God for the Church all over the globe. It is amazing to go and see its endeavors and missionary work; India is one of the greatest beneficiaries of that. The Church has given the world music, festivals, fellowship, the community, and caring. Of course our human weaknesses also are expressed in Christianity and many wrongs have been done in the Church's name. But that wasn't Christianity—that was the failings of human beings. As long as we are in the world we will always have failures, shortcomings, examples of the weak.

But in the media today, every time a pastor falls, it always hits the front page. Why? Because we find it easier to pull down than to build, to destroy than to uphold. You don't often hear of the sacrifice and the efforts and the commitment of the many. The media fails to do that. Too often, the only image upheld before people is one of duplicity, not one of fidelity.

I believe a Christian (separated from all of the ecclesiastical trimmings), is a follower of the Lord Jesus Christ as his Savior and Lord in the person and work of Christ.

✢ 6
MOTHER TERESA

I pulled into a Travel Center, bought some gas, and then parked in the midst of a herd of resting semis. As I lay in the back of my motor home trying to sleep, I couldn't help but think of the differences and similarities between the Jesus of Ravi Zacharias and that of Dominic Crossan. Both were passionately dedicated to the Jesus they found/and were finding, and both had set the course of their life using *the* Truth of Jesus as their compass. For a moment, I wondered where my exploration of Jesus would lead me.

I looked up at the ceiling, sighed deeply, and then rolled over and reached into the drawer next to my bed. I pulled out some mala beads and held them in my hand. The beads had a grainy texture, and were actually seeds from the bodhi tree, each about the size of a pea and strung together like a rosary. The thread that had held them together had broken a few years ago. They looked so disconnected and estranged from each other; so self-contained and yet lost, that I vowed to restring them first thing in the morning.

As I rolled one of the beads between my forefinger and thumb, I remembered the way she held my hands in hers, while looking up at me with her clear, gray eyes . . .

Back in 1990, the bus ride from Dharamsala to New Delhi took almost a day. We traveled a winding road through mountains that were both breathtaking and deadly. It wasn't unusual to see the remains of a poorly driven bus at the bottom of a ravine or cliff.

In New Delhi, I hopped on a train to Calcutta. Years before I had traveled third class and loved being among the common people. Third class is an austere experience that connects a person to the simplicity and salt-of-the-earth, day-to-day existence of Indian life. There the seats and sleepers are plain wooden boards, hanging by chains. This time I again opted for third class, and although I paid for a sleeper for myself, there were other people sharing the space with me. The train was packed. We sat shoulder to shoulder in a car without air-conditioning, and everyone sweated together. After a day of intense heat, my romanticism melted away. I slipped off the train anonymously, paid extra, and boarded the second-class air-conditioned car.

I was given a sleeper across from a wealthy Indian businessman. I tried to make small talk, but he didn't say much. He had an air of superiority and seemed distant. The only thing we seemed to have in common was our balding heads. "So," I asked, "when did you start losing your hair?"

He looked at me, and his face softened. It was the first time he had smiled. We spoke for the next few hours about baldness cures and politics.

"Would you take a pill if it cured baldness?" I asked.

"Most definitely," the man replied without hesitation. We laughed together and lay awake in our sleepers till deep into the night, talking like two brothers.

When the train arrived in Calcutta, I asked an Indian man for directions to my hotel. He showed me the line for taxis and waited with me. After thirty minutes, a taxi came. When I asked if he wanted to share the taxi, he said no, that he had waited in line only to make sure I continued my journey safely.

The first mass at Mother Teresa's mission started at five forty-five. As soon as I stepped out of the taxi, beggars surrounded me. "Are you a Christian?" they asked.

I nodded in affirmation.

"Me, too. Let me show you her door."

The mission's door was halfway down the alley; there, the beggars held out their hands, expecting payment. It was hard to refuse a beggar in Mother Teresa's doorway.

The chapel inside the mission was very simple. There were few chairs; most people sat on the cement floor. Mother Teresa sat near the back wall deep in prayer and looked as though she had been sitting there for a hundred years. She seemed so normal, so ordinary. How did a person of her simplicity ever become famous? Even at her age, she sat on the same cement floor everyone else at mass sat on, except me—I cheated and brought a blanket.

After a while, Mother Teresa got up and walked to the altar. She wore a blue and white habit, there were no unnecessary distractions in her walk. It was simple and deliberate, like a bride about to be married.

Perhaps in Mother Teresa's walk was the secret of her life. Mother Teresa didn't appear to be a visionary with grand ideas and the need to complete them. Instead, her life was a series of steps; with each step, she accomplished what God presented to her. And because her Beloved was *here* in the midst of life and not in the future or some heavenly realm, Mother Teresa was also *here,* in this present moment. For Mother Teresa, each step on her way to the altar was done in God's presence. Each step was a communion.

After the mass, I lost Mother Teresa in the crowd of people who gathered around her. When the people dispersed, I told a nun I was there to see Mother Teresa.

"Oh," she said, motioning to her right, "she is right here." I was surprised to see that Mother Teresa had been standing only a few feet away. If you didn't know she was a "saint," you probably wouldn't look twice at her.

I told her why I had come. "I don't do interviews anymore," she said, waving her hand. "So many interviews."

My excitement suddenly turned to disappointment. Without Mother Teresa's interview, I felt that the book would be incomplete. It wouldn't be the way I planned. I wanted to ask her again—to use my traveling such a distance and to use my suffering and the suffering of the world in order to persuade her to do the interview.

I wanted to beg her, because I didn't want to go home feeling I had failed myself and anyone who might read this book.

I handed her the letter she sent me. Perhaps she didn't realize she had already consented to do an interview. She glanced at the letter and gave it back to me. Then she took my hand and held it lovingly in both her hands and pulled me close to her. Her gray eyes looked into mine.

"I'm not feeling well," she said. "And I'm tired."

When she said that, it was as though God was telling me she was going to die. My concern for myself suddenly shifted to her. And by looking into those eyes, I saw it and took it in as though it were a gift: It was *suffering*. In some strange way, I felt the vast suffering Mother Teresa had witnessed. It was a suffering I had experienced before but rejected, because it had been too much for me. Now, years later, the suffering had returned. It had come full circle; only now I had grown enough to accept it.

"Do *everything* for God . . ." Mother Teresa continued. "God has given you many gifts—use them for the greater glory of God and the good of the people. Then you will make your life something beautiful for God; for this you have been created. Keep the joy of loving God ever burning in your heart, and share this joy with others. That's all."

I barely heard her; there was something deeper overwhelming me. I had come all this way with my mind set on interviewing Mother Teresa, but now that all changed because she was asking for something from me. Her eyes conveyed this. After having understood so many, I realized that Mother Teresa also needed understanding.

Mother Teresa in all her wonderful loving presence now appeared to me in a different way. She was no longer a saint; she was more than that. She was a human being. She was what we, as human beings, were meant to be all along. She was so deeply human and ordinary that she had touched that part of humanity that touched God, a humanity that can suffer, cry, laugh, and even die while staying connected with that essence that infuses us.

"Anyway," Mother Teresa continued, "you have the Dalai Lama. He's enough!"

As she said that, she waved her hand in the air as though to say, "Go on. It's going to be all right; you've got everything you need."

She turned and walked slowly back to her room. Her walk was just as it was the first time I saw her—nothing special. In some ways, her presence was also nothing special. It was a presence of utter simplicity. I doubt whether there has ever been a human being as ordinary as Mother Teresa, but it is precisely this quality that has made her so extraordinary.

Out in the hallway, people sat on benches that lined the walls. They waited to get a glimpse of Mother Teresa and smiled at me when they realized I had met the person they came to see. Today, I was proud to be a human being—because Mother Teresa was one.

The next day, I went to see Mother Teresa again. I wanted her to bless the malas, which are prayer beads similar to Christian rosaries. I figured it would be a nice gift for my friends—prayer beads blessed by the Dalai Lama and Mother Teresa. I met with the nun who was Mother Teresa's assistant. I asked her to give the malas to Mother Teresa to bless. "Oh no," she replied, "I can't do that."

When I asked why, the nun said they were Hindu and not Christian rosaries. I tried to tell her that they were Christian to me, but she didn't seem convinced. "Can you take them to her anyway?" I asked. But she refused again, until I told her that I didn't think Mother Teresa would mind. Then she relented and begrudgingly took the prayer beads to Mother Teresa.

I sat in the dimly lit waiting room. I found it hard to believe that one of Mother Teresa's nuns would make this distinction. If here, in such a place as this, people still believed in the illusion that religions are so different, what could we expect of the outside world?

Just then, the nun returned, smiling. She said Mother Teresa had blessed the prayer beads without hesitation.

✤ 7
WHO CAN SEE
THE REAL JESUS

I've met a lot of rich people in my life—especially religious rich people—and as Jesus said, "It is easier for a camel to go through the eye of a needle than for a rich man to enter the kingdom of God." But I don't mean *money* rich, I mean *belief* rich. They have many beliefs, and they cling to those beliefs as a rich man clings to money. Clinging to concepts and beliefs, whether religious or nonreligious, will keep a soul out of the kingdom of God just as easily as money.

If we look hard enough, we can see the difference between beliefs that express wisdom, truth, and compassion and beliefs that hold one fast so that the deeper, riskier business of further soul growth is ignored. If Jesus were here, it's possible he would remark that certain beliefs about him might keep people from knowing him or our Father, who sent him.

Even before Jesus, the ten commandments warned human beings about making our beliefs into idols.

"You shall have no other gods before me. You shall not make for yourself an idol in the form of anything in heaven above or on the earth beneath. You shall not bow down to them or worship them."[1]

Idols aren't only statues that sit on an altar, they're also the beliefs and thoughts on the altar of our mind, which we often hold more dear than God. These idols keep us from the experience of God, Jesus, and life. So the real question is, *Do we love God enough to let go of our beliefs about God and thus drop eternally into the God we don't know?*

The same can be said of Jesus: Do we respect him enough to look at him with new eyes? Or are we clinging to the beliefs about Jesus that were taught to us long ago? Because if you hold fast to the idea that you're Catholic or Lutheran or fundamentalist or Jewish or Baptist or Buddhist or New Age, then all you'll see is a Catholic or Lutheran or fundamentalist or Jewish or Baptist or Buddhist or New Age Jesus. There's an old joke that says, "if a pickpocket were to see Jesus, he would only see Jesus' pockets." Which means *we tend to see what we're looking for.*

I've had to fight hard in order to let go of my concept of Jesus, otherwise this book's Jesus would be limited by my perceptions. I hope that I can allow the real Jesus into this book and not just the Jesus I want to find. As I travel from town to town talking with mystics, scholars, and evangelists about Jesus, I am struck by the differences in who they see. During my quiet moments on the road, I wonder—*who can see the real Jesus?*

✠ 8
MARY MORRISSEY

WILSONVILLE, OREGON

"You don't have a choice about whether you are going to build a life," Mary Morrissey said, "you only have a choice about what life you are going to build."

1. Exodus 20:3–5.

I met her at the Living Enrichment Center, which stood on ninety-five forested acres in Wilsonville, Oregon. Each week over three thousand people attend her Sunday services there, while her radio show reaches over eighty countries. She is the author of *Building Your Field of Dreams* and *No Less Than Greatness*.

"I had to walk on some water to help create this place," she said after I pointed out a picture of "Jesus walking on water" in her office.

"The water Jesus walked on," she said, "is like fear. If you focus on the fear, you're going to sink."

Two thousand years ago, I'm sure there were people who said that Jesus' version of Judaism was "the Judaism of the future." Mary Morrissey's way of understanding Jesus may be the Christianity of the future.

"The Second Coming," she said, "is the coming of the Christ in every one of us; the realization of the divine spark that is within us all and not the coming of any specific person."

Because of ideas like that, some Christians might roll their eyes at her, but two thousand years ago Jesus prayed to God and asked, "that all of them may be *one*, Father, just as you are in me and I am in you."[1] Therefore, if we are all one with Jesus and the Father, who is it that will come again?

Who was/is Jesus?

There was a collective longing for a great being, for God incarnate—the Messiah. This Messianic energy took form because the longing of humanity called it forth. This "calling forth" was a track that delivered to humanity a soul who could incarnate and demonstrate the level of living that Jesus did. I don't think of God as sending Jesus down, because where is down? God is everywhere.

Jesus taught universal spirituality, the core of which is: *This life is love.* That is the curriculum in this realm, learn how to love, learn how to be love, learn how to express love, learn how to give love.

---

1. John 17:21, NIV.

We are all sons/daughters of God. Jesus wasn't fundamentally different from us. He was the highest version that we have seen of what it is we are all supposed to become.

It's interesting, because you mention that you came to the experience of love and what Jesus may have taught through exploring Eastern teachings. When I grew up we went to Baptist, Presbyterian, whatever church was nearby, and I didn't always believe in the Jesus that I was being taught there. It was only after I read *Autobiography of a Yogi,* that Paramahansa Yogananda introduced me to a Jesus that *rocked.* I thought, "Oh! This is the Jesus that I believe in!"

Jesus' teaching is simple. He taught that wherever we put our *attention,* we are putting our *intention,* and he said, "Seek ye first the kingdom of God."

One of the practices he gave was forgiveness, which is really giving or exchanging one perception for another. That's what forgiveness is. Instead of being a victim of circumstance, you take that same circumstance and find a different way to think about it and see it and you are no longer a victim of circumstance because you glean the gift out of it and you refuse to be victimized by that circumstance. You stand in your own authority, as a child of God yourself.

Love is like the highest frequency of thinking. We have labels for frequencies of thought, so this unconditional love—we could call it unitive consciousness, Divine mind—is where you are connected to that realm that is available to all of us. You know the old song says, "Love lifts you up, higher and higher"? Well, it is that; you think beyond the borders of your own skin and consider what is good for all of us, that we are part of something that is magnificent and wonderful, that is bigger than any one of us.

When we experience love, it is because we have attuned to our true nature. It may be in the context of an experience with another person, so then

I say, "Oh, I love you," when actually what I am saying is that in your presence and through our exchange I am touching that place in me where love lives, I am touching that experience of connecting to what is true about me, about this life, about our experience together.

"Love one another," a warm feeling
or a state of being?

Love absolutely has to do with a state of being, it has to do with a recognition that, in fact, what it is essentially that makes you, you, and what essentially makes me, me, is the same thing. I honor, respect, and hold the highest regard for that in you; it has nothing to do with behavior, it has nothing to do with personality, it is way beyond behavior and personality. It is filtered through behavior and personality. But beyond that, it's the essence, and when I am in that place in me and you are in that place in you, then we can really recognize the true essence of each other together, but either of us can recognize it even alone.

Emotional love is a form of love and we can experience love that way, but unconditional love is a presence, it is a name for the presence and power of God.

Jesus' religion?

Certainly Jesus had Jewish roots, but he was taught a universal spirituality. He knew there was one Presence and one Power but one God was viewed differently for different people—that we have different approaches to experience this one presence and one power.

Did Jesus intend to start Christianity or
just bring some life into Judaism?

It doesn't appear to me that he meant to start Christianity. I think he meant to start a world awareness that would wake up anyone who heard the message. And when he said, "The truth shall set you free," that was true. When you touch this truth, it sets you free from the life you've known.

Jesus would be amused at Christianity! Because I am a minister, people sometimes try to make me responsible for the good thing that happens in their life when all I am doing is helping them develop a relationship with God. And I really think that what Jesus asked us to do and what his teaching was meant to do was to say, "Do this and get your own connection and become aware yourself. I am just showing you what is possible and how to practice your life in such a way that you, too, will have the same experiences."

It is very difficult for a finite mind to have an infinite God, so while we have access to infinite mind, we operate from a finite perspective—it's easier to imagine God like Jesus than to imagine an infinite presence. For me, it is an earlier developmental stage in terms of learning how to relate to God, that you see Jesus as God, like kids see their parents as God and hopefully they mature and grow out of that.

Jesus said, "By their fruits, you shall know them," and I think that is true. Do people who follow the Buddha have evidence or the fruits of that kind of spiritual life Jesus spoke of? I think so. I have known some of the most beautiful, awake, generous, giving, loving, kind Buddhists. I call people like this mystical practitioners of their faith, whether it is Buddhism or Hinduism or Jainism, Islam, the Sufis, or Christians. Those who practice their faith on a mystical level are beyond the borders of the dogma. They experience the true spirit of transformation that is available in a personal, profound relationship with the Spirit.

It is important to contextualize what Jesus said because you can take anything and make it sound a certain way, and Jesus spoke to many different levels of awareness. For example, when he said, "I am the way, and the truth, and the life and no one comes to the father but through me" (John

14:6, NIV), he spoke from the realm of Cosmic Consciousness—here the "I-am" or "Cosmic Consciousness" *is* the way and the truth and the life and no one *does* come to the Father or the creator except through that "I-am" awakened consciousness. It is through the "I-am" that is within each of us that we have a relationship with the creator. We know Jesus was also making the connection to the Exodus story where Moses was told that God's name was "I Am what I am."

What is a mystic?

A mystic is somebody who is able to live in the two worlds at the same time, who is able to live in this earthly realm but not be bound by it. It is best described in the quote we attribute to Jesus where he said, "Be in the world but not of it," A mystic has the ability to be in this world but not be trapped by the limitations of perspective that often come by living in this world.

Virgin birth?

The virgin birth is a metaphor. We all have an immaculate conception, and by that I mean I think each one of us is conceived in perfection. In the mind of God we are all perfect and nothing is missing and nobody has any more than anybody else. To develop and bring that into conscious awareness, which is what it appears to me this life is about—earthing it, bringing it into form in an awake state. So we see people in various stages of awakeness in this realm of existence we might call earth school.

Accuracy of the gospels?

Divine truth has a frequency to it so that when you read the gospels, you can feel their truth. Certainly any of us who have studied the historical trail the Bible has gone down can see moments where it was altered or shifted or changed, where things were deleted and added, where an organization's needs and considerations took preference over what seemed to be the highest truth that was accessible in that document. But there is certainly enough truth there that a person who is trained and has a true heart will find that truth. It is absolutely one of my favorite texts, because within it I find constant inspiration, tremendous help, hope, inspiration, guidance.

Jesus' lost years? Was he perfect?
Did he have to learn things?

We do not know a lot about the early childhood of Jesus. Our first accounting of him as a teacher was at twelve years old when he was in the temple demonstrating extraordinary awareness with the rabbi basically sitting at his feet. We know then that there is something magnificent about this being. But I wouldn't say he necessarily was perfect, I just think he came with extraordinary awareness and he never had it trained out of him. While no one we know had his awareness, there is a natural knowing in all of us.

Did Jesus ever sin?

"Sin" has been described as an archery term that meant missing the mark. If Jesus had his life to live over again, he'd probably say he would do some things differently—so I think the answer to that question is "yes"— he made some sins, some errors.

Was Jesus ever married or did he
have an intimate relationship?

I have always felt that he was a totally, fully human being, therefore, it would have been very odd if he was completely out of touch with his sexuality. He might have been so driven by his mission that he transmuted and moved that energy toward his mission. But I have never thought he was out of touch with his own sexuality.

We know he had a special relationship with Mary, and that love comes through in the gospels we are handed. Sometimes we make a lot out of sex, and it is certainly a wonderful expression in the human realm. But whether he did or didn't, just isn't really so important to me. What is important to me is that the Jesus I know was fully alive, fully human, and fully divine.

Jesus had a physical resurrection. I have a sense that it is actually possible for a being to resurrect because our being is life; this body is just a mass of molecules and that is enlivened by the Spirit. We don't live in our bodies, our bodies live in us. So if this is, in fact, true, then why would it not be possible to disconnect, leave it dormant, and then call it back into life? Jesus was at a level of consciousness where he could demonstrate that the Spirit that you are is greater than anything—even greater than death. That Spirit in him, and in us can even calm the sea and heal disease.

We make such a big deal out of the physical aspects—Did he literally walk on water? Did he literally lift up his body from the dead?—that we get stuck in the more limited forms of what his teaching could really mean to us. Using the Christ power, that energy that is in each one of us, to call forth that which looks like it is dead, is what you and I are to do in our own lives today. Maybe you have a project that looks dead but if you don't want it to be dead, you have the power to literally breathe life back into it. You have the power to breathe life back into anything should you call it forth.

Forgiveness?

You begin to forgive by separating the human being from the behavior. The behavior itself may be despicable and the behavior itself may be not anything you ever want to repeat or allow into your life again. But the being who perpetrated that behavior is still worthy of your love. In any place in my mind or heart where I have a person or experience where love doesn't live, I have cut a portion of myself off. So the opportunity in forgiveness is for me to learn a level of loving that wouldn't be available to me if there weren't that really difficult experience. If all my experiences were easy, I would never have to dig deep in myself to really call forth the greater capacity for loving. And a love that goes beyond behavior, that goes beyond the borders of what I have known, is transformative.

There is a love available that can be applied to every circumstance. There is a way of seeing and experiencing everything through the realm of pure love. And this makes possible the experiencing and bringing to bear in this life the highest of what life can offer.

First he had his own prayer practice of simply making contact with God alone—there was the practice of the inner work. Second, there was the practice of the small group. He had a little mastermind group, a group of twelve people that he hung out with who were his close intimates. I call them "partners in believing." People that believed with him and for him. So if you want to stay in the Presence and that awareness of "I-am", you need to have people who believe with you and for you, whatever your own dream may be. Third, he had the work he did in the world.

Fear killed Jesus. It wasn't a group of people, it was just fear. It is interesting because in some ways the message is still being killed today. I mean the fear that this power could live in each one of us, that we each could do these things and greater things still. It is still being put down and hidden and kept from people.

I resonate with the Gospel of Thomas in a great way. I really think one particular line that is often quoted—"If you bring forth what is within you, it will save you, and if you do not bring forth what is within you, it will destroy you"—is absolutely true.

Within everything is a thread of truth, so the thread of truth in original sin is the idea that we are all born into the garden and the garden is the garden of unity of consciousness. But then we begin to eat from the tree of knowledge of good and evil, right/wrong, we move into comparison, we move into the world of separation, and in the world of separation, we step out of the garden. Jesus represented the one who taught us that you can live in unity of consciousness.

There are basically three levels of awareness.

The first level is people who are really asleep to who they are and I call this the "to me" level because it feels as if life is happening "to me." Look what happened to me! Look what my parents did to me! Look what my boss is doing to me! It's very victimy and it is very powerless.

The second level is thinking "by me." If you can give up your victimhood, then you can move into the second state, which is "Oh, I'm a co-creator!" It is the first stage of waking up, of perceiving that I am part of something that is magnificent and I am part of this life. It is here we begin to use our own creative energies to create things we want. But usually this is a very ego-driven stage. We are still immature spiritually, so we manifest from a self-centered perspective. A great deal of the world is driven by this level of consciousness. If I only get more and more, then I will be happy and safe.

The next level is called "through me." In order to move out of that self-centeredness, you have to give up some control by submitting your ego to your soul or to your spirit, so that you bring your ego in alignment with your soul. When you move onto this level you give up control of the ego and you walk through the doorway into the stage we could call "through me." Now I am listening to higher guidance and letting those messages move through me. I am aligning my energies in the way Jesus meant when he said, "Put love first." Check things out, does this feel loving? If it does—do it. If it doesn't feel loving—then let it go.

In the beginning of the through me stage there is often a rational or logical kind of thought processing. Is this the right thing vs. the wrong thing? Eventually, the heart becomes involved and we begin "to catch" this Divine love and partner with it. At this point you're sensitive to this leading of the Spirit and it's like having constant contact with God. You don't have to process what you are going to do or not do because if you start to do something that isn't in alignment with that stream of energy that is loving, you feel a decrease in your own energy. Basically, you feel more alive when you are in touch with your own life force and less alive when you are out of touch with it. Seek first that kingdom—because *the kingdom of aliveness and the kingdom of God or life are the same.* So if you are seeking the kingdom of aliveness, then you know you are on the right track when you are feeling more alive. We are created so that we will feel more alive when we are on the right path and heavy and uninspired when we are doing things we are not supposed to be doing. *We have to pay attention* because we don't have a choice about whether we are going to build a life; we only have a choice about what life we are going to build.

Second Coming?

The Second Coming is the coming of the Christ in every one of us, that realization of the Divine spark within us all, and not the coming of a specific person.

✢ 9
BILLY GRAHAM AND THE DOOR

MADISON, WISCONSIN

It was 4:30 P.M. and I was at home in Madison, Wisconsin. I had come home to regroup for a few weeks, or was it a few months? At any rate, I had run out of money again, so I went home to work for awhile. But working to pay the bills is like treading water, and I didn't get anywhere on my book while time passed.

After a while I called my sisters, and they gave me a couple of credit cards to use. I felt like crying because they had faith in me despite my less than stellar financial history. I got the generator on my motor home fixed and packed up, then I pointed my motor home in the direction of Montreat, North Carolina—the home of Billy Graham. I had written him several times requesting an interview and the answer was always "no," but if you're writing a book about Jesus and his friends—*you've got to have Billy Graham.*

After a little detective work, I found out the name and location of the church Billy Graham attended whenever he was home. "I'll just go there and ask him for an interview about Jesus," I thought to myself. "Maybe I'll only get ten minutes or twenty minutes—*but I'll go.* What do I have to lose? Even if he said 'no,' at least I got to see where the great man worships." Why is he great? Because he has integrity, fortitude, and devotion. I may disagree with a point here or there, but Billy Graham is sincere and preaches without the malevolent side I saw in some of the other evangelists. Have you ever heard of Billy Graham getting in trouble? Me neither. Usually, preachers get in trouble one of two ways—women or money. *Sometimes it's both women and money.* From what I've heard, though, Billy Graham is honest enough to open up the accounting books of his religious organization to the public and smart enough not to meet alone with an unknown female. I called the church while driving my motor home.

"Mr. Graham comes here when he's in town," the young lady said. "But I don't know if he's in town or not."

I hesitated. Should I continue to drive all the way to Montreat, North Carolina, if Billy Graham wasn't even going to be there?

"On Easter Sunday," the woman continued, "we have a pancake breakfast at seven forty-five."

The woman's friendliness and Southern accent convinced me (she had a voice like soft butter) as well as the fact that I could already smell those pancakes and steaming cups of coffee, while envisioning young children wearing their Sunday best playing tag as the adults went back for seconds on the sausage. Pancake breakfast?! Zow! I'm there. I looked down at the speedometer—my hulking house was speeding. I slowed down a little and told myself to relax. There was plenty of time, the breakfast was two days off, the pancakes hadn't been mixed yet and the grill was still cold.

A little after midnight the next day, I drove into Montreat. I slept in the parking lot of the church until 5:30 A.M. My plan was to attend all the services that day plus the pancake breakfast and hope Billy Graham showed up. The first service was at six forty-five, and I was there five minutes early, but there was no one around. Instead, they were all upstairs eating pancakes—*but wasn't that scheduled for seven forty-five?*

"This morning was daylight savings time," a smiling young woman said, carrying a plate of pancakes past me. "Clocks were set ahead. It's almost eight o'clock."

I looked around. There were about twenty to twenty-five tables with people chowing down. I didn't know anyone, and I felt *very alone.* But then it dawned on me that since I didn't know anyone, I could sit anywhere—and suddenly I felt *very free.* Hmmm . . . I still felt a little insecure, so I took a deep breath, and remembered that I am always in God's presence and loved no matter where I go. More important, *I felt loved*, despite being in a crowd of strangers.

I saw a table of attractive women all dressed in their Easter best. But for some reason, I steered away from their table and walked over to what appeared to be a family.

"You mind if I sit here?" I asked. They welcomed me warmly and introduced themselves. For a while, our conversation was just a surface courtesy. We talked about the usual things without any real connection until I noticed that the father, whose name was Peter, had an unusually large black watch.

"That's a big watch you got there," I said. Suddenly he sat up and came alive.

"It's a compass, a barometer, and an altimeter," he said proudly.

"Wow," I said. "I need one of those—I'm always getting lost."

"Look, Mom," their pretty daughter said. "Finally, someone who likes Dad's watch."

"My family bought this for me," Peter said as he took off his watch and handed it to me.

"We called all over," the wife said, speaking for the first time. "And eventually found it at a store in Asheville—it's made by Sunto—a Finnish company."

I pressed the various buttons as Peter explained each function to me.

"This is amazing," I said. "When I travel, I never know which direction is which, but now I can see that north is directly behind me and the altimeter says that Montreat, North Carolina, is 2,700 feet above sea level."

We made more small talk while I gobbled down some pancakes.

"Well," I said, getting up, "I'm off to the eight-thirty service."

A few flights of stairs later, I sat down in the chapel—about midway between the pulpit and the back door. The walls of the chapel were made of stone and the stained-glass windows were closed, but they were opened midway through the service after the congregation said "Christ has risen" twice. It was a nice effect, the colored sun streaming into the church just as "Christ has risen" was spoken.

Billy Graham never showed up, and I yawned throughout the service because I hadn't had enough sleep. After the service, I made a beeline for my motor home—and took a nap. I woke up ten minutes before the eleven o'clock service and since I was still tired, I did some quick math. If Billy Graham showed up, he wouldn't speak until the sermon at eleven-thirty, and that meant I could sleep another half hour. I hit the snooze button and went back to bed. At eleven twenty-five, I jumped out of bed and walked a few hundred yards to the chapel. Unlike the eight-thirty service, the chapel was packed, and when I stood on my tippy toes and peered over the heads in front of me, I saw that he was there! Billy Graham was up at the pulpit and he talked about Kosovo—and his voice was soft, more like warm milk than soft butter. His gray hair looked wild and thick, and with his Harry Caray glasses, he came across differently than I'd expected. I thought he'd appear stern and sound judgmental—but instead his voice conveyed warmth, hope, and acceptance.

He wasn't young and cocky, like the other preacher. Nor was he arrogant enough to think he knew God's Word. Instead, his melodious voice carried his words—and his words were prayers that expressed humanity's mistakes. There was no hate or disdain for our mistakes, only a wish to overcome them. When he finished speaking, he turned and took a seat behind the pulpit. Once seated, a gray-haired man next to him momentarily put his hand on Billy Graham's forearm. Billy Graham turned slowly and looked at the other man, then they smiled broadly at each other. They looked like two old friends who just as easily could have been in a small boat—fishing together, or on a porch somewhere—rocking away.

At the end of the service, Billy Graham sneaked out the back door before I could catch him. I attended the lunch buffet after the service, but he wasn't there. I talked with some older ladies who suggested I try his radio station—"It's just down a few miles."

I walked out into the parking lot knowing the radio station wasn't the best idea because I'd probably run into an administrator or two who, while only trying to do their jobs, would just get in the way rather than help. You can give the most heartfelt and logical reason to an administrator for meeting someone like Billy Graham, and either Billy Graham won't get the message or what you're doing gets so watered down by the time it gets conveyed to him that it sounds like a few useless lines at the end of an overly long obituary.

About thirty feet to my right, an older man was getting into his rather large Buick. *What the heck? I thought. You never know.*

"Excuse me," I said, "do you know how to reach Billy Graham?"

The man's clear blue eyes looked at me for what seemed like an eternity. Whatever he was looking for in me, he must have found.

"Last house on the left," he said, "down a few blocks. A man named Calvin Theilman lives there. He's the former minister here at Montreat—he'll know."

I jumped into my motor home and drove up and down the block a few times looking for the right house. I almost gave up and finally just guessed at which house was the right one. Then I parked my twenty-eight-foot motor home (inconspicuously I hoped) in a vacant lot around the corner. As I walked down the street, I wondered how easy it was to tow an illegally parked motor home.

My backpack contained everything I needed or might need: my tape recorder, two microphones, cassettes, power cord and batteries, my list of questions, a couple copies of my first book, and—now that my generator was fixed and my printer worked—four copies of a letter to Billy Graham.

There was no name on the mailbox of the house, but there were two doorbells and above one was a piece of tape with the word "doorbell" scrawled in black ink. I rang the doorbell, and almost immediately the door opened.

10
CALVIN THEILMAN

MONTREAT, NORTH CAROLINA

A woman opened the door on Easter.

"I'm looking for Calvin," I said.

"I'm Calvin," a gray-haired bear of a man said as he stuck his head out from behind the door. I quickly explained myself to the man.

"I'm a writer working on a book about Jesus and I'm trying to find Billy Graham . . . and I'm sorry to bother you."

"Come in," he replied with such a welcoming and open-armed attitude that I swear I felt at home even though I was a thousand miles away from my home.

He took me to his study, where there were large sunny windows stretched across the whole back wall. He went up to the glass and looked out, then he turned and motioned for me to join him at the windows. The study overlooked a large backyard where a group of children played. A stream ran through it, and beyond the stream was a hill, with trees that went all the way to the top.

"I built this room a few years ago," he said. It felt strange standing there next to him because even though I had just met him, he had no fear of me; he trusted me in a way that I can only describe as giving me *my* space within *his* house. I had a wonderful feeling just being in his presence.

I showed him my first book, and gave him some more details about what I was doing. Then he stopped me, went to a screen door, and called to his three sons.

"Come in here," he said. "I want you to hear this."

Then he looked back at me.

"They're all Ph.D.'s and two of them are M.D.'s."

After they came in and sat down, Calvin said, "Tell them what you're doing."

I started talking as Calvin showed them my book.

"It's hard getting published," his son Dave, a New Testament scholar, said. "How did you do it?"

I explained that, and how I was in a Tibetan monastery when I first got the idea for *Tying Rocks to Clouds.* After some friendly conversation, the sons excused themselves and went out to their families. Calvin stayed and talked.

"Well, Bill," Calvin said, "you seem like a compassionate man."

"I've suffered," I said, "and I suffered till I surrendered. That's when my heart and soul opened to God's presence. After that I became more aware of other people's suffering."

"That's true, Bill," Calvin said with such a feeling of empathy that I knew that at some point in his life he had been broken open too.

"You know, Bill," Calvin continued, "there are some people who say my beliefs are too narrow. When I say, 'My God is the only way,' they say I should change my beliefs. *But this is what my God tells me to believe!* How can I choose to change those beliefs when those are the beliefs that God tells me to live by?!"

"If that's what your relationship with God demands you believe," I said sincerely, "you can't change your beliefs to please other people."

Calvin sighed.

"Thank you for saying that," he said. "Some people want me to be tolerant of their beliefs—and yet they won't tolerate mine."

✛ 11
A DOOR

Calvin Theilman and I made a few phone calls, but one of Billy Graham's assistants said a meeting with Billy Graham wasn't possible. I was disappointed, but I'm persistent, so I decided I'd come back and try again in a few months. I drove to Black Mountain (which was a small town right next to Montreat). I left there a little after 4 P.M., and since I had to be in Newark by 11 A.M. the next day, it was going to be six hundred miles of continuous, hard driving. I should have left Black Mountain earlier, but I liked hanging out at a coffee shop named Mountain Java's. If I didn't know better, I would say Black Mountain was an oasis, a place at the end of the earth where old hippies, poets, wanderers, and the lost tribes all end up. Kathmandu, Bangkok, Berkeley, and Maui were also like that, places where directionless people congregated until they decided where to go next. For example, there was a woman named Lorna who was always at the coffee shop. She was in her mid-fifties, didn't have a job, and lived off her sister's credit card.

"I don't know what to do next," she said in between puffs on her cigarette.

There was an older gray-haired man named Joe who did handyman work part time, drove a 1978 Toyota pickup, and always wore a baseball cap that said "Joe" on it. He often talked about the Civil War.

"Some people around here call it 'the War of Southern Independence,'" he'd say between sips of coffee, "or the War of Secession or the Great Rebellion or . . ."

Once he told me about his first marriage. "I had just bought a new motorcycle," he said, squinting his eyes. "It must have been about 1962 or 1963. Anyway I was going to drive the cycle across the United States, but then I met a woman and married her six months later. Never did go on that trip and sold the motorcycle pretty quick after I got married."

Then there was the young poet named Jimmy, whose intense love poems reminded me of myself twenty years ago. He liked to call women "goddesses" and used phrases like "dark love," "insane jealousy," and "heart-rending purgatory" to describe his intimate relationships.

And, of course, Roger, an ex-Baptist minister turned medicine man. He had long gray hair, a gray beard, and a medicine bag around his neck.

"Thirty years ago, I was preaching the Bible," he said while rolling a cig-arette. "Now I'm a medicine man—a healer in an Indian tribe."

Day after day, I met them and others at the coffee shop. Some of them seemed to be stuck there, unable to get on with their lives. Then I realized that while most places on this earth have many doors in and many doors out, places like Black Mountain only have doors in and no doors out—*you have to make your own door out.* That's where Jesus came in, because Jesus was a woodworker—specifically he worked on and built doorways. That's true, and you can look it up. So Jesus knows a lot about doorways, and he can help you find the courage to point yourself in a direction and to go, to just go and create an opening where none existed before—because resurrection is bringing life to a place that had been dead and an opening to that which has been closed.

✛ 12
DEEPAK CHOPRA

LA JOLLA, CALIFORNIA

I was semi-delirious. It was probably the lack of sleep together with too much caffeine. After only several hours sleep the night before, I had gotten up at 5 A.M. and driven from Thousand Oaks, California, to La Jolla, Cali-fornia, in order to meet with Deepak Chopra. It was only a hundred-and-fifty-mile drive, but throw in the unpredictable state of California highways together with several espresso stops and you get four hours of driving.

With an hour to kill before my interview I debated about which would be more beneficial to my wakefulness during the Deepak interview: Hatha Yoga and a bit of prayer and meditation? Or a large cup of strong coffee? I decided on the yoga, meditation, and prayer. And then five minutes before the interview—*I ran across the street for some coffee.*

His assistant, Carolyn, led me into Deepak's office. He was seated behind a desk, wearing spectacles and peering into the glow of a computer monitor while clicking a mouse with his right hand and simultaneously turning some pages of a book with his left hand.

Deepak Chopra is a smart guy. A smart and calm guy. Smart people are rarely calm since they are usually enamored by their own thoughts—in the way that dancing partners rarely let go of each other. This constant movement does not lend itself to peace and the subsequent calm that comes from it.

But I expected Deepak's calm and his understanding of what it meant to have a relationship with God. Since he is Indian and brought up as a Hindu, I was surprised however, to find he was very familiar with Bible verses and could even translate a few verses from Aramaic (the spoken language of Jesus) into English . . . Consequently, I mentioned to him how Jesus had said, "Blessed are the meek, for they shall inherit the earth," during his Sermon on the Mount and how the word "meek" had always bugged me because it conveyed to me a meaning of weak or wimpy, and why should the weak inherit the earth?

Deepak simply reminded me that "meek means innocent and open. It refers to those who have surrendered to the will of God and the infinite Spirit."

His answer was so simple that it was almost disturbing. Later when I told a friend what Deepak Chopra had said about the word "meek," my friend reminded me that he had just said that same thing to me a few weeks before. And *that was even more disturbing,* because I think I paid more attention to Deepak Chopra's words than my friend's because Deepak Chopra is famous and my friend isn't.

So often in life, and very often just within this book, the Spirit of God is staring us right in the face. But even though we read and hear the words, we really don't see them or hear them, because we are looking for God's word in a certain kind of person or a certain kind of Christian. But Jesus' story of the Good Samaritan reveals the Truth. God often works through the person you least expect and often through a person not of your religion or belief. Within this book, that "messenger of God" and friend of Jesus may be Jerry Falwell or Billy Graham, or Deepak Chopra or Marianne Williamson—or perhaps it may even be the next person you meet or the person who is beside you now.

Deepak Chopra is a renowned physician and author of twenty-five books that have been translated into thirty-five languages. *Time* magazine selected Dr. Chopra as one of the Top 100 Icons and Heroes of the century. He is the founder of the Chopra Center for Well Being in La Jolla, California.

Who is/was Jesus?

In the Eastern traditions there is the concept of avatars or bodhisattvas—enlightened beings. In Buddhism, the idea is that these enlightened beings are at the edge of what is called the dharmakaya and the sambhogakaya. The sambhogakaya is the realm of enlightened beings and the dharmakaya is beyond that event horizon where there is the infinite intention of all that is, was, and will be. When beings reach this edge between the sambhogakaya and dharmakaya, they are at the door and have a choice to go beyond the event horizon and disappear from our realm or to come back and help others to where they are. In Hinduism, or the Vedantic tradition, they are called avatars, while in Buddhism they are called bodhisattvas because they have infinite compassion. As you know compassion is also an important aspect of Jesus. In many parts of India, depending on your vocabulary or semantics, Jesus is considered to be a bodhisattva, an avatar, or an enlightened being who has infinite compassion and wants to help others come out of their suffering. Jesus introduced the idea (which was very foreign to the older traditions of Judaism) of forgiveness, of love, of equality, of salvation rather than the Old Testament God that was like a dysfunctional parent.

Some Christians and fundamentalists refer to Christ as the only savior. I did research on this in response to a letter I received from a fundamentalist who demanded proof of what I believed. When people claim Christ to be the only savior they are almost always referring to verse 14:6 in the Gospel of John in which Jesus said, "I am the Way, the Truth and the Life, no man cometh unto the Father but by me." But when we quote this, we must remember that these words in English are very different from the original words in Aramaic. When these words appear in the King James Version it is sixteen hundred years later. When Jesus spoke them, he spoke them in Aramaic, which, along with Babylonian and Hebrew, is one of the original Semitic languages. In Aramaic "I am" is translated as *ena-ena*. In other words, it is repeated. It refers to the "I inside the I," the essence, the Spirit, which is universal. The word "way" in Aramaic was *urha,* which means light. The word "truth" in Aramaic was *sherara,* which can mean "Spirit" or "the light of pure knowledge." And the word "life" in Aramaic is *hayya* or "sacred life force," known in the Eastern tradition as *prana*. And the phrase "but by me" is also revealing in Aramaic because it refers to mortal forms and physical forms that pass away and which provide a vehicle to move from one reality into another. So if you follow the original Aramaic, my interpretation is that Christ said "the I in everyone is the essence of the essence, *ena-ena*. It is the Spirit that is universal; it is the light of pure knowledge and it is the source of the life force and it is through physical forms, that is, the human body and human nervous system, that we unfold the unmanifest into the manifest." But in the West, almost two thousand years after the original words are spoken, many people, particularly fundamentalists, have taken the words of Christ to mean that *he* as a *person* is the only means to salvation or enlightenment.

After I posted this on the Internet, a woman e-mailed me and said, "If the King James Version was good enough for Christ, it's good enough for me!" But as we all know, the King James Version was written sixteen hundred years after Jesus.

Jesus' religion?

Jesus wasn't any religion. Jesus wasn't a Christian just as Buddha wasn't a Buddhist and Mohammed wasn't a Mohammedan. Jesus was beyond institutional religion. Jesus was experiencing and giving others the experience of a domain of awareness that was universal and, therefore, could not be something that could even be called a religion. Spirituality is a domain of awareness that goes beyond dogma and ideology and narrow domestic boundaries.

Jesus' lost years?

There are many stories about Jesus traveling and spending time with the great spiritual masters of India. He was known in India as Isa. There is also a school of thought in India that his disciple Thomas was actually one of Jesus' teachers. In many paintings, including the ones in the Vatican, Thomas is represented as being very dark, he is brown, he's black—because according to many legends in India, Thomas is supposed to be from Madras. And Thomas's attitude toward Jesus was not one of pure adulation because he had been Jesus' teacher—that's why after the so-called resurrection Thomas doubts. At any rate, according to these legends Thomas and Jesus came back to India after Jesus' resurrection along with his mother, Mary. Jesus is believed to have been in India until he was over ninety years old. He is thought to be buried in a tomb in Kashmir, outside of Srinagar and people still go there to see it. Mary is buried in a tomb near Murree in Pakistan.

Why are people afraid to question
the validity of the Church

It's simpler to just accept something and not have to go within and ask questions. It also is fear-based and political—there is a lot of money behind the Church.

Why didn't most Jews accept him as the Messiah?

Like most populations, the Jewish population was influenced by its authorities, and the Jews who were influential did not accept him as the Messiah because he threatened their authority. Messiahs are usually accepted only after they have been martyred. Even Jesus said ". . . in his own house is a prophet without honor."

Who killed Jesus and why?

The Romans decided it would be expedient to get rid of Jesus because he was a renegade. Besides being a great spiritual being, he was a savvy political activist. He was trying to restore independence for the Jews in many ways.

So the traditional Jewish people and the rabbis were uneasy about this young man who was trying to stir things up and get rid of their power. They and the Romans were nervous because he was threatening their authority. It was convenient that Jesus go away—for the Pharisees, the moneylenders, and all the people who he was questioning.

Jesus died for our sins?

Karma means experience. In this case, saints or martyrs consciously or unconsciously take on the experience or karma of a collective psyche and by doing so they change the course of history. Martin Luther King took on the collective suffering of the black people in America and as a result of his martyrdom there is a change in history of that race.

Mahatma Gandhi took on the collective suffering of the Indian people. It's not like he's atoning for their sins, but Mahatma Gandhi took on the collective experience, and because of him, India got a new surge, a new resurrection, a new pride among the peoples of the world. Enlightened beings sometimes do that consciously, sometimes unconsciously. By doing what Jesus did, he introduced the ideas—which was very foreign to the older traditions of Judaism—of forgiveness, of love, of equality, of salvation, rather than God being a dysfunctional parent who often punished his creation.

In India, there is a long tradition of yogis who can go into a deep state of consciousness. They can decrease their metabolic rate to almost zero and appear dead. In this suspended animation state you can take a yogi and put a knife through his hands or through his flesh and it won't bleed. I believe that's what Jesus did when he appeared to die. Afterward, Thomas and Mary came, got him out and escaped through Egypt into India.

There are references to Jesus' marriage in Indian mythology; he had a very loving relationship with Mary Magdalene. There is also this whole description of Mary in the Christian Bible washing his feet and rubbing his feet with oil—a custom that was basically restricted to those who were in a very intimate, sensual, and possibly sexual relationship. Not only did she wash his feet and anoint them, she wiped them with her hair.

The word "born again" actually is similar to resurrection, and it really means to let go of the old self and create a new self. I believe that many, many people have their own second coming and Christ is a metaphor for that.

I never think of events as happening in space or time. So when I look out on the street and see the city of La Jolla, that's not a location in space and time, it's an event in my awareness. Ultimately, every event is an event in awareness and depending on the state of awareness you're in, you experience the event in a different way. I think Jesus Christ himself is a state of awareness that we could all aspire to, that there is such a thing as Christ Consciousness. Christ Consciousness is a worthy goal because it talks about the essence of unity. "Do unto others as you would have them do unto you. My father is in me, I am in you, I and the Father are one, love is the most important thing." That state of consciousness is what Christ is to me and it's something that is a worthy goal to aspire to because if we have that aspiration, not only will we be different but the world will change. So

Christ Consciousness can change the world and hopefully will. *That* would be the Second Coming of Christ, if you have a critical mass of people in Christ Consciousness, the world will change, *that* will be the Second Coming of Christ, changing our collective psyche.

We have so many versions of God and Christ because they are all different projections or fragments. The God of any religion is only a fragment of God, but is so complete as to create a unique world, each with a different relationship. So when someone asks, "Is there really a God?" the most legitimate answer is "Who is asking?" And ultimately "Who is asking?" is just another stage in the quest for God knowledge. God has approached in stages because otherwise one could never close the huge gap between him and us.

If you see yourself as one of God's children, then his relationship to you will be as a protector or a maker of rules. This relationship shifts if you see him as a creator—then you start to share some of God's functions. You stand on a more equal ground. Finally, at the stage of "I am," you see the same pure being that is common to God and humans. I believe we progress toward God in seven stages and gradually the wide gap between God and his worshipers becomes narrower and eventually closes. Therefore, we keep creating God in our image for a reason that is more than vanity; we want to bring him home to us, to achieve intimacy. If you look at the Old Testament, all the seven stages of projection are there.

1. In the first stage, Jehovah or God banishes Adam and Eve from the Garden. He is upset with Cain because Abel gave him meat and Cain gave him grain. *At this stage God may be seen as punitive or as the protector of those who see themselves in danger.*

2. In the Book of Moses, God is in a reactive mode and makes rules and laws. *God is the almighty who appeals to those who want power and accomplishment (or lack any way of getting power).*

3. In the Psalms, God goes into the restful-awareness response.

"The peace that passes understanding." *The God of peace brings peace . . . to those who have discovered their own inner world.*

4. In the New Testament, you can see God as the intuitive response, "Ask and you shall receive, seek and you shall find, knock and it shall be opened unto you." *God is seen as the redeemer . . . to those who are conscious of committing a sin or aware of growing and evolving to our full potential.*

5. The Book of Genesis is the creative response. God the creator said "Let there be light and there was light"—it's all about creativity. God as a creative response also exists in the New Testament in the form of Jesus. Jesus "creates" healings and miracles. Eventually the apostles learn to create miracles and live creative lives.

6. The Book of Moses is about a visionary response. The visionary response is in both the Old and New Testament. This is the God of miracles . . . when the laws of nature are suddenly revoked without warning.

7. The sacred response is in the Old Testament when Moses asks God "Who are you?" and he says, "I am that I am." This stage is where pure being allows us to revel in the infinite creation of God. Here the mystic Jews searching for the Shekinah[1] meet the Buddhists in their search for satori, and when they arrive, the ancient Vedic seers will be waiting in the presence of Shiva, along with Christ and his father. This is the place which is both the beginning and the end of the process that is God. As Jesus said while being the *"I am"* of pure being—"I am the Alpha and Omega."

These are all stages of human projection till the final stage when you realize that the essence, *"ena-ena"* as Jesus says, the essence, which is pure spirit, is God and the whole universe is a projection of that God. When you

---

1. God has a presence known in Hebrew as Shekinah—sometimes translated as "light" or radiance. Shekinah formed the halos around angels and the radiant joy in the face of a saint. Shekinah was feminine though God was interpreted in the Judeo-Christian tradition as masculine.

get to the core of your essence, it is the same core as my essence, and the same core essence of everything in creation.

The universe is constantly being generated from that essence. Genesis wasn't "once upon a time." Even as we speak there are millions of galaxies and there are giant stars that are exhausting thermonuclear energy and disappearing into black holes and exploding on the other side through wormholes into new galaxies. Creation is a projection—its maintenance, destruction, incubation, and resurrection are an ongoing phenomenon through which that essence operates, and all that we experience in the material world is the projection of that essence. It's all projection. How you see this universal projection depends on the level of individual projection you are perceiving from. Are you projecting from the level of your senses, or are you projecting from your ego? Are you projecting from the level of silent witnessing awareness, or are you projecting from the collective domain of our consciousness—are you projecting from the universal? It depends on where you are projecting from.

How do we not get caught in only one level of projection or experiencing?

Just by being aware. Every time you have any experience you can ask yourself—*Where am I coming from right now?* Immediately you will see that all of life is projection and it becomes more nurturing to yourself and to the environment if you start to project from those domains of awareness that are not personal. Because in the end you realize there is no such thing as a person, there is only the universal pretending to be a person. That's why we have so many versions of Christ, they are all different projections. All concepts or ideas of God are projections of human beings. The absolute, which is God, by definition can't be conceptualized because as soon as you conceptualize God you limit God. Concept is a boundary; God has no boundaries.

✢ 13
BISHOP SPONG

At 10 A.M., I pulled into the parking lot of the office of the Episcopal Diocese of Newark, New Jersey. My meeting with Bishop John Shelby Spong was scheduled for ten-thirty so I had just enough time to take a bird-bath in my kitchen sink. Since it had been an early winter in Madison, Wisconsin, my motor home was winterized (which meant it had no running water because the water tank and the pipes had been emptied of any water to prevent freezing). So I took out a pot, lit my propane stove, and then heated some water I had kept in a jug. I used the hot water to shave, then I washed my face and under my arms.

Bishop John Shelby Spong was the Episcopal Bishop of Newark. He's the author of fourteen books including *Born of a Virgin, Why Christianity Must Change or Die,* and *Liberating the Gospels.* One of the reasons Bishop Spong has been seen as a rebel is a statement like "I don't see organized churches or synagogues making it." But his wisdom is not just rebellious—it is also mature. And unlike many people who blindly reject all of what Christianity is/and has been, Bishop Spong also sees the positive side of Christianity.

"There is a tendency," he said, "to denigrate life-giving structures when they stop giving life. My sense is that you honor the thing that gave you life in the past, even though it cannot give you life now."

Though he often finds himself debating with fundamentalists, like Jerry Falwell on "Good Morning America," he remains thankful for his early upbringing as a Southern fundamentalist.

"My father was an alcoholic and my mother was troubled," he said, "and I'm not sure I would have made it if I hadn't had this keen sense that I had another parent in the sky who was going to take care of me—which is a fundamentalist way of looking at things."

Eventually, a young John Shelby Spong studied science and philosophy after encountering Galileo, Copernicus, and Isaac Newton. The biblical conception of God lost its hold on him.

"You know," Spong said, "if you want, you can have an absolute hold on the God of the Bible, because his Will is described there and all you have to do is master it and then live according to it."

But Bishop Spong's yearning to know God was more powerful than his need to control God, and thus through the years he was led to a God who is "an invitation into a higher consciousness, a journey into mystery beyond all of my symbols. To me, God is a wondrous sense of life that constantly invites me to live and love more fully, while encouraging me to be who I am more fully, and allowing others to be who they are."

This realization has led Bishop Spong to "fight for gay and lesbian justice—because for me to be a heterosexual, is to be who I am. To be black is to be who you are. To be a woman is to be who you are. To be gay is to be who you are."

Then John Shelby Spong discovered the Anglican Church, which taught him that he didn't need biblical faith, only faith in the Church. "It was another form of biblical faith," he said, "just a little more sophisticated."

Eventually, Bishop John Shelby Spong rid himself of all the explanations of God, but "I couldn't get rid of God."

While Bishop John Shelby Spong continued to write more books, his beliefs became quite simple.

"God is part of consciousness," he said, "so that the more deeply one enters Consciousness the more one sees God. I really have increasingly become a mystic."

"I grew up with all those guys." Bishop Spong said when I mentioned that I was going to try to interview Jerry Falwell, Pat Robertson, and Billy Graham. "Billy Graham was about ten to twelve years older than I and lived about a half mile down the road. I know Jerry Falwell from the time I served a church in Lynchburg, Virginia, in the late sixties, and Pat Robertson's father was beaten by my first cousin in a race for the United States Senate."

There is very little that is literal about the gospels, but that doesn't diminish them. If you worship the Bible as infallible truth, then you may think I'm saying there is nothing true in it. But the Bible, or the New Testament to be more specific, is an attempt to capture the experience and language of people of that day in a way they would understand.

Jesus started his life as a follower of John the Baptist, which is clear from the scriptures, but that embarrassed the Christians and so they wound up having John the Baptist say, "I'm the one that ought to be baptized by you but I'm going to baptize you anyway." That does not make any sense. There is a lot of negativity to John the Baptist in the Bible because they could not get rid of the fact that Jesus had originally been a disciple of his.

There has been a lot of talk about the Jesus Seminar, which bases its whole argument on the early documents of Q and the Gospel of Thomas, but I think the Gospel of Thomas is a second-century document and it does not say anything new. I do not think the Q document existed either. The gospels are actually outlined according to the liturgical life of the synagogue because Christianity grew up as a movement in the synagogue. The Jesus story was preached when Christians celebrated Yom Kippur and the Jesus story was preached when they observed the Jewish Pentecost and when Tabernacles and Rosh Hashanah were celebrated. When those clues are opened up, the gospels are illumined.

Who was Jesus? Was he sent down by God,
or God incarnate or a wise man who realized
his relationship with God?

The traditional myth says that "the theist God beyond the sky" invaded human history through the virgin birth in the person Jesus. He did a lot of Godlike things like walk on water, feed five thousand with five loaves, and probably the most gory part of all—he somehow paid the price of sin, which assumes there had been a "good creation" corrupted by a fall into sin. We

67

were captured by the bondage of sin and that somebody, usually God, demanded that a price be paid to overcome that. Jesus paid the price, then cosmically ascended up to heaven, which is the realm of the theistic God.

But I believe that myth was an attempt to explain an experience and this explanation speaks to the way the people in the first century understood God as an external supernatural force. They created the idea of the virgin birth in order to provide a landing field for God to get into the world. Then they needed a way for God to get back out of this world, so they gave him a launch pad—which is the cosmic ascension. Jesus was portrayed as the incarnation of the Divine—a sort of human visitor for thirty years—but really he is God in disguise. But if you see God as the emerging consciousness, a sense of transcendence, the power of life, the power of love, then you look at Jesus from the full human point of view and you see him as totally alive and incredibly loving and a deeply real person who had the capacity to be himself. If that is so, then Jesus becomes a channel through which you experience the ultimate meaning of life—which is what God is. I do not have any difficulty with the ultimate Christian affirmation, namely that somehow, in Jesus, God has been encountered.

The problem is not what happened, but the explanations of what happened. In my book *Why Christianity Must Change or Die* I point out that even in the New Testament the explanations vary.

First Paul (writing to the Romans in the fifties C.E.) says that God designated Jesus, Son of God, by the spirit of holiness at the time of the resurrection. Basically, God adopted the Holy Jesus into being part of who God is.

Then the Gospel of Mark (written in the early seventies C.E.) says God poured out the divine Spirit on Jesus, but says it was not at the resurrection, it was at his baptism, when the heavens opened and the Spirit descended and the voice proclaimed him God's Son.

But Matthew, writing in the early eighties, and Luke, writing in the late eighties or early nineties, said, "Oh no, he was God from the moment of conception."

Lastly, John, writing between 95 and 100 C.E., said, "Oh no, he was God from the foundation of the world, he was the Divine Logos who spoke when the world was created and then this Logos was simply enfleshed in the person of Jesus."

All of them were trying to deal with the experience they had when they believed they encountered God in Jesus. I have been accused (accurately and inaccurately) of being a heretic. The place where I would be accurately described as a heretic is that I would argue that Jesus is not different from you or me in kind, he is different only in degree, and Meister Eckhart in the fourteenth century articulated that point of view. My particular mentor, a man named John A. T. Robinson, an English Bishop and scholar also held this point of view. It has been a minority point of view within orthodox Christianity over the centuries, but I suspect it will emerge as a dominant part of Christianity and may even become the new orthodoxy.

Original sin?

In 1859, when Darwin published *The Origin of Species,* he changed the landscape and the Church has not yet realized it. He said human life is an emerging process, a work in progress, an unfinished creation. Does that mean that sin is not real? Of course not! Human beings are capable of doing the most incredible evil to one another. One has only to look at ethnic cleansing in Kosovo, at the Holocaust, or at the people Christians have burned at the stake over the years, the killing of Catholics and Protestants by each other in Ireland, or the fact that Matthew Shepard was murdered in Wyoming or James Bird in Texas, and evil is apparent. Human beings are capable of incredible evil. But is its source something called full or original sin?

Original sin is an ancient myth. We did not fall, we just are not yet finished. We have had to survive four and a half billion years of evolutionary history. We have had to put ourselves first; that is the survival technique. What this has done is breed a creature who has expanded self-consciousness and who is radically self-centered. Human beings will kill anybody who gets in their way and threatens their being deeply. Our difficulty theologically is that Church saw this behavior, interpreted it against the mythological background of their understanding of the goodness of God's creation. So they postulated a fall into sinfulness, and the need for a redeemer to lift us back to what God originally intended us to be.

If, however, one takes Darwin seriously, then the whole Christ story must be retold. I do not think Jesus was a sacrifice to overcome the sin of the world. He is a new consciousness of God emerging in human history calling us beyond our boundaries, our tribal identity, our sexual diversity, our gender orientation, and our fear of people that are not like us. All of that is part of humanity, that is the humanity that the Christ calls us beyond. To me the mark of the Christian life is the ability to give ourselves away. I can do that for the people I love—I could die for my wife if I had to, I could die for my children. To me, the Christ life is to call me beyond my boundaries, my fears, my prejudices, and my stereotypes so that I can live for other people and become an agent of life and be, in effect, part of what Christ is. That is, to me, the way I think we have got to redevelop and rechart the Christian faith to make it live in the next millennium. The traditional symbols I do not think will make it.

Is Jesus the only Son of God?

People who believe in the traditional symbols are like a man who is in love and who says, "You are the only one for me." In his case it is an accurate expression inside that experience, but when you try to make your experience everybody else's—then it becomes inaccurate. Obviously, my wife, whom I absolutely adore, is not the one for everybody else—but she is *the* one for me. I do not mind saying "Jesus is *the* only way to God for me," but I do not think I own God. I am deeply grateful that I have this Jesus relationship but I would never want to say to God, "You have to reach everybody the same way you have reached me!" But that is what happens when you say, "Jesus is the only Son of God."

When Christians say that Jesus is the only way to God, usually they quote John 14:6 where Jesus said, "I am the Way and the Truth and the Life. No one comes to the Father except through me."

But that is to misread John. John's gospel was written in the tenth decade after the fracture between synagogue and church. It was written by Jewish Christians who were excommunicated from the synagogue and who had to deal with the fact that the Orthodox Jewish tradition said to them, "We have the true God, the I-am God of the Exodus experience, the burning bush, the God of Abraham, Isaac, and Jacob, and you are apart from that." So these Jewish Christians countered by saying, "Oh no, the God who was of Abraham, Isaac, and Jacob and the burning bush has been met anew in Jesus of Nazareth so we are not apart from that." So John took the "I-am" name of God and put it into the mouth of Jesus every time he could.

Only in John does Jesus say, "I am the Way and the Truth and the Life. No one comes to the Father except through me." It is a polemic dividing revisionist Jews who later became Christians from Orthodox Jews. One day we read these words outside the context of that polemic. Then we claimed that these literal words were the ultimate Word of God for all people and all time. If one believes that, then he or she must go out and convert people. I am not in favor of conversion efforts. In the first place, these conversion efforts have been a failure. The Christian Church has not really penetrated Buddhism, Hinduism, Islam, or even Judaism in two thousand years. The Jews who converted to Christianity did so because their lives were threatened by Christians. Sometimes their children would stay with that new tradition. We have never really converted other religions to our own. There is something arrogant when anyone says, "I have the truth." I do not think Jesus said any of the "I am" sayings. Only John has Jesus say such things as, "Before Abraham was, I am" (John 8:58, NSV).

John also has Jesus say, "when you see the Son of Man lifted up, then you will know—I am." The translators did not understand what Jesus meant here so they translated it "I am He." What John was saying, however, was "when you see the Son of Man lifted up, you will see the God 'I Am' that Moses saw at the burning bush." The temple was destroyed by the time John was written and so the Christians had Jesus claim to be the new temple. In the past, the temple was the place where God and human life came together. Since the temple had been destroyed, the Christians began to say, "We don't need to rebuild it because we have a new place where God and human life come together. It is in the person Jesus of Nazareth."

Virgin birth?

The idea of the virgin birth was an attempt to say that we have met in Jesus something human life alone could never have produced. In the first century, people believed that the whole life of the newborn lived in the sperm of the male and that if one wanted to talk about a divine origin, you only had to get rid of the human father. You never had to get rid of the human mother, because they didn't believe that human mothers contributed anything. So in the first century, to talk about Jesus being the Divine Son of God, you got rid of the human father and put in the Holy Spirit—you didn't worry about the fact that the mother was a human vessel. In 1724, we discovered that women have egg sacs and that women are cocreators in the genetic content of a life. We are made up of 50 percent of our mother's gene pool and 50 percent of our father's gene pool. The virgin birth died at that moment, though we haven't realized it. It doesn't make any sense anymore because if the virgin birth took place, knowing what we know about egg cells, then Jesus is neither human nor divine, he is half human and half divine, because Mary has to be acknowledged as a human mother.

Remember the virgin birth was a first-century attempt to talk about a Divine origin and to make sense of the experience. It makes no sense now, just as the cosmic ascension was a first-century explanation that doesn't make any sense in the space age.

Did Jesus learn things? Was he perfect?

Of course he learned. The problem comes when we can't separate the Christ who transforms our understanding of God and life from the Jesus who walked in history. We've gotten those two confused. But it's through Jesus that we came to see the Christ. Marcus Borg does a good job of that when he separates the "Jesus of history" from "the Christ of faith." The Jesus of history was human, but the Christ of faith is an understanding of God that is so deeply connected to Jesus that we've debated that forever, about how he was both God and human. I suspect he had to have his diapers changed, and everything else.

Was Jesus married or in an intimate relationship?

Was he perfect? When you read the gospels, Jesus made a whip out of cords and drove people out of the temple, so he certainly was capable of getting angry. Absolutely, I think Mary Magdalene was his wife. That's why she is always portrayed as the first among equals of his female apostles and why she is portrayed as the chief mourner at the tomb. That's why in John's gospel she even asks the person she thinks is the guard for access to his deceased body, which would be absolutely out of bounds if she were not the nearest of kin. In the gospels, Jesus is called rabbi, and he couldn't be a rabbi if he weren't married.

In the first twenty-five years of the second century, Magdalene is trashed and that's the same year Mary, the virgin mother, who is pure and sexless, emerges to take her place as the primary woman in the Christian movement. Christianity did that because it was beginning to interpret itself in a neoplatonic world where the flesh was evil. I talk about that in my book called *Born of a Woman*.

What religion was Jesus?

He was Jewish—absolutely, I don't think there is any doubt about that. The irony being that anti-Semitism is a Christian gift to the world. I don't think it would be here if it wasn't for the Christian Church. Religion is as destructive as it is creative in the world. If you look at history, we've done some rather dreadful things.

Look at the difficult periods in history, in this country and in this world right now, there is a religious connection at the bottom of every one of them. In Ireland, it's Catholic and Protestant; in the West Bank, it's Jew and Muslim; In Lebanon, it's Christian and Muslim; and in Pakistan and India, it's Hindu, Sikh, and Muslim.

I did a radio program a few weeks ago, and the call-ins were universally hostile and life-threatening. At the end of the program, they announced that I would be lecturing that night at the Knox United Church in town. That church then had so many hostile calls from fundamentalist Christians that they thought I might be in danger so they decided to hire a bodyguard. He was a six-foot six-inch Sikh with his turban on and I thought the irony of that was kind of incredible. Here's a Christian Bishop being protected from Christian fundamentalists by a Sikh. But there's violence in religion, and the violence is actually caused by a lack of faith—not faith. If it makes you angry when someone raises a question about religion, that means your faith is shaky and you're trying to defend what you know you really don't have. God doesn't need to be defended, God can go on quite all right without defense.

I've thought about that a lot and it could have been just an accident. He traveled with a group of basically Galileans and everything in the Bible indicates the Galileans carried swords and were armed. Therefore an armed group of Galileans in Jerusalem on Passover would be a threat because Rome had to constantly put down rebellions up in Galilee. The Galilean problem actually broke out into full-scale war in 66 A.D., but the tension was even there when Jesus was killed.

I believe Jesus was the pacifist of the group, because he was constantly portrayed as saying, "You're not going to win this by arms, and put up your swords, this is not the way to do it." But I think there was a sweep by the Romans and his death could have been an accident. The sense that the innocent one was put to death is also an idea that permeates the gospel story. They had to come up with a reason why it was that God allowed the innocent one to be put to death. That's when Jesus was interpreted as the Passover lamb that's put to death to break the power of death itself, just as the lamb of Yom Kippur is put to death to overcome the sins of the world. Jesus became the sin bearer, the one who takes away the sins of the world and in later evangelical tradition, they attributed to his blood all sorts of power: "We've been washed in the blood—the shed blood of Jesus is what saves." But isn't that grotesque? It portrays God as some Middle Eastern sultan who demands a human sacrifice.

Resurrection?

The resurrection was important because it meant that people really did understand who Jesus was, that he had broken every human barrier and now he broke the barrier of finitude. He lifted them beyond the limits of human life. It's the defining moment. The disciples had all forsaken Jesus and fled, but then something reconstituted. The disciples were all Jews and something forced them to say, "In Jesus we've met the Holy God." They could no longer talk about God without talking about Jesus as part of who God was.

The first meaning of the resurrection in the New Testament was not being raised from the dead and back into life, from which you have to eventually be ascended into heaven—the first meaning was that God raises you from death into the meaning of God. Through the meaning of God the resurrected Lord is seen, and this has nothing to do with the physically resuscitated body. The proof of that is in 1 Corinthians 15, where Paul talks about those who have seen the risen Lord. He says it's Peter, James, the apostles, the five hundred brethren, and he includes himself. Nobody argues that Paul saw the resuscitated Jesus (a body who walked out of the grave). He saw the God who was beyond the limits of life and a body. That's a very powerful symbol. Without the resurrection, Christianity would never have emerged. But since then, we've literalized the explanation of the resurrection and I talk about that in my book *Resurrection: Myth or Reality?*

Second Coming?

The Second Coming is a myth, but the mythology isn't unreal. Mythology stands for something. Jesus lived in a Jewish world and was seen as the first sign of the coming kingdom of God. Therefore, there has to be a Second Coming.

If you go back and read Jewish apocalyptic literature about the end of the world, you find all sorts of clues that are later attributed to Jesus. In the battle of Armageddon its says, the forces of evil and the forces of good will meet at Armageddon in the final cataclysmic battle and the forces of evil will prevail and there will be darkness over the whole world. Then every gospel writer says that when Jesus died there was darkness over the whole world—the sun went out. That's a symbol lifted out of that literature. Jesus is also said to have been in the grave for three days, and that is also taken from the apocalyptic idea that the darkness would last three days. It then says that at dawn after the third day, the heavens would open and the kingdom of God would descend out of the sky and it would be the first day of the new creation. That's the mythology of the Jewish apocalyptic tradition, and that's also the story of Jesus' resurrection when the grave opens and it's the first fruits of the kingdom of God. What we've done is to literalize it, then lose its context—until we pray for "the kingdom to come" in the Lord's Prayer. Jesus never said the Lord's Prayer and he didn't teach that prayer.

It's an interpretation of Jesus as the first fruits of the new creation, placed into the mouth of Jesus by the gospel-writing tradition. It's a wonderful symbol, but literalized it's nonsense.

Did Jesus try to start a new religion?

If Jerusalem hadn't been destroyed by the Romans in 70 A.D., Christianity might well have stayed a part of Judaism and maybe even come to dominate Judaism. The original Christians were Jewish revisionists and they were liberals. They were people who believed God had done a new thing. They worshiped in the synagogue and were in the process of relating Jesus to the ongoing Jewish tradition. That's why the gospel stories were so Midrashic, because most of the gospel stories were originally sermons about how Jesus related to the Hebrew tradition. Then in 70 A.D., the Romans destroyed Jerusalem, the city, destroyed the state and destroyed the priesthood. All the Jews had left was the Torah. Then the Jews did what every threatened religious group does—they became literal about their one remaining icon. Therefore, the revisionist Jews were not tolerable any longer and tensions grew between approximately 70 and 88 A.D. The tensions grew until the Jews finally said, "We can't tolerate you revisionists anymore," and they excommunicated them. It's not unlike what I see going on in the world today, where Christianity is threatened and shaken, so the religious right is more and more brittle and anybody who doesn't agree with them, they are ready to kick out.

But you can't see that when you are insecure, and your religion feeds your security system—then you can't stand any threat. So Christianity became a new religion in the tenth decade. The split between synagogue and Church didn't take place any earlier than 88. But by 100 A.D., twenty-five to thirty years after the fall of Jerusalem, Christianity had become almost totally a gentile movement because Judaism had become more and more rigorously right-wing Orthodox and Jews who weren't going to do that had drifted into the melting pot of the world, so Christianity became gentile. When it became gentile, then they began to literalize the Jewish stories that are in our New Testament because they didn't understand the Jewish stories. Today, Christianity is divided between liberals (who deny the literalism) and conservatives (who assert the literalism) and both of them are wrong. Instead of fighting the old battle of whether it's true or not, we ought to be looking at it from a totally different point of view. For example, what was the experience underneath these various explanations which caused these explanations to be born in the first place?

What spiritual practices or techniques did Jesus teach?

Jesus taught the crossing of boundaries; the breaking of barriers we've created. In the Jewish world, there was the division between the Jew and the gentile, and the way the Jew survived was to define the Jew over/against the gentile. Yet, Jesus is portrayed as stepping across that barrier, he heals the centurion and the servant. The common thread that lies behind the gospel stories is that he healed them both—a Jewish healer crossing the boundary and healing in a gentile context. He is portrayed in Matthew's gospel as saying only one thing after the resurrection and that is, "You've got to go to the gentile's race, you've got to go to all the people, go to all the world and proclaim the gospel." So that barrier got relativized in him.

The barrier between the Jew and Samaritan was another powerful barrier. The Jews would do anything to avoid speaking to or even walking in Samaria; they would literally go across the river and down the desert to come back in to avoid breathing Samaritan air. The Samaritan was everything the Jew didn't want to be. The Samaritan was a half-breed, while the Jews were pure Jews. The Samaritans were corrupt worshipers of God, while the Jews were true worshipers of God. Yet Jesus crossed that barrier. The Parable of the Good Samaritan is an incredible parable—whether Jesus said it or not is not important—it's attributed to Jesus because of who he was, and he said that a Samaritan who acts according to the Torah with compassion and love is more deeply a child of Abraham than the priest and the Levite who passed over to the other side. That's revolutionary. He also tells the story about the people being cleared of their leprosy and only one person returns—it's the Samaritan who understood that you acknowledge the source of your holiness.

Then there was the male-female barrier. A Jew wouldn't cross that one either. Yet Jesus is portrayed as talking to the woman by the road. Jesus clearly had disciples who were female. Christianity sometimes tries to discount that but women are significantly and definitely in his ministry.

How important is the mystical experience?

My difficulty is that I don't really know how to talk about God except ecstatically. There aren't any words that are quite big enough. My experience is that when people throughout the world have an ecstatic experience of God, they inevitably interpret it within the framework of their own faith traditions; Buddhists have experiences that are quite Buddhist, Roman Catholics and Protestants always get the sweet Jesus in the white tunic. In the Cabalistic community of the Jewish tradition, the mysticism has a very distinctive Jewish flavor. That ought to tip us all off to the fact that there is something ultimately real about the God of spirit and something radically unreal about everybody's explanation.

I have great affection for Judaism—it's wonderful—because in the last analysis it is also mystical. The strict Jew will not even pronounce the holy name because to pronounce the holy name is to act as if you know it, understand it, or can control it. The first commandment, and heart of Judaism, is that they can make no representation of the Holy—that's interpreted as no idols. We make representations or idols of the Holy verbally and after we've done that, we claim that our representation is infallible or without error.

Can the Bible be an idol?

Absolutely. The Bible is the Protestant idol. The Pope is the Roman idol; or, if not the Pope, then the traditions of the Church. There was an article in the *New York Times* magazine section last Sunday about Roman priests and it was amazing that they were still taking the point of view that the Church cannot be wrong. I mean, despite history, where the Church has been wrong over and over again, they still say "the Church cannot be wrong."

Almost all the positive letters about my book *Why Christianity Must Change or Die* came from lay people who are church dropouts. People who are either on the edge or have actually left the organized church. They're ecstatic and they're saying, "You have given me a way to come back or to see God." The 25 percent who are negative are almost totally from the ordained, and they are incredibly hostile. It really surprises me how hostile ordained people can be. I've been called a heretic, an atheist, an agnostic, an apostate, a whore—I thought that was a really interesting one. I thought a whore was usually a woman—but that's neither here nor there. But this person said, "At least a whore respects the source from which her income comes and you are destroying the Church and still drawing a salary from it, so even a whore is better than you."

> *The word "respect" comes from a Latin root that means "to look again." Therefore, if you respect God, you keep looking at God again and again and allow God to grow. Why don't people respect God or their religion more?*

People do respect God, but what is happening is they no longer think the Church is the place where they ought to be looking. I've done three lecture tours in Australia and New Zealand. They're interesting countries because they are incredibly secular, more so than the United States and even more so than Europe. But whenever I spoke at a church in Sydney there would be mediocre attendance, and whenever I spoke in a public lecture hall it would be jammed. More people come to a public lecture hall than will come to a church because they have a sense of what they are going to hear if they go to a church and they don't want to hear it anymore. But in a public lecture hall they feel free of that. And yet, at the end of the lecture, during the question period, inevitably a question will be, "Where can I go and practice the thing that you're talking about, is there a community?"

My call is for a reformation that is so radical that it will change the very nature of the way we talk about God and it will also obviously change the way the Church organizes its life—and I think that's beginning to happen. For a long time, the Church organized for the external supernatural God above the sky—that's why we built steeples. Until very recently the Western Catholic tradition had the priest bringing the Eucharist back to the people, who looked up in the sky at God. Today, we've turned this around so that the priest is now looking at the gathered people to say, "We see God more in the gathered community than we do out there in the sky."

To my delight certain liturgical churches have stopped their kneeling. Kneeling is an interesting posture for worship. In human intercourse, kneeling is the stance of a slave before a master or a peasant before a king. It's not, in my opinion, an appropriate response between a worshiper and a deity, unless the deity is conceived of as an authority figure sitting up on the throne from whom you need a boon of some sort, so you approach on your knees and back off on your knees. But if you think of God as the Ground of Being and emerging in every human life, then I'm part of God and you are a part of God and you don't kneel before a God for whom you are part of. One church said, "We are not going to kneel in this church, we are going to practice the joy of our religion and so we are inviting everybody to stand in the attitude of praise when you pray."

> *When Jews sacrificed animals at the temple,*
> *was it because by giving up something*
> *valuable, they thought they would be forgiven?*

At Yom Kippur, the power of sacrifice really comes out. At Yom Kippur, the Jewish people had this sense of their unworthiness to come into God's presence, so they were taught that they had to offer God a perfect offering and if God accepted the perfect offering, maybe God would accept the imperfect people who offered the perfect offering. That's why they developed all these liturgies about the lamb. The lamb had to be scrupulously inspected to be physically perfect, no broken bones, no scratches or blemishes—it had to be a physically perfect specimen. But they also began to develop the idea that the lamb was sinless, because lambs live below the level of human freedom, lambs cannot choose to be evil, so lambs are morally perfect, physically perfect, and we portray Jesus as the lamb of God all the time. The part in the New Testament that says none of his bones are broken is deliberately designed to convey that he was the symbolic lamb, and the developing tradition that he is/was the sinless one. You find that in "Hebrews," which is the book of the Bible that most puts the sacrifice of Yom Kippur into the Jesus tradition, it says that he was tempted in all things and yet without sin, he's the sinless one. So Jesus was young, he's a male, he's physically perfect, no broken bones and he's morally perfect, even though he's above the level of human freedom. That was the attempt by the original disciples (who were Jews) to say—Jesus is the Yom Kippur lamb of God who takes away the sins of the world and if God can accept the perfect offering of the lamb and then accept us imperfect people, how much more would God accept the perfect offering of a human being and therefore accept those of us on whose behalf the offering was made. That's very Jewish and it made sense in the first century, but it doesn't make sense to people today. Animal sacrifice is anathema to people today, and yet we still talk about Jesus, a human being, as the sacrificial offering to overcome the sin of the world.

14
FOOD AND FALWELL

The interview with Jack Spong went so well that I wanted to celebrate. *Pancakes!* That's what came to me, *I wanted pancakes.*

"Pancakes?" Bishop Spong's assistant asked, "You want pancakes?"

"Yeah," I said. "I'm in the mood for pancakes."

"Ain't nowhere around here that'll serve pancakes after noon," she said.

Now if I have any gifts at all, persistence is one of them. Mix persistence with a bit of divine inspiration, and that's how I do what I do. So when Bishop Spong's assistant told me there were no pancakes around here after noon—well, she didn't know whom she was dealing with.

I left my motor home at the Bishop's office and went for a walk along Main Street in search of pancakes. I stopped at a Greek restaurant, but the waitress said, "No pancakes after noon." The other restaurants all said the same thing. Then I thought of Interstate 95—*truck stops usually have breakfast all day!* I ran back to my motor home, drove to the interstate, and twenty minutes later I stopped at a truck stop. The Hispanic waitress said, "No pancakes after noon." Then one of the assistant managers (who was also Hispanic) yelled back in Spanish to the kitchen, "Blah, blah, blah, pancakes, blah, blah?" I could hear the cook reply in Spanish. "Blah, blah, no pancakes, blah." The waitress looked back at me, "No pancakes after noon."

I walked back to my motor home and sat down. I sighed deeply as the harsh reality slowly sunk in—*there would be no pancakes today.*

✢ 15
THE PLAN AND MORE FOOD

I-95 SOUTH

I left New Jersey and drove south on 95 toward Virginia. Jerry Falwell and Pat Robertson lived there. Reverend Falwell in Lynchburg and Pat Robertson in Virginia Beach. The chances of interviewing them were slim, but I had to try. Why? Because the book would be incomplete without them. Many liberal people I know said to forget these two preachers because they taught hatred and not love as Jesus taught. But even if they did teach hatred (which is debatable), they're just as much apostles of Jesus as anyone.

When Jesus asked the apostles, "Who do you say I am?" they all had different answers. So aren't Jerry Falwell and Pat Robertson's conceptions of Jesus just different answers to Jesus' question? Jesus was wise enough to listen to all the answers given. Are you? Am I? Is Pat Robertson or Jerry Falwell?

But I needed a plan, because it wasn't easy getting interviews—especially with well-known religious figures who are worried about getting misrepresented by the press. I had been rejected by Falwell's office a few times by mail, so I decided to ask Jerry Falwell directly by approaching him after his Sunday service in Lynchburg, Virginia. Over the years, he's probably learned to size people up pretty quickly and I figured my sincerity together with whatever help Jesus might be giving me gave me a shot. But I decided to increase my odds of getting an interview by appearing more conservative. I planned to wear a white button-down shirt, a V-neck sweater, a pair of dark slacks and wing tips. Then I'd just walk up to him and say, "I'm traveling the world talking to people about Jesus for a book I'm writing. Will you talk to me about Jesus for thirty minutes?"

How could he say "no"?

If Jerry Falwell and Pat Robertson said "no" to that—then I'd fall back on my second plan and hand them a card that said, "Jesus have mercy." That's a short prayer I repeat over and over to myself from time to time. It was recommended to me by Brother David Steindl-Rast, who is a Benedictine monk. The idea about handing them the card isn't entirely my own idea. It came from a story I read about a man named Paul Reps who went to Japan to study Zen Buddhism after WWII. The military wouldn't allow visitors into the country so when an officer at immigration denied him a visa, Paul Reps took out a card, scribbled on the back, and handed it to the officer. It said, "Making green tea, I stop the war."

The officer looked up at Paul Reps and said, "We need more people like you in this country," and approved his visa.

If the "Green tea–Jesus have mercy" thing failed, then I would resort to telling them that Jesus wanted me to write this book—which I really think is true, but it sounds so crazy that I'd rather not have to say it. If all that failed, I would offer them each five hundred dollars for thirty minutes (five hundred dollars I don't have by the way). I got that idea when I was told a story about a minister who traveled around and offered five hundred dollars to various religious figures for thirty minutes of their time. Supposedly they all said "yes" without taking the money.

Finally, if truth, Jesus, and cash don't work—I'll just park my motor home outside their churches and wait.

I drove all night filled with hopes of interviewing Jerry Falwell and Pat Robertson. At about 3 A.M., I stopped somewhere between New Jersey and Virginia on Highway 95. I was so tired that I don't remember the name of the town, but the name on the diner was Frank's Diner and I had a fantastic turkey omelet. The potatoes were seasoned just right, the coffee was better than most, and Frank was a black gentleman, an ex-military guy who was buffing his own floors at 3 A.M. The waitress had to tell me he was the boss.

"He runs a tight ship," she said.

He used that buffer like a maestro. An easy left-to-right gliding motion that swept across the tiled floor about three feet. It was a ballet, a meditation—*it was the owner buffing his own floors at 3 A.M. in the morning.* The reason I'm telling this story is because I want to go back to Frank's Diner sometime, but I was so tired that it was like a dream and I don't know where it was. If you know Frank's Diner, please let me know where it is and tell Frank I said, "Hi."

✠ 16
THOMAS ROAD
BAPTIST CHURCH

RICHMOND, VIRGINIA

"Ain't nothing between here and Lynchburg." The cashier at Vic's grocery in Richmond, Virginia, said after I asked her about espresso.

Whatever you do, don't start drinking espresso or cappuccino because you won't go back to regular coffee. That regular coffee will taste like brown water after drinking espresso. My usual choice of caffeine imbibing was three shots of espresso over a cup of ice. Then I dump in my fake cream and two fake sugars. I also add one or two real sugars just to fool myself into thinking the fake sugar tastes like real sugar. This might sound like a lot of sugar to put in coffee, but when coffee is iced most of it sinks to the bottom. If I remember from my science class correctly, it has something to do with "solubility."

On the way to Lynchburg, I dewinterized my motor home—which meant that I had running water and I could take a shower. I pulled into Lynchburg early the next morning, napped for a few hours, and then had my first shower in a week. I had stopped at a clothing store the day before, but I couldn't find a decent V-neck sweater, so I wore a purple and black plaid sweater vest, a white long-sleeved shirt, dark pants, and a pair of wing tips.

After being directed to the wrong church, I finally found Dr. Falwell's Thomas Road Baptist Church. I was thirty minutes late for the nine-thirty service and Jerry Falwell was already preaching when I sat down. I agreed with 95 percent of what he said during this particular sermon, as, for the most part, Jerry Falwell said things like, "Do God's will" or "God is love."

Every so often, he said something that I either had to translate in my own mind into what I thought he meant or I just disregarded altogether. My eyes teared up because I realized he was sincere, he was devoted, and he thought he was doing the right thing. We had that in common even if I disagreed with him at times. And there was no denying the devotion and sincerity of his congregation—it was beautiful and holy.

It had been the same way four months before in Arizona when I met a young man at a Christian bookstore whose beautiful devotion and longing for God transcended whatever disagreements I had with him about religion. Why was his spiritual longing beautiful? Because it was not twisted by anger and disappointment. It was hopeful and open, not angry and closed.

After the service, I watched as Dr. Falwell met and greeted people. He appeared genuine. Since I was nervous, I breathed deeply a few times while silently asking Jesus if he was with me—his answer was to smile at my doubt.

Dr. Falwell waved me toward him in a way that I can only describe as ingratiating. *Bingo! So far so good.* He welcomed me warmly and listened intently as I slowly explained (I hadn't found any espresso in Lynchburg so I was pre-caffeine and not thinking quickly).

"I'm traveling around the world, writing a book for Doubleday . . . about Jesus—I would like to speak with you. This is my first book," I said, handing him a copy of *Tying Rocks to Clouds*. "In it I interviewed Mother Teresa, Norman Vincent Peale, Robert Schuller . . ."

I intentionally mentioned only the Christians I'd interviewed and avoided mentioning the Buddhists or the atheists like B. F. Skinner.

"What's your name again . . . ?" Dr. Falwell asked.

"Bill Elliott."

"Well, Bill," Dr. Falwell said, taking out a card and writing a number on it, "here's my number. Call Kathy in the next few days and we'll meet."

I felt like crying—not because of Jerry Falwell—but because my vision, my dream, was one step closer to being realized and at moments like that, gratitude swelled my heart until I wanted to burst into tears. On the way out I met Deryl Edwards, the president of the Liberty Alliance. I explained about my books while two older ladies listened.

"What's your first book about?" one woman asked.

"I talked with Mother Teresa, Norman Vincent Peale, and the Dalai Lama," I said, and realized I had mentioned the Dalai Lama—a Buddhist. Would they disapprove? I looked at Deryl for a sign of disapproval or concern.

"You actually talked with the Dalai Lama?" Deryl asked, genuinely excited. "How did you do it? Often we try to speak with these people, and we can't locate them."

"Persistence," I replied. "Do you know how to contact Pat Robertson?" I asked.

"I have a contact for you," Deryl said. Then we talked about Billy Graham. "I have another contact for you there, too," he said. I almost cried at the helpfulness he displayed, and as I walked out into the afternoon sun, I felt I was being watched over. If Jerry Falwell had said "no" to an interview, would I still have felt watched over? I don't know, but I do know one thing, I wouldn't have stopped there. I would have tried the next day and the next until he denied me—dare I say "three times"? Either way, I would have gotten back into my motor home and continued on to Virginia Beach, Pat Robertson, and the rest of my book.

I don't quit.

17
MY HEART SANK

LYNCHBURG, VIRGINIA

I called Dr. Falwell's office first thing Monday morning and Kathy, his assistant, set up the appointment for 2 P.M. the next day. I kept my fingers crossed and my hopes were high, but something in me said, "Don't get too happy till it happens."

Sure enough, at 10:30 A.M. the next day, I got a call from his office.

"Dr. Falwell can't do it," the voice said. "Can we do a phone interview in a few weeks?"

My heart sank. I wondered if I was being blown off, and this was just an indirect way of doing it. I called Deryl Edwards, the president of the Liberty Alliance, because I wanted to know if the real answer was no and they were just trying to be nice by putting me off until I gave up. Deryl said he'd vouched for me as much as he could, and that I should send some more information and references.

The toughest thing about interviewing people is the waiting. I have to push, push, push, and then wait. If I could have interviewed Falwell that next day, a part of me would have relaxed, knowing his interview was done. Now his "potential interview" would sit in the back of my mind—waiting. It's a sense of incompleteness. The unanswered question. The open-ended longing. I suppose any endeavor can be a spiritual one, and this book is for me. I can't get too up or too down, I have to persist and always keep going. It was a big financial risk for me to invest everything I had into this book, and the psychological risk was just as great, because I don't like calling people on the phone and being rejected. That was/is the beautiful danger that comes from attempting to manifest one's dream. Anyone can dream, and anyone can do, but "to do one's dream"—that's a tough one. Especially a dream that began in the soul. To take something as sensitive and as private as one's soul and to extend it out into the world, well, sometimes when you stick your neck out, your head gets chopped off. That's happened more than a few times and whenever it happens, I talk to God, talk to myself, and then talk to my friends and pray. Again and again, I return to these sources for strength and renewal; to cry, to get angry, to complain, and to be loved. Out of this, I spring again—resurrected, complete with a new head! Ready to stick my neck out once again.

My faith comes from the experience of God's presence. Without this faith, I wouldn't have the strength to write my books. It's grace to have faith like that because the man of no faith must hold firmly to his life—it's the only one he's got and he can't risk it. But at the bottom of our soul, beneath the river of time, there is a depth that stretches through Holy Ghost territory and into the heart of God. If you know this place—the true fountain of youth—then you can die continually and you can die each day and in your death, you will actually be given a new and better life.

God doesn't pour new life into old wineskins, instead he waits for the sense of self to die so that a new life can be poured into a new sense of self and into new wineskins. I hate dying as much as the next person, but when has my new life ever been less than the one I gave up?

✟ 18
SERPENT AND
DOVE WITH HEART

VIRGINIA BEACH, VIRGINIA

Now it's off to Pat Robertson's. I would have felt more settled and confident if Dr. Falwell's interview had been done, because then I would have had that credential. People look at credentials. We all do. Do I know you? Do you know me? As my sculpture teacher said, "Everything you do tells people who you are," and a completed interview with Jerry Falwell may have been a credential that told Pat Robertson that I was someone he should talk to.

A couple hours later, I stopped at Regent University, which is Pat Robertson's college and the Christian Broadcasting Network. It was a large complex and obviously expensive. Despite what people say about Mr. Robertson's religious views, no one ever criticizes his business smarts. As I walked around the campus, all I saw were women in skirts and men in suits. In the main office, an assistant told me Pat Robertson was away—in New York promoting *The Book,* a simpler-to-read version of the Bible. I gave a letter and a copy of my first book to the assistant, but I doubted that Pat Robertson would ever receive them.

A lightbulb went off a few minutes later, when a clean-cut Asian man pointed to a large house that was surrounded by a high fence and said, "That's Pat Robertson's home right over there." I started the quarter-mile walk to the house and turned down a road with a sign that said, PRIVATE ENTRY ONLY. I figured I'd leave the book by his door, and that way when he got home he couldn't miss it. I took my time walking; I tried to look like I was just another student out for a walk on a sunny day, dressed in my sweater, white shirt, and wing tips. As I walked down the road, I wondered if there were hidden cameras. I mean, if there were a few people killing abortion doctors, there must be a few people out to get Pat Robertson for his views on gays. To make a long story short, the gate surrounding his house was too high to get beyond, but I stopped and admired the horses Pat Robertson had on his property. One horse, white as snow, took a few steps toward me but stopped and seemed to say, "You don't look interesting enough to visit."

The grounds of Regent University and Pat Robertson's home are impeccably kept. Together with those horses and rolling green fields, it's a picture fit for a painting. It's just too bad there wasn't any room in that picture for an interview.

The next morning I woke up with the words "innocent as a dove but sly as a serpent . . ." running through my head.

Here was my plan. My editor told me that another Doubleday author, Señor Garza who wrote *The DNA of God* would be on Pat Robertson's "700 Club" the next day. Bingo! First, I'll call Señor Garza and tell him that I was also a Doubleday author, that I was writing a book about Jesus. Then when we met for coffee, I would casually say, "Do you mind if I come along to 'The 700 Club'?" Bingo! I'm in the front door and I hand Pat Robertson a copy of my first book and my credentials.

But the plan eventually failed because after many phone calls Señor Garza is nowhere to be found. The moral of the story is that that kind of thinking is how you accomplish difficult tasks—but you have to stay connected to a right motivation. We all have a hell of a serpent inside us, and the point is to marry our serpent to a dove with a good heart.

✦ 19
REJECTION AND SURRENDER

While working on my book, I get rejected a lot. Sometimes I think this means it's not meant to work out—that God is somehow against me.

But maybe that isn't true . . . perhaps God just wants me to learn to push myself, to persist and get stronger even as I let go and surrender.

✣ 20
RABBI HAROLD KUSHNER

BOSTON, MASSACHUSETTS

I was brought up to believe that Jesus wasn't Jewish, he was Christian, and that the Jews killed Him. How blind I was. After reading and rereading the New Testament, and studying what the scholars and mystics have said about Jesus and the creation of the gospels, my eyes were opened. Often I wondered who blinded me and why? *". . . who sinned, this man or his parents, that he was born blind?"*[1]

I had interviewed Rabbi Harold Kushner, the author of *Why Bad Things Happen to Good People* back in 1988 for my first book. But this time I hesitated before calling him for an interview because I didn't want to offend him. As Neil Douglas-Klotz, Bishop Spong, and others have said, Christians have blamed the Jews for killing Christ and that helped lead to the Holocaust. Since I have many Jewish friends, I've seen the hurt in their eyes whenever I mentioned the name Jesus. It is as though Jesus had been used to scourge the Jewish people, and any mention of his name just reopened old wounds. So when I finally called Rabbi Harold Kushner, I was nervous. I also wasn't sure if he'd remember me.

"Yes," he said affectionately. "Of course I remember you. We met in New York City eleven years ago."

For some reason, I wanted to preface my request for an interview about Jesus with an apology. But suddenly, I remembered a passage from the gospels.

"What do you want me to do for you?" Jesus asked a blind man.

"Rabbi," the blind man said, *"I want to see."*[2]

When I finally did ask Rabbi Harold Kushner (and many of the people in this book) for an interview about Jesus, it was in the spirit and humility of *wanting to see.*

1. John 9:2, NIV.
2. Mark 10:52.

Rabbi Harold Kushner is the author of seven best-selling books and is best known for his international best-seller *Why Bad Things Happen to Good People*. He is Rabbi Laureate of Temple Israel in Natick, Massachusetts.

Who was/is Jesus?

It's very hard for me to know who Jesus was because we have so little reliable information and much of what we have was written long after he lived and filtered through the belief systems of the people who were writing. My understanding of Jesus is that he was God's instrument for bringing the moral teachings of the Torah to all of humanity rather than having them be the property of the Israelites alone.

I suspect he was a charismatic teacher who sincerely believed that the world was about to end. Therefore, he felt the urgent need people have to cleanse their souls and be on the right side of God when the judgment comes. The ethics he taught were not the sorts of things a person might be able to keep forever. He thought in terms of a moral sprint rather than a moral marathon—give away all your possessions, don't marry, turn the other cheek, and don't hate anybody. People can do that for a couple of weeks, but not for a lifetime. Christianity has a tension that is partly caused by people who have tried to live their whole lives with these urgent ethics, but feel like moral failures when they find out they can't do it.

Jesus' religion?

Oh, clearly he was Jewish. He was an observant, committed Jew.

From what we know about first-century Judaism, there was a very wide spectrum of belief systems and behavior systems. I suspect that everything Jesus taught can be found somewhere in those systems, though his combination or charisma may have been unique. I tend to agree with Albert Schweitzer that what Jesus taught was an ethic of the last days. That means he was part of a substantial fraction of the Jewish people who, because things were so terrible, believed that the Messiah was going to come and the world was going to end very soon.

Why didn't all Jews accept
Jesus as the Messiah?

Because Jesus didn't fulfill the predictions of the Messiah. For example, he didn't usher in a world of peace.

Second, for Jesus to have ridden into the city on the donkey and to have people gamble for his clothes after his death were the least important of the Messianic predictions—if in fact they were Messianic predictions. The real Messianic prediction was that the Messiah would be a just and fair ruler who would usher in an age of peace and justice—and Jesus didn't do that.

Accuracy and authorship of the gospels?

Don't forget, you're talking about documents that are almost two thousand years old with a very different notion of truth. We tend to think that people have always believed in the nineteenth- and twentieth-century definition of truth—a newspaper account of what actually happened that probably started with Hegel. But two thousand years ago, truth was reported with the intention of conveying a higher truth—accuracy of the truth was less important. Therefore, the gospels probably are not a reliable newspaper account of the life and teachings of Jesus.

Is Jesus the only Son of God?

No, I couldn't possibly accept the formulation that he was the Son of God. That's a pagan idea and that's part of Paul's bringing in Greco-Roman mythology and grafting it onto the Judaic tree.

Virgin birth?

I don't believe in the virgin birth, and actually it only says in one gospel that Mary was a virgin when Jesus was born. The concept of the virgin birth only became important later. What's interesting is that the concept of a virgin birth is the sort of thing that would have scandalized the Jews of the first and second century but would have appealed to the Romans.

The Romans obviously did. Crucifixion was a Roman form of punishment. They did it not only to Jesus but to thousands of other potential troublemakers. During Passover, when hundreds of thousands of pilgrims would come into Jerusalem and celebrate their Divine deliverance from slavery to freedom, the Romans in authority were very nervous; they were ready to kill anybody who looked like a potential troublemaker, and Jesus was probably one of hundreds of troublemakers who were picked up and killed rather than being allowed to cause trouble. The Procurator Pontius Pilate made his reputation by keeping the taxes coming and keeping civic order. The best way to lose his job and become Procurator of Outer Mongolia would have been to call in the Roman army because he couldn't control the natives. Therefore, he was very quick on the trigger. My interpretation of what happened to Jesus is that he was brought to the Sanhedrin that night, not to try him and condemn him, but to warn him that if he went around talking about the revolution and the coming days of God's judgment, he was going to be picked up and killed by the Romans. But years later, that episode was written (through the filter of Jewish-Christian enmity and competition) so that that night visit to the Sanhedrin turned into a trial and condemnation of Jesus.

Can the idea of resurrection be found in Jewish belief?

There was no idea of resurrection in early Jewish belief, though there was a very controversial first-century belief that in Messianic times, the dead would collectively be brought back to life. It was so bitterly debated that there were fistfights breaking out in synagogues between people who were praying for the resurrection of all the dead and people who didn't believe in it. The resurrection is a very non-Jewish idea. But I've had visitations from people I have loved who have died—they were very real and it felt as though I could touch and smell them. Perhaps people who cared very deeply about Jesus saw him in their dreams and in their daydreams afterward.

Was Jesus married or
in an intimate relationship?

Again, we know so little about him, except what the gospels tell us. I find it very hard to think that a significant detail like that was universally filtered out, that if true, it wouldn't have sneaked through someplace. I suspect he refrained from being married because he really believed the world was going to end soon.

Second Coming?

Since I don't believe in the First Coming, I can't very well believe in the Second!

I do have a friend who says the argument between Jews and Christians will be resolved very easily—just wait for Jesus to come, and then ask him if he has ever been here before.

Most important teaching of Jesus?

First of all, I make the same distinction a lot of theologians make, between the religion of Jesus and the religion about Jesus. The religion of Jesus is left-of-center, first-century Judaism. Again, I look at all his teachings and all of them are pretty mainstream Jewish, colored by this sense of urgency that the world is going to end.

His most distinctive teaching, the one where he diverges from mainstream Judaism is the Sermon on the Mount. There he's essentially giving a sermon on the ten commandments and moving the locus of sin from the deed to the thought. "The old commandment is don't kill—I give you a new one, don't hate. The old commandment is don't commit adultery—I give you a new one, don't even look lustfully at a woman." That's a very non-Jewish teaching because first of all, the Jewish orientation is that you can control your deeds better than you can control your thoughts. For example, it's a lot easier for me to keep my hands to myself than it is for me not to fantasize about an attractive woman. It's hard for me not to be angry or envious, but it's very easy for me not to do harm to another person. It's more realistic to ask a person to control his actions than his thoughts.

Second, we can judge other people by their behavior but we can't really read their hearts. It's sort of like the umpire who has to decide whether the pitcher was deliberately throwing at the batter or if the pitch just got away. You can judge where the ball went, you can't judge a person's motivation.

I don't think there is anything original in the teachings of Jesus that isn't found in Jewish teachings. When he said the most important commandment is "Love thy neighbor as yourself," he was just repeating Leviticus 19:18, which says, "Love your neighbor as yourself." What was most effective was how he put the whole package together and then exemplified it.

There are people who simply by their presence convey a message that they don't have to put into words and I'm prepared to believe that Jesus was that kind of individual.

✣ 21
JERRY FALWELL

"That was your Waterloo," Jerry Falwell said when I told him about how years ago I had found myself in a deep depression. He also told me about his "Waterloo" and for a moment, we rested silently together in the truth of our own human frailties and our subsequent experience of God's presence. We had that in common, and I realized Jerry Falwell was my spiritual brother. Sure we had differences of opinion, but we also had a shared appreciation for spiritual surrender and a shared knowledge of how our suffering led to that surrender—how, in that place where human beings come to the end of themselves, there's the chance that they will encounter God. No wonder Jesus said "Blessed are the poor in spirit," because it's when a human being is weakened that the strength of God can emerge.

Anyway, Jerry Falwell and I rested in the presence of holiness together without thinking or clinging to ways of defining it. I had learned "non-grasping" from the Buddhists, and Jesus had spoken to Mary about much the same thing when he told her after his resurrection "to not hold onto me." Because although Jesus had been resurrected, he still had a body and he didn't want her clinging to the physical or conceptual notions of who he was. He wanted her to wait until after his ascension when he became pure spirit, because the surest way to stay out of God's presence is by clinging to God's perceived presence. God is to be experienced—but not clung to.

So, Jerry Falwell and I just sat there and smiled as we rested in our experience of God together. *But then it happened.*

"Bill," Dr. Falwell said, "I think you've had some genuine spiritual experiences, but I don't think you're fully 'born again' yet."

I felt the moment drain away as he labeled it and judged me as not knowing God as well as he. We looked at each other for an eternal moment and I thought about how I had studied with Sufis, Buddhists, Hindus, Sikhs, Jews, and other religious practitioners around the world. How I had felt God in their presence. How I had done a silent, ten-day retreat each year for the past fourteen years. How I had done these things, and if Jerry Falwell only knew what I knew—he would be even wiser—and he would be more . . . *more . . . like me!*

That's when I almost burst out laughing because while Jerry Falwell had looked at me and thought I wasn't wise enough, I had looked at him and thought he wasn't wise enough either.

In 1952, Jerry Falwell was a sophomore in college studying to be a journalist. One night, while listening to Dr. Charles E. Fuller's "Old-fashioned Revival Hour," he became convinced that he would have a relationship with God and that that relationship must be established through a new-birth experience and the Gospel of Jesus Christ. Despite the fact that his father was an agnostic and his grandfather was an atheist, Jerry Falwell began looking for a church that taught what Dr. Fuller preached. In his hometown of Lynchburg, Virginia, on January 20, 1952, Jerry Falwell attended a Sunday-night service at a little Baptist church, and as a result of the message preached, he walked down the aisle and gave his heart and life to Jesus Christ.

The next day he purchased his first Bible and two months later he felt called to the ministry. In September 1952 he enrolled in the Baptist Bible College of Springfield, Missouri. In 1956, he started Thomas Road Baptist Church in Lynchburg, Virginia.

I met Reverend Jerry Falwell at his office on the campus of Liberty Baptist University. Meeting him, I was reminded of a lesson I had learned in 1986 when I met Bhagwan Rajneesh in Kathmandu, Nepal. Bhagwan was an Indian guru who had lived in various places: Greece, India, Nepal, and even Oregon, where he'd collected followers along with over one hundred Rolls-Royces. Back then, I had developed a negative attitude about Rajneesh even though I had never met him, heard him speak, or read anything he had written. But after I had attended his talk in Nepal, my attitude about him changed and though I never looked at him as my teacher, I was able to glean some wisdom from him. My experience with Rajneesh taught me to be aware of making judgments based on what I'd been told by others or by the media.

It was the same with Jerry Falwell because a month before I had had a negative attitude about him even though I had never met him, or heard him speak extensively, or been to his church in Lynchburg, Virginia. I had allowed my opinion of him to be created by what the media had told me about him.

While on this journey to understand who Jesus really was or is, I realized time and time again that each of us has to ask in a deep soul-searching way, the question Jesus asked Peter.

"But what about you?" Jesus asked. "Who do you say I am?"[1]

Who was/is Jesus?

I believe Jesus Christ was the promised Messiah of Israel and that he was and is a member of the Godhead. He is the second person of the Trinity—the Father, Son, Holy Ghost. I believe that in the beginning he was with the Father, and then God sent him to the earth. He was born through the Virgin Mary. He was both God and man, the God-man, perfect God, perfect man. I believe that he lived a sinless life and that he died upon the cross to atone for the sins of all humanity for the just and the unjust—past, present, future. I believe that he is coequal with God the Father in all attributes pertaining to deity; that he was God's instrument in the creation.

1. Mark 8:29, NIV.

I believe that after he died upon the cross, he was buried and on the third day, by his own power, rose from the dead. Later from the Mount of Olives, he ascended back to the right hand of the Father, where he today is seated at the right hand of God the Father as an intercessor for all the saints on the earth. He will come again.

Jesus the only son of God?

I believe that Jesus is the only begotten Son of God: John 3:16. But all who place their faith in God through the crucifixion, the burial, the resurrection of Christ, believing the gospel is the atonement for their sins, become adopted sons of God.

Jesus' lost years?

From his childhood until the beginning of his ministry at about thirty, I believe that he grew up with his family, much like any boy grew up in Nazareth, with his mother, Mary, and her husband, Joseph. I think he was aware of his deity and since his father was a carpenter, he probably learned carpentry. Luke's gospel tells us he grew in stature and in wisdom, therefore he developed, grew, and matured like any child would, except that he was incapable of sin.

Did Jesus ever make mistakes?
Or learn things?

Jesus was perfect and while growing up as a child, I think he stumbled, crawled before he walked, and I believe that his physical body matured like all of ours and went through all the natural processes of development. All of it occurred without sin.

I believe that he did learn. It says that he grew in stature and in wisdom, therefore, I believe that he learned how to do things just like any child would. I believe he grew educationally and intellectually as other children. The only difference was, as deity, he was incapable of sin. I believe that when he entered his ministry at thirty that the Holy Spirit came upon him and that was manifested openly at his baptism when the Heavenly

Father said, "This is my beloved son in whom I am well pleased, hear ye him" (Mark 17:5, KJV). I think at that point in time, that he was limited (by choice) by natural laws and that he ate, lived, slept, walked, talked, and performed as any man would, but with the powers of deity within his hand.

Was Jesus married?

I don't think that he was ever married. First of all, there is no biblical record of it, and second I believe that he was married to the will of his Father.

Jesus' religion?

I'm not much of a religionist. I don't believe that Jesus was religious. I believe that he was in total submission to his Heavenly Father. He said, "I've come to do thy will, oh God." I don't believe that Pharisaism or Judaism or the Sadducees of that day, or any religion that may have existed, had any attraction for him. He came to give life, he came to teach a relationship and provide a relationship with his Father through himself.

I'm not a religious person, I'm a spiritual person. We are all spiritual beings and I'm more interested in a relationship with Christ as a person than I am in being a member of any church or organized religious effort. The organized church is fine if, in fact, it is delivering God's message and is lifting up Christ, and not its own programs—unfortunately that's rare today. But I am totally committed to knowing Christ and making him known to others. I am totally committed to witnessing to every person in the world, and that's why I do the talk shows. They're not in church on Sunday morning but they are there watching late-night television. There are many people who tell me the first time they ever heard what I'm saying was on a show like "Politically Incorrect."

Did Jesus intend to start Christianity?

The word Christianity is not in the Bible. The word Christian is in the New Testament three times. Jesus came in order to create believers in and followers of himself. All that we have added since then has been human addition. There were no church buildings in the New Testament era. The ec- clesiastical headquarters, the high priest and Old Testament Judaism, were created and established before he got there. *I do not believe it was his in- tent to create organized religion.*

Why didn't the majority of Jews accept him as the Messiah?

I believe the Jews did not accept him as Messiah because they were looking for a king. He came as a servant, a lamb. John the Baptist identi- fied him: "Behold the Lamb of God which taketh away the sin of the world" (John 1:29, KJV). But they expected him to come in power and great glory—he will later. They misinterpreted Old Testament prophecy and did not understand that before he could come in power and in great glory, he must be the Lamb of God, who at Calvary takes away the sins of the world.

Who killed Jesus and why?

The sins of all of humanity had to be atoned for through his death, only the blood of the deity could atone for the sins of the world. Therefore, every person who has ever lived has equal liability in the death of Christ. It was not the Jews, the Romans, or any organized religion of the day—but it was the sins of all of humanity; every one of us was equally and mutually re- sponsible for his death.

Who wrote the gospels and how accurate are they?

I believe the entire Bible, Genesis 1:1 through Revelation 22:21 is lit- eral and inspired of God, without error and infallible. I believe that Matthew, Mark, Luke, and John were written by those four men and they were inspired by the Holy Spirit. They were human instruments whose per- sonalities come through and whose skills and background are all unveiled in the writings by their similes, metaphors, and their illustrations. Each of them has a different perspective as though created through a prism. All four gospels were written exactly as they were inspired to be written, and, therefore, are the Word of God.

Second Coming?

The rapture of the Church is the first phase of the Second Coming. After the rapture the anti-Christ shall appear and there will be seven years of tribulation on the earth and it will be a time of purging, of preparation for the establishment of the kingdom of heaven on earth. At the end of the tribulation, the battle of Armageddon will be fought and Christ, with all of his saints of all of the ages, will come down from heaven in power and great glory. He will defeat the forces of anti-Christ and Satan will be bound for a thousand years in the lake of fire. Christ will rule upon the throne of David in Jerusalem for a thousand years and the saints shall rule with him. At the end of which, the heavens and the earth as we know them today will be passed away and new heavens and new earth—Revelation 21 and 22: "And the New Jerusalem will come down from God out of heaven, prepared as a bride adorned for her husband. The former earth and heaven will pass away and eternity will be ushered in and Christ will reign for ever."

Why do some Christians evangelize so forcefully?

Because of Jesus' final words in Matthew 28:18, 19, 20. He said, "All power, all authority is given unto me in heaven and in earth. Go ye therefore and teach or make disciples out of all nations, baptizing them in the name of the Father, Son and Holy Ghost and teaching them to observe all things." Then he said, "If you do that, lo, I am with you all the way, even to the end of the age."

We call that "the great commission," and his final words commanded that we give the gospel to every person in the world in our generation.

As a Christian, the only way to pray is to pray to the Father, in and through the merits, and in the name of his Son, Christ, whose death, burial, and resurrection I have accepted as the atonement for my sins. The Son of God, the only begotten Son of God, becomes my Savior, but God becomes my Heavenly Father. When I pray to the Father, it's in and through my own merits, I have no right to approach the throne, but through his, my relationship with his son, and by the Holy Spirit who helps me pray from the heart. In a nutshell, prayer is to the Father, through the Son and by the Holy Spirit. And that's the Trinity—Father, Son, Holy Ghost. And we must always, the best we know, do it unselfishly in the will of God—praying for a new Cadillac probably won't impress him too much. *But praying for food, the necessities of life, safety, the well-being of others, and the ability to be more of a blessing to humanity*—that's what God's interested in. The relationship God wants is an intimate and personal one, so that we converse and have intercourse with him more intimately than we do with anybody on earth.

What Spiritual techniques did Jesus teach?

Jesus taught us to realize that everyone is a sinner, not some of us—all of us. As soon as we are old enough to know right from wrong, we do wrong—all of us. That's why a new birth is needed. Once I realize that I am a sinner and that I have broken God's laws, then I can go to the Father and say, "Yes, I agree with you that I'm a sinner." Romans 10, verses 9, 10, and 13: "For with a heart man believes unto righteousness with a mouth confession is made unto, or because of, salvation." Romans 13: "For whosoever shall call upon the name of the Lord shall be saved." As an eighteen-year-old college sophomore, I didn't understand much about it but I acknowledged to God that I was a sinner and that I wanted to be born again. I asked Jesus, through his shed blood, to wash my sins away, come into my heart and save my lost soul. God will move heaven and earth to answer a prayer like that. Conversion and the new-birth experience occur when we genuinely, sincerely repent of our sins, receive Christ as our Lord Savior and believe the atonement has paid our sin debt in full forever. We are already children of God by creation, but we then become children of

God through faith. We become children of God by relationship and by spiritual welding. At that moment, God becomes our Heavenly Father spiritually. We can call him Father, we can talk to him, we can look to him—that's where the Bible comes in. The Bible is God's Word, it's his way of talking to us. Prayer is our way of talking to him.

When Billy Graham gives the gospel invitation in a crusade and people come down, they come with simple childlike faith. They repent of their sins, they receive Christ as their Lord and Savior, they get God's forgiveness, and they start a brand-new life in the Lord.

By admitting your sins and your mistakes,
you let go of your pride?

That's what it is. It's acknowledging and agreeing with God. God says, "You are a sinner," and you've finally come to the place where you say, "You're right, I am a sinner and I want to do something about it." We are still sinners until we die, but we are forgiven sinners and that's a difference.

I was raised to relate to God directly,
without putting Jesus' face on God.

That's exactly what I was saying, probably on "Politically Incorrect," that I'm really not impressed by religion as such. You know, all the high-church, low-church ritualism. To me, I'm driving my car down the road and I've got a family need or one of my kids is going through a tough time or whatever, or I am, and I just talk with the Lord about it like I would talk to you. I know he's there and I know he's listening. I claim the victory of this and I claim the provision in that.

Most of us don't know what to do past five minutes from now, so I just seek divine wisdom. But it's in and because of that experience I had on January 20, 1952, and I would say the one you had when you were twenty-one where you entered into a relationship with God as the personal Christ. Somebody else will tell us later what we are, if we're a Methodist or Baptist because we like this church or that church. But that infrastructure is purely that, it's a place for you to develop relationships and friendships and so forth and to grow, an incubator. But it has nothing to do with establishing a relationship and that relationship is something far higher than any church you'll attend or any pastor you'll listen to.

There is nothing deader than dead orthodoxy. We can very easily bring in all the two-year-old children of Lynchburg and spend the next ten years teaching them the Westminster Confession and the Orthodox beliefs and so forth, but unless at the end of that ten years each of them has established a relationship with God through Christ, they are going to have a head religion and not a heart religion. Without the heart, when they hit the storm out in the world—it's dissipated very quickly. That's what preaching is all about. That's why Billy Graham holds crusades, and that's why I do TV and pastor a church. That's why personal witness is about putting my arm around somebody privately and saying, "Let me talk to you about the Lord." *I want to help people connect what they've got in their head with faith in their heart and suddenly it's a transforming experience.*

How does a person know they have a true experience of God? Someone like Adolf Hitler thought he was doing the right thing.

There is nothing more dangerous than religion without Christ. That's exactly what's happening in Northern Ireland and in the Balkans. *Those so-called Christians who are killing the Muslims in the name of God only have knowledge, because their heart would never let them do that if they were spiritual men and women.*

You've got to go right to the book, the Bible, the authority. Someone who says, "Show me what the Bible says and I will do it." I show them John 1:11 and 12: "He came unto his own, Christ came to the Jews, his own, the Jews received him not, but as many as received him, to them gave he power, authority to become the Sons of God, and that is, those who believed on his name." And then Romans 10:9: "That if thou shall confess with thy mouth the Lord Jesus, and believe in thine heart that God hath raised him from the dead, thou shall be saved, for with the heart man believeth unto righteousness and with the mouth confession is made because of salvation . . . for whosoever"—that's Bill Elliott, Jerry Falwell, Billy Graham—"whosoever shall call upon the name of the Lord, shall be saved." That's exactly what the Bible says. You've got to go back to the fact; has there been a time when, regardless how I feel tonight, regardless of what I'm going through right now, regardless of my mistakes through the years, *was there a time when I sincerely, as a sinner, honestly before God, called upon him and asked him to come into my heart as my Savior?* If you've got a little question about that, then you ought to right here and now just pray that prayer and give your heart and life to Christ. That doesn't mean you weren't saved back there, it just simply means that you are tying the knot, you are reconfirming what you did back there so that the rest of your life there is always that blessed insurance that maybe I didn't know at twenty-one fully what I was doing, but I know now and I've taken Christ as my Lord and my Savior.

✢ 22
MY PRAYER WITH JERRY FALWELL

LYNCHBURG, VIRGINIA

After the interview, Dr. Falwell asked me to pray with him. He asked with such sincerity and devotion that to say "no," never crossed my mind. In Sufism, they believe that God has ninety-nine names or qualities. These qualities are reflected in human beings and that is why the Bible says we are made in God's image. No one exhibits or manifests them all, but it's enough sometimes to see one of God's qualities in another. I saw devotion clearly in Jerry Falwell, so when he asked me to pray with him, and then to repeat his words, my soul never hesitated. Instead it became spacious, and everything Jerry Falwell prayed I held in my spaciousness, a spaciousness that is found only in accepting the ninty-nine names of God, and not one or two.

"Heavenly Father," Jerry Falwell said as he held my hand, "I pray for Bill Elliott—you brought him here today . . ."

Jerry Falwell was right. I was in Lynchburg, Virginia, and I had no doubt that God had guided me. So far Jerry and I agreed.

". . . He's writing about your Son, Jesus Christ . . ." he continued.

". . . and the world is going to read his book and, Father, I pray that you will help him right now to know your son . . ."

I was starting to get uneasy. It sounded as if Dr. Falwell assumed I didn't know Jesus.

". . . I pray for Bill right now, that you will give him that blessed assurance, that blessed hope and faith that alone saves."

"Bill," Jerry said, "I'm gonna pray a prayer now and just from your heart sincerely follow me."

Now I have to tell you I gulped a little when Jerry Falwell asked me to follow him. I gulped because he wanted me to repeat *his prayer*. And when I pray—it's *my prayer*. My prayers are honest and heartfelt. How was I going to be honest in *my heart* when I was repeating *his words*? But then I remembered: I have meditated in Buddhist monasteries and chanted and danced with Sufis. I've learned that it is the purity of the heart, of the surrender behind the name or word, that invokes God's presence—not the name. God was here with Dr. Falwell and me, just as God was in the Tibetan monasteries or Sufi dances.

"Dear Father in heaven . . ." Jerry Falwell began.

"Dear Father in heaven . . ." I repeated. Which was easy enough because I believe in God.

"I believe that you are . . ." Jerry Falwell continued.

"I believe that you are . . ." I repeated.

"I believe that your Son came to this earth."

"I believe that your Son came to this earth," I said, while reminding myself that God sent all his sons and daughters to earth.

"Died upon a cross . . ."

"Died upon a cross . . ."

"Rose from the dead . . ."

"Rose from the dead . . ."

"I believe that the blood of Jesus . . ."

"I believe that the blood of Jesus . . ."

"Washes away the sins of mankind . . ."

"Washes away the sins of mankind . . ." I repeated, and I had a slight problem because I don't believe God demanded Jesus' death in order to forgive our sins. That was too much like a business deal—"If I get this, then I'll give you forgiveness." But I let go of that need to know, and trusted that *somehow*—Jesus' life and death (in ways that no one can conceive of) brought us closer to God.

"I receive Jesus right now . . ."

"I receive Jesus right now . . ." I said, opening up to the companionship of Jesus.

"As my Lord and my Savior . . ."

"As my Lord and my Savior . . ." I said, as I realized what a difference words made. Jerry Falwell was comfortable with the word "Lord" whereas it reminded me of the Middle Ages when *lords* had *serfs* whom they often treated terribly. I preferred to think of Jesus' words *"call me friend."* And Savior? What exactly was a Savior? How does a Savior "save"? Does a Savior carry you out of the hell you've been in? Does he do it for you? Or does a Savior show you the way out by showing you how to align with God, and thereby be saved?

"Come into my heart, Lord Jesus . . ."

"Come into my heart, Lord Jesus . . ." I repeated, feeling the presence of Jesus.

"Forgive my sins . . ."

"Forgive my sins . . ." I repeated, knowing that Jesus had already forgiven my sins—and just waited for me to do the same.

"Save my soul . . ."

"Save my soul . . ."

"I will serve you, Lord, the rest of my life . . ."

"I will serve you, Lord, the rest of my life . . ." I repeated, knowing I continually strive to serve God.

"As you give me the strength to do it . . ."

"As you give me the strength to do it . . ."

"In Jesus' name . . ."

"In Jesus' name . . ." I repeated, asking for Jesus' guidance and advice in my relationship with God.

"Amen."

"Amen."

"Don't ever again doubt," Jerry Falwell said. "You'll have bad days and the older you get—sometimes you'll be lonely and all screwed up. But don't doubt. I never got in real trouble until after I became a Christian. And then I wondered, if I'm a Christian, how in the world could I do this? But you know, we're still human beings."

In that moment, I saw Jesus in Jerry Falwell—and that's the irony. He probably thought he was doing Jesus' work when he preached, but I saw the humility and divine humanity of Jesus in Jerry Falwell when he was just being honest and humble.

"I'm seeing Franklin Graham tomorrow," Dr. Falwell said at the end of our interview. "I'll tell him to meet with you."

"I've got a little something for you," I said, holding up a small sandalwood bead. "Mother Teresa and the Dalai Lama blessed this."

Then I placed the gift in the palm of his hand, and as he looked at it, a smile appeared on his face.

23
THE OTHER LEAD

"You follow a trail of evidence that leads to the man," my brother the detective said.

And there seemed to be at least several trails or ways to know Jesus.

One was through reading the gospels, various books, and in meetings with scholars, mystics, and evangelists.

A second way was through *helping others as Jesus did,* and that's why I worked in helping professions.

And a third way was by *walking where Jesus walked.* Thus, there was only one thing to do.

24
O'HARE AIRPORT

CHICAGO, ILLINOIS

"Why do you have this?" The head of Israeli security at O'Hare Airport asked while going through my bags. He was talking about the two quarts of nondairy creamer I had stuffed in my luggage.

"I'm allergic to dairy products," I said.

"They have this in Israel," he replied.

How was I supposed to know? All I knew was that I liked coffee with cream in the morning, and if I didn't have my fake cream . . . well, it just wouldn't be good, so I didn't take any chances, and I brought my own. But the fake cream was the least of my problems. Actually the problem had started an hour ago when Matt Cohen, the head of Israeli security, approached me after I had answered a few questions put to me by the first wave of Israeli security.

"We have a prob-blem," he said, looking at me intensely, and I smiled for a second because this was usually the way one of those spy novels started—but he didn't smile back. At least I was comforted by the fact he said "we" had a problem, that it wasn't just *my* problem.

My brother had dropped me off at O'Hare Airport because I was on my way to Jerusalem. Little did I realize my trip to Jerusalem would bring back memories of the Dalai Lama. Why? Because when I met with the Dalai Lama in 1990 he was surrounded by a bunch of guys with machine guns—and I was frisked twice by bodyguards. Now that I was on my way to Jerusalem I was stopped by Israeli security and asked questions. The problem began when I couldn't produce any paperwork or letter about the pilgrimage tour I had signed up for.

"It was all done through e-mail," I told a woman who was part of Israeli security. She asked to see an e-mail from my laptop, and then she freaked out when she saw that the tour organizer had a Muslim name. In truth, he was a Sufi and named "Zahir" by one of his spiritual teachers— actually, his name was something like Michael "Zahir" Smith or something like that.

"That's a Muslim name," she said.

"No—it's more of a Sufi name," I replied.

"What is a Sufi?" she asked. I began to explain, but I could tell right away that she wasn't getting what I was telling her, and so she just stared at me. In the same way as when the dog *really* does eat your homework and you try to explain it to your teacher, she just *stares at you.*

"Where are you staying in Jerusalem?" she asked.

"At a YMCA across from the King David Hotel," I said. "I think it's the Three Arches or something . . ."

"The Seven Arches?" she asked.

"I thought it was the Three Arches," I replied—not really sure of the name.

"I have heard of the Seven Arches," she said, "but not the Three Arches."

I figured since she was from Israel, she must be right and I must have gotten the name wrong.

"It could be the Seven Arches," I said.

Later, I found out that that was about the worst thing I could have said because there are two hotels in Jerusalem with the word "Arches" in the name. The Three Arches is a hotel in the Israeli section of town, but The Seven Arches is a hotel in the Palestinian part of town. When Israeli security telephoned Jerusalem in order to verify my story, they called The Three Arches and, of course, they had no reservation and had never heard of me because my reservation was at The Seven Arches.

That's when the Israeli security man named Matt Cohen came up to me and said with an Israeli accent, *"We have a prob-blem."*

That's when I smiled, not a big smile—but enough to arouse suspicion. Why did I smile? I guess because I've always smiled whenever I was in a peculiar situation. It began after both my parents died when I was a kid. When I went back to school everyone kept saying, "I'm sorry to hear about your parents."

And I was in such shock over their death that all I could do was smile, and then they would say, "Your parents just died—*why are you smiling?!*"

"What do you want me to do?" I would reply. *"Cry?"*

Since then, whenever I am in a strange or uncomfortable situation—I smile. This was especially disturbing to the dean of my high school. Whenever he called me in for disciplinary action—I'd smile. Of course this irritated him, and the madder he *got—the more I'd smile.*

Anyway, to make a long story short, Israeli security went through my luggage for twenty-four hours and I had to delay my departure until the following day.

"Excuse me, sir," Matt Cohen said just before I left the airport. "I have a question for you. You are taking this amazingly well—why?"

"Well," I said, "I've spent a lot of time in Buddhist monasteries meditating and in 1990 I went to Calcutta to interview Mother Teresa. She had sent me a letter six months before saying she would do an interview and so I traveled seven thousand miles to meet her and when I got there, she told me she was too sick and tired to do an interview. What was I going to do?

Argue with her? Tell her to 'toughen up'? That's when I learned that it's best not to get upset about what's out of my hands."

Matt Cohen looked at me and smiled.

"Besides," I added, "I'm a writer and I actually found all this interesting [I almost said *amusing*] because as an author it gives me something to write about."

The next day before I got on the plane they made me take off my shoes and my shirt while they frisked me. That's why going to Jerusalem is like meeting the Dalai Lama. They're both surrounded by security and I got frisked both times. Why? Why was all this necessary? Because there are people out there who in order to further their own political-religious beliefs, will kill the Dalai Lama or blow up Jerusalem.

Holy people and holy places will always be endangered by people who have never encountered the holy inside of themselves. That's why I've tried to understand every view of Jesus in this book, rather than try to defend what I believe and kill that which I don't.

✠ 25
A TOUCHING FLIGHT

"I was six years old when my family left Poland in 1936," Miriam Julius said. She was a seventy-year-old Jewish American who sat next to me on the plane to Jerusalem, and she had a vibrant energy that made her so alive she seemed closer to fifty than seventy.

We first started talking over our dinner meal because El Al Airlines had included a nondairy creamer with the coffee.

"Fantastic," I said.

"What's so fantastic?" she asked.

"The creamer," I replied. "It's imitation, it's fake—that's great."

"That's because it's against Jewish dietary law to eat dairy with beef," she said. "So in Israel and around the world, many Jewish people use nondairy products."

During our flight, I gave her a copy of my book *Tying Rocks to Clouds* to read and when she read the beginning about how my parents' death had devastated me when I was twelve years old—she didn't say like most people—"That must have been hard." Instead she said, "Didn't you know that people don't live forever? Didn't anyone tell you that—or didn't you realize that?!"

I was momentarily stunned—what made her think like that? Then I realized—she was a Polish Jew and at six years old she'd fled Poland—just a few years before Hitler began exterminating millions of Jews, many of whom were Polish. To her, death would be expected—especially unfair death. I guess when millions of your people were shot, burned, or gassed, the death of the parents of a twelve-year-old boy in Chicago doesn't surprise you.

"Didn't you know that people all over the world are dying and starving?" she asked.

I just shrugged my shoulders because like most kids I probably just thought about my own little world.

"I believe in science," she continued, *"not God.* But you know, my son is studying to be a rabbi."

When I told her I was staying at the YMCA, she said it's pronounced "AIMKA" in Jerusalem.

"No one will understand Y-M-C-A," she assured me.

Later as we watched a music video on the overhead screen—she started to cry. Since the video was in Hebrew, I asked her what the woman sang about.

"She sang about how all the windows to my past are open now."

"So that's why you cried?" I asked. "It reminded you of the past?"

"No," she replied. "That wasn't it. It was the beauty of her voice that made me cry."

Toward the end of the flight, I saw her crying as she read my book. She looked over at me.

"The chapter about your grandmother," she said tearfully, *"about how much you loved her . . ."*

She stopped talking, bit her lower lip, and closed her eyes. Then she lightly placed her fingertips on her chest—right above her heart—and we talked no more.

26
THE SHIRUUT AND OLD FRIENDS

"Remember to take a *shiruut* from the airport in Tel Aviv to Jerusalem," my friend Miriam Julius had said. "A cab is too much money."

I made it through customs easily and outside the Tel Aviv airport, I looked for a *shiruut*, which is a small van that taxis people to and from the airport. It was much cheaper than a cab because they squeezed eight people into it. Initially I sat next to a Jewish man and woman from New York. They were both tiny, impish folks whose friendliness and affability were as palpable to me as scents are to an animal.

"Excuse me," the cabdriver said, "you have to change seats because there are religious people here."

I looked to my right and saw two Orthodox Jewish men. They're easy to spot—they all wear the same clothes.

"It's a kind of uniform," the old Jewish imp next to me said.

The "uniform" of an Orthodox Jew begins at the head with a round-brimmed black hat that made me think of a Billy Jack movie. Their entire wardrobe is black: a black suit, long black trench coat, black shoes and socks—except for a white dress shirt. The most distinguishable feature is the hair. Two long curls hang down under the hat—one on each side—and they all have beards.

Anyway, I was disappointed because I had to move and sit in the back with all the men, while the women had to sit in the front. Part of Orthodox belief is separation of sexes.

"See," the old Jewish man next to me said loud enough so that everyone in the cab could hear, "they wear those clothes and have that hat and beard in order to stay in their own world."

"They want to keep to their own and separate themselves," he continued. It was obvious he was hoping to instigate a fight, putting out a nibble—but the two Orthodox Jewish men didn't bite.

"They're Orthodox like me," he said. "But more extreme, more to the right."

I looked at the two "extreme" Jews. The one man in his fifties had eyes that gleamed, as though he experienced a holy, mystical joy—but then again, it could just as easily have been a self-satisfied, holier-than-thou look. I couldn't be sure. The other man looked to be around seventy years old and acknowledged no one; instead he stared straight ahead as though focused on some unseen goal. Their two daughters sat in the front with my impish friend's wife. I called him friend because any man who's pushing eighty years old and is willing to entertain the idea of seeing through the rituals of his religion, while retaining the spirit that they portend to protect, is a friend of mine. And even though I hadn't met him before, I learned that as I move throughout the world I meet many kindred spirits who seem oddly familiar.

"Am I allowed to talk to the women up front?" I asked.

"No," my Jewish friend said. "They keep their women separate so as to control them and who they talk to. But I think they mainly keep them separate from men—especially themselves—because I think they're afraid they'd fall in love with them. You need rules when you don't know your God and don't trust yourself. But if you know your God and yourself, then you're free—you don't need all those rules."

27
WHERE JESUS WALKED

JERUSALEM

I arrived at my hotel a day before the rest of the tour arrived. There were no reservations for me. The desk manager said it was $120 a night, but after some debate, he gave me the room for $60 a night, provided I talked with the manager in the morning.

The next day I got up at 6 A.M. and went for a short walk before breakfast. I kept the hotel within sight so that I didn't get lost—which reminded me of why the Sufis say the remembrance prayer, *"La illa ila la hu,"* to remember where the soul came from.

As I walked along, I constantly wondered about the significance of everything I saw. Did Jesus walk here? Did Jesus sit there? How old is that building over there? Or that wall over there? As an American, I was easily impressed by the age of things because in America, anything older than two hundred years is a big deal. I wondered which of the older walls and buildings were special, and which were just old.

I returned to the hotel and ate breakfast. One by one, two by two, people walked into the hotel's restaurant, sat down, and talked. I heard many languages—but no English. Since I was your typical American, I was language-illiterate. If you travel abroad, you realize the whole world knows that about Americans. There's even a joke about it.

"What do you call someone who knows three languages?
Trilingual.
What do you call someone who knows two languages?
Bilingual.
What do you call someone who knows one language?
American."

Occasionally I did hear a "good morning," and once, when the waitress spilled a pitcher of milk at the table next to me, she softly said, "Oops." Then the gentleman seated at the table also said, "Oops." For a moment I felt more connected to other human beings through spilled milk and "Oops."

After breakfast, I walked for five hours through the crooked streets of old Jerusalem. It reminded me of India or Nepal because there were many small stores and bazaars, and the storekeepers called out, "Hello," "Need help?", or "Wake up! Over here!" in their efforts to sell me something. I followed the occasional and haphazardly placed signs to the Western (or Wailing) Wall, which is all that remains of the Temple. A little boy, of perhaps eight years old, saw me searching.

"I will take you there," he said, and then he began leading me without asking because he obviously wanted to make a shekel or two. Usually, I would have played along, but I wanted to find the Wall on my own. I wanted to take my time walking toward the Wall, and I wanted to reflect as I walked toward what may be the holiest of places for Jews.

"I can do it myself," I told him several times. But he didn't listen.

"Alone," I told him. "I want to go 'alone.'"

"You give me one shekel," he replied.

"I don't have any," I said because I didn't have anything less than a twenty-shekel note in my pocket. "But I'll be here for two weeks—if you see me again—ask."

Finally, he left me when I sensed I was close to the Wall. I like to think it was my intuition that told me I was close, but I'm sure I just noticed the increasing number of machine-gunned police and soldiers all around—and God do they look young. Some looked barely out of their teens and yet they were expected to skillfully deal with crowd and terrorist problems. My brother became a Chicago cop when he was twenty-one years old and he was shot with a shotgun when he was twenty-two. I guess no matter how young you are—getting shot, or the possibility of getting shot—matures you.

After walking past hanging slabs of meat, sweet shops, and new Internet cafés, I turned a corner and there was the Western Wall in the distance. I was still several hundred yards and several stories above the square, but because of the Wall's size (it's 486 meters long) it seemed as though I could reach out and touch it. I walked down several flights of stone stairs, through a narrow corridor, and past a metal detector and several Israeli guards. Then everything opened up into a huge square where a few thousand people walked about. Children raced around while a vast array of Jewish people talked, chanted, or prayed. The women were dressed in everything from conservative dress and "babushkas" to tight leather pants with high heels, heavily made-up faces, and dyed hair. The men were just as creative and, of course, there were many Orthodox Jewish men dressed in black. Since many of the Jews didn't have a yarmulke, there was a box of cardboard yarmulkes by the entrance to the Wall. I laughed as a teenage boy with spiked hair tried to rest the cardboard yarmulke on his hair without messing it up. The yarmulke sat precariously on his stiffened, sticklike hair until a sudden breeze sent it tumbling off his head.

There were two sections at the Wailing Wall. One was for women and the other for men. Both sections were fenced off from the general public, and all I could do was watch from an elevated area just behind the fence because I wasn't sure if it was acceptable for me—a non-Jew—to go into those areas.

Just beyond the fence, a group of men gathered around an open text—a scroll contained in an embossed metal cylinder. A rabbi stood toe-to-toe with a young boy and yelled at him in a language I couldn't understand. He seemed to be teaching him. I figured it was part of a bar mitzvah.

A group of women next to me began throwing what looked like handfuls of small rocks at a group of men carrying another cylinder. The rocks bounced off their heads and chest, while the men squinted their eyes hoping not to get hit in the face. When the rocks fell to the ground, several young boys scrambled and fought over them. It was then that I realized that the "rocks" were actually candy-covered almonds.

Amid all this religion, the machine guns were ever present. On the rooftops that surrounded the Wall were groups of soldiers. Down below, soldiers walked here and there, and I was surprised to see one machine-gun-toting man with a ponytail, wearing a baseball cap backward.

When I had traveled to India and Nepal years ago, my heart was immediately and often opened by the people, the places, and the wandering Buddhists or Hindus I encountered. But here in the homeland of my native religion, I didn't feel much in my heart even though I realized how important Jerusalem—especially the Wall—was for others. I hadn't seen or felt the fruits of spiritual practice in the people around me. Where was the compassion, joy, and peace?

Was it me? Was I so deadened that I couldn't feel it? I respected that others thought of Jerusalem as holy. But when I looked at a map of Jerusalem and saw the words "Mount of Olives" with the word "Hotel" added to the end, I couldn't help but think Jesus would have trashed this place as he did two thousand years ago. That Moses would have come down from his mountain and seen the golden calf everywhere. That Noah would have had to escape all over again—the flood of "doing"—in his wish to find the Being of God.

✤ 28
BEGINNING TO FEEL

JERUSALEM

I went to the Western Wall again, but this time I went past the gate where I had stopped yesterday.

"You must have something on your head," the guard told me. I put on a cardboard yarmulke, but it kept sliding off. I held it on with one hand while I walked toward the Wall. With each step closer to the Wall, I felt an intensity grow. Finally, I stood at the base of the Wall. Looking up I saw folded-up pieces of paper placed in the cracks of the Wall—between the stones. Slowly I looked from one end of the Wall to the other, and then from the top of the Wall to the bottom. Every inch of space had a folded piece of paper placed in it. Thousands, probably millions, of letters and prayers placed there over the years. Messages sent to whom? It must be God—messages sent to God through a Wall that was all that remained of the temple that was the center of Judaism.

I walked over to the Wall and placed my left hand on the ancient stone, then my forehead against the back of my hand. It felt like many small bubbles in my mind. Then chattering. A growing voice. Many voices—praying together. A thread of voices spanning thousands of years, existing before I was born, and most likely continuing many years after I die. For a moment, I had dipped myself into the river of Judaism, the Ganges of the Holy City. The one stream of many voices and many prayers. Was it the Wall that made this place holy? Or the voices of people whose hearts/souls impressed upon this place a holiness—or is the holiness always present—asleep almost, until a human heart awakens, becomes a doorway for the presence of God to "set up Her tent."

It is said that Jesus' presence allowed the Great Presence to be born through him into this world. That is called being "born again" and it is by being born into spirit that we reenact the virgin birth because this birth of spirit does not come through the union of man and woman, but through the union of man or woman with God.

There is a difference of spiritual energy here at the wall. It is more active. More determined. More anxious. More conflicted. In India, I once sat underneath the Bodhtree and I can tell you there was a difference of atmosphere. In Buddhism, you sit in one place until the realization comes. Here at the Western Wall, the Jews are moving up and down—"davening." While acceptance and union are a key component in the East, in the West, and in Judaism—conflict and relationship are key. Being able to argue with the Supreme Being is accepted and it is a valid way to relate to the Supreme Being. While this appears to be a less peaceful method, it does lead to a more human experience.

At one time, I sought the peace, the Being of the Buddha. The Buddha taught me to relax back into Being. Now I seek the experience of Being Human or Human Being. Obviously there's a reason why we are called "human beings" and God is called "the Supreme Being"—it's Being that's stressed and most connects us to our soul, true nature, and God. But somehow this search for Jesus was bringing me into relationship with all the human and religious conflicts I had tried to let go of. It seemed like lifetimes ago that I was sitting in a monastery somewhere in Asia. There, for a moment, I let go of all my "doing" in order to experience a moment of Being. It was then that suddenly I understood the wisdom of the Tao Te Ching that said, "The wise man does nothing and yet nothing remains undone."

But in Judaism (and also in some ways its child Christianity) the idea is that God, the Supreme Being, created everything—and yet left creation unfinished. It is up to us, the many expressions of the One Being who are made in the image of God, to finish creation.

✢ 29
BETHLEHEM

I finally found a place that immediately struck me as holy. What's holy to me? I suppose it's a place, person, or thing that reminds me of that silent prayer that was whispered into my ear at the moment of birth. The Church of the Nativity in Bethlehem was built at Jesus' birthplace in 325 A.D. by Emperor Constantine. Today many modern scholars say Jesus was actually born in Nazareth, but anyone who knows anything knows that doesn't matter. What matters is that that same Spirit that was born in Jesus is born in us,[1] and it can be born anywhere.

Beneath the Church of the Nativity there is the cave. In that cave there is a gold star embedded in the floor at the place where he was born. Many people stood around that star taking pictures, but I was drawn deeper. I walked around the cave until I found a spiral staircase that had been carved out of the rock. It turned this way and that as I descended. At

---

1. John 14:20, NIV. "On that day you will realize that I am in my Father, and you are in me, and I am in you."

the bottom was a catacomb and upon exploring farther—a small chapel. The chapel and the thirty chairs in it were empty. I sat in one. A mosaic on the wall was the last thing I saw before I bowed my head and closed my eyes. My sense of self seemed to rise up from the depths, and slowly I sacrificed all thoughts of self until something even deeper emerged. Immediately I sensed the presence of those souls of old, and I asked for their guidance in birthing my holy child. I stayed there until their blessing was complete. Then I opened my eyes, stood up, and ascended the stairs with—how do I say this?—less of myself, but more of what I am.

✢ 30
DOUBT: DENIED

A letter from the Wisconsin Arts Board was forwarded to me. It said I didn't get one of eight grants offered. What's going on? I mean, one of the largest publishers in the world wants to publish my book, and the Wisconsin Arts Board says it's not good enough for a grant?

"My life isn't working," I said in my motor home the night before I was to meet with Marcus Borg.

"I give up," I said to no one in particular. For the past year while writing the Jesus book I've had to make choices like *which bills to pay*, and *which to pay late*.

"Money, going to work, car payments—even writing this Jesus book— it's all just crap," I said as I fell onto my couch. "The only thing that seemed to matter was this book . . ." I said, looking up at the ceiling, ". . . and I can't do it. It's all a waste and nothing ever works out," I said in total despair.

I felt like my soul and my dream were dying, and I had come to the end of myself. And when I tried to look beyond myself—I saw nothing. For an eternity, I was in that "in-between" place, the place between the old life that died and the new life that had not yet come—in the tomb of Jesus. How did I get here? Did I bring myself, or was I led here?

My Judas, my best friend and betrayer, helped put me here. Who was my Judas? My Judas was "my concept of life," and eventually, my concept of life—our concept of life—will always betray us. Because a concept is a fixed idea about life, while life is always changing—and that's why Jesus said, "The son of man hath no place to lay his head" (Luke 9:58). He was wise enough not to rest or lay his head on the pillow of concept. Instead Jesus lived the words of Psalm 62:1: "My soul finds rest in God alone."

As much as I tried to have faith, that night I fell asleep on a bed of doubt and confusion.

✣ 31
MARCUS BORG

"Bill, let's eat something before we talk," Marcus Borg said. "You're not a vegetarian are you?"

"No. I'm a recovering vegetarian," I replied. I had been a vegetarian for six years, and I was trying to be one again. But then Marcus pointed across the street.

GRANNY'S CHICKEN PALACE, the sign read.

"I've heard it's the best fried chicken in North Carolina," he said.

I guess *"vegetarian Bill"* would have to wait till tomorrow because I was a sucker for any restaurant called "Granny's" or "Grandma's." It brought back memories of my grandmother, and since I loved her if that was Granny's restaurant, I was going to eat there. But there was a problem. I only had fifteen dollars in cash and an American Express card. I wanted to treat Marcus Borg to dinner because he was kind enough to give me his time, but the restaurant didn't take American Express.

"Don't worry, Bill," Mark said. "I'm treating—I probably have more money than you."

I did the usual hemming and hawing about him paying, but he was certainly right. He did have more money than I did, and for a moment, I wondered how he could tell. Did I look poor?

During dinner, I confided in him that I was broke and that I had already borrowed money from my relatives.

"I think you're on to something with this Jesus book," Marcus said, "by putting all these people into one book, you're doing something no one else has done. My advice is that you get the money to finish this book even if you have to go to a loan shark."

A plate of fried chicken was brought to the table. Without discussing who would eat what and how much, Marcus and I each proceeded to take one breast, one thigh, one leg, and one chicken wing each. We were respectful of each other's pieces. After sharing our meal, like Jesus did at the last supper—though I suppose there was no fried chicken in Jerusalem— we returned to the motel and talked about Jesus while seated in rocking chairs outside Marcus Borg's room. As we watched a few children shriek and jump into the swimming pool, Marcus Borg lit up his pipe.

"I can't write or think without it," he told me.

Marcus looked thoughtful as he puffed on his pipe, and so I fantasized about getting a pipe too. I imagined interviewing myself while I smoked a pipe. It was a pleasant image. I was drawn toward it. I, like Marcus Borg, would look thoughtful and reflective. I imagined I was a college professor with a few dedicated students around me. They anxiously awaited my next words as I puffed and contemplated.

I continued to relax into that image until my mind was suddenly flooded with cancerous thoughts, and then my body went rigid. I recalled stories of partial removals of people's jaws, lips, tongue, and mouth . . . and what about the yellow teeth? Then I thought about my grandfather, who had smoked a pipe. He didn't put tobacco in his pipe, instead he put a cigar in it so that it stuck straight up. It made you think that he was kind of nuts, and to make matters worse, he constantly said, "I want pizza pie with bananas on it."

Now you might think that he was a cute, harmless old guy, but this was also a guy who would hit you in the face with a flyswatter while you were sleeping and say "Oh, I missed that fly," and think it was funny. He also was known to chew tobacco and spit the juice in your ear while you slept. So I fled from my image of being a cancer-jawed old man who constantly asked for banana-covered pizza pies, into the sweet-smelling smoke of Marcus Borg's pipe. I looked across from me and saw Marcus Borg waiting for the first question.

Marcus Borg is a nationally known Jesus scholar and Hundere Distinguished Professor of Religion and Culture in the Philosophy Department at Oregon State University. The *New York Times* described him as "a leading figure among the new generation of Jesus scholars." Chairman of the Jesus section of the Society of Biblical Literature, the oldest and largest association of Biblical scholars in the United States, he considers himself "a deeply committed Christian, nonexclusionist, nonliteralistic—but deeply committed." He is the author of numerous books including the best-seller *Meeting Jesus Again for the First Time* and *Reading the Bible Again for the First Time*. He is a member of the Jesus Seminar, a group of scholars examining and voting upon the historical accuracy of the words and deeds attributed to Jesus.

Some people have a problem with the Jesus Seminar and other kinds of biblical scholarship, but if one's faith is strong and is built upon the experience of God's presence then no scholar can destroy that truth. What will be destroyed instead are all the things we've added. For example, in chapter 16 of the Gospel of Mark (which is considered to be the oldest of the gospels and the most reliable), Jesus is resurrected and seen. But if you read the Bible's footnote you will see that it says (due to the work of scholars), *"The most reliable, early manuscripts and other ancient witnesses do not have Mark 16:9–20."* Therefore, the oldest gospel does not end with a risen Jesus being seen, it ends with an empty tomb. Does that lessen the power of the Jesus story? Not if you listen to scholars like Marcus Borg.

"The story of the empty tomb," Marcus Borg said, "first showed up in Mark's gospel, which was written around the year 70. One way of reading it is that Mary Magdalene; Mary, the mother of James; and Salome went to the tomb and it really was empty—it's history remembered. Another way of reading the story is to say that *it is a parable of the resurrection and makes the point that you won't find Jesus in the land of the dead—the tomb is empty—death couldn't hold him. He is among the living, not among the dead."*

Who was/is Jesus?

Jesus was a Jewish mystic and the Christian Messiah. He was a Jewish mystic in the sense that he had vivid and frequent experiences of the sacred. His mysticism was the foundation for everything else he did.

He was a healer, an enlightened wisdom teacher like the Buddha and Lao-Tzu, and his wisdom came out of his mystical experience.

He was a social prophet and a movement initiator. He was a movement initiator because of the charismatic presence that comes from being a mystic in the Jewish tradition.

"Christian Messiah" is shorthand for all of the exalted titles given to Jesus in the Christian tradition, which would include "Messiah," "Son of God," "Word of God," "Wisdom of God," "Lamb of God," and so forth. All of those titles are Christian metaphors. Put another way, I see all of those titles as post-Easter products of the early community, speaking about the significance of Jesus.

I don't think Jesus thought of himself as the Messiah, or said he was the Messiah. Jesus was to religion what Mozart is to music. My impression of Mozart is that he was somebody whose psyche was unusually open to music coming from somewhere, so that he could virtually transcribe it. I would speak of Mozart as a musical genius and I think of Jesus and Buddha as religious geniuses. Jesus, like Mozart, is a human possibility.

Jesus is no different from any other human being, but just as a Mozart comes along only very rarely, a person like Jesus comes along very rarely.

I see Jesus as a human possibility, but not a human achievement. I can work extremely hard to be open to the Spirit like Jesus, but it doesn't mean I'll attain his spiritual genius, just as none of us, by working really hard at it, could become a Mozart.

What religion was Jesus?

Jewish! Deeply Jewish!

There isn't anything that Jesus taught that necessitated the creation of a new religion, but there is a boundary-shattering quality to the experience of the Spirit and in the teaching of Jesus. A lot of the sharp social boundaries of his day were undermined or negated in his teaching. One of the sharp social boundaries was the boundary between Jew and gentile, but I don't think Jesus had very much contact with gentiles and I don't think he saw himself as having a mission to gentiles.

The boundary-shattering quality of his own movement during his lifetime and then immediately after his death led the movement relatively early on to discover that the boundary between Jew and gentile was not a sacrosanct boundary. Then, the more successful the Jesus movement became among gentiles, the less credibility it had as a Jewish movement among Jews. The consensus among scholars is that the reason it became a religion separate from Judaism is because of its success in the gentile world.

But don't overestimate how quickly it became gentile. Although there were gentiles included very early on—probably within ten years, maybe even less—at the end of the first century, it was still primarily Jewish in its makeup. By the end of the first century, it was probably still 80 percent Jewish and maybe 20 percent gentile. *Even as late as the year 250, half the people in the Jesus movement were still Jewish.*

The anti-Jewish statements that are in the New Testament are Jews calling other Jews names. It's like Southern Baptists fighting with each other, in the sense that Southern Baptists might say the most terrible things about each other but if people who aren't Baptists start using that language about Baptists, then we have a very serious situation on our hands!

Authorship and accuracy of the gospels?

We don't know the name of any of the authors of the gospels with the possible exception of Luke. Luke may have written Luke, but the other ones are all anonymous documents that were given names in the middle of the second century.

The gospels, with the exception of Luke, are all in-house documents, which means they come out of a community and they were written for a specific community. They are not written for outsiders, but for insiders.

There is a huge distinction, of course, between the first three gospels, Matthew, Mark, and Luke, known as the synoptic gospels, and John's gospel.

John's gospel is not very historical at all, and I don't think Jesus talked the way he talked in John's gospel. I don't think he said any of the great "I am" sayings or "I and the Father are one" (John 10:30, NIV) or "Anyone who has seen me, has seen the Father" (John 14:9, NIV), and so forth.

I see John as a very powerful voice and witness to what the risen Christ had become in the experience of that community.

I see Matthew, Mark, and Luke as a mixture of "history remembered," on the one hand, and "history metaphorized" on the other hand. By history remembered, I mean some of their content is in there because it really happened.

By history metaphorized, I mean that *the gospel writers are interpreting the significance of Jesus* as well, and the language they use to do the interpreting is the language of symbol and story, not a conceptual language. In other words, they don't say what something means in abstract concepts; instead they use a metaphorical narrative. Sometimes a story will be a mixture of history remembered and history metaphorized.

It is not that some material is only history remembered and other only metaphor. A classic example: Jesus really did restore sight to some blind people, so those stories of giving sight to blind people are history remembered and have a basis in history. But the way those stories are told metaphorizes the history in such a way as to suggest that what Jesus is really about is helping sighted people to see as well.

There is a wonderful example in Mark's gospel. The great central section of Mark's gospel from 8:27 to 10:52 is the story of Jesus' journey from Galilee to Jerusalem, and the whole section is dominated by the Way or the Path and stories about disciples following him on the Way.

Mark frames that great central section with two stories of people getting their sight. Mark 8:22–26 is the story of the blind man of Bethsaida who comes to see gradually, and Mark 10:45–52 is the story of blind Bartimaeus, a blind beggar on the side of the road in Jericho. Bartimaeus calls out to Jesus and Jesus comes over to him and says, "What do you want me to do for you?"

Which is a wonderful question to be asked by a numinous figure, and Bartimaeus says, "Rabbi, I want to see again."

Mark, by framing that great central story with these two stories of restoration of sight, is saying that coming to see again involves seeing the Path, the Way of Jesus, as the way of transformation. It's an enlightenment motif, even though I think it is based in history remembered.

Some parts of the gospels are purely metaphorical narratives not based on anything that happened. The birth stories, the multiplication of loaves, walking on water, stilling of the storms—they are metaphorical narratives. They are history metaphorized without any historical basis, except the significance of Jesus in the lives of the community.

How do we know what Jesus really said,
as opposed to something the author
might have put in his mouth?

I believe the wisdom teachings of Jesus were historically said by him. These wisdom teachings fall into two main categories: the aphorisms, which are the short, memorable sayings of Jesus—the great one-liners— and then the parables, which are short stories.

But even then, the authors of the gospels sometimes apply those in a certain way so that the application is the work of the evangelist, even though the saying itself or the parable itself goes back to Jesus.

Within the discipline right now there is a spectrum of opinion on how much goes back to Jesus and the spectrum ranges from maximalists, who would say almost everything goes back to Jesus to minimalists, who would say very little does.

The minimalists would include Burton Mack and Robert Funk. The maximalists would include people like Tom Wright from England and Ben Witherington. Dom Crossan and I are in the middle of that spectrum, which of course is exactly where you would want to be!

Is Jesus the only Son of God?

The language about Jesus being the "Son of God" underwent development in the first couple of centuries of the Christianity tradition. Initially, it was a relational metaphor that described the intimacy of Jesus' relationship with God as a mystic.

It became a biological metaphor in the birth stories and then ultimately became an ontological claim in the development of Christian doctrine that speaks of him as being one substance with God.

I don't think he was the only begotten Son of God; I see that as a Christian way of speaking about the ultimate significance that Jesus had come to have within that religious tradition.

Why did early Christians make him
into something more than a person who
had a relationship with God?

A lot of that has to do with the fact that Jesus was experienced after his death within the community. I don't believe those experiences involved the resuscitation of a corpse or the reanimation of a corpse but I do think those experiences included visions. Paul clearly had a vision of the risen Christ on the Damascus road. Other people in the community, no doubt, had visions as well, and Paul even gives us a list of people.

Resurrection?

I don't think the resurrection of Jesus has anything to do with something happening to a corpse, and so it is irrelevant whether the tomb was empty or not.

I do believe there were visions of the risen Christ in the early community. The presence of the risen Christ was strongly felt. I don't think those experiences are the same as the experiences that people sometimes have of their deceased spouse. Studies suggest that roughly 50 percent of people will have at least one experience of a deceased spouse that is so vivid that they are absolutely sure they saw the person. But those experiences don't lead people to say, "My deceased spouse is Lord and God!"

But, there the Jewish tradition or "Son of God" or as "One with God" is because of the post-Easter experiences of the risen Christ within the community. It evolves out of that, and then comes the extension of "Son of God" language to being "One with God" and then "the only Son of God."

Was it actually the risen Christ or
an experience of the Divine within them
and naming it Jesus?

The Divine, or God, or the Sacred is sometimes known within us, but I don't think of the Divine or the Sacred as being within us more than it is outside of us. Instead I think of us and everything that *is,* as being within God.

God is the one in whom we live and move and have our being, to use a line from the New Testament itself. These people were experiencing the presence of the Spirit and I would say that the Spirit is always present; it is just that most of the time our eyes are blind to it and we don't see it, or our hearts are closed to it and we don't feel it.

During the public part of Jesus' life, I think his followers sometimes experienced the Spirit in and around him. After his death, they continued to experience that same Spirit, which is why they said, "It's Jesus," instead of simply saying, "It's God," or "It's the Spirit"—they recognized a similarity of presence. It is the continuity of *felt* presence that accounts for them saying that it is Jesus and not simply the Spirit within.

Some of my colleagues think that the "apparition stories" as they are called, or the "appearance stories," are basically legitimization-of-authority stories. Whomever Jesus appears to, whether it's John or Peter, legitimizes their authority as leaders. But not all these stories are legitimization-of-authority stories, some were just the natural language of ancient people whenever they wanted to make a point.

Something I often wonder is *how literally did they believe their own stories?* Were they hearing or reading them as history remembered or history metaphorized? For example, the story of the empty tomb showed up first in Mark's gospel, which was written around the year 70. One way of reading it is they went to the tomb and it was really empty, it's history remembered.

Another way of reading the story is to say that it is a parable of the resurrection and it makes the point that you won't find Jesus in the land of the dead—the tomb is empty—death couldn't hold him. He is among the living, not among the dead—an empty tomb story is a wonderful way of making that point.

Another example is the story of the Emmaus road, where two disciples are walking and talking with Jesus after he's died, and they don't recognize him. Do you think that story is reporting the kinds of events that could have been videotaped or filmed?

The point of the Emmaus road story is that the risen, living Christ journeys with us, whether we are aware of that or not, realize that or not, and there are those moments of recognition when we do become aware of that presence. It is perhaps even more powerful when the historical is forgotten and the symbolic is understood.

Let's take the doubting Thomas story, which some people would take literally. I hear that as a more evocative and enigmatic story and like any good story it is probably making more than one point.

Thomas is never condemned for his doubt and once you set that aside, you realize that what Thomas desired was his own firsthand experience of the risen Christ. He didn't want to go on secondhand testimony, and his desire was granted. It is a story legitimizing that desire for your own firsthand religious experience, and affirming that the risen Christ comes to those who want to know Him so badly that they can taste it.

I want to reaffirm that there is no condemnation of Thomas in that story, but a negative spin has been put on it—that the only thing worse than being a doubting Thomas was to be a Judas! That's a misunderstanding of the story.

Virgin birth

I don't think the virgin birth happened, but I do think the stories of the virgin birth are profoundly true.

Stories of Jesus having a special birth are only in Matthew and Luke and both of those gospels were written quite late—near the end of the first century. Nobody else in the New Testament mentions it. The Gospel of Mark, which is the earliest gospel, the Gospel of John, which is maybe the last gospel written, and Paul—none of them mention it. Minimally, this suggests that the story of Jesus' birth wasn't thought all that important.

The most likely explanation is that the stories hadn't been created yet. If you compare the two stories, there are a whole set of differences between them. Matthew has wise men and the star; Luke doesn't have wise men and a star, but he does have shepherds and angels singing in the night sky.

The genealogies in the two birth stories are very, very different. Matthew has Jesus born at home, because the family lives in Bethlehem; Luke has the family living in Nazareth, but then journeying to Bethlehem because of the census and so he is born in a stable. They both agree he was born in Bethlehem, but they have different reasons for the family being there.

Matthew has the slaughter of the innocents, which Luke doesn't have at all.

These are reasons for saying these don't look like historical reports. But there is truth in the stories in that they convey the significance of Jesus by making use of ancient religious imagery.

For example, the ancient religious imagery of light coming into the darkness. This is an archetypal image, and it's in Matthew with the star shining in the night sky. It's also in Luke with the Glory of the Lord shining upon the shepherds out of the night sky as the angels sing to them.

The birth stories are also tales of two lordships. In Matthew's story, it is the lordship of Herod vs. the one who is born King of the Jews. Here Matthew echoes the story of Pharaoh and the Exodus in the story of King Herod, who orders the death of all the Hebrew baby boys under two. Matthew's story symbolizes the conflict between the lordship of Pharaoh (which represents the kingdoms of this world) and the true Lord (Christ, or God as known in Christ).

Luke has a similar theme. The shepherds are told by angels that a Savior has been born who is the Son of God and who will bring peace on earth and this is good news to men of good will (as the old translation has it, or to people of God's favor as the new translation has it).

Now the amazing thing is that the words "Savior," "Son of God," who has brought peace on earth, and that this is "good news" ("gospel") were found on an inscription in Asia Minor describing the Roman emperor, Augustus. But Luke is using that language very deliberately to talk about Jesus. He is raising, in a provocative way, the question, *Where are you going to see the true Lord?* In the glory, power, and wealth of empire? Or in this Jewish peasant baby? Where are you going to see the manifestation of the Sacred—in an empire or in Christ?

This is truth, but not the truth of historical factuality. The trouble is modern people have difficulty with a metaphorical reading of scripture because they identify truth with factuality. Both biblical fundamentalists and liberals, to a certain degree, agree on that.

What was Jesus' mission?

The gospels and creeds say the mission of Jesus was to die for the sins of the world. I don't believe that for a moment. I see that as a post-Easter retrospective interpretation of his death, and only one of at least five major interpretations of his death that we find in the New Testament.

We have to keep in mind that the public activity of Jesus was very, very brief. One year if the Synoptic Gospels are right, three or four years if John is right. So when we try to discern whether Jesus had a mission or purpose, we are only looking at a small portion of his life. If he had another ten years or forty years of public activity like the Buddha did, we might be able to say with great certitude what his mission was.

From what we do have, we can say his wisdom teaching offered to peasant people (who are marginalized or untouchables) a way of being in relationship to God that didn't depend upon institutions, the temple, or upon measuring up to conventional standards of what a religious person should be.

Jesus was also a social prophet, who like the social prophets of the Hebrew Bible was a radical critic of the domination system of his day. He was also an advocate of an alternative social vision that was more inclusive and egalitarian, so we can speak of his mission as also being a challenge to the domination system. That's what got him killed.

Jesus' lost years?

We can only speculate what might have developed if he had been active for another ten or twenty years. I see him not as some kind of wandering flower child who rejoices in creation, but as someone with a passion and deliberateness. If you combine the Dalai Lama, Martin Luther King, and maybe Mother Teresa—then you begin to approach the magnitude of Jesus' mission of compassion, challenge, and enlightenment.

I don't think he went to Egypt to study with Egyptian healers and I don't think he went to India and I don't think we have to go outside of the Jewish tradition to account for anything we see in Jesus.

I do think he must have been on a religious quest during those years, because that is the only reasonable explanation for why he went out into the wilderness to check out John the Baptizer.

John the Baptizer was doing a very unconventional thing out in the wilderness. He was the head of an anti-temple movement. He didn't want to destroy the temple, but John was claiming that his baptism was a way of dealing with and forgiving sins, while up to that time, the temple was the official way of atoning for sins.

By saying his baptism does forgive sins, John is challenging the temple's claim to have an institutional monopoly on forgiveness. This is an unconventional movement, a movement that is viewed by some people as a dangerous movement—including Herod Antipas.

I don't think you go out and spend time with John the Baptizer unless you have been on a religious quest for awhile. Jesus went through something that amounts to a conversion experience with John.

Did Jesus learn things? Was he perfect?

Jesus had to learn everything he knew through the same means that we do. Of course, as a child he sometimes got angry at his playmates or angry at his parents, and he may have bopped people over the head.

Presumably, as an adolescent he had sexual fantasies, what we would call impure thoughts or lust.

The notion that Jesus was perfect basically comes from the literalization of a metaphor. The metaphor is that he is the sacrificial lamb and within the Jewish tradition, a sacrificial animal had to be spotless and without blemish. In other words, you couldn't sacrifice your three-legged lambs or your sickly lambs, otherwise it wouldn't be a meaningful sacrifice.

The idea that the sacrificial lamb must be spotless and without blemish was literalized and thus you got a spotless and without-blemish human being—one free from sin. Once again, the Christian tradition made a mistake of literalizing their metaphors.

Very early on we metaphorized our history and then we forgot we did that and historisized our metaphors.

Was Jesus celibate?

It wouldn't bother me at all if he had a sexual relationship with Mary Magdalene or anybody else for that matter. In fact, I would kind of be delighted if he had! It is kind of charming to imagine him as this passionate, itinerant wisdom teacher and healer who crusades for social justice, who is also regularly sleeping with this intelligent and perhaps gorgeous woman. But then, I immediately have to say that as a historian we have no basis for thinking one way or another on that.

The Gospel of Philip says that Jesus "used to kiss her [Mary] often on her mouth."

We know that usually a Jewish man would enter into an arranged marriage around age eighteen. This would typically be arranged by his father or if his father were dead, by an uncle. This was so common that ancient Hebrew and Aramaic didn't even have a word for bachelor.

But that tradition did not extend down to the lower levels or radically marginalized class of peasants who lacked the financial means to support a family. Now if Jesus was in the really marginalized peasant class, it's possible that he didn't marry because financially it was impossible.

First of all, nobody would be interested in giving their daughter to somebody who couldn't support a family.

Second, even if there were radically marginalized peasant daughters around, they would have had nowhere to live and could not have started a family and raised children. It is possible that Jesus wasn't married because of his radically impoverished social class.

There is also a recent scholarly book that argues since Joseph died and Jesus was the oldest son, Jesus then had the responsibility for his siblings and for Mary, and this responsibility kept him from entering into a marriage. But that presumes that Jesus was the firstborn and we don't know that he was the firstborn. If you take the virgin birth story literally, then he has to be the firstborn, but without that, we have no idea about birth order.

As a historian, we have no basis for saying he was married or not married or involved in a sexual relationship. I don't think Jesus would have seen it as sinful. In spite of him saying, "You know you have heard it said, 'You shall not commit adultery but I say unto you, anybody who lusts after a woman in his heart has committed adultery already.'" I don't think that is a stern prohibition of impure thoughts. It was a way of saying, "You people who think you're righteous, if you have even lusted, you're not!"

Who killed Jesus and why?

The synoptic gospels say the cause for his arrest was overturning the tables and driving out the moneychangers. That is historically plausible. I see what he did there not as a fit of anger or a "temple tantrum"—as if he were surprised by what he saw there and spontaneously lost his temper—

but as a deliberate act, and more like the symbolic actions performed by the prophets of the Old Testament. It was a protest against the role of the temple in the domination system.

The temple was not only the religious center but also in many ways the economic and political center of the country. Jesus was executed because in both word and deed, he challenged the domination system of his day, which was economically exploitative, politically oppressive, and legitimated by temple theology. He was killed because he was a social prophet. He wouldn't have been executed if he had been just a mystic, a healer, and a wisdom teacher. As a social prophet he challenged the ruling elite and that got him in trouble.

Look what happened to John the Baptizer. The reason he was killed, according to Josephus, is because he criticized Herod Antipas, and Herod feared his influence with the people. It was because he offended the authorities and seemed to them to be a potential threat, that he was executed.

Why did Jesus disrupt the temple? He must have known that would lead to execution.

Maybe he thought there was a chance he'd get in trouble—rabble-rousing prophets from the Old Testament sometimes got put into the stocks—but really didn't expect to get killed. Or he knew for sure that he'd get arrested and executed if he did that, but he was willing to get himself killed in order to show the bankruptcy of the domination system.

Why didn't all Jews accept Jesus as the Messiah?

First of all, because he didn't think he was and didn't say he was, and second it wouldn't have been obvious to anybody that he was. According to the gospels themselves, there were many perceptions of Jesus. His family thought he was insane. His hometown wasn't impressed. Some of his critics believed that he had healing powers but said he was doing it through an evil spirit. Others who encountered him felt they had never encountered the spirit in such a powerful way. This variety of responses to Jesus suggests ambiguity about Jesus as a historical figure.

One might compare the different attitudes toward Martin Luther King during his lifetime. Now, most people are willing to grant that Martin Luther King was a heroic figure, but this wasn't the case when he was alive.

The deeper meaning of Crucifixion?

First of all, thousands of people in the Jewish homeland were crucified in the first century, so the cross shows how brutal the domination system is willing to be.

A second meaning of the cross in the New Testament is when the cross and resurrection are seen together, as Good Friday and Easter. The cross and the resurrection are a metaphor for an internal psychological spiritual process that involves dying to an old way of being and being born into a new way of being.

It is interesting that Paul is already speaking about the cross in this way by the '50s of the first century. In Galatians 2:20 Paul says, "I have been crucified with Christ, it is no longer I who live but Christ who lives in me." Here, then, Paul refers to himself as having undergone an internal death in such a way that Paul is no longer alive but Christ lives in him. Perhaps he's referring to the death of his ego identity . . .

A third meaning, once the completed Christian story is in place (by that I mean that Jesus has become "the beloved Son of God" in Christian thought), is that the cross becomes a demonstration of the depth of the divine love for us—to use the old Hallmark greeting card slogan, "When you care enough to send the very best!" The cross becomes a demonstration of God's love for human beings and that God was willing to part with that which is most precious to God for our behalf.

A fourth, common understanding of the cross in the Christian tradition is as a sacrifice for sins. In a first-century context, this is a profoundly subversive notion and to see the subversive meaning of that statement, we have to set it in a first-century context where temple sacrifice is still going on.

The temple claimed an institutional monopoly on the forgiveness of certain kinds of sins. Some kinds of sins could be dealt with without the temple, but some kinds of sins and impurities, from the standpoint of temple theology, could be dealt with only through temple sacrifice. In that setting, when the early Christian movement said, "Jesus is the sacrifice for sin" they were saying, "You don't need the temple." It is an anti-temple statement. It undermines the temple's claim to have that kind of institutional monopoly. Therefore it proclaims an immediate access to God—apart from institution and temple mediation. The wisdom teaching of Jesus also speaks of the immediacy of access to God—apart from institution and apart from tradition and apart from convention.

Another meaning is: Seeing Jesus on the cross, as "the Son of God," is a way of saying that God participates in human suffering. It can become a powerful metaphor for saying, "God knows our suffering because God has partaken of our suffering."

Second Coming?

When the New Testament and the Creed speak of Jesus coming again they talk about him coming in glory to be the judge of the living and dead. I don't believe that for a moment.

I don't believe it's that literal, although I know some people do. I saw a fund-raising letter once, sent out by a well-known televangelist, that was raising money to support a twenty-four-hour-a-day airborne helicopter, television crew in the Middle East, because they were quite fearful that when the Second Coming happened the major networks wouldn't cover it. That's pretty strange.

Jesus comes again in many metaphorical ways. There will not be a singular, future Second Coming; rather Jesus comes again and again and again and again and again. One can speak of Jesus coming into one's life. He comes again each year in the liturgical season of the church year, namely in coming each year as the season of Advent and Christmas. One can speak of him coming to us in the Eucharist, which happens how many tens of thousands of times a day around the world?

Do people today have more of an experience of
God than people did two thousand years ago?

Probably less, because the conditions of modern life get in the way of our experience of the Sacred. Quiet and the experience of nature—not just of the beauty of nature, but sometimes the naked fury of nature—helps in experiencing the Sacred. We are insulated from all of that. We live with constant noise and, as Paul Tillich said, the spirit of the modern world teaches us to live on the surface of things.

Tillich then said that God or the Sacred is known in the depth of our existence and not on the surface level. As modern people, we live much more on the surface level than premodern people did. Even being a farmer now is different. Consider the difference between being in a field with a scythe and only the sound of nature around—nothing but the swishing of wheat. Compare that to harvesting in an air-conditioned combine with headphones and a refrigerator with a six-pack of beer in it—it's not as natural.

Well, the beer is natural— it's made from grain, isn't it!

Don't get me wrong, I have nothing against beer!

Sometimes I find it hard to believe people in the Gospels were so ignorant, and that they needed Jesus to explain everything to them.

The point you're making leads me, for the first time, to think that to some extent a teacher like Jesus may have been legitimizing something that people already knew. That when he said, "Your sins are forgiven" and that you have access to God apart from tradition and apart from the temple—it gave legitimacy to something that people already knew or felt.

What spiritual practices or techniques did Jesus teach?

His public activity was brief, so he never developed an eight-fold path like the Buddha or systematized his teaching. There are traditions in the gospels that suggest that Jesus practiced a form of contemplative prayer. I presume he taught his followers to do that as well.

Central to his teaching was the notion of a life centered in the sacred and not centered in tradition—the how-to is, to a large extent, the content of his wisdom teaching. His wisdom teaching regularly invites a radical perceptual shift, a radical change in the way you see reality and some of his teaching seems deliberately to use the language of paradox to do that. For example, "The first shall be last, the last shall be first, the humble will be exalted, the exalted will be humbled."

His parables and aphorisms consistently invite people to see things radically differently. Jesus' wisdom teaching subverted "measuring up" as a way of living one's life—implicit in that is trust your own experience. Jesus said, "Judge for yourself what is right"—it's the opening line of a parable.

One of his most characteristic practices was his inclusive meal practice—Dominic Crossan calls it "open commensality." For marginalized people, that may have brought about some radical change in their sense of who they were. One could speak of inclusive meal practice as a technique or strategy for changing people's perceptions of themselves and of God.

How did studying Jesus change you?

There was a massive deconstruction of the understanding of the Jesus I had gotten growing up in the church. It was really liberating because my old beliefs had already become highly problematic for me. Being given another way of looking at it, together with a series of mystical experiences that made the notion of God or Spirit seem profoundly real to me, created the possibility of putting it back together again in a new form.

✢ 32
THE HUKA PIPE

JERUSALEM

"I want to huka!" Jez, my British friend, said. I had met him along with an American who wrote Japanese poems, while on a group tour one day.

"Huka?" I asked.

"Yeah," he replied. "You know—smoke Turkish water pipes."

"With hash?" I asked.

"No," he said, making a face. "They smoke tobacco here and it's mixed with charcoal and different bits like apple and such. The pipe is filled with water and is about three feet tall with a hose that you puff on."

"It's called a huka pipe?" I asked.

"I don't know what it's called," he replied. "But I call it huka."

Later that night I was introduced to a man named Abraham—he was Palestinian—and Abraham was pronounced "EE-BRA-HEEM." He was a short, roundish, bald man with less than perfect teeth. In the West, we're taught to look at appearance first but if you can look past that—you'll see another's soul—and Abraham had a good soul. Although he was a Muslim, one of my tour guides, Christa, introduced Abraham as "a little bit Christian, Jew, and Muslim—all together."

The Brit wasted no time and spoke up. "Can you take us for some smoke?"

"Yes," Abraham replied, smiling.

"Awesome," the Brit said. Fifteen minutes later we were in Palestine at a "huka bar," toking on water pipes the size of baseball bats. I was surprised by the reception. We were three "white boys" walking into a Palestinian bar, and while there were eyes watching us, none were staring. I also didn't feel any hate or disdain—just curiosity. Whether it was the fact that we were with Abraham, who seemed to be everyone's brother, father, or cousin, or whether Palestinians are more friendly and accepting than the five o'clock news would have us know—who knows. All I know is I felt safe and I felt liked. Is that possible? To feel liked just because I was another human being? My brother, Ed, used to say, "Everyone's my friend until they prove otherwise," and that's what I felt in the "huka" bar.

"I'm hungry," Jez said while waiting for the huka pipes to come.

"Do you want some bologna?" Abraham asked, getting up from the table.

"Sure," Jez replied.

It didn't take long for me to get a buzz off the tobacco—mainly because I never smoke. After puffing for about fifteen to twenty minutes I got dizzy and felt a little green. As I looked around at all the Palestinian faces I thought I would be really embarrassed if I passed out or puked.

"Here is your bologna," Abraham said as he handed Jez a plate full of sliced meat.

I had to look away because I almost lost it right there. We left a few minutes after that and Jez was so nauseated that he had to hang his head out the window the whole taxi ride home. As we passed a police car, Abraham pointed out that in an attempt to cooperate many police cars in Palestine have one Palestinian soldier and one Israeli soldier in them.

"This is the Mount of Olives," Abraham said, pointing to an archway on our right. "Behind that door is where Jesus was in the Garden of Gethsemane."

Now the place I wanted to see the most in Jerusalem was the Mount of Olives. That place, for me, held the greatness of Jesus' soul when he said, "Father, if you are willing take this cup from me . . ." (Luke 22:42, NIV). Jesus was afraid that night; he didn't want the life and destiny he was given by God. And don't we all, from time to time, feel that way?

But Jesus finished his prayer as all skillful prayers should be finished. ". . . but not my will—thy will."

So I wanted to go to Gethsemane and weep like Jesus wept, pray like Jesus prayed, and want out of this life as Jesus wanted out. Never did I imagine that my first contact with the Mount of Olives would be after smoking too much at a "huka bar."

Less than an hour later, I was lying in my bed back at the YMCA, and the room was spinning. Within the spinning, my thoughts ran rampant. Maybe Jesus didn't say "Father, . . . take this cup from me," at Gethsemane; maybe he really said, "Take this pipe from me."

I immediately cringed at my irreverence, but if God didn't have a dark sense of humor he wouldn't have made the Dome of the Rock in Jerusalem the holiest place for Jews, the third holiest place for Muslims, and the place that some Christian extremists say will spark the apocalypse.

As I drifted off to sleep, something deep in my soul smiled.

✛ 33
HOLY SEPULCHER

Naturally one wants to feel something in the Holy City of Jerusalem. Whether standing in front of a two-thousand-year-old Wall, or hearing the Islamic call to prayer five times a day, or seeing the tomb of Jesus—at any of these, a pilgrim wants to feel the presence of God. I worked hard to feel the presence, but it didn't come easy.

When I returned to the Western Wall, I was immediately approached by a man who placed a white shroud on my shoulders.

"American?" he asked. I barely had time to nod before he and two others whisked me away.

"Come. Come," he said, and I was taken to a small chamber to the left of the Wall where many Jews prayed amid a small library of books. I stood in a semicircle with the three men, while one of them read from a book and asked me to say "Amen" several times. I felt special, singled out by my spiritual brothers. The man motioned for me to kiss the Wall. As I did, I was filled with brotherhood until . . . he asked for money.

"Donation—please," he said anxiously.

"Yes," another said. "You are American—donation please."

I felt stunned and misled as I reached into my pocket. Then I paused and looked into their eyes. Instead of seeing sincerity, I saw shifty eyes filled with greed. It was then that I remembered Jesus' anger at the moneychangers. I waved the two men away, left the Western Wall, and walked toward the Holy Sepulcher, which is the most important shrine in the Christian world. The church was built by Constantine's mother in the fourth century, and Roman Catholics, Armenians, Greek Orthodox, Coptics, Ethiopians, and Syrian Orthodox all share rights to the church.

I began to feel something there, and for a moment I thought I'd cry. It wasn't the place, it was the people and what they felt and yearned for in this place. Whether it was the Greek Orthodox monks singing amid smoky incense and clanging bells, or just the pure, simple yearning of the people who had traveled hundreds, if not thousands of miles to be here, it reminded me of holiness—a holiness that began to grow.

Inside the Holy Sepulcher, there is a place where it is believed Jesus was entombed. My friends tried to take pictures and immediately were waved away by the keepers of the Holy Sepulcher.

"It is being cleaned," they said. "Go away."

We moved twenty feet away, and tried to take pictures again. But that still wasn't far enough, so they came over and rudely told us to leave. My friends and I looked at each other in disbelief. We had come thousands of miles to see Jesus' tomb, and the caretakers were telling us to go away.

I left my friends and explored the various floors, stairways, and smaller chapels within the vast church. Then I walked back toward the main entrance to the Holy Sepulcher. Recently, a second exit was put in and from what I heard the different Christian groups represented at the Sepulcher had fought for years because they couldn't agree on where the exit should go. I also heard another strange rumor. Since the Christian groups couldn't agree on who should have the keys to the Holy Sepulcher, a prominent Palestinian Muslim family kept them and opened the church every morning.

On the way out, I passed the place where Jesus was crucified. Two pilgrims knelt there; their heads were bowed to the ground, and their devotion touched my heart. Just then, a janitor came by with a broom and tapped them on the shoulder.

"I have to sweep here," he said.

Unlike the inside of the Holy Sepulcher, which was constantly noisy and run by monks and housekeepers who were not very friendly, the rooftop is one of the most quiet and reflective places in Jerusalem. There is a small church on the roof along with a small Ethiopian community and monastery.

One day, after ascending the ancient stone stairs, I found a monk walking slowly along a wall on the left side of the monastery. He wore a hat, robes, and sandals and the requisite beard of most monks here. He prayed as he walked, which inspired me to do the same. I walked slowly, aware of the sensations as I placed each foot on the ground. I also paid attention to my breath. In Aramaic, the language Jesus spoke, the word for "spirit" is the same word as for "breath." Thus when Jesus spoke of the Holy Spirit, he just as easily could have been speaking of the Holy Breath. When Jesus blessed his disciples, in the Gospel of John it says, "And with that he *breathed* on them and said, 'Receive the Holy Spirit.'"[1]

Occasionally, I looked over at the monk, so as to assure him I wasn't mocking or mimicking him. I just wanted to be with him while being in myself. His eyes occasionally glanced in my direction. For a few moments and an eternity, it seemed as if we were two brothers of spirit and breath, connected through movement upon the earth.

The following day, I returned to the Holy Sepulcher. As I walked around the church, a place where many believed Jesus was crucified, buried, and resurrected, I heard the words, *"At once the Spirit sent him out into the desert, and he was in the desert forty days . . ."* (Mark 1:12, NIV).

I stopped and looked around at the inside of the Holy Sepulcher. It looked like a museum because anything that couldn't be swept away by janitors seemed to have been gold-plated until the place of Jesus' death and resurrection looked like a golden, garishly framed 3-D painting. I suddenly felt like a customer at a mall—window shopping and buying nothing.

"At once the Spirit sent him out into the desert, and he was in the desert forty days . . ."

In the Holy Sepulcher I wanted to find a corner to hide, to be alone and feel whatever spiritual atmosphere was there, but there was no place to turn—at least for me. I spotted what looked like a Greek Orthodox monk seated on a bench and suddenly I knew what I had to do.

"Excuse me," I said, "may I ask you a question?"

"Yes," he said, stroking his beard as I sat down next to him.

"Do you know anything about Mar Saba monastery?" I asked. Brother David Steindl-Rast, a Benedictine monk back in America, had mentioned Mar Saba, a 1,500-year-old monastery just outside of Jericho.

"Of course," he said, "I know of Mar Saba."

1. John 20:22.

"I want to stay at Mar Saba for forty days," I said.

"No, you cannot stay for that long," he said. "Maybe a day or two you can stay."

The stone bench wasn't very comfortable and when I changed my posture and crossed my legs, the monk said, "Don't do that. You can't do that here."

"She shouldn't be doing that either," he said, pointing to a woman seated next to me who also had her legs crossed. I leaned over and informed her of the custom.

The monk and I talked for a while. When I saw him smile, I asked again.

"I want to stay in the desert for forty days like Jesus. I heard Mar Saba was the place to stay."

"I don't know if you can do that," he said. "But you must talk to a monk there named Father Edward."

The next day I called Father Edward, and after haggling with taxi drivers outside my hotel, I rented a taxi to Mar Saba with a couple of friends from the tour.

After only a few minutes of driving, our taxi passed through a desert landscape of various shades and colors—from off-white, to tan, and then golden brown.

Did you ever have the feeling you were on your way to a place that would change your life? That's how I felt on the way to Mar Saba Monastery.

As we approached Mar Saba's entrance, an old man, two younger men, and a donkey greeted us. Actually it was mainly the donkey that greeted us, because the human beings seemed disinterested. I wasn't sure if it was just the desert sun's brightness that caused their scowls and squinty eyes or if these men had just grown up in the land of milk and honey—minus the honey, with the milk gone sour.

The door to the monastery was painted blue, and in order to enter we had to duck our heads. While the taxi driver stayed in his car and napped, I told one man that I had spoken to Father Edward on the phone. We were led to a courtyard, and waited on a stone bench for Father Edward. Ten minutes later a monk came down the stairs. He didn't look especially happy to see us. If first impressions count, I would say this one did not bode well.

Father Edward remembered my phone call and was kind enough when he showed us around the monastery. But he seemed like a troubled man.

"I came here thirteen years ago," he said, and it struck me that his monastic stay had as much to do with him being an introvert as anything.

As our tour of the monastery came to an end, I was disappointed, because I knew Mar Saba was not the place for my forty days in the desert. Over the next few days, I visited several other monasteries and though the monks were always kind, something just didn't feel right. In my search for a place in which to spend forty days in the desert like Jesus, I was struck by three things.

One was that Jesus didn't spend his days and nights in a monastery that was full of busyness, smoky incense and iconic images of God, angels and saints. Jesus was out in the desert with God. The desert was bare, stark, empty, and yet full of nature and God.

Second, when I went to Mar Saba and other monasteries, I was asked if I was Greek Orthodox. When I said "no," I was given "the look." The kind of look that said, "You can't stay here because you're not one of us."

Which brings up my third point. If Jesus were to come to their monastery, they would have asked, "Are you Greek Orthodox?"

"No," Jesus would have replied, "I'm Jewish."

I wonder if they would have given him "the look," and shut the door.

✝ 34
LUIS PALAU

FARGO, NORTH DAKOTA

"I've got an answer that will kill yah!" Luis Palau said enthusiastically when I asked him about the virgin birth. "Absolutely kill yah!"

And that's what I love about Luis Palau—how excited he gets when talking about the Spirit.

"I just came up with an explanation of the virgin birth while taking a shower the other day," he said, "and I was hoping someone would ask me about it!"

Later in our meeting, when Luis Palau quoted C. S. Lewis's famous line, "Jesus was either a liar, lunatic or Lord . . ." I just had to tell him about my recent revelation.

"C. S. Lewis forgot the most important 'L' word of all when describing Jesus," I said. "Jesus was a *lover*. Because if you read everything Jesus said, he spoke as someone in love with God. And when you're in love with someone or something, there are times you become that love—and since 1 John 4:16 (NIV) says, 'God is love' whenever Jesus became love, he was one with that love that God is. That's why Jesus could say, "I and the Father are one" (John 10:30, NIV). "He was a lover and one in love with God."

"Hmmm," Luis Palau said, squinting his eyes and caressing his chin between his forefinger and thumb. Suddenly his eyes opened wide with enthusiasm.

"That's very good!" he said. "I've got to write that down. *Liar, lunatic or Lord . . . and you say, 'lover'!! This guy's got insight!*"

Luis Palau was so genuinely enthusiastic that I just couldn't stop myself.

"And in 1 John," I continued, "it says 'God is love' (4:16, NIV), that 'Love drives out fear' (4:18, NIV), and that 'punishment has to do with fear.' Therefore, since God is without fear, God must be without punishment. But when Adam and Eve ate from the tree of the knowledge of Good and Evil, they were given the ability to judge—and the first thing they did was judge themselves as bad, and then they judged God as punishing them. But they were wrong on both accounts. Why were they wrong? Because the mistake Adam and Eve made was that when their eyes were opened, *they judged first*—whereas God *loves first* and *judges second*. Jesus came in order to teach us to love first and judge second, and then as 1 John 4:17 (NIV) says, 'In this world we are like him.' "

"Oooooh, that's good!!!" Luis Palau said excitedly.

Luis Palau is known as "the Billy Graham of South America" and is the author of forty-four books and booklets in English and Spanish, including *Where Is God When Bad Things Happen?* and *God Is Relevant.* I met with him in Fargo, North Dakota, where his two-day crusade drew thousands of people. But it was a small crowd by Palau standards, because in 1982 he spoke to seven hundred thousand people in Guatemala City. And in Hong Kong, just before the city reverted back to China, he spoke to over one hundred thousand people.

Originally from Argentina, Luis Palau became a U.S. citizen in 1962. He has proclaimed the message of the gospels in sixty-nine countries over the last thirty-five years. What I love about Luis is his openness and his yearning for God, which was stronger than any belief. Time and time again Luis Palau surprised me with the depth of his spiritual insights about God and our relationship to Jesus. Along with a handful of other evangelists, Luis Palau is not only one of the most gifted speakers but one of the wisest. I saw a Holy Spirit in him that is not restricted and imprisoned by past interpretations of God. I saw a Holy Spirit that is alive in ways that reveal the new revelations and interpretations Jesus had promised. In my opinion, Luis Palau is the best of what evangelism can be—all it can be when it's based on the love and freedom of God, not the condemnation and arrogance of sclerosed and legalistic interpretations.

Who was/is Jesus?

Jesus was and is God the Son who became incarnate through the Blessed Virgin Mary and by the work of the Holy Spirit. He is the creator and the only Savior of the world. He is my greatest friend, the guide of my life, and the one who fulfills my life like nothing else or anybody else ever could. I love my wife, but Jesus is even better than my wife.

Is Jesus the only Son of God, or are we all
sons and daughters of God?

Jesus is the unique Son of God. God the Son is a better way of saying it than Son of God, although both terms—properly understood—mean the same thing. But he is unique. He is God who became man.

One begins to understand the mystery of the Trinity when you understand that you, I, each of us is a human person created in the image and likeness of God. The Bible says that we are created in the likeness of God and we are much like this: Father, Son, and Holy Spirit. We are created body, soul, and spirit. We tripartite as human beings and yet we are one. We speak about parts of ourselves in the third person and yet it's us. For example, we say, "I broke my finger," even though it would be better said, "I broke myself at my small right-hand finger." I say "my head aches," and yet it is me, speaking about me. So there is oneness in Trinity and Trinity in oneness. Jesus is Almighty God, the creator, the Savior, alive, sitting at the right hand of God; and yet through his Spirit he's living in me, and in millions of others. By understanding Jesus we understand ourselves, and then by understanding ourselves better, we actually understand Jesus more.

I've seen through my travels around the world that Jesus Christ truly fulfills the mind as well as the spiritual and emotional life, that the deep questions of the human mind are best responded to by the person and the teachings of Jesus Christ. Christ answers those basic questions.

Is Jesus the only way to God?

God knows the heart and he knows any person, under any circumstance, whose heart is right toward him, hungry, honest, humble, broken by his or her own unworthiness. I believe that anyone who has heard a properly presented Jesus Christ (because Christ has been used with many tones, turns, and colors), and who has heard with an honest, hungry, humble and broken heart will say, "This is It."

Consider how, in chapter 10 of Acts, the apostle Peter said, "I now realize how true it is that God does not show favoritism but accepts men from every nation who fear him and do what is right." He said this to a Roman officer who was a good man and who did good deeds for the poor but was probably a pagan. Now, does that mean that the sacrifice of Christ was wasted? Absolutely not! God could not accept men or women from any nation unless he died on the cross. Does that mean the resurrection is meaningless? Absolutely not! If there was no resurrection, Christ would have been just another dead man. But remember, the Bible says, "Man looks on the outward appearance, God looks on the heart." If people in a non-Christianized culture fear and trust God, and they may not even say there is one god or three in one—they just say there's got to be a creator because look at the sun, the moon—if they say this and do what is right, I believe that God looks at them and says, "They fear me and are doing what they know to be right. On the basis of the death of my Son, his dying for them and resurrecting for them, I will forgive them, I will accept them. Because I love them as much as the people who have heard and repented." That conviction gives me great peace. It gives me a great sense of—Wow! That helps me breathe—otherwise I couldn't sleep at night.

In my travels I've seen that in many other countries and cultures there is a hunger for the eternal one . . . for forgiveness, for the real thing. In these places Jesus often appears, and they know it's Jesus, don't ask me how. I've heard their stories, from people in Africa, the Middle East, Egypt, Arabic people living in Germany, in England, Libyans, all sorts of people! And they see this picture of Jesus: almost always dressed in white, with music in the background and a beautiful setting, and they sense that God is saying, "I am the way, I am your Savior, trust me." It gives me great comfort to know God has not abandoned the nations of the world.

The revelation of God through Jesus Christ is the complete and final revelation. When you analyze the good things in Hinduism, Buddhism, Islam, Judaism, they leave big lagoons. In my simple mind, Jesus leaves no lagoons.

Once a sick woman who lived near the Himalayas went to a village where she cried in the plaza. A man asked her, "Why are you crying?"

"I'm sick," she said. "I came from the other village and thought I might find a cure. But I have not found one."

"You know," he said, "I've heard of a man by the name of Jesus and, in his name, you can be healed."

"Where can I find him?"

"I have no idea," he replied. "I just know that in the name of Jesus you can be healed."

So she said, "Jesus, they say you have the power to heal—please heal me." And just like that—she was healed. She returned to her village where other sick people also invoked the name of Christ, and everybody sick in that village was healed. They all said, "We believe in Jesus," even though they had no idea who he was. Then one day a Bible-school student came into the village and talked about Jesus on the street corner. The whole village came and was converted to Jesus Christ.

That is a true story and you can check it out. But that's how God loves;

he is a God of love, if not, he wouldn't be God. And he loves every one of us.

I believe in the virgin birth! Billy Graham once said, "If God is God, I believe he could easily make a big fish to swallow Jonah. In fact, if God is God, I believe he could have helped Jonah swallow the fish!" If God is God! It's an extreme statement but it makes a point. Just look at women today—they can get pregnant and have babies without ever having sex. Why? Because some smart scientist takes a sperm from a guy, gets a syringe, and goes zip, zip at the right time of the month. She never had sex. So if a scientist can do it, God Almighty can do it. What's the big deal? It's great to see science "coming to the rescue" of the biblical account. If scientists are able to impregnate a woman without sex, then God could certainly do it.

Why couldn't Jesus be born regularly? I don't know the reasons. God chose to do it that way. We all have arguments, and some of them sound very plausible. Remember, God wanted to become vulnerable and truly human. Mostly, Jesus called himself "the Son of Man" which means I'm fully human—and only occasionally "Son of God."

Jesus used that in turning the tables on several self-righteous religious leaders. That verse explains that when we receive Christ, we receive the Holy Spirit. We become children of God and are indwelled by the Spirit . . . 1 Corinthians 6:17 says, "Whoever is joined to the Lord becomes one spirit with him." It's not that "we are gods," it's that we are created in the image and likeness of God. Now, rescued by Christ, we are restored. And when we are perfected at the Second Coming—when the bodies raise from the dead—and body, soul, and spirit are reunited—then we truly shall be like him! It's an amazing statement! Because we shall see him as he is.

The Spirit led the writers of scripture to write what he wanted written without manipulating their personality. Inerrancy is the end result: The content of scripture is solid without error. But within that, the Gospel of John is the one I recommend to everyone. The Bible is 1,000 pages, but if you start by reading the Gospel of John and his Epistles, and the Book of Proverbs—you'll be okay. With John you've got the relationship with God, and with Proverbs, relationship with man.

Are new Revelations still being revealed?

New revelation was as Jude 3 says, "Once for all, given to the saints." 2 Peter 1:3 says, "God has given us everything we need for life and godliness." Therefore, the Holy Spirit left us a complete revelation of all we need for life and godliness in written scripture.

Some Christians do use the word "revelation" for new insights, but they mean "illumination." Revelation as the New Testament teaches was once and for all given to the saints. This revelation can be illumined through the Holy Spirit and meditation. In these ways we understand that revelation and then have insights into life, problems, and a deeper understanding of God. Any illumination (or, if you want to call it revelation) that contradicts what is written, cannot be of God, because God is not going to contradict himself. It's amazing how God can speak to us and illumine scripture! For example scripture says, "Don't you know that you will judge angels!" My goodness! And 1 John 5:11–12 says that God has given us eternal life, this life is in his Son, whoever has the Son of God has life, whoever doesn't have this life is not condemned by God—*we condemn ourselves.*

> *Grace is realizing we are already forgiven*
> *and already loved.*

Grace is sitting there waiting to be embraced. Hell was originally created for the devil and his demons, not for humans. I don't know *why* people reject Christ! Give me one good reason why you should not receive and follow Jesus Christ! Give me one!

Jesus didn't have a religion, he had a relationship with God. When I preach, I never talk about religion, though I know what the listener's thinking—he's thinking of an organized something or other. Are you this, are you that? No, I'm not into that, I'm not into religion. I'm into a relationship with God. I don't support, endorse, approve of religion because it is run by humans who are very flawed.

Jesus was born "under the law," which meant his religion was Judaism. But Jesus truly came to complete the law that ended with John the Baptist. "From then on, the kingdom of God is . . . The last of the prophets was John the Baptist." The fulfillment of the law was the crucifixion of Jesus Christ and the resurrection. He came—under the law, born of a virgin—and then when he died and rose from the dead, he fulfilled the law, that is, the old covenant. And then the new covenant came into operation and that, of course, is repeated several times, you know—"Your sins and evil deeds I remember no more, I'll put my Spirit within you, I'll give you a new heart, I'll make you walk in my ways."

For the same reason that not all gentiles accept him as Messiah. There is too much self-righteousness in us all. People feel this is too good to be true. They prefer the religious box they have created, within which they are comfortable and from which they are afraid of stepping out.

People then allowed themselves to be led blindly by their religious leaders, without listening, without thinking, without looking, and without meditating. They just said, "Crucify, crucify him!" Those people allowed themselves to be brainwashed—just like today. People today are more afraid of peer pressure than they are of God Almighty. They are more concerned about what their neighbors are going to think than what the creator thinks.

In a sense it doesn't matter. The real meaning of the crucifixion was that God chose to incarnate himself and be the substitute for the fallen human race because we could not pay for our own sins, atone for our own evil behavior. If it had been left to us, we would have had to pay forever for our fallen-ness, our disobedience, and the way we have stained the moral universe by our wrong behavior. Who put the nails physically into Jesus' hands and feet and who physically put the crown of thorns on his head aren't really the main issues. The words that clearly express this are in John, where Jesus says, "No one takes my life from me, I lay it down of my own free will, I have power to lay it down and I have power to take it up again, this commandment I received from the Father" (John 10:18). It was a voluntary, knowing acceptance of the crucifixion.

Jesus' lost years?

He was just a normal young man, working with his father in the carpentry shop. Joseph probably was his mentor.

Second Coming?

In the New Testament alone, the people who have time to count these things say there are four hundred references to the Second Coming. That's enough to convince me he is coming again. It's prophesied even in the Old Testament, that he was coming with power and glory to rule the world, but first he had to come in humility and in a despised form, ending up on the cross and then resurrection and ascension. The climax of history and the end of the world will be the Second Coming of Jesus Christ.

My favorite quotation is from a Scottish theologian from the last century who used to open up his cottage window every morning, look up to heaven, and say, "Perhaps today, Lord Jesus, perhaps today." We should be waiting for him as though he is coming today, so that you live fully, freely, happily. If he comes today—glory—if he comes tomorrow—fine! But we are supposed to wait for him every day and then one day, he's coming.

My faith was originally based on belief, but now it is also based on experience. It all started when my father and mother said to me, "We know God" and I said, "Oh! If Dad and Mom know God, I want to know him, too." They gave me all this information about God and then one day I met him myself. I was twelve years old and a counselor sat with me and said, "Do you want to be with God forever? Do you want to go to heaven, or do you want to be forever lost?"

"No!" I said, "I want to know God, I want to live with him, I want to know God. My father and mother know him, I want to also." At that moment, I experienced God in a dramatic way, and over the years I have had many more moments that have been vivid and dramatic. I've experienced steady growth, but there are also plateaus, and then more growth followed by another level and plateau. Right now, I feel that I'm in a growing mode in my knowledge of the Lord.

I think the thing holding others back from experiences like this is fear: the fear of what other people think instead of just growing, perhaps daily and perhaps forever, and expanding your knowledge of God.

John Wesley said, "I learned more about God from my mother than all the theologians of England," which is a very humbling statement for theologians. But I could say the same thing. I learned about God just seeing my mom enjoying God in the days of wealth and then in the days of poverty and then in the final years of her life. A woman from MSNBC called me up about a year ago and said, "We want to do a week of half-hour shows answering one question. We are going to have a Buddhist, a Hindu, a Muslim, and also a Jew and would you like to represent Christianity?"

"Great!" I said. "What's the theme?"

"Is God alive?" she said.

Then she suggested we go over the theme "Is God alive?"

"Yes," I said. "God is alive."

"How do you know?" she asked.

"I talked to him this morning," I said.

"Oh, that's a great answer!" she replied.

But this is a basic Sunday school answer, and yet it's true. I talked to him this morning, I talked to him half an hour ago, I talk to him all the time. It's real. It's not an illusion. I walk with God, I talk with God, I enjoy him. There are times when I fail him, so I ask for forgiveness and I'm on my feet again. God is as real to me as my wife or my friends or anything.

What spiritual techniques did Jesus teach?

If we look for Jesus in the scriptures, we will find him because the scriptures are the Word of God: *the incarnation of God in words.* In Jesus, you have the Word of God, incarnate in a man. There is a beautiful psalm that says, "You have exalted your name and your word above all things" (Psalm 138:2). Jesus says, "If you want to encounter me, then one way is to read the scriptures and wait for me—because I am there and I will speak to you."

I find when I read the scriptures, I forget myself. When I read the New Testament, in particular, it's like the Lord is speaking to me. Even the Old Testament is that way although many passages are very historical and need careful interpretation. But when I read the Psalms, the Book of Proverbs, certain passages jump out at me, and I feel the Lord is saying, "Luis, today, this and this, this is going to happen, you're going need this memory, this particular truth is for you today, this is the way I want to use you or speak to you or protect you, I'm there . . ."

Second, believing in Jesus is more than intellectual ascent. The term you used—"lover"—is great because you connect with a lover in love. My favorite Bible verse is "I stand at your door and knock, if you hear my voice and open the door, I'll come in to you and eat with you and you with me" (Revelation 3:20). To me, it is a *beautiful* picture, of Jesus coming into your life. Jesus is really saying, "If you open the door I will come into you and we'll have a party that will never end. I'll eat with you, you eat with me, this is life!" If every believer believed that, the revolution would be utterly amazing, the outpouring of love and power would be unbelievable!

Get on your knees by your bed or wherever you are, open the Bible to the Gospel of John and say, "God, I want to know you, speak to me, I am absolutely open to you." Often within fifteen minutes, you will meet God through Jesus. The most important thing is to open your heart while reading the Word—*then he will come in and from then on you will know him di-rectly.* As Romans 8:16, says, "The Spirit Himself witnesses with our spirit that we are God's children."

✢ 35
PILGRIMAGE

JERUSALEM

Being in Jerusalem, I realized I was on a pilgrimage to holy sights. What's a pilgrimage? It's a moving meditation, a flow of reflective moments, a prayer rosary whose beads are places, and whose places point to one place—*the heart.*

The heart can hold all places if asked, and a pilgrimage asks only one thing. It asks the heart to remember the original place, and in this original place is found the original intent—this intent was breathed, whispered into man by God at the beginning of time.[1] To hear that whisper is to know the first place, and that is the place Jesus spoke from when he said, "Before Abraham was born, I am!"[2]

While in the desert for forty days, Jesus remembered this first place when he heard God's whisper amid the desert winds and clear dark nights. At times Jesus teetered on forgetting, but God sent angels[3] who eternally echoed this holy sound of original intent and blessing. Jesus then ventured into the city and whispered what he had heard to anyone who had the ears to listen.

If I, or anyone could hear this whisper but once, our walls would crumble and our world would crack open—like an egg—out of which we would emerge, born again.

In my quietest, stillest moments, I pray to be broken open in this way, to be poor in spirit a thousand times so that I may hear the sound that cre-

1. Genesis 2:7, NIV. "The Lord God formed the man from the dust of the ground and breathed into his nostrils the breath of life, and the man became a living being."
2. John 8:58.
3. Mark 1:13, NIV. And he was in the desert forty days, being tempted by Satan. He was with the wild animals, and angels attended him.

ated all life. Yet I fear that very thing that would save me because no human being wants to lose his life.[4]

Yet isn't that our deepest heart desire? To be lost in God till we know only God? And then, like Jesus, we can wipe away the bloody sweat, and take the cup back from our outstretched hands—drinking life from the Holy Grail. This fluid life is both wine and blood, joy and suffering. If Jesus had not accepted his cup, he would never have known the sweet taste of a soulful life.

✣ 36
MATTHEW FOX

OAKLAND, CALIFORNIA

Matthew Fox has been a priest since 1967. He was dismissed from the Dominican order in 1993 because, among other things, he would not change his stance on original sin, which he wrote about in his book *Original Blessing*. He has a doctorate in spirituality, summa cum laude, from the Institute Catholique de Paris and is founder and president of the new University of Creation Spirituality in Oakland, California. He is also editor in chief of *Original Blessing—A Creation Spirituality Network Newsletter,* and author of twenty-one books. In 1995 he received the Courage of Conscience Award by the Peace Abbey of Sherborn, Massachusetts. Other recipients of this award include the Dalai Lama, Mother Teresa, Ernesto Cardenal, and Rosa Parks.

During our meeting, whenever Matthew Fox criticized the Catholic Church I felt validated. I was so angry at Christianity and especially Catholicism, that it felt good throwing stones. In his latest book, *Confessions: The Making of a Post-Denominational Priest,* he listed various aspects of the Church's shadow side such as "Clericalism, not teaching mysticism in church, lack of curiosity, witch burnings, the silly stance on birth con-

---

4. Matthew 16:25, NIV. "For whoever wants to save his life will lose it, but whoever loses his life for me will find it."

trol and consequent ignoring of global population crisis, the condemnation of condoms (which can lead to AIDS), treatment of native peoples in their religions, anti-Semitism, homophobia," and the list went on.

Along with validation, I felt a warm delight. But something Marcus Borg had said came back to me. I had asked Marcus Borg, "What would Jesus think of Christianity today?"

"Like me," Marcus Borg replied, "Jesus would probably have a mixed judgment about it. I assume he would find much of it reprehensible and he would also be able to discern that the tradition also works in the lives of some people."

I realized that I was so angry at the Church that I couldn't see anything positive about it, but Marcus Borg was right, there must be something positive about Christianity—only *I was so blinded by resentment that I couldn't think of anything!* Then I continued to read Matthew Fox's book *Confessions: The Making of a Post-Denominational Priest* and though he was critical of Roman Catholicism in his book, toward the end he listed the good things he'd experienced in the Roman Catholic Church. He praised Catholicism for "the mystics, Mary—our own Christian goddess, spiritual disciplines, the word spirituality, Chartres Cathedral, the mass, Gregorian chants, some strong women, tactical ecstasies for prayer such as fasting and abstinence, Thomas Aquinas, John the XXIII and the thrust for ecumenism (while it lasted), spiritual disciplines, the word spirituality and the quest for holiness."

While I read this list I had to keep reminding myself to breathe, to relax, and to acknowledge the positive. As I had discovered, "respect" comes from the Latin *to look again.* If I wanted to be a decent and balanced human being, I had to look at the hard stuff—even the things I had already made up my mind about. Whether it was Christianity, Jesus, or God—I had to look with new eyes; however, he was also the following:

Who was/is Jesus?

Let's talk first about who he was not: He was not Paul, and so much of Christian theology came from Paul. I respect Paul because he was a fighter and a genius and:

1. He was Greek-educated, which means he was intellectual but he was heavily influenced to think in the Greek way, which unfortunately is dualistic, i.e., flesh vs. spirit.
2. He was a zealous Jew.
3. He was a Roman citizen, which meant he was politically protected.
4. Lastly, he became a follower of Jesus. Therefore, Paul brings together the four great powers and the neuroses of the time and this makes him terribly interesting and very complex. Was it Otto Rank who said, "Paul is the extrovert and Jesus is the introvert"? It is important to separate Paul from Jesus because Paul never met Jesus. This is especially important for Protestants because Protestant theology has relied so much on Paul and Augustine—after all Luther was an Augustinian monk—and neither of them met Jesus.

Second, Jesus was not present at the Council of Nicea in 325 A.D., which is when the Catholic Church created so much of what we know of Christianity. This interpretation of Jesus and the Christ is filled with the cultural language and the philosophical categories of Greek thinking. Jesus is not necessarily the Christ of the Nicene Creed, except in a very metaphorical way.

So who was Jesus? Jesus was a Jew who was very much, consciously and unconsciously, tapped into the prophetic tradition of Israel—and he was prophetic. Jesus tried to simplify his religion at a time when things were getting very complex. He tried to respond to the needs of people he met. For example, he took both his religion and his culture to task for the abuse of women and he focused on some of the basic tenets of Israel, such as "Love your neighbor as yourself," which had gotten lost under the barnacles that religion adds to the core message of faith. He tried to strip down his faith to its essentials. Jesus was deconstructing religion in his time. We always have to go through a deconstruction and a reconstruction. Jesus was spiritually motivated. He was an artist and he chose telling parable stories as his way of awakening people. His basic message was that we are all sons and daughters of God and that we should start acting like it. Jesus knew the wisdom tradition of Israel profoundly. That tradition is creation-centered and feminist. Jesus therefore was both mystic and prophet. Wisdom is the source of a Cosmic Christ consciousness.

At the Nicene Council in 325 A.D. the Catholic Church tried to make Jesus the only Son of God, but that distorts the message that the Cosmic Christ is in all beings, and Jesus was trying to wake us up to that. The Christ was in Jesus, and Jesus was waking us up to know that Christ is in all of us, in all beings and all of creation. Jesus was a mystic and a prophet and he tried to wake others up to their dignity, nobility, and responsibility.

Given the fact that he did this in just a few years, it is astounding the amount of influence he has had after his death. When the Roman Empire and others crucified him, they gave an archetype to the world that is not easy to dispose of. All kinds of poor people through the centuries have been able to identify with this story of a good man being shot down by the powers that be. It is an archetypal story and there is power in that and you can even say there is redemption and grace in that. There is healing in that story because it shows that hatred and envy do not have the last word. That is the Easter message.

*Can a person get too caught
in our Christ story?*

Too caught in the story? There is such a thing as religious fanaticism, which we see in fundamentalists. They want to make it an exclusive story and are totally caught in the story that *Jesus is the only Son of God, Jesus is the only Christ, and no one is saved except through this method.* But one of the charges against Jesus at the time was that he was ecumenical—he talked to Samaritans and to women and to Roman soldiers and he was not sectarian.

Jesus did not teach fear or control as fanaticism does. Jesus was the opposite. Jesus was driving out fear. Jesus was not building religion, and he certainly wasn't building a religion on fear. He was trying to draw from people their own spirit, their own better selves, and their own profound relationship with the Creator of all this. A religion should be God-centered and not sin-centered, which is seen in redemption religions and is so anthropocentric and narcissistic. Jesus' stories and his life were about waking people up, not about condemning them.

Was Jesus actually sent down by God or
was he a human being who realized and
developed his relationship to God?

It isn't either/or. God does things directly and indirectly. God sends someone *and* the human being also responds—it's cocreation. God works through our study and through the mentors that we meet, and through history.

In fact, the whole idea of the miracle consciousness—God zaps!—including zapping someone into history, is typical of the modern era because the modern era sees the world as a machine and the whole idea is that the only way you can stop that machine is by zapping it. But recently, we have come to rediscover the universe is not a machine, it is more like an organism; it unfolds, and so the wisdom behind the universe, another name for which is *God,* works through the unfolding of things, not just through zapping. There has been too much emphasis, especially in the modern era, on the zapping thing and we have distorted the meaning of miracle. Meister Eckhart is right when he says Is-*ness* is the miracle, existence is the miracle. In fact, the more we learn about this vast universe the more it seems to be quite a miracle that this planet has happened with its delicate balance of ozone and oxygen and all the things that make it possible for our species and many others to survive here. A creation story teaches that more and more existence itself is the miracle and Jesus' coming is part of that brilliant unfolding. And so were Buddha's coming, Martin Luther King's and Gandhi's coming. Were they all sent by God? I think so, but they had to respond—as Jesus did. He responded, he gave himself to the task.

Accuracy of the gospels?

The Jesus Seminar scholars tell us that only 15 percent of Jesus' words in the gospels are Jesus'. This liberation does not mean that 85 percent of the words are irrelevant and stupid. No! It means 85 percent came from the community, came from the faith experience, came from a Cosmic Christ experience. Then the question becomes why aren't we writing our own gospels? The early Christians didn't hesitate to put all these words in

Jesus' mouth; they trusted their own mystical experience. But today, we don't trust our mystical experience and the Church doesn't even teach our mystical tradition. Our seminaries don't teach it. When we really reconnect to the historical Jesus and to the intention of the first followers who experienced the Spirit of the Cosmic Christ, we will get our courage back and our imaginations back.

A good example is the Celtic Christianity that made a home in seventh-century Wales, where it created mystical poems to the Cosmic Christ: "I am the waves of the sea" and "I am the giant oak growing" and "I am the wild boar fighting." These are "I am" poems and when you compare them to the "I am" sayings in John's gospel, you are dealing with the Christ, not with the historical Jesus. "I am" is a goddess name and is in all of creation and is represented by the essential message of Jesus. Now, why is it that our seventh-century Celtic ancestors had the courage and imagination to create these poems and all our fundamentalists today are like parrots or tape recorders, just repeating, "I am resurrection and life, I am the way"? Because in the last thirteen hundred years we've lost all of our religious imagination.

Virgin birth?

A birth happened, whether it was a virgin birth or not, I think the question is really—why this emphasis? Why is it important?

The brilliant psychologist Otto Rank says that the virgin birth was important for the following reason. Early Christianity, like many religions in the first century around the Mediterranean, was a goddess religion. But in most of those goddess religions the Divine Mother gave birth to a son who later had intercourse with the mother. The Virgin Birth of Christianity discounts such an incestuous story. Instead, Jesus, in prophetic fashion, *leaves home* and goes into the world to love it. He leaves his mother behind. Thus the cycle is not closed but open and service to the world rather than incest results from the birth of the divine son from the divine mother.

Now Otto Rank was not a Christian but a Jew. Yet this is the only explanation I have ever encountered that made sense of the Virgin Birth story at all.

I believe in resurrection, and even modern science says that everything in the universe lives, dies, and gets reborn. For example, supernovas live for billions of years and then they explode and in their explosion they seed elements for other forms of life in the universe. In fact, the elements of our bodies come from such an explosion five and a half billion years ago.

The mystery of the life, death, and resurrection of Jesus is not just about Jesus, it's about the Cosmic Christ and therefore it's about the universe itself and it's about you and me. We live, we die, and we seed others. Now, exactly how and what form resurrection takes, we don't know. It's a mystery. One point I make in my book on the Cosmic Christ is that the people who reported seeing the risen Christ did not say, "We have seen the historical Jesus." They said, "We have seen the risen Lord," and Lord means governor of the universe. It is a Cosmic Christ tale, not a Jesus tale. It is very important that the one who resurrected was the Christ in Jesus. The issue of resurrection is a problem if we don't have a Cosmic Christ theology. The Jesus we talk about is not just the historical Jesus, there is also the Cosmic Christ, who found a home in Jesus, as 1 John says, "Set up its tent." This is Sophia, this is lady wisdom, who sets up her home all over the place but found a special home in Israel and in Jesus.

It's not whether the resurrection happened, it's how it happened, and the fact that it is happening all the time. Thomas Aquinas has a great teaching about resurrection that I've never seen anywhere else. He said, "There are two resurrections; one is waking up in this lifetime and the second you don't have to worry about if you've done the first." The second comes at death. I like that because the resurrection is about the awakening of our psyches and souls.

What spiritual practices or techniques did Jesus teach?

Jesus taught people how to pray and he taught the Good Samaritan story. He taught how to love your neighbor. He took and adapted the strategies, the spiritual strategies of his Jewish faith: "The Sabbath is for the people, and people are not for the Sabbath."

But was he teaching Eastern meditation, as some people think? I rather doubt it. He was teaching by parable and aphorism—ways of artful involvement of his listeners.

Jesus taught by example. He obviously did a lot of inner work. He knew the prophetic tradition and wisdom literature, which is the basis of Sophia and the Cosmic Christ tradition. He prayed the psalms and he prayed in nature, observing the revelation behind nature very carefully and drawing profound lessons from it. It appealed to him because it is very universal, and it is not at all sectarian. This is why East meeting West is so valuable. We have things to teach one another and that's what is so sad about Protestant/Catholic, East and West splits—both are damaged by the splits. They both can be stronger if they would start getting together instead of pronouncing that only one has the way.

My mother raised me to talk with God
and not as much with Jesus . . .

I remember lecturing in Australia a few years ago and a young man asked me, "Do you believe that Jesus is the Son of God?"

And I said, "Yeah, and so are you and the woman next to you." It's a heresy to leave out God the Creator and God the Spirit. That's why the Trinity tradition has a lot to offer us—because it is an alternative to purist monotheism and God can come in a human form while also coming in other ways. This phrase that I got from Père Chenu, my mentor in France, "continuous incarnation and continuous creation."

Was there a conscious decision to control
people through religious beliefs?

Those who control religion are trying to freeze the creation. But they can't—it's still going on! And why should they? Why freeze the incarnation as if God was incarnated only in Jesus? Divinity gets incarnated in all of us, hopefully. This zeroing in only on Jesus or the tradition of the second person of the Trinity is idolatry or Jesus-olatry or what Dorothy Solle, the theologian, calls Christo-fascism.

We must remember there is a political agenda today, just as there was in Jesus' day, and we see it in Jerry Falwell's relationship to the right wing. This political agenda is about control and it's about sectarianism. It's about leaving out people of other faiths.

Why are so many Western Christians indoctrinated into the theology of original sin when the word never dropped from Jesus' mouth? The idea of original sin came from the fourth century A.D. St. Augustine was the first guy to use the phrase. No Jew believes in original sin and Jesus was a Jew. Jews believe in the original blessing—that the entire universe is a blessing. Yet Christians know more about original sin than they know about original blessing. Why is that? Because it plays a political role and if you are going to run an empire, which is what happened in the fourth century when the Church took over the Empire, it really behooves you to teach original sin because then you get people in their place and you can control them and they will obey and doubt themselves.

A lot of things happen almost unconsciously, but that doesn't mean they don't happen. In fact, they become more violent because they are unconscious. These things carry on century after century and when you critique them as I did with my book *Original Blessing*, you have someone like Cardinal Ratzinger, who rose up in total fury and denounced me. I realized I pushed an ancient button and what someone like Cardinal Ratzinger is really saying is if you take original sin away from us, we may not have a reason to exist.

What religion was Jesus?

What religion was Jesus?! Obviously he comes out of Judaism and he never denounced his religion. He didn't think in terms of religion, he thought in terms of spirituality. He tried to relate to the Spirit, the Creator, and respond to the truth as he grasped it. He paid a price for it and he was smart enough to know the path he had chosen was going to get him into trouble. But it didn't deter him. He was a man of great courage, integrity, and creativity in making up stories and adapting stories. He was like many artists and very responsive to what was going on around him. Jesus was like water—fluid and sensitive.

It was a great metaphor, wasn't it! We remember it two thousand years later. This is what prophets do in Judaism—rile things. Jeremiah took his clothes off and streaked around the city to draw people's attention. It's about drawing people's attention in order to wake them up. The commercializing of religion was a real issue in Jesus' day and it keeps coming up in our own. Why am I thinking of "The 700 Club" right now?

Second Coming?

The emphasis on it is misplaced. The Second Coming is meant to happen in all of us. We are all called to be other Christs and it will be not only a Second Coming, but five billion comings.

People have an addiction to the fall-redemption religious mentality that says something from outside is going to save us from ourselves. This is contrary to everything Jesus is talking about. He said, for example, "impurity doesn't come from outside, it comes from inside," and so does purity. He is trying to get us back to the inside of things, including the inside of creation itself.

When the Book of Revelation was written, the Christians were really under persecution, attacked and made powerless by the Empire. In response, there are some wild images and wonderful stories in the Book of Revelation—but to take them literally is crazy. It makes no sense. I heard Jerry Falwell say just the other day on television that Jesus wrote every word in the Bible! That's strange, the Bible was written over a seven hundred-year period. Jesus would have had to have been seven hundred years old.

Some books were written long after Jesus died, especially the Book of Revelation, so they were distorted by so-called Christian writers.

I don't know if Jerry Falwell deserves to be called a theologian, but at least he is a pastor, and as a pastor he should be trained to know the difference between Jesus and the Holy Spirit. To say Jesus wrote every word is really strange. What about Paul? Does that mean Paul didn't write his own letters? That's how we began this conversation. So the inability to see distinctions is a problem.

He died for two reasons. He stepped on secular, political, religious/ political toes and he pressed buttons. He was killed because he stepped on imperial toes by raising questions about the real kingdom versus the Roman kingdom that was going on in its perversity—and it was perverse in its treatment of so many people and tribes, including his own. Also there was a religious animus against him because the logic of his message meant that many people who were profiting from the religion of that time would profit less if his words were taken seriously. That's why Gandhi was shot by fundamentalists of his own religion, and, of course, why King was shot. We have had plenty of experiences of this. It doesn't take much imagination to see that when people announce the freedom and liberation of others, some of them cannot take it. They are very happy with the way things are and when they are threatened they overreact.

We are brought up with the idea that
Jesus was somehow a Christian and
that the Jews killed Jesus.

Jesus was not a Christian. Buddha was not a Buddhist and Jung was not a Jungian and Aquinas was not a Thomist. We have to get this in our heads, Jesus was a Jew. Christians love to skip over that, which shows more of the shadow side of Christianity with anti-Semitism that we have not dealt with. And it's there, obviously it's there. Hitler did not happen out of the blue. Hitler happened in a so-called Christian country.

Was Jesus ever married or
in an intimate relationship?

I wouldn't discount that—one of my theories is he may have been a widower. He certainly had an understanding of women that was very unique and very deep and my guess is that some women were very important teachers to him in his life. But it's speculation—what do we know about something as concrete as that? It's one of those things you can't really prove or not prove, it seems to me.

Of course, Jesus had to learn and that's his genius. What he chose and what he let go of. My take is that he observed that John the Baptist, who was probably a mentor to him, didn't succeed very well and so he chose not to go the "in your face" route; he chose the parable route and the story route and he lasted longer than John the Baptist. Like every one of us, he had to make a lot of choices in his life and I suspect that those years were years where he observed a lot of things. Some people speculate that he went to India or something. Pretty hard to prove but I think it is very possible that he communicated with people who knew something of the East. It doesn't mean he had to go there physically, but I think in those years he obviously did a lot of living and a lot of observing.

Jesus' opinion of Christianity today?

Jesus wouldn't be too proud of the record of the inquisitions and the wars and the wiping out of native populations and religions—this destruction of the planet. And a certain amount of the responsibility for these things does lie with Christianity because Western culture has developed the technology to do these things, and how we treat other beings is a spiritual issue.

A lot of our history is testimony to our failure to understand Jesus' primary message and a record of the detours that have gone on in terms of guilt, of trying to get to heaven, usually on the bodies of others. There have been and are some gross distortions in the name of Christ. At the same time, there have been some beautiful people and some powerful movements. Take, for example, Francis of Assisi, whom I really admire. My reading of his story is that he did indeed try, like Jesus, to create an alternative form of spirituality within his own religion and that was the fraternity that he founded. However, before he died the Church took it from him, started ordaining his brothers, which he did not want, and frankly broke his heart. The stigmata was also a result of a broken heart. Those who have tried to live Jesus' message most deeply and purely have invariably paid the price. After all, Meister Eckhart was condemned the week after he died and he's still on the naughty list, and he probably understood Christ's message as well as anybody.

What did Jesus mean when he said, "I am the
Way and the Truth and the Life. No one comes
to the Father except through me"?

That is from John's Gospel and it is not the historical Jesus speaking, it is the Christ speaking. If the Christ is present within all creation then it's right to say Christ is the Way and the Truth and the Life. No one comes to the Father except through Christ because it is through creation that we get to the Creator. This means the way to God is through the way, the truth, and the life of creation itself.

✢ 37
NOBODY INTERVIEWS
THE POPE

OAKLAND, CALIFORNIA

When I met with Matthew Fox, I asked him if he had any contacts at the Vatican. He just laughed because in 1993 he was dismissed by the Dominican order for taking on the Vatican.

"It's like standing in front of a train," he said.

But I was desperate, and the Pope is really hard to talk to, I mean when was the last time you saw an interview with the Pope?

Never. Why?

Because *nobody* interviews the Pope. But you know what? Some of my friends said my first book of dialogues would never happen because "you're nobody" they said, "and famous people don't waste time on a nobody."

As I said, *nobody interviews the Pope,* and maybe that's where my strength lies—in being nobody. Maybe nobody can get on a plane and fly to Rome and then nobody can just walk invisibly past those helmeted Swiss guards. Nobody is hard to stop sometimes.

But really, how does a person go about interviewing the Pope?

You start by making contacts, any contacts. I called my editor at Doubleday because they had just published a book by the Pope.

"I don't have anything for you," my editor said. "We never talked to him. Everything went through an agent of the Vatican."

That didn't stop me.

"Just give me a name," I pleaded. "Any name, and I'll take it from there."

"I'll see what I can do," he said.

For the next three weeks, he wouldn't answer his phone, so I called him several times a week and left messages on his machine.

"This is Bill," I said, "give me a name! Any name!"

He never called me back.

Then I called an operator in Italy and got the phone number of the Vatican in Rome. I called the Vatican and they gave me a fax number.

On June 4, 1998, at 1 A.M. I faxed the Pope. That afternoon, I told people, "I faxed the Pope today."

They laughed. They always laugh.

"He's not going to do an interview with you," just about everyone said.

When people say that, I don't answer them, because if the Pope refuses to grant me an interview, maybe I'll tell him he owes me because of that crappy "It was God's will" answer one of his priests gave me twenty-seven years ago.

So if I do get into see the Pope, I have a secret plan. After I ask him my Jesus questions, I'll thank him and get up to leave. But just before I walk out the door, I'm going to turn around and say, "I have one more question. When I was a small boy, both my parents died. Why did that have to happen?"

I'm really going to ask him that because even though the adult in me doesn't need an answer, the child in me still does.

A few days later, I got a reply from the Pope.

PREFETTURA
DELLA CASA PONTIFICIA

IL PREFETTO

The Vatican, 17 June 1998
Fax: +39 6 6988 5863

Mr. William J. Elliott
489 Blackbird Lane
Madison, WI 53704
U.S.A.

Dear Mr. Elliott,

I am replying to your letter of June 4 in which you have requested an interview with His Holiness to discuss your forthcoming book.

Unfortunately, because of the Pope's heavy commitments, this will not be possible.

With my best wishes,

Yours sincerely,

(+James M. Harvey, Prefect)

39
ANDREW HARVEY

The night before I met Andrew Harvey for an interview, I was invited to a wine tasting at Christie's Auction House, which is famous for auctioning off expensive wines and forty-million-dollar Van Gogh paintings. A friend who worked there invited me and I had to laugh to myself because I was sure I would be the poorest person at that wine tasting.

I was late for the event because I couldn't decide what to wear. I didn't bring a tie or a sport coat on my trip so I decided to wear a black turtleneck. I figured if I was the only one there without a tie, then I would try to look like an artist who couldn't be bothered by ties or sport coats. Anyway I was half running/half walking up Rodeo Drive toward Christie's when I passed a man in a wheelchair. He wore old clothes and looked weathered like a street person.

"Excuse me," he said.

Strangers had stopped me many times since I had been in California, and they always wanted money. I didn't have any money because I had spent it all traveling around and working on my Jesus book, and yet I was on my way to a wine tasting at Christie's. I had an American Express Gold Card in one pocket and a cell phone in the other.

"I don't have any money," I replied as I hurried past him.

"I wasn't asking for money," the man called after me. This froze me in my tracks and I turned and walked back to him.

"Those are my cigarettes," he said, pointing at the ground. "Will you give me one?"

I bent down quickly and picked up the cigarettes. When I looked back at the man, he just looked at me calmly and a strange feeling came over me. Even though I was in a hurry, something in me wanted to slow down and be present with this man. I handed him the cigarettes, but he lifted up his hands and showed me that his hands didn't work. I took a cigarette slowly from the pack and respectfully placed it in his mouth. As I lit his cigarette,

I really looked at him—as though for the first time. We talked for a few moments, and when I walked away, I saw everything clearly.

The next day I met Andrew Harvey in a bar at a small casino just outside of Las Vegas. I liked him for two reasons. First of all, he didn't hold anything back. He was passionate, outspoken, and proud of being a mystical scholar. Second, he said my book was "incredibly important for the millennium" and *you've got to like that.*

After talking for a few moments he said, "Let's go to the desert!" We drove my motor home out to the desert, and then walked and talked as Andrew Harvey pointed out blood-red mountainpeaks amid the barren peacefulness of the desert.

One problem I had had with Christianity was the whole idea of Jesus as "Savior." But then Andrew Harvey said, "Jesus is my Savior, not because he is some avatar who came here and breezed through life, but because he, like me, was a human being who discovered his Divine identity and who was living it with an unbelievable integrity, ferocity, purity, and passion—while showing me how I can do the same. He saved my life by being a fellow human and Divine being as well as my sacred brother and my sacred friend and my sacred beloved and a sacred presence within me that has nothing to do with somebody outside of myself or in another dimension."

Something in me relaxed when Andrew Harvey said that, and consequently my relationship to Jesus became more trusting and deeper—while my understanding of Christianity became greater.

After our meeting, I dropped him off at his new home in suburbia. It was on a street where all the houses looked the same. After living in big cities and being seen as a spiritual teacher, Andrew Harvey now seemed happy to be just another hardworking homeowner. Before I drove away, he gave me directions to the best casino buffet in Las Vegas.

Andrew Harvey is a poet, novelist, mystical scholar, seeker, and teacher. He is the author of more than thirty books including *Son of Man: The Mystical Path of Christ, The Way of Passion: A Celebration of Rumi,* and *A Journey to Ladakh.*

Jesus was not an avatar, and I don't believe in the concept of avatar and if you think of him as an avatar, the whole point of his radical life gets lost. It is much, much more challenging and far closer to the truth to think of Jesus as somebody who is "Christing" himself in the most extreme, clear way and giving us a final and beautifully accurate diagram of how to do that ourselves. That is a much more interesting concept to me than some avatar coming in and floating through and leaving a kind of calm, pure teaching. Jesus' life was torn apart—bloody, scarred, and frightening in its intensity— while being very, very pure. His life had all the signs of somebody stagger- ing from discovery to discovery and from illumination to illumination. That's what makes Jesus so unbelievably moving, and so unbelievably help- ful! Because that's what we are all doing, and this makes him far more a Savior than the avatar figure. He is a Savior because Jesus took that jour- ney of waking up and the spiritual bomb went off. It has gone off in hun- dreds of thousands of people. I have seen it in many people and it's not the privilege of any group. Every human being has the bomb of Divine love in the core of himself/herself and is waiting for the moment when it explodes, and for those ever continuing and greater explosions that go on and on in cosmic scale. The One being is waking up to the oneness in all of us.

Accuracy and authorship of the gospels?

They are four great sacred poems, written by four sacred poets. They contradict each other and are not accurate in that sense. But they are ac- curate in the way a great poem is accurate; they are accurate in register- ing the sacred emotions that the presence of Jesus must have created. If they are read in that spirit then we see Jesus as a personality of absolute incandescent mystery, a mystery that is reflected in the gospels in mar- velous ways. But if you take the gospels as letter-by-letter accurate tran- scriptions of what Jesus said or did, you're completely misreading them. You're missing the full experience of the Jesus that is behind them, the mystical Jesus.

People who think Jesus was a Christian have lost their minds. Jesus was beyond all religions, because all mystics wake up to that which is beyond all religion. They wake up to the reality of the Divine presence in themselves and in the external world and its absolute primacy over everything.

How could his realization be contained by any word? That's why I call it "the Christ Path," because those are the only words that don't betray what is being talked about. What we are talking about when we talk about *Jesus in the Christ* is a realization that transcends all signs, forms, names, and possibilities of the human imagination. It goes on and on, expanding beyond time and space. What Jesus birthed in himself is a crucial birth of the whole of humanity, far beyond the limits of mere Christianity.

Why do people keep the same beliefs they had
as children without questioning them or
allowing them to evolve?

Because they lose the mystical dimension. If you lose the mystical dimension, you lose everything, especially mystical initiation. If you lose the mystical initiation that the mystical dimension brings, then you are condemned to believe in the letter of the law, to follow forms, to obey rules, to be trapped in hierarchies and beliefs. The mystical initiation is the volcanic eruption of Divine love in the heart and with that volcanic eruption comes the destruction forever of all boundaries that exist between you and other beings. That initiation is Christ Consciousness, and that is what Jesus strove to incarnate completely on earth. Jesus realized and is one with Christ Consciousness and is instructing the whole of anybody who wants to turn to join him. Christ Consciousness has nothing whatever to do with dogmas, laws, rules, or any kind of elitist authoritarian structure. If you get trapped in any of those structures, it is proof that you have no understanding whatsoever of who Jesus is.

Jesus is not the only Son of God. Jesus never claimed to be the Son of God. That is a fantasy and a disastrous evasion of the reality of Jesus' mystical message and it has resulted in this terrible famine that we see around us called Christianity. He claimed to be *the son of man* and that is a very complex and rich title. The revelation that was birthed in him told him that his revelation was not just for him but for all of humanity, for absolutely everyone. Jesus realized everyone had Christhood in them. He knew it was everyone's destiny, everyone's goal, and everyone's end. But those in charge realized early on that if people were empowered by the full intensity of the revelation of the Spirit, then they would become impossible to control because they would all be released and initiated within the core of their own lives, and led to great awakenings by the Spirit itself. Therefore, people wouldn't need priests, experts, Church-identified saints, or institutions— they would have liberated themselves from all that.

Christianity made a disastrous decision, either consciously or half-consciously, to support structures rather than the living experience, and you see this in the destruction of the Gnostics. This was a demonic decision that created seventeen hundred years of drought. A drought that is punctuated by a few very great mystics. If those original Christian authorities had chosen to live in Spirit rather than structure the world might have been transfigured by now.

What spiritual practices or techniques did Jesus teach?

He taught the Lord's Prayer and he taught how to pray it unpretentiously, silently and quietly while knowing that you are the direct child of the Divine and praying directly to the Divine. Jesus taught a direct path, a direct connection between child and source. He gave the ultimate prayer, which expressed all the different relationships he wished for people to experience. Jesus taught through the Lord's Prayer and it contains an astonishing sense of universality: the calling down of God's laws to earth, the calling out for God's protection, the calling out of gratitude for all the graces that are given and the expressed desire to be safe from evil.

Jesus taught simple meditation techniques *by example* as when he could be observed sitting in the quiet of the landscape. He transmitted his realization mystically to his disciples, as when he says in the Gospel of Thomas, "He who is near to me is nearer to the fire." The disciples were near his spiritual explosion and they must have caught fire from it. There are great mystical experiences that come in dreams and from just being in the presence of someone like Jesus.

You can only model learning, and if you model learning with humility, wonder, and great joy, then you will become a kind of living fire sign, you will become infectious, and you will be giving off the perfume of the sacred like a flower gives off perfume and people will inevitably be moved by that.

Like anybody who is awake, Jesus can help other people awake. Because the direct path doesn't mean not having mentors or not revering or not loving or not learning immensely from someone who may be farther on than you. What it does mean is not getting them to, or thinking they are going to, do the work for you or deifying them, but taking total responsibility for your relationship with the world, which includes your relationship with them.

I have visited people I consider very high, almost saint-like people like Bede Griffiths, and I knew that he was much farther on than I was in many, many ways and I didn't think of him as a god or totally deified. I thought of him as somebody who was on an immensely beautiful journey from which I could learn everything important. I thought of him as a human being who was still struggling and seeking in the most dazzling and most beautiful way. Bede Griffiths taught me how to learn and true lovers of God share their love like wine. When two people are in love with the Divine, they can share their love like a feast, like wine, like bread, and then they both get filled by that activity and they both get help. This is a relationship that has nothing to do with power and everything to do with love, joy, and celebration.

When you truly love you are in a perpetual state of infinite receptivity, which is ecstatic and extremely painful and has to be held with a container of calm, just as the Divine does, otherwise you would explode.

Spiritual practice is the container in which you can have the explosion. You need a daily practice of prayer and meditation that constantly strengthens peace, trust, and confidence because as the heart opens to sacred reality, it also opens to the agony and suffering of the world. That's why the mystics have always stressed the necessity of a humbling practice that creates a container. This container creates a kind of mother around you, which enables you to develop at the right pace and gives a crucial balance. Earlier when we were driving in the car, you said that I was extreme. Actually I am both extreme and balanced because otherwise I would never be able to live like I do or write like I do. *You have to be very balanced to be very extreme.* Because to love extremely, you have to be extremely clear. That's what enlightenment in Mahayana Buddhism is—the marriage of wisdom and compassion. Love on its own without Gnosis or Divine knowledge is going to go crazy. Gnosis is what steadies and fills love with transcendent peace. Love frees Gnosis so that it is not constricting and vice versa. It has to be a marriage of the two: ecstasy and the illumined mind or reason. The illumined mind catches the soul and enables it to soar more profoundly.

Virgin birth?

There wasn't a virgin birth, but it was an amazingly powerful metaphor for the real birth of the innermost Christ Consciousness. What it means is that the innermost Christ Consciousness, the consciousness of Divine love, is born out of the utter love, freshness, and purity of the Divine feminine. Out of that final purity, that final tenderness, that final bliss, is born the complete love consciousness that is the Christ. The virgin birth certainly happens, but it happens in the soul and not in the body.

What happened to the Divine feminine in Christianity?

Much of my book *Son of Man* is about the loss of the feminine, and what I say is that Jesus is as much the "son of the mother" as "son of the father" because he believes in an embodied love, and love that is embodied transforms the world. Jesus wants people and their relationships transfigured. He is incarnating on earth the maternal passion of the motherhood of God for the earth, for life and for beings. Jesus fused within himself the complete awareness of the transcendent with the utter devotion toward the eminent that the father has for the mother. This Divine lovemaking went on in the depths of his soul and produced the sacred in him, which we call "the Divine Child." Jesus wants us all to become embodied lovers of the Divine and agents of transformation.

Second Coming?

Christ is returning, but not as a Savior or avatar—that is part of the old fantasy that belongs to the same set of concepts that have distanced him as a Savior in the first place. The Second Coming will be the birth of Christ Consciousness in millions of beings who have taken the journey toward that naked radical love—that is the only kind of Second Coming that could change anything. That's what is either going to happen or not. If it happens, the world will be preserved. If it does not happen, the world will be destroyed. I feel we are at this amazing moment where we could actually birth the Christ Consciousness, because we have been through enough of the patriarchal deformations to know that they have it all wrong! It's not being born that way!

People have to be brave enough to embrace what they recognize. People are most sacred, in my experience, of love. Pain and joy also scare people because they dissolve control, but the great force that dissolves control is love. Love terrifies because it sends you mad, because letting go into love means abandoning your inhibitions, your restraints, and the separations that keep you conveniently safe. When you start loving, who or what would you leave out of your circle of love? Could you, as fundamentalist Christians have done, stand outside the funeral of Matthew Shepard saying, "God hates fags!" It's an obscenity and a blasphemy beyond all comprehension! How could anyone who has ever had a moment of the real experience of God want to exclude gay or black people or whoever else they want to exclude. How could you have it and even think about excluding anybody! Because if you tasted one drop of the wine of what Christ was handing out in his life, then it sends you drunk for the whole of reality. All you want to do is to kneel in front of everybody and hold everybody to your heart and wish absolutely every creature on the planet total health, happiness, and long life!

Jesus is in a state of perpetual crucifixion because his teachings were destroyed. But since Jesus is realization, and the realization of the Cosmic Christ transcends all teachings, all religions, and is the absolute reality of this whole universe—then there is an aspect of it that can never be trampled because it is the eternal reality.

Did Jesus' teaching go farther than the Buddha's?

Jesus' teachings went farther than the Buddha's despite the enormous wisdom and sophistication of the Buddha's realization. There is running through all of Buddhism a contempt for the body, a secret disillusion at the nature of reality, and a not-so-secret desire to transcend reality altogether into a state that has total timeless peace at its very foundation. That is a one-sided realization and is fundamentally a patriarchal realization and is only one half of the complete realization. The other half involves embodiment, involves embracing the sacred feminine, involves opening to the fullest nature of the sacred heart and living in time, in a body, with Divine ecstasy. Jesus fused what the Buddha knew with the radical wisdom of the sacred heart that he himself came to discover and embodied. He produced a wholly new, wholly original vision, which was actually the discovery of a nuclear force. The Buddha discovered a way of transcendence. Jesus discovered the equivalent of Hiroshima, Nagasaki, and all the neutron bombs, in the internal psyche. The explosion of the heart will forever alter reality and give people the fuel with which to transfigure reality into a living mirror of Divine love. That is a very fundamental difference, because fundamentally in Buddhism there is a turning away from the world, a seeing of the world as a dream, as maya, as illusion, as a fading transient show.

Jesus is different. He has a mind-shattering sacredness for each pebble, each tree, and each human face. The experience of Divine ecstasy in the Divine creation is far more important now that we are in danger of destroying nature. We need to reintegrate the masculine and feminine.

Jesus' path was of descent. The Buddha took the path of ascent and there is tremendous compassion and awareness radiating from the ascended position. But Jesus actually specifically refused the path of ascent. That's what I think he is doing in the desert. The devil, in a way, offers him the guru position, offers him the imperial guru position, world leader, world charmer, world enslaver, and he could have been like one of those gurus we see today. But Jesus saw through that and chose the maternal path of descent. He chose to embrace life, to embrace ordeal, to embrace the difficulty, and that deepened his realization immeasurably. If the whole point of creation is to divinize matter completely, and thus create a great evolutionary scheme through which matter becomes more and more divinized, then Jesus' discovery of this lure of sacred passion is a discovery that enables that fusion to take place. His discovery allowed creation to become more and more conscious of its Divine origin and, therefore, merge with its Divine origin.

Jesus was also at war with the world, but the world he despised is the world of inherited assumptions and the blindness of conventional wisdom. He shattered that world in order to get to "The World" and "The Kingdom," which is all around us and which is the living experience of Divine ecstasy and Divine love. We can do as Jesus did, which is be the living experience of Divine manifestation.

We must remember that the Buddha didn't get it wrong, he got it unbelievably right, in the dimension that he got it. There is a great difference in the story of the Buddha in that he wakes up to the fact of time and death in the rather sort of mathematical way, doesn't he? He lives in these luxurious apartments and then he sees the four things: the old man, death, sickness, and the sadhus.

But Jesus' life is a life of unbelievable pain. Now I am not glorifying pain, but there is something in suffering that expands wisdom. On the other hand, the Buddha seems to have discovered a technique for ending the kinds of suffering that Jesus found transforming. And the suffering of Jesus took Jesus farther into the core and heart of life, so that he became one with both matter and spirit. He didn't refuse matter, he experienced matter as being just as Divine as Spirit.

Jesus was able to do what no one else ever did, which is to achieve the resurrected body. The meaning of the resurrection is that Jesus fused heaven and earth together forever. That fusion has forever altered the whole relationship between matter and spirit. It allowed for the possibility of the final birth of the Spirit in matter, which means the final transfiguration of matter by the Spirit, which means the carrying of this dimension fully conscious into complete divinity—which is what Mary is doing in the assumption. Jesus' revelation goes beyond all the others.

Was Jesus ever married or
in an intimate relationship?

All his relationships were intimate. He could have easily been either celibate or sexual, but at a level and in such a way that we cannot even begin to imagine because his consciousness was so far above our basic consciousness. That level of consciousness dissolves the kinds of categories that create words like celibate and sexual. If he was celibate, he was celibate at a level of pure erotic Divine joy and if he was sexual, he was sexual with a desireless, sweet, ecstatic intelligence. When you get into the consciousness of Christ Consciousness, how could those categories mean anything? They don't. You cannot simply repress sex, and you cannot simply express sex. What you have to do is consecrate your entire being to Divine love, at which moment sexuality is transfigured, not necessarily into celibacy, but into a wholly different force of initiatory love.

I don't think Jesus was celibate. I hope there was a hidden Tantric transmission and he could have been bisexual. There is a homosexual mystical tradition through John and a heterosexual mystical tradition through Mary Magdalene and if there wasn't, then I think one of the responsibilities for a modern mystic taking the Christ Path is to receive that transmission from the Cosmic Christ.

If the historical Jesus didn't have transfigured Tantric relationships, I know that the Cosmic Christ is totally capable of initiating anyone who wants to have one of those relationships.

Can people be happy without having that
cosmic Christ experience?

No! Of course not. Because that's why we are here, to have that experience and to realize it and in its fullness, as far as we can in the body.

The things that most people are smiling about can be destroyed, but the joy that Jesus birthed in the soul cannot be destroyed by time or by death. It's the eternal joy. Divine experience is in every aspect of life; it's making a meal for a friend, it's talking to somebody who is sick, it is sharing a happy walk with a dog, that's all Divine . . . everything is Divine. *Learning how to smile and be happy with God's face and God's heart is the great mystical challenge,* isn't it? Jesus is always, always, trying to lead people farther into an experience of ever-expanding love. It always grows.

God is so merciful that many scraps fall from the table for everyone. Many beautiful things are given but only a very few wake up to who is giving those beautiful things and those who do are the lovers and the mystics and they are lucky because then they know that they are the beloved of God.

Is it grace that wakes us up?

It's a mixture. Grace comes but you have to work with grace, just as rain falls on the field but you have to plow the field. Both together. More and more I think at the high levels it is grace, because my experience is that you can do all the work, you can sweat and practice, but you can only take yourself to a certain level, only God can take you beyond that level and that's what grace does. What your work does is symbolize your receptivity and your humility before the Divine and create a kind of emptiness in which you can receive revelation, and then the revelation will be given. But revelation is always a pure gift and it is always experienced with a dazzling wonder, awe, gratitude, and joy. The authentic mystic is always talking about the grace of God, while the inauthentic mystic is always talking about his or her own experiences because the mystic still hasn't got it.

40
WEEPING WITH JESUS
IN GETHSEMANE

JERUSALEM

"Can I have that card?" the voice behind me asked.

I was at a park near my hotel and I had just made a phone call at a public phone using an Israeli phone card. Since the telephones in Israel don't take coins, you have to use cards, and they cost anywhere from five to twenty dollars.

I turned and saw a middle-aged woman with long reddish hair. Although it was warm out, she wore a winter coat and she carried two bags which appeared to contain her whole world.

"I don't have any money," she said. At first I offered her the use of the card because I had just purchased the card and it was worth a lot of money. I certainly didn't want to give it to her, but then I looked into her eyes . . .

I had visited most of the holy sites in and near Jerusalem during the past week with the hope of feeling the spirit of my Christian roots—more specifically I wanted to feel the spirit of Jesus. It had been more of an effort than I had originally thought to feel the holy in this acclaimed holy place.

. . . but then I looked into her eyes, and I saw her pain, and my heart slowly cracked open and crumbled. From working on a psych unit for many years—I've developed the ability (like many of my coworkers) to look into another's eyes and sometimes see their psychological pain and torture. When I looked into her eyes, that's what I saw—a tortured soul.

I handed her the phone card as delicately as I could. She took it from my hand and then looked up at me with eyes that for a moment filled with peace, as though the tortured soul within her had temporarily been pacified. Her cheeks suddenly flushed red, and she glowed as a smile slowly dawned upon her face. Then she thanked me and walked away.

My body shook as I wept, only a few paces from where Jesus had wept almost two thousand years ago. I had found a place in the corner of Gethsemane—the place where Jesus sweated blood. I closed my eyes and immediately felt his presence. But he wasn't near enough. How? I thought, how do I get closer to Jesus?

I want to get closer to you, I prayed.

Why? he asked.

Because you understand what it means to be human, I said as I began to cry.

I felt him watching me—not from a distance, but next to me. I knew he felt my pain because he had suffered too.

Are you with me?

"I'm here," he said, as I felt his supportive hand on my back. I wept harder. And one by one, the disciples came over—and I invited them to heal me—to help me to open by their touch. I invited them to touch me, and they in turn, invited me to open. I wept. I wept for all the tension that had squeezed the life out of my soul. I wept for all the lost faces I saw around me and especially for my own "lost face." I wept because God was around me, and because Jesus and my brothers had not forgotten me.

Do you remember who you are, brother? they asked. You are our brother, and we are here with you.

Then Jesus held my face in his hands and looked at me—straight in my eyes. "Wake up!" he said. "Wake up! Can you hear me? Wake up. Look at me—Wake up!"

During his forty days in the desert, Jesus found a heart that didn't weaken in the face of temptation. But in the Garden of Gethsemane, Jesus found the deep human heart he had forever sought. In Gethsemane, he found the heart that broke, like the heart that broke in me, and as it broke in me I sweated blood. Not the blood of fear, but the blood of life pouring out through pores from an awakened, renewed heart that only suffering can midwife.

"The suffering heart sweats the blood of new life," I whispered to myself.

Without Gethsemane, Jesus would have been just another prophet who pretended he was human. Jesus was human—so human that he wept, and through his weeping birthed himself into a deeper humanity. In the desert Jesus had plucked and uprooted the devilish weeds of his soul. But in the garden his life bloomed. Red. Alive. In ways he never imagined.

✢ 41
RABBI ZALMAN
SCHACHTER-SHALOMI

Jesus was Jewish! Jesus was Jewish! Jesus was Jewish! It was only after many months of writing and reading about Jesus that one day I woke up and realized *Jesus was Jewish!* I know that might be obvious to some people, but not to me. I was brought up to believe he was Christian and that somehow all these other people (who were Jewish) didn't understand his wisdom and so they killed him. *The Jews killed Jesus*—that's what I had always been taught. But *Jesus was a Jew.*

When I mentioned to Marcus Borg how blind I had been to this insight, he said it was common.

"In a workshop," Marcus Borg said, "I mentioned to people that Jesus was Jewish. Then a woman raised her hand and said, 'But what about his mother Mary—surely she wasn't Jewish!' "

As Christians, we're often brought up ignorant of the fact that all the heroes in the gospels were Jewish—all the apostles, Mary and Joseph, and even the writers of the gospels were Jewish.[1] Given that, why have Christians blamed the Jews for so long? In reality, we Christians should thank the Jews for Jesus. Especially when historians and biblical scholars tell us that crucifixion was a Roman method of execution and that *the Romans killed Jesus.*

Since Jesus was Jewish and called "rabbi" in the New Testament, I knew I had to interview rabbis. Years ago, I had interviewed Rabbi Zalman Schachter-Shalomi for my first book and what had impressed me was *he*

---

1. Except for Luke, who may have been Greek.

was his wisdom. You felt it. He wasn't reaching for intellectual answers or depending on scripture, instead his answers came from *who he was.* He helped me realize that many answers to life's questions can be found in oneself.

Rabbi Zalman Schachter-Shalomi was born in Vienna in 1924. He is the father of ten children and twenty-two grandchildren. His book, *From Aging to Sage-ing: A Profound New Vision of Growing Older* deals with what Rabbi Zalman calls *spiritual eldering.*

"Instead of preparing for our elder years," he said, "we back into aging with fear and ignorance. Life has to be harvested to be completed. If people in the November or December of their lives close down their consciousness, they sleep through the end of their lives."

Like Jesus, Zalman Schachter-Shalomi is a rabbi who knows the Jewish scriptures and possesses a mystical understanding of life and scripture.

Who was Jesus? Was he God or man?

That question can't be answered. Ultimately, it is only God interacting with God and nothing else exists. There is a level at which a person can become so transparent to God, that God flows through and you don't see a person talking to you—you see God talking to you.

At times, when I would consult with my rabbi and hear him teach, I would have the feeling that he was not just an individual but that he was totally transparent to God. But I never made it into a theological abstraction even though there were moments in which his identification with God was so complete, because I realized it was just a moment of experience. I imagine there were some people who experienced that with Jesus.

I take issue with Christianity because they have taken Jesus and lifted him out of totality and built everything around him. We (the Jewish people) had ten people who were more horribly killed by the Romans than Jesus and we call them "the great ten martyrs of the State." Yet Judaism did not make any of them a God.

For example, Hinduism is a vast, vast religion, and in fact, it is not a religion, it is a religious civilization, in which there are many religions at home. There are many teachers in Hinduism. One person who was particularly gifted and had wonderful charisma became a great teacher and he is the founder of the Buddhist faith—the Buddha. What did Hinduism do with the Buddha? In Hinduism, the Buddha is reabsorbed into the pantheon of the many avatars and is not seen as so special. But in Burma, Japan, China, and Korea they began to see the Buddha as the only one. They embedded the Buddha into each local religion, like Shintoism in Japan, the Bon religion in Tibet, and Taoism in China.

Jesus was also embedded. The Irish embedded Jesus in the Celtic religion, and in Brazil, Jesus is embedded in Candomblé.

So what happened in Judaism? In Judaism, the same thing happened. There were some Jewish Christians, but when the pagan Christians took over and pulled it so far away, the Jewish Christians weren't comfortable anymore—they returned to their Jewish roots.

It is easier to promote a religion with one person as the ideal. You see everybody has a higher self and that is one's ideal. "Nobody cometh unto the Father" except through one's higher self. But this higher self is hard to recognize as our own higher self, so we project this higher self onto another ideal person. It is much easier to focus on one individual, especially if that one individual doesn't come burdened with a lot of cultural baggage. In Christianity very little of the Jewish cultural baggage was transmitted. In Buddhism, very little of the cultural baggage of Hinduism was transmitted. That is why Buddhists are not into having a sacred cow or having different castes. In Christianity there are not the Jewish dietary restrictions.

It is easier to take a mythic figure who represents the ideal that everybody holds in their heart and hold them up and make them the one and only.

Is everyone a son or daughter of God?

"The Son of God" is an idea that is repeatedly talked about in the Old Testament. God says, "Send my son, Israel, my firstborn son." The whole people were considered children of God. Ultimately, the whole universe is a child of God and to create the idea around Jesus—saying he is the only one—I don't agree with that.

They were silent years—*he* wasn't "lost." *We* lost track of him. Jesus spent time in the desert, he is baptized by John, and after his bar mitzvah in the Gospel of John, he disappears until he is about thirty years old. Where is he? The answer might be that he went to the Dead Sea Scrollers and stayed there and did his spiritual hot-housing.

Virgin birth?

For God it is possible that a woman who has not had intercourse with a man should have a baby. And it is not only possible for God, it is now possible for science to do that as well.

But that whole business of the virgin birth is clearly a misreading of the word *parthenos*, which is itself a misreading of the Hebrew word *alma* (which means a young woman) and which certainly is not the word *betulah* (which means virgin, one who has not been with a male). The virgin birth idea began with an Isaiah prophecy. But Jesus was born four hundred years after that prophecy and *that prophecy was dealing with an immediate future, it wasn't talking about the birth of Jesus four hundred years later.*

On the other hand, have you ever been present at a birth? It can be the holiest moment. I was present at the birth and assisted in the labor of four of my children. There is a moment after the crowning of the baby, until the baby finally flips out and takes its first breath, that there is such a holy silence in the room that if one were a Catholic, one would make the sign of the cross. I was so full of awe, that I wanted to kneel in front of that woman and to honor her with prayer.

"Hail, hail, mother full of grace, the Lord be with you, blessed are you, blessed is the fruit of thy womb."

Then when I saw the labor, the agony of birth that is almost like dying—yet brings forth life—I had to say "Holy mother, pray for us at the hour of our death."

So the process that occurs when *any* woman gives birth, evokes such a deep mystical feeling that I have to say, "I believe in the virgin birth," because every mother who gives birth has the potential to be in that holy and pure virgin place.

Original sin?

I believe in the "original blessing" as Matt Fox said rather than in "original sin." Original sin is an old, old story. If Momma says, "Don't touch the cookie jar," that kid is going to touch the cookie jar, right? It is very clear that the Garden of Eden story is a setup.

Resurrection?

I don't believe in a grave opening up and all these guys coming out like zombies in comic books. Every time a child is born, there is a resurrection going on because if you believe in reincarnation, that is a resurrection.

Right now, our mind is such that we hardly pay attention to the body. But could you imagine, on a beautiful day you feel sort of zip-a-dee-doodah in your body, and you feel ecstatic about things and you love God and you love the world and you can't wait to hug somebody and share your blessing. That's what I call "the body of the resurrection," as in "I sing the body electric" from that Walt Whitman poem.

Was Jesus married or in an intimate relationship?

I can't imagine that Jesus didn't have a love relationship with somebody. The question always comes up as to whether Mary Magdalene or Martha had a relationship with him.

He said Mary had the better part when Martha was running the kitchen and Mary was just "gaa-gaaing" over him—something must have happened there. Even if they didn't have sex, there was certainly love there. It would have been unusual at that time for a man his age not to have been married.

What religion was Jesus?

It is clear that Jesus was a Jew and his teachings did not betray Judaism. Moses said to God, *"M'cheini nah misifr'cha asher katavta,"* which means "Erase me from the book you've written." Moses was willing to be the atonement for the people, to take on the sins of the world, and to be the lamb of God just as Jesus did and this is a very Jewish idea.

Most important teaching of Jesus?

That question doesn't work because the special thing about Jesus is that whatever he was doing at the moment was the most important thing.

Once, a Hasidic master was asked what was the greatest thing he learned from his teacher.

"Whatever he was doing at that moment," the Hasidic master replied.

Who killed Jesus and why?

What was written at the top of the cross? *King of the Jews.* Crucifixion was not a Jewish form of capital punishment. It was Roman, and it began in Greece. It was done because it was so painful, and the Greeks and Romans figured this agonizing way of dying would scare people and they would think twice before opposing the government.

The notion that Pilate washed his hands of Jesus' death is ridiculous. That people were saying, "We want Barabbas" is funny because the word "bar" means son and "abba" means father. So when the people are saying we want Barabbas, they are saying, "We want the son of the father." I don't know how this was interpreted that the people actually wanted someone named "Barabbas."

Furthermore, could you imagine a Roman Procurator asking the people, "Do you want me to let this rebel go?" or "Which one of the rebels do you want?"

And the people reply "We want the most dangerous-to-the-Romans rebel," and Pilate would say "Okay, you can have him!" This story is sort of twisted.

*Why wasn't Jesus accepted by
Judaism as the Messiah?*

There is a job description, a Messiah description, which says when the Messiah comes there will be peace on earth, the lion and lamb will lie together, and kids won't go around in school yards shooting other kids and that hasn't happened yet. So, why claim the Messiah has come? Even Christians say they're waiting for the Second Coming. My point is, if Jesus fulfilled the requirements of the Messiah, why is the Second Coming needed?

I don't believe that one individual will be the Messiah. As a totality, we all will become Messiah. Just like Farid-Ud-Din Attar describes in the *Conference of the Birds*. We are getting so much closer but people can't see it because it isn't available in theological language. Gaia is waking up and there is something happening to the planet. The planet is becoming more alive than it has ever been.

Teilhard de Chardin books have a beautiful vision of the divinitization of the planet—what he calls Christogenesis. He was not hooked on one guy appearing from the clouds and saying "It's me!"

Jesus' opinion of Christianity today?

I think Jesus would be in pain. I believe that every religion has an angel. When I talked with the Dalai Lama, it wasn't only Zalman Schachter-Shalomi and the Dalai Lama talking—it was the angel of Tibet and the angel of Judaism talking together. I believe there is an angel being of Christianity and at this time that angel being is in agony. This angel is being crucified by the number of conflicting denominations. On the right side is the Western Church, on the left side is the Eastern Church, and all over there are those little cancers that are the different denominations—none of them want to be part of the greater body of Christendom.

Jesus said "the kingdom of Heaven is within."
Why don't people believe that?

It isn't that people have a hard time believing that—it's that churches have a hard time running a church when the kingdom of God is within. If the kingdom were truly within, then there would be a much greater freedom of conscience. And the kingdom within would control it, not the kingdom without! But many religions don't want that. For instance, the Vatican is the kingdom without and to this day it will not allow people a lot of latitude in how they relate to Jesus. It has to be according to the way in which *the Vatican* calls the shots.

There is a misunderstanding when someone says, "Master, how shall we pray?" and Jesus answers, "Our Father, who art in heaven."

What they have done with that is make this verbal form of prayer the only kosher way of praying. When in reality, he was demonstrating how a common, simple prayer often spoken in those days, should be done.

When Jesus said "Our Father," at that moment he connected so strongly to the Father, that Jesus and some of the people around him could feel the vibes of the Father. That's what Jesus was demonstrating, the feeling, the energy behind the words—not which words to say.

*When Jesus said, "I am the Way and the Truth
and the Life," what did he mean?*

When Jesus says, "I and the Father are One," he could have as easily said, "I and Gaia am One."

When Jesus said, "I am the Way and the Truth and the Life," he wasn't saying, "I Jesus am the only way." He was saying, "Do what I am doing. Look at me! I am a model of someone who is living in the presence of God. Be like me!"

But fundamentalists aren't going to buy it, so what are you going to do? Fundamentalists need to have the Christ outside of themselves, not within, because they are people who don't trust.

It's the difference between autonomy and heteronomy. Heteronomy is when somebody outside of you is calling the shots (telling you what to do and what to believe) because God is not experienced and felt within. Autonomy is when I experience and feel God within me. I hear Jesus saying, "Autonomy—find God within." But I see the people who hated Jesus and wanted to get rid of him as not having that inner experience of God, and so they believed in heteronomy and then they said, "Look, Jesus is against heteronomy!" And of course they were right! *Jesus was against heteronomy!* And yet today, it is the fundamentalists who want God outside, who believe in heteronomy—it is they who enshrine Jesus in heteronomy instead of autonomy. *Think about that and then think about it some more.*

42
FAKE CREAM REAL BLOOD

The following morning, I went searching for my nondairy creamer in the Jewish Quarter of Jerusalem. Since it was against Jewish dietary practices to mix beef and milk, the Jews have developed some fine dairy imitations. Fake whipped cream, fake regular cream—they got 'em and I was in search of them.

I walked through the butcher section of Jerusalem. It was a long block of various gutted animals, entrails, and occasional boxes filled with heads. The smell of blood and guts was everywhere. At the end of the street, just as I turned a corner, I spotted two men with blood running down their faces. They both held handkerchiefs to their heads.

"Do I have it in the right place?" the one man asked an Israeli cop. The two were surrounded by four or five police. Arabs and Jews alike just stood by and watched. I kept walking and as I did, I followed a trail of blood. Evidently the two men had been hurt some ways away and had walked to where I had seen them—leaving a trail of blood that I now followed.

The storekeepers, shops, and tourists continued their working, and it seemed that only I was aware of the trail of blood. I followed it from the center of the Old City up the steps as it led to the Jaffa Gate. A hundred yards or so from the gate, the blood trail ended.

I walked through the Jaffa Gate, turned and stopped. The Old City of Jerusalem—the City of Fire—the Holy City—the City of God—was also the City of Blood. Animals, people, saints—all bloodied, all butchered.

In the place where three major religions converge, our humanity shows its true heart: The Western Wall prayers of the Jews. The five-a-day prayers of the Muslims. The Holy Sepulcher pilgrimage of countless Christians. That's the light of man.

The butchered animals, the moneychangers, and the butchered human beings—that too is human.

When a human being is filled with God, he or she is filled with the holy blood from head to toe, from heart to hands. But what is also found in Jerusalem is blood on the hands—when man kills neighbor in the name of God. The true crucifixion of man is that the blood of God flows *into* our hands, while the blood of man is found *on* our hands.

✠ 43
E. P. SANDERS

"Ed Sanders," the voice answered.

Ed Sanders? But I'm calling E. P. Sanders, the world-renowned New Testament scholar. Could this "Ed" Sanders be the E. P. Sanders who taught at Oxford University? Who wrote the acclaimed *The Historical Figure of Jesus* and whom John Meier called "America's most distinguished scholar in the field of Jesus-research today"?

I expected a highbrow voice infused with academic authority culled from years of struggling with ancient text and undergraduate students. I expected a voice and manner that said "I am E. P. Sanders and I know more about the New Testament than you will ever know about your own name."

But he wasn't that way. He was just plain old Ed Sanders.

But that was two weeks ago, and now it was the day before our appointment and I had to phone him and change our meeting time. I was worried because I had already changed it once, and like I said he's considered by some to be the most famous New Testament scholar in the world and I was afraid he'd yell at me—well, he wouldn't yell, he'd be dignified and all, but still . . .

"Mr. Elliott," I imagined him saying, "E. P. Sanders is never kept waiting. I'm in demand all over the world. I am the foremost, most highly regarded New Testament scholar in the world. My time is valuable. I can't be waiting around for you—especially, when you have no money and Marcus Borg has to buy you dinner at Granny's Chicken Palace."

Nevertheless, I phoned him again in order to change our meeting time, and braced myself for the worst.

"Ed Sanders," the voice on the other end said.

"I'm sorry," I said, "but I had to drive eighteen hours today to try and meet with you—I'm not going to make it."

With that, the exhaustion I felt seeped into my whole body, and I was so tired I didn't care if he got angry.

"I'm exhausted," I added, as I prepared myself for disappointment.

"I'm sorry you had to push yourself driving," he said with sympathy that was so real that I felt momentarily nurtured. Then he calmly changed the time and gave me directions to his house.

A few hours later, I made the turn off onto E. P. Sanders's street. When I pulled into his driveway, he was walking among his rosebushes.

"Japanese beetles," he said, showing me one he held between his thumb and forefinger.

"They wreak havoc on rosebushes," he said as he squashed the beetle between his fingers. He tossed it aside and suddenly this Bible scholar was "the terminator of Japanese beetles."

As expected, during our meeting Ed Sanders was articulate and knowledgeable. He was friendly and funny. When I told him that my father and brother had been detectives and that I felt like a detective in search of Jesus, Ed Sanders said, "Biblical archaeologists and other biblical scholars often regard themselves as detectives."

After the interview, when Ed went to answer the phone, I paged through some ancient-looking books that were piled on the table. I couldn't make sense of any of it—it looked like Greek to me.

"What language is this?" I asked him after he came back into the room.

"That's Greek . . ." he said, pointing to a paragraph, ". . . and that's Aramaic and that's Hebrew and that's . . ."

Afterward, he walked me out to the motor home.

"If you see any Japanese beetles . . ." he started to say.

"I know," I replied. "If I see the Japanese beetle on the road—kill it."

Who was/is Jesus?

The main thing for people to understand is that while discussing the topic of Jesus, they actually have different subjects in mind.

I am a historian. I try to study the life and teachings of a man who walked around Galilee for about thirty-five years, around about two thousand years ago. My methods are limited to the methods of the historian and my sources are limited to the sources that would be used by a historian of any subject matter.

I am trying to re-create the life of the historical Jesus in just the same way that one tries to re-create the life of Alexander the Great, Herod the Great, or someone less famous and less noble. But most people, when they think about Jesus, have at least partly in mind a person whom Christianity believes to have been the second person of the Trinity—a supernatural or partially supernatural person who had powers that go beyond the normal run of human powers.

Who we think Jesus was affects why we think he died. For example, did he die because he made a ruckus in the temple during a pilgrimage festival, when the city of Jerusalem was packed, when Roman troops came up to the city specifically to keep peace, and when troublemakers (like him) were put down in a hurry?

Or did he die because he was the designated sacrifice for the sins of the whole world? If so, Jesus then becomes the incarnation of God. God designated him, and God accepted Jesus' death as atoning for the sins of the world.

Now, it is not necessarily the case that one of these answers is right and the other one is wrong. They can both be true, but when you are reading about it, you need to know what you are reading.

Are you reading about the plain vanilla ordinary life of Jesus? Or are you reading a discussion about the Divine plan and Jesus' role in it—which cannot be studied historically? Not only is it not verifiable or unverifiable, you can't study it at all. You simply cannot study the plan of God. Historians don't do that!

I am a real, sure enough, ordinary, plain vanilla sort of historian! I am not dealing with theological questions. Although, I do want to add one very brief point, which is that a lot of Christians think that Jesus was, as I just indicated, more than a mere man, that is, that he combined human attributes with Divine attributes and that the Divine attributes enabled him to do supernatural things. This is, in fact, a heresy. But that is what most Christians believe.

What the Christian's creed requires Christians to believe is that Jesus had two 100 percents; he was 100 percent human and he was 100 percent

God and that these two 100 percents were not intermingled or confused. That is, one did not tamper with the other. So it is actually a heresy to say that Jesus' supernatural 100 percent changed the specific gravity of his body so that the human feet could go skimming across the surface of the water. Whether or not you believe in supernatural beings, that is actually a heresy; it is saying that Jesus was neither human nor Divine, he was half and half, and that used to get people burned at the stake! Speak hyperbolically.

Christian dogma, left all to itself, says that, with regard to his human side, Jesus was precisely as we are, except without sin. Sin is the only distinction between the human 100 percent of Jesus and the human 100 percent of all the rest of us.

Accuracy and authorship of the gospels?

Different people wrote the gospels. Of course they have different names—Matthew, Mark, Luke, and John—but the names don't necessarily indicate the authors. They were all written anonymously. They were not given names until the second half of the second century, when between the years 150 and 180 they suddenly picked up names.

Were the names that the Church gave them between 150 and 180, the correct ones? Do they actually reflect their authorship? Nobody knows.

Jesus died around 30 A.D., and the gospels were probably written between the years 70 A.D. and 90 A.D., about 35 to 40 years after his execution. Are they accurate? Well, they accurately reflect what the author wanted you to read. What does that mean?

First of all, the authors had sources. They had stories that had been circulated about Jesus and sayings of Jesus that had been previously collected and gathered, edited, and polished.

Second, they had the needs of their own churches and communities to consider.

Then they combined their sources with the needs of their communities and churches. That's how the gospels were written. They are not the lives of Jesus in the sense of a modern biography. That is, they are definitely written with the then-present needs in mind and they were written on the basis of sketchy sources.

For example, we do not know the actual occasion of most of the events in the gospels. Why do I say we don't know the occasions? Because they change in each gospel. In Mark, a saying has one location or setting, while in Matthew the same saying is in a different setting. And if Matthew, Mark, and Luke changed these things among themselves, we must assume that the Christian tradition had been doing that long before they wrote them. For example, everyone believes that Jesus said, "Love your enemies."

Now, what was the circumstance in which he said it? The historical answer is that we do not know. Therefore, we do not know if this is an admonition for all of Israel to "Love the Romans" or an admonition to love the local moneylender or an admonition to love your neighbor with whom you had been quarreling over the fence.

Now, from the point of view of a sermon it doesn't matter, because the preacher of the sermon and the author of the gospels apply that saying as present circumstances require. So it is a marvelous saying because it will float; it can go from this setting to that setting to that setting. That's the way it will happen in modern sermons and that's the way it happened in first-century sermons. But we don't know what occasion in Jesus' own life triggered it. For a sermon that isn't important, but if you are a historian and you say, "I want to reconstruct the life and teaching of Jesus. In which circumstance did he do this?" The answer is, we usually don't know.

The only time we can become really certain of circumstances is when we reach the last chapters of the gospels, his final week in Jerusalem, where suddenly, we now have a coherent story. *They did this in the morning, this in the afternoon, and this in the evening. They slept here, they got up, they went there.* You just don't have that kind of detail in the gospels until you get to the last week.

Even if we knew that Jesus said every single saying in the gospels and that they are 100 percent accurate—we still don't know the individual circumstances that sparked each statement. We still wouldn't know precisely what he was up to and what he meant.

Just look at the evidence. It is simply the fact that a saying or a deed in one gospel will appear in a different location in another.

For example, both Matthew and Luke place Jesus' birth during Herod's reign. Herod died in 4 B.C.

But Luke also uses the census of Cyrenius in his birth story and that was in 6 A.D., which was ten years after Herod died. Is there any chance that we are wrong about when Herod died and when Cyrenius was governor of Syria? No. There is just far too much evidence, overwhelming, from all kinds of sources about those dates. So, what do you have?

Was Luke or Matthew a liar? No, they're not liars.

Luke, or the person who wrote Luke and Acts, knew a lot of things about Asia Minor and was almost certainly from Asia Minor. But he didn't know much about Galilee or Palestine. He wasn't quite sure where Sumeria was, vis-à-vis Galilee and so on. He lived in Asia Minor and was writing his books sometime after 70, probably sometime after 80. Now, in the '60s there had been great destruction because of an enormous war, the first great Jewish revolt against Rome, in Palestine.

This culminated with the temple's destruction in 70 A.D.; all the records were destroyed. Galilee had been ravaged. People had died and survivors had been sold into slavery. So here we have Luke in Asia Minor, and number one, he doesn't have maps.

Number two, there is no newspaper archive. Number three, there are no encyclopedias. Number four, if he went to Palestine, he couldn't find anyone who knew anything about this. Number five, because of the war, whatever records there may have been about Jesus, his father, his family, mortgages that his father took out, the marriage certificate of his father and mother, etc., all that stuff was lost.

What was Luke supposed to do? Was he to write a story and say, "I don't know anything about these early years"? Or was he going to try to tell a story about what he knew and then fill in the rest? The answer is, of course, he would rather tell a good story. This is not dishonest, he just wanted to give some specific events and add color to it. I think his background color is really quite good.

For instance, when Luke describes Jesus taken to the temple and the prophetess Anna worshiping there, he writes: ". . . she was eighty-four. She never left the temple but worshiped night and day, fasting and praying."[1] That is just marvelous stuff.

> *Why did they choose these four gospels and not the other gospels like Thomas or Peter?*

The canonizing process, the process of deciding which books were sacred to Christians (in addition to the Hebrew Bible in its Greek translation, which was already considered sacred), took hundreds of years.

The first time anyone offered a list of the twenty-seven books in our New Testament as being *the* list that should be read in church was the Festival Letter in 327 A.D.—three hundred years after Jesus died.

Finally, church councils decided on our list of twenty-seven books late in the fourth, early in the fifth century. In Syria, Eastern Christianity struggled with this debate into the sixth century and then in the sixteenth century Martin Luther did a little revision.

The books chosen proved useful to the churches, while those not chosen didn't prove useful enough to churches and antagonized some of the major parties in the first few Christian centuries.

One example of this antagonism was the gospel attributed to Thomas, which is known as about a third-century manuscript and is a sort-of Gnostic gospel. The Gospel of Thomas was more acceptable in Alexandria (which was the second main church of early Christianity), than it was in Rome (the first main church of Christianity) or Antioch, Syria (the third main church of Christianity), so it didn't make it into our modern Bible.

The choosing of the books that got into the canon was a political struggle. The Gospel of the Egyptians, of which we only have small fragments, was probably very popular in Egypt, but Egypt didn't carry the day. Alexandria was against the Book of Revelation, and Rome was against the Book of Hebrews. Rome pointed out that Paul had not written it and Alexandria pointed out that John, by whom they meant the same John who wrote the gospel, had not written Revelation. Many of the arguments in favor of these

---

1. Luke 2:37, NIV.

observations were grammatical and linguistic, just like those scholars of today. In the end, both were accepted as scripture. Each side had to give up a little bit in order to get one of its favorite books in.

The gospels chosen couldn't be proved not to be by disciples and they couldn't be proved to be by disciples, but they were attributed to disciples or to the disciples of disciples. For example, Luke's writings got into the canon because first of all, Luke was thought to be a disciple of Paul and no one could disapprove that. Second, the churches found Luke's gospels useful and they didn't offend one of the major groups in Christianity too much. In the case of the gospels, this kind of bargaining ended up with our four Gospels of Matthew, Mark, Luke, and John—while others were left out, though perhaps over protests.

Was it necessary to create Christianity or could Jesus' teaching be accommodated within Judaism?

Jesus' teaching, as we have it in Matthew, Mark, and Luke, could have been accommodated within Judaism. These gospels depict him as a striking, compelling teacher and healer, but most of the material that they contain could be ascribed to a prophet: Elijah and Elisha, for example, were both miracle-working prophets. Since about 1850, scholars have relied on the first three gospels in reconstructing the life and teaching of Jesus, and so most would join me in saying that the teaching of the historical Jesus could have been accommodated within Judaism.

The separation between the two faiths came as the result of processes that went on over a substantial period of time. There was never a moment when all the followers of Jesus—the "Christians," as they came to be called—got together and decided that the teachings of their great leader required them not to be Jewish anymore. That result was not achieved in the first generation. Probably by 150 A.D. most people realized that there were now two separate religions, but it was a few more centuries before all followers of Jesus accepted the divorce.

Two factors led to the separation. In the first place, some Christians began to say things about Jesus as Son of God that could not be fitted within Judaism. The title itself was not the problem, as we discuss below.

But to say that Jesus was the incarnation of the eternal divine communication (the *logos*, "Word of God"), as in John 1:1–17, begins to stretch Jewish views and terminology to the breaking point.[2] More generally, the Christian view that God accepted Jesus' death as covering the sins of the entire world gave him an importance that Judaism could not accept. Thus one of the developments that led to the divorce of the Christian movement from Judaism was "Christology," the various theological claims that were made on behalf of Jesus.

The second factor was the success of the Christian mission to Gentiles (non-Jews). There were many Christian missionaries to Gentiles, but the one we know a lot about was Paul. Paul was of the view that the promises that God had made to Israel were being fulfilled in his own day and that Jesus was central to them. One of these promises, often made by Israelite prophets, was that the day would come when Gentiles would turn to worship the God of Israel (for example, Isaiah 2:2–4). The prophets did not say that these Gentiles had to become Jewish, only that they would worship the God of Israel. And so Paul arrived at the view that his Gentile converts needed only to worship the God of Israel and believe in his son, Jesus, in order to share in the blessings of Israel. They did not have to accept circumcision, food laws, sabbath restrictions, and many other parts of the Jewish law. The Gentile converts to the Christian movement accepted that the law in the Hebrew Bible was given by God, but they thought that the prophetic promises to Gentiles meant that many of the requirements of the divine law did not apply to them. Christians continue to have this view: God inspired the Old Testament, but they are exempt from many of its laws.

The missionaries to Gentiles were much more successful than the apostles who tried to persuade Jews to believe in Jesus. Gentiles could attain valuable aspects of Judaism (monotheism, a high ethical code, community support for poorer members, and the like) without dramatically altering their life-long habits, and many signed on. Finally, decades later, it was the sheer weight of numbers that made Christianity a largely Gentile religion and that thus led it to break decisively with Judaism.

2. These verses in John are not entirely without precedent in Jewish literature. Philo seems to have thought that Moses was the incarnation of the divine communication (*logos*).

I am a historian, and there isn't any historical way to evaluate whether Jesus was born of a virgin. But I can explain the purpose of the story. In a Greek readership, it puts Jesus in the line of the mighty heroes, and as we know the author of the Gospel of Luke was Greek. It isn't a very Jewish story. This is one of the parts of Matthew and Luke that is not very Jewish and it is perfectly at home in the Greek-speaking world where Christians had begun to win converts.

For example, Alexander the Great (even in his lifetime) was believed to be the son of Zeus. Furthermore, all the Macedonians regarded themselves as Sons of God, and that the progenitor of the race had actually been a god. In one story the Greeks claimed that Zeus assumed the form of the swan in order to have intercourse with Leda, a human woman. I don't know why a swan would be especially enticing but still, that's the point of the story. So, throughout Greek mythology the Greek gods are bounding around, having intercourse with humans and begetting these kinds of superduper offspring—it's really a Greek idea.

Another reason for the story is that it works as a kind of defense against the accusation in the New Testament that Jesus was illegitimate.[3]

Is Jesus the only Son of God?

In a Jewish context, "son of God" does not mean "more than human." The Hebrew Bible uses the term "sons of God" to refer to Israelites, as in Psalm 82:6, Hosea 11:1, and Exodus 4:22. The singular "son of God" is somewhat less common, but it was sometimes used of an individual, such as a king of one of the Patriarchs. The king is addressed as "son of God" in Psalm 2:7. In a first-century Jewish work, Joseph is called "son of God," "first-born Son of God," and even more dramatically "the sun from heaven," that is, the incarnation of light.[4] Whereas in Greece, "son of God" was used

3. In the Gospel of Mark Jesus is called "the son of Mary." An accusation that in ancient times meant Jesus had no father and was thus illegitimate. In the Gospel of John Jesus' illegitimacy was questioned again when his accusers said, "We were not born of fornication," while implying that Jesus was.
4. *Joseph and Aseneth* 6:2–5; 21:4, trs. & ed. C. Burchard in James Charlesworth, ed., *The Old Testament Pseudepigraph* II (New York: Doubleday, 1985), pp. 177–247.

literally and meant "descended from a union of a god and a human, but nevertheless fully mortal," in Judaism the phrase was used metaphorically. In Jewish custom "son of God" referring to a group meant "people of God," while it meant "specially favored by God" when it applied to an individual. In the New Testament the Greek usage is found in the birth narratives of Matthew and Luke, where it appears that God supplied special spermatazoa to impregnate Mary. In most passages, however, the title seems to be Jewish, that is, metaphorical, as it is in Rom. 1:4 ("declared to be Son of God in power"). Whatever the meaning, however, Jesus is depicted as living a fully human life: he eats, sweats, suffers, and dies.

Like everything else, when it is studied closely the question "was Jesus the Son of God?" becomes complicated: what does one mean by the term? Christianity insists on the title, but it has not always defined the title in the same way. Speaking entirely personally, I have considerable difficulty with Jesus as Son of God in the Greek sense: a hybrid offspring produced by joining divine and human reproductive elements. The Jewish usage presents me with no problem: Jesus was "Son of God," meaning that he was very specially favored by God.

Perhaps it is worth pointing out that Christian dogma, as decided in the fourth and fifth centuries, rejected the Greek view (a God-human hybrid) and insisted on a metaphysically double person: Jesus had two complete essences: he was entirely divine and entirely human. There is nothing about two essences in the Bible, and Greek metaphysics here (as often) led to a basically un-Biblical formulation. This is, however, orthodox Christian dogma.

There is nothing in the first three gospels that approaches fifth-century Greek metaphysics, but John requires separate discussion. This is where we find the statement that Jesus is the "only Son" of God (John 3:16) and where Jesus says such things as "the Father and I are one" (10:30) and "before Abraham was, I am" (8:58). To later ears, this seems to be the same as fifth-century Christian dogma: he was of the same essence as the Father. But John's view was different from that. Being *one with* the Father (8:30), it turns out, meant being "in" the Father (8:38). This union was based on love: the Father loves the Son and the Son loves the Father (10:17; 14:31; 15:9). On the other hand, the Jesus of John is also *one with* the disciples: he and they are "in" each other (15:4–5) and they love each other (14:21).

The consequence is that, in John, Jesus is the intermediary who brings the disciples and God together: disciples and God are united by love (14:23) and are "in" one another. Just as God is "in" Jesus and Jesus is "in" God, the disciples are "in" Jesus, and Jesus is "in" them (14:20). This relationship, which ultimately unites God and believers via Jesus, is expressed primarily by the verbs "to love" and "to be in," and it does not naturally lead to the conclusion that Jesus had two essences, much less that Jesus and God were *identical*, which is what many believe about the message of John. On the contrary, the Jesus of John states that the Father is greater than he (14:28) and that he has no authority on his own (5:30–31; 12:49). Although some sentences in John strain the Father-Son metaphor, the metaphor still dominates the gospel: the Father sends the Son, the Son obeys the Father. Being "Son of God" in John is not identity with God, but a relationship of obedient love and mutual indwelling. The relationship is that of a mystical union rather than metaphysical identity.

Thus John presents a complicated view of Jesus as Son of God. He is not Son of God in the Greek sense: there is no birth narrative that describes God as Jesus' sire. Jesus is "one" with God by being "in" him, and the primary definition of "being in" is loving with complete and utter devotion and obeying perfectly. The disciples should have the same relationship with Jesus, which means that they too, through Jesus, are joined with God in a relationship based on love and obedience. Claims of Jesus' pre-existence (before Abraham was, I am) may push John beyond the metaphorical meaning of "Son," but they still do not add up to metaphysical identity with God.

I do not intend by this digression on the complexity of the Gospel of John to say that the historical Jesus actually made all the statements in that gospel. I join the vast majority of historical scholars in thinking that John presents theological meditations on themes and is not a collection of the sayings of the historical Jesus. As sayings, the material in John cannot be reconciled with that in Matthew, Mark and Luke. In John, Jesus speaks in long metaphorical monologues, the only topics being his relationship with God and with the disciples; he almost never speaks about the kingdom of God. In the synoptic gospels (Matthew, Mark and Luke) Jesus speaks in brief parables and aphorisms, not long monologues, and the topic is the kingdom of God, not himself. He declines to say who he is, but rather asks who people say he is. Even the miracle stories are different. The "signature" miracle in the synoptics is the exorcism of demons; there are no exorcisms in John.

You have asked a difficult question, whether or not Jesus was the Son of God. The answer has to be complicated. In the birth narratives of Matthew and Luke, Jesus appears as Son in the Greek sense, a hybrid of God and human. Mostly in the New Testament he is Son in ways that could be metaphorical, meaning a person especially close to God. John is the most difficult: Jesus is "Son" in the sense of being united in love with the Father, though statements of pre-existence go beyond the metaphorical meaning. We don't know what John would have made of the later creeds. He would probably have insisted that a union based on verbs is better than use of the noun "essence" (of the same essence as the Father). Most difficult of all is the question of what the historical Jesus thought of himself. He clearly thought that he knew the plan of God and that he was authorized to be God's final messenger. We do not know whether or not he went beyond this.

Why didn't all Jews accept
Jesus as the Messiah?

All Jews didn't accept Jesus as Messiah for two reasons.

First of all, he did not fulfill any Messianic expectations, which is a complicated response because there was no one single Messianic expectation in Judaism. The notion that everyone in Judaism was sitting around waiting for a son of David to rise up and be a great warrior like David is not true. Most people didn't expect a Messiah at all and those who did thought he would be more of a teacher than a king. But whether they wanted the Messiah to be a military leader or simply a sage teacher who would teach people how to live in the world—that Messiah, that kingdom didn't come. This was the great nonconfirmation of Jesus' career. It is a fact that the kingdom for which he prayed "thy kingdom come, thy will be done" did not arrive and so the normal Jewish viewer could not regard him as someone who brought in the kingdom of God, whether military or not military.

The other thing is that while he might have been regarded by many

Jews as a great prophet and teacher, he got bad press in the Jewish world because his movement quickly became gentile and gentiles did not observe many of the requirements of the law of Moses. Jews always suspected the gentile Christians of being a little too close to idolatry and once they started calling Jesus the Son of God and the second person of the Trinity, the Jews could say, "You guys are not monotheists at all, we worship only one God and you've got two!" And then Christianity said a few centuries later, "We've got three! Father, Son, and Holy Spirit!"

Was Jesus married or in an intimate relationship?

Marriage was regarded as a religious duty. Genesis says, "Be fruitful and multiply," and Jews were expected to fulfill that command. But there were people who took vows of chastity as well as others who were celibate of their own volition. Like Paul, who wrote in 1 Corinthians 7:1 "It is better for a man not ever to touch a woman, however, if you think you have to, it is better to marry. I wish you were as I am." The Qumranians also seem to have been celibate. Philo writes about a group that is celibate, so celibacy was known and Jesus could have been one of them.

Jesus' mission?

To prepare people for the kingdom of God that he thought was on its way. Did Jesus think the end of the world was coming? No, not immediately. We don't know if he ever thought about the end of the world one way or the other.

Paul did; he thought that first Jesus would return and reign until all of his enemies were destroyed, and then he would turn the kingdom over to God. Now that sounds like a two-stage resolution of history: One, Christ reigns and straightens the world out; two he defeats death itself and turns the kingdom over to God. Now, we don't know that Jesus had this kind of two-stage end definitely in mind. The only evidence we have of his thinking on this is stage one, that the kingdom of God would come, but he does not describe this specifically, and thank goodness he didn't! Because later, when Christians during the Crusades decide they would do it for him, you are really embarrassed.

The trouble is, so often when people try to imagine things that have never been seen or occurred they are limited to analogies. When people wanted to imagine brand-new beasts in the Bible, for example, what did they do? Well they said, "It will have the tail like a bull, shoulders like an ox, a head like a lion, a body like a horse, and a single horn in its head like a narwhal."

That's human imagination—they use what they already have experienced, very few people can imagine something that has no analogy with what they know. When you get people imagining what the kingdom of God is like—they are just hopeless.

When Jesus described the kingdom of God he used general terms. People would love one another, the twelve tribes of Israel would be reassembled, foreign arms would no longer oppress the people of Israel, he and his followers would be in charge, and the world would be run according to the principles of the Sermon on the Mount.

Will the kingdom of God come about by the slow transformation of humanity, one by one? Jesus thought God would intervene soon. When people asked, should we help him by swinging our swords and cutting off a few Roman heads? Jesus said no: "If you pick up a sword, you will perish by the sword, don't do that. Leave this to God." He is on the leave-it-to-God scale of Jewish expectation which ran from "if we fight the war, God will help a little" to "wait."

His point was if God wants to improve the world, he will do it—but don't do anything—start living now, as you will live in the kingdom of Heaven.

What spiritual practices or
techniques did Jesus teach?

We don't know of any, except his admonition to pray. It would be surprising if he had trained his disciples in meditation because they surely would have passed it on and we don't have any record of it.

Very near the end of his life, there is the admonition to have the supper. "Do this in remembrance of me." I think he actually said this and he meant his disciples to actually follow it and there is still a token supper in most branches of Christianity.

In Jesus' time the typical spiritual technique taught in Judaism was to recall the commandments twice a day in some kind of summary form and to pray. A few especially pious people may have prayed three times a day.

Who killed Jesus and why?

Pilate, who was the Roman Prefect in Judea, ordered Jesus to be executed. If you were of nobility, you would be beheaded, the cleanest, simplest execution. People like Jesus were crucified.

Pilate normally lived in Caesarea in Herod's former palace, but brought his troops to Jerusalem for the festival because the city of Jerusalem went from around thirty thousand to around three hundred thousand during the festivals, and tent cities sprang up outside the city. Latrines were dug and so on, as pilgrims came to observe the three pilgrimage festivals.

The biggest of the three festivals was Passover and it was at that time that Jesus was executed. Why did Pilate do this? Because he needed to control Palestine. By controlling Palestine Rome controlled trade. Rome didn't get money out of Palestine, it probably spent more than it got on maintaining law and order, but it was absolutely vital to the Empire because it lay between Asia Minor and Egypt.

What did Rome want? Stability.

Did it want the citizens to become Roman? No. I mean you could hardly get a decent Roman to move there to live—the climate was inhospitable, the people difficult, and so on. I mean, they were not trying to Romanize the place, there were no Roman schools, Roman laws, Roman religion, Roman temples, and so on. No, no, no, they just wanted peace on the border. They would strike with absolute efficiency at the first sign of trouble and they were very good at it.

Whenever a prophet arose—if he gained a following—he was dangerous. It didn't matter what he said; a following got you killed. He would not live very long unless he was extremely quiet and disbanded his following overnight. So Jesus' following was Rome's concern.

How did Rome conduct their policy? There wasn't any Roman in

Jerusalem directly governing. Government was in the hands of the High Priest. The High Priest had governed the Palestinian Jews since the return from exile in the sixth century B.C. except for the time originally when Herod became king. When the Herodian line failed to secure Palestine Augustus decided to take Judea over, not Galilee but just Judea (the area around Jerusalem). He sent a minor official to govern it but he put the day-to-day running of the place into the hands of the High Priest.

Who governed Jerusalem? It was the High Priest and the temple guards. They took care of whatever needed to be taken care of, except that in the kind of province that Judea was, *the only one who* had the sole power to execute was the Prefect. He could execute even a Roman military officer without a Roman trial. It was martial law.

Jews responsible for Jesus' death?

The Jewish people were not responsible at the time and are not responsible now.

The crowds are depicted as playing really diverse roles in all of this. First, they hail Jesus on his way into Jerusalem on Palm Sunday and then they stand outside Pilate's courtyard yelling, "Kill him, kill him."

But a crowd does not represent the collective and intentional will of a nation. All you are talking about, at best, is a mob, and one doesn't accuse a whole nation because of what a mob may have yelled.

In any case, it wasn't what the mob yelled that got Jesus killed, it was Caiaphas's recommendation to Pilate. And his concern was upheaval in Jerusalem—*Kill this man now*, he's not going home peacefully. Do I believe the idea of Pilate worrying and fretting about Jesus' death and then washing his hands?

No. In fact, the historian Philo wrote that Pilate was finally dismissed because he executed and punished people without reason! Pilate wouldn't have hesitated. The reason that story is in the gospel is because the Christians wanted to shift blame from Rome to the Jews.

At the time the gospel was written, the Christian church was trying to make its way in a Roman world. It didn't want Rome to see Jesus as being a revolutionary or a troublemaker and it didn't want its members to feel hostile toward Rome.

Jesus probably helped his father with his carpentry, went to school, and learned to read the Hebrew Bible.

Did Jesus learn things?

I'm a historian and study human beings. If he wasn't a human being, I can't deal with him. Besides that, the tenets of Christianity require me to think he was 100 percent human, just as human as we are, except that he was without sin. This would seem to rule out foreknowledge of the world, complete knowledge of all science and medicine, and so on—so, yes, he had to learn things.

Jesus' opinion of Christianity today?

I would suppose he would have had mixed reactions. Christianity does not have an entirely glorious history. But he would have approved of Christianity's main tenets, as I am sure he approved of the main tenets of the Judaism of his day. Because Jesus got his two great commandments from Judaism—from the Hebrew Bible. "Love your neighbor as yourself" is from Leviticus 19:18 and "Love the Lord your God with all your heart and with all your soul and with all your strength" is from Deuteronomy 6:5.

If you had asked Jesus "What do you think of the Judaism of your day?" he would probably have said, "I don't like everything, but I like the main principles of love of God and love of humanity."

What would Jesus say about Christianity today? Well, he probably wouldn't like that one set of his followers is killing a bunch of other people in the Balkans right now. He'd regret the Crusades and the Holocaust and pogroms against Jews in Europe.

He would see people go to church and pray to his Father and use his name in their prayers, but his actual concern would be about what is in their hearts and the way they live when they go home. He would have the same problems with modern Christianity that he would have had with ancient Judaism; namely that it has great principles but not very many people actually live up to them. There is an awful lot of hypocrisy in the world.

Which resurrection? *In the best manuscripts of Mark, which is the oldest gospel, there is no resurrection story.* In the other sources, how do you reconcile irreconcilable locations and lists? And what does it mean to say you "believe" it?

Most Christians think that what Christians have to believe is that the corpse of Jesus stood up and walked around and that it was still obviously Jesus. Now there are, in fact, six resurrection traditions in the New Testament, Matthew, Mark, Luke, John, Acts, and 1 Corinthians. What is noteworthy about these is that they disagree with one another. They don't agree on who saw him. They have different lists. Peter is in all of them. But there are women in Paul, and you have James (Jesus' brother) in Paul—but you don't have James in the gospels. Look at the ends of each of the gospels and 1 Corinthians. Write down the list of appearances and compare the list and you'll see the discrepancies for yourself. Anyone can do this.

Where did Jesus appear? He doesn't appear in Mark.

Matthew is quite clear and straightforward: "Tell them I will meet them in Galilee." And then in the appearance story, Matthew 28, that is actually what he does. The disciples hightail it to Galilee, and Jesus appears near the tomb and meets all the disciples.

In Luke, none of them ever leave Jerusalem. They most definitely do not go to Galilee. They are in Jerusalem, nearby in Bethlehem, and on the road to Emmaus and so on.

What is even more striking than the discrepancies in the lists of names and locations of the appearances, is the description of the person who appears.

In Matthew, you would think there wasn't any problem, he is recognized as Jesus.

In Luke, there is a substantial problem. He walks with two of his followers on the road to Emmaus, talks to them all afternoon, sits down with them to eat, and they don't know who he is until he breaks bread, at which time he disappears. Then he appears a few miles away, in Jerusalem with his other disciples. It isn't so clear as to what it is that these two disciples saw. They were with a man they knew, all afternoon, and they didn't know him.

Paul's Corinthian converts don't believe the resurrection is of flesh, skin, and bone. They believe in the immortal soul, because they are Greeks. Greeks generally believe that every human has an immortal soul that will live on—in either a good place or bad place.

So Paul has come to this fairly Greek community in Corinth and he is telling them Jesus was raised and you will be raised, and they say to him, "That's not true, all you have to do is go to the graveyard and dig around and you will find that the bodies have decayed." Paul is faced with this and meets them a large part of the way by saying, "It is a spiritual body."

In Christianity, the resurrection of Jesus is a foundational event. No story of resurrection plays the role in Judaism that the story of Jesus' resurrection played in Christianity. Historically, some Jews believed in resurrection. In Jewish resurrection, the person's body dies and then lives again, while the Greek idea is that the body dies and the soul floats off to heaven or to Hades. Christians combined the Jewish and Greek beliefs: The body dies, the soul departs and goes to be with God. Then on the last day, the bodies will be raised and reunited with the souls.

Second Coming?

Jesus depicted the Son of Man as coming in the future. He said to Caiaphas: "In the future you will see the Son of Man sitting at the right hand of the Mighty One and coming on the clouds of heaven."[5]

What does he mean by Son of Man? I don't have a clue. Is it composite Israel? Is it himself? Because in other contexts, Jesus refers to himself as "Son of Man," such as when he says "Foxes have holes and birds in the air have nests and the son of man has nowhere to lay his head."

Does it mean that whenever he says "Son of Man is coming on clouds" he means I will be that Son of Man? Anyone can use the same word in two different meanings and in different contexts. We don't know for sure what Jesus means, but we know what the early Christians thought. Because Paul, in 1 Thessalonians 4 takes it to mean that Jesus will return (just as in Matthew) except he has the Lord coming instead of the "Son of Man."

5. Caiaphas (Matthew 26:64, NIV).

Paul thought the Second Coming would take place in his own lifetime. "Some have died but we who are left, we will be snatched up together with them to greet the Lord in the air and so we will be with him always." Paul thinks the world will be changed soon and that the Lord, when he comes, will reign until he destroys all enemies including death. He is urging people to hang on and wait for this event. One of his main pieces of behavioral advice is, "Don't change." If you are circumcised, don't disguise it, if you are uncircumcised, don't be circumcised. If you are married, stay married. If you are single, stay single; if you are a slave, stay a slave—don't change.

Why not change? Because Paul believes there is no time. Paul is expecting that he and most of his converts will still be alive. Well, Paul was wrong on the timing of the Second Coming, so if he is wrong on the timing, is he wrong on the idea of whether or not the Lord will come? We are now into speculative theology. Right? This is like debating the doctrine of the Trinity. Is God really three persons in one substance? And the answer is—I'm a historian, I can't tell. I can only tell you what Paul thought.

✠ 44
FRIDAY EVENING AT THE WALL

JERUSALEM

On Friday evening I went to the Wall for the last time, and I heard the noise from a block away. When I arrived, there was a large crowd near the base of the wall, and it was all lit up. While the majority of people were solemn, two groups of men danced and sang. Since they sang in another language, I couldn't understand the words—but it looked like fun—and more than fun, it felt like a *celebration*.

On the seventh day, God rested after six days of creation. And on that day, we also rest—*we rest in God's love*. So Friday night at the wall was a time of celebration and great joy. Friday is the end of God's creative love and the time to celebrate that creation. Thus they sang and danced.

One of the two groups of men who danced were dressed in black. They looked like Orthodox Jews, and they shouted loudly as they danced. The other group of men had their arms around each other as they danced in a circle and sang. They looked to be having the most fun, and their ring leader was a rabbi dressed in a ridiculous-looking gold robe and yarmulke.

At first I just watched and thought about what they were doing until my mind sucked all the life from my body in an effort to understand them. The more I thought, the stiffer my body got.

"Do you think they'd mind if I joined them?" I asked my friend Atum, one of the tour guides.

"Do they look like they'd care?" Atum replied. So I took a deep breath and joined the circle. While I sang the words to Hebrew songs I couldn't understand, I looked up at the Western Wall, and saw that the floodlights had illuminated the thousands of tiny prayers tucked away in the cracks and crevices.

✦ 45
THE FLIGHT HOME

FROM TEL AVIV TO MADISON, WISCONSIN

While I waited to get on the plane, I spotted a rabbi who allowed a young boy to board before him. He seemed kind, and later when I saw him on the plane, I asked him a few questions about Judaism and Jesus.

"The problem with some Christians," the rabbi said, "is that they made an idol of Jesus."

"I agree that happens sometimes," I said. "But what about the Torah—can't that be an idol also?"

"The Torah's different," he said. "The Torah is God's Word."

Of course I didn't reply because you can't have a conversation with a man who thinks that only "other" religions are idol worshipers.

"I *used to* do drugs," the young man who sat next to me on the plane home said. He was Jewish and studying to be a rabbi. "Then I rediscovered Judaism and the Torah."

He looked happy, intense, focused—the way people do when they first find their path and fall in love. I too, have fallen in love with God—only it is a faceless God, and so I have a tendency to want others to understand that God is a faceless God. That he only wears faces so that human beings can see him, and these faces are different religions, and that religious beauty is in the eyes of the beholder. But too often, we end up killing each other while arguing about whose beloved is the most beautiful.

"It sounds like you're still searching," the young man said after I told him about my Jesus book.

He didn't get it. He just didn't get it, and I must admit that it bugged me whenever someone said, "You're searching," because what they usually mean is you're lost. And the truth is I'm exploring not searching, and I'm exploring because I'm found. I'm exploring God because *God is explorable.* Can you tell me why I can see God in Judaism, Christianity, Buddhism, Hinduism, while some people see God only in their own religion?

"If you're in love," I tell the young man, "you keep trying to understand your beloved in deeper and deeper ways—and that's why I explore God."

He nodded, but I still think he thought I was an older man without a religion and without a God.

"If I were to give you advice," he said, "it's not to listen to others—do like you were going to do. Go to the desert and leave the middleman out. Just you and God."

As I tried to fall asleep on the plane—in that place between sleep and wakefulness—a sequence of scripture verses came together.

"God is Love."[1]

"The Father and I are One."[2]

Therefore, *Jesus is Love.*

So when Jesus said, "I am the Way and the Truth and the Life—no one gets to the Father but through me." He was saying, *"—no one gets to the Father but through love."* Because *Jesus is Love.*

Just as it all came together, something in my heart relaxed, and I fell into a deep sleep.

1. 1 John 4.
2. John 10:30.

✠ 46
MORT'S HELP

This was it. I was dead in the water. For the umpteenth time, I had come to the end of myself and my financial resources. But this time was different because the weight of my endeavor and the weight of my bills were too much and I didn't know what to do. I had maxed out three or four credit cards, along with $25,000 in other high-interest loans. My publisher had offered an advance, but I couldn't accept it since it wouldn't cover the debts I had already incurred or allow me to finish the book. I was done, and yet somehow I had to go on.

For a few days, I just wallowed in my inability to continue and then the doubt came, like a black cloud from over the horizon. It settled above me and cut me off from any connection I felt to the heavens. Why is it that human beings associate heaven with something above them? Particularly when Jesus said, "the kingdom of Heaven is within"? But the gospels also said "As soon as Jesus was baptized, he went up out of the water. At that moment *heaven was opened,* and he saw the Spirit of God descending like a dove and lighting on him. And *a voice from heaven said,* 'This is my Son, whom I love; with him I am well pleased.' "[1]

And that's it, isn't it? We all want to know, and not just know—but *feel* that God loves us. We especially want to feel God's love at times when we feel despair and pain. But for whatever reason, it seems that human beings aren't always able to feel God's love. What do we do then?

Whenever I feel disconnected from the Spirit, especially the Spirit of inspiration and hope, I look for a positive thought that supports my will to go on. And even if I don't feel the love—I try to *remember* a thought that tells me that I'm loved and hold on to that as I also tell myself to "keep going."

But how could I keep going? I had applied for several grants and been

---

1. Matthew 3:16–17, NIV.

denied. I had already borrowed from friends and relatives, so those avenues were spent.

But I did know two wealthy people. One was a woman named Pat and the other was a man named Mort.

Pat had inherited millions after her husband died. She was open-minded, kind of "New Age," and sort of a friend. Mort was one of the wealthiest businessmen in Madison, Wisconsin, and although we had played golf together twice, and I liked him, he was a long shot because I really didn't know him that well. His circle of friends were mainly bankers, developers, and assorted businessmen who played golf at country clubs while I lived on the east side of town in a mobile home park. Besides, I had heard that he had very conservative Christian beliefs, and while my Jesus book would not intentionally offend or oppose conservative or liberal Christian views, I did not want to be put in a position where I had to deny the truth of what I found just to appease any point of view. Therefore, I figured Pat was probably a better bet than Mort, and she was probably the one who would help.

I contacted her and, after a few days, she sent me an e-mail that said, "Sorry, but I can't help you," and the shock was like someone had thrown cold water in my face. Mort was the only option left, and it seemed like such a long shot that I almost didn't bother. But then I called him on the phone the next day and explained my book.

"Make an appointment with my assistant," he said, "and we'll talk."

I had actually contacted him a few years before, because one of his businesses sold computers and I thought maybe I could get a deal on one—but it didn't work out. Why would now be any different?

When our meeting came, I prayed beforehand. It took everything I had to ask Mort for a grant: I needed the guidance of Spirit, together with the vision of an artist and, of course, the prudence of a businessman. Most of all, I couldn't be stuck in any of the three.

At our meeting, I handed him an estimate of how much money I needed and for what. Then I gave him the proposal, and what I had written so far. Finally I said, "If you help with this book, it won't be because you're thinking with your head, but because doing so speaks to your heart. God may tell you to help me, and God may tell you not to help me."

"Contact me in a week," he said, "and we'll see."

A week later, I stepped out of the elevator on the third floor of Mort's office building. Moments later, I was in his office, where he sat behind a big desk in a high-backed leather chair. He stared at me for a moment and then leaned back in his chair and looked up at the ceiling.

"I'm inclined to do it," he said, without looking at me.

My eyes misted up, and I barely heard what he said next.

"I'll give you three thousand a month through next year," he said, squinting up at the ceiling, as though reading the words from some heavenly cue card.

"And that twenty thousand-dollar loan you have on the motor home at 19.9 percent," he added, "I called my banker and he'll refinance it for you. In return, maybe you can give me a hundred copies of your present book, and a few hundred copies of the new book when it comes out. I can give them out to friends. Maybe put me in the acknowledgments, so I can feel I was a part of it? A little personal pride?"

Then Mort leaned forward in his chair and looked at me.

"Maybe we can learn from each other," he said warmly. "You can do the book however you want. Just send me a letter once a month and let me know how you're coming. I want to feel a part of it.

"I know you're not the greatest money manager," he added, "so maybe I can even help you with that."

When I left Mort's office, I felt like crying. Not so much because I got the money I needed—it was more than that, Mort had treated me with respect. The thoughtfulness and trust he displayed when he said, "You can do the book however you want," just amazed me. Most of all, *he believed in me,* and through his belief, *I felt God hadn't forgotten me.*

✣ 47
NEIL DOUGLAS-KLOTZ

MADISON, WISCONSIN

"For example," Neil Douglas-Klotz said, "when Jesus said to Nicode-mus, 'You have to be born again,' the Aramaic says you have to be born not *'again,'* but born *'from the first beginning.'* That first beginning is the 'I Am' and when you touch this 'I Am' place by remembering the Jewish creation story, then all of the different levels of your life light up and are made clear."

My talk with Neil Douglas-Klotz, an Aramaic scholar, illuminated many things. Once again, I was reminded how language and the translation of language change everything—especially the meaning of Jesus' words. Be-cause it cannot be stated too often that when Jesus spoke to his disciples and to crowds of people he most likely spoke Aramaic, and not Latin, Greek, or English. That changes everything. For example, did you know that the word for Spirit and breath are the same word in Aramaic? Thus whenever Jesus said "Holy Spirit" he also may have meant "Holy Breath." What an immediate difference that knowledge can make, and does make in my life because as I go about my daily business, occasionally I will think of my breath as being Spirit. *I, and each of us, breathe in and out Spirit.* No wonder Jesus spoke so intimately of the Father or Abba—the Spirit of God, to Jesus, was as close and as vital to him as his own breath. This also brings new meaning to Jesus' words when rereading John 20:22: "And with that he *breathed* on them and said, 'Receive the Holy Spirit.' " Or Genesis 2:7: "the LORD God formed the man from the dust of the ground and *breathed* into his nostrils the breath of life, and the man became a living being."

"The first spiritual technique Jesus taught," Dr. Neil Douglas-Klotz said, "was remembering the Jewish creation story. Jesus taught that you should go back and relive the Jewish creation story in your meditation. That's what it means to be 'born again'—born from that beginning place. You remember the whole creation story, and go through that unknowing, that chaos, that darkness . . . then you come into the light, that is, 'Let there be light.' "

Which sparked in me a remembrance of the major depression I went through many years ago—and I realized that my depression was in some ways an incomplete re-creation story. My previous psychological and spiritual life had died, and I had become depressed, stuck in the "unknowing, that chaos, that darkness . . ." aspect of the creation story. It took me another few years before I completed the rest of the story and got to the part that said, "let there be light."

Dr. Neil Douglas-Klotz is an international scholar of religious studies and psychology specializing in Middle Eastern spirituality and mysticism. He is currently co-chair of the Mysticism Group of the American Academy of Religion. His books include *The Hidden Gospel: Decoding the Spiritual Message of the Aramaic Jesus; Desert Wisdom,* and *Prayers of the Cosmos.* In 1982, he founded the International Network for the Dances of Universal Peace, which is dedicated to helping bring peace through the arts. He currently lives in Edinburgh, Scotland where he co-directs the Edinburgh Institute for Advanced Learning. Information about his retreats and lectures can be found on the Internet at the site of the Abwoon Study Circle, www.abwoon.com.

His work arose out of his own spiritual practice and is partly an attempt to make sense of his unusual upbringing, which he said was "partly Jewish-speaking, but mostly Christian."

Who was/is Jesus?

In the Jewish or Semitic language the word for prophet (*nabi* or *nabiyun*) means the person receives from the Divine and then gives to the people, almost in a shamanic sense. Jesus is an expression of this prophetic impulse, which cannot be separated from the mystic impulse. In Jesus' time, the word for mystic and prophet was the same—a prophet was a mystic and a mystic was a prophet. In modern Western times, we have separate words for prophet and mystic because of our Western language set. In Jesus' time, a prophet was trying to make changes in society while also being a person who retreated at times to go through his own spiritual process in order to reach other states of awareness. You go on a certain vision quest and then (as the Hebrew/Aramaic word *nabi* indicates) you receive from the One, and then you give to the people. The spiritual journey has to be both—not just the mystic sitting alone in his cave or the prophet who is out there among the people trying to change conditions in society. It's got to be balanced and both.

Who wrote the gospels and
how accurate are they?

There are two answers to that question. First, some fundamentalist Christians will tell you God wrote all the gospels and some will even tell you that God was sitting on the shoulder of all the translators, like the King James translators, as they were translating, so even the translation from the Greek into the English is divinely inspired.

The historical Jesus and the postmodern scholars will say the gospels are written by people, and sometimes those people are not even real people. In the case of the gospels, they say, you can't identify a real Matthew or a real Mark or a real Luke or a real John. Those names are used, but they are just collections of different opinions that are enmeshed with politics and culture.

I agree and disagree with both sides. I agree with the fundamentalists that ultimately any sacred scripture or any inspired scripture or any inspired writing is going to come from the human relationship to the cosmos, to the Great Mystery; and if you want you can call that great mystery "God," that's fine with me. I believe the relationship of human beings to their cosmos and the Great Mystery has produced all the sacred literature in all cultures. Thus all divine scriptures, all sacred scriptures, all inspired poetry, is all written by God, and I tend to see God as the Only Being rather than some thought-form or some Supreme Court–like judge who is sitting on a cloud somewhere.

I also agree with the postmodern or historical Jesus folks, because humans are writing these reports down and they are remembering things in different ways. There is no doubt about the fact that things have been added to the gospels at various layers of their writing and editing. There is no doubt that each of the four gospels is influenced by the different opinions of their time. So I agree with the historical Jesus people that they are written with a certain agenda, but I also believe that inspired words and stories are enmeshed in that reportage. In the journalistic reportage, there is some essence of Jesus as a mystic and that is best viewed through his native language, which was Aramaic.

So Jesus definitely spoke Aramaic?

In Jesus' time, Aramaic was the common spoken language of the Middle East. There was some Greek influence by way of Alexander the Great, but Jesus and the majority of his hearers were all speaking Aramaic and understanding things from a Semitic language worldview. Aramaic replaced the Old Hebrew of Abraham and the biblical prophets, which for the most part died out after the Hebrew peoples had gone through captivity in Assyria and Babylonia. This happened between 300 and 500 years before the time of Jesus. By studying Jesus through an Aramaic and Hebrew lens, we can begin to recover some of the mindset of the earliest people to follow Jesus, whether we call them Jewish Christians or the "Jesus movement." For these people, their primary practices—before any written accounts of his life surfaced—were to memorize his words, to repeat them to each other and to act like him—healing the sick and welcoming the outcast.

The oldest physical copies of the gospels are in Greek and that's what you could say prejudices the Western scholarly approach—that the gospels in the Aramaic language are a hundred years newer. But the Aramaic-speaking Christians, of which there are perhaps half a million in the world today, would say that the reason for this is that the Aramaic culture did not keep old relics. That they ritually recopied a manuscript when it was getting frayed or tattered around the edges, and then burnt the old one. European Christianity developed as a relic-based tradition in which you try to keep old things and venerate them.

How do they date manuscripts?

Western scholars look at the handwriting, which is called *paleography*, and where possible they do carbon dating on the manuscript. Paleography can be misleading, because if you are writing down a manuscript you could use an old handwriting form or you could use an old piece of parchment. But the age of a physical document isn't as important as the fact that when Jesus spoke he didn't speak in Greek, Latin, or English—he spoke Aramaic. Therefore, we need to look through the Aramaic language for possible other meanings to what Jesus was saying. It's a question of what scholars call hermeneutics, or interpretation.

Jesus' religion?

The Jewish (or really Hebrew) religion at the time of Jesus, and even before, was not a monolithic, uniform cult; it was a collection of all sorts of different ways and interpretations. The Samaritans were "Jewish," by a broad definition, except they didn't honor the temple in Jerusalem. They honored the One Being, they had a dialect of Hebrew, they honored the dietary laws, and they had many of the same sacred books.

The Essenes, Pharisees, Sadducees, Zealots and others all had different ideas about how to continue and honor the tradition of the Hebrew prophets. As a number of scholars have pointed out, at this stage of history, you can't talk about "Judaism" as a religion, any more than you can talk about "Christianity." Only after the destruction of the Jerusalem temple by the Romans in 70 C.E. and again in the 120s do you begin to see the development of the Christianity and Judaism that we know today. Really as they develop, they begin to define each other.

This also affects the way we see other noncanonical accounts of Jesus' life and teachings. For instance, scholars are currently reevaluating the nature of the Gospel of Thomas, which most estimate to as old as any of the other gospels. At one time Thomas was said to be a Gnostic text and that label by many scholars placed it safely away from the development of early Christianity. But now some scholars have reevaluated this whole point of view. They say that Thomas is not an expression of some Gnostic heresy that split off from idealized, normative Christianity. The Thomas community was just another way to be Christian or Jewish-Christian at that time and it was just as valid as any other way. Christianity as a monolithic idea was still unformed. What we have later—the so-called accepted Christian texts—*is simply the winners writing history with prejudice against the losers.*

Probably the destruction of the temple. This was a major holocaust and it happened twice. The Romans first destroyed the temple in the 70s and then again in the 120s—during two civil wars. There wasn't much left and the whole Hebrew tradition had to reevaluate itself—this led to the rise of the Jewish rabbinic tradition that we know today.

Simultaneously, there was more than one ongoing Jesus movement. The Jewish-Christian and gentile-Christian communities continued from Jesus' time for hundreds of years until basically Constantine intervened and said, "That's enough. If we are going to run an empire based on this we have to have a tradition that makes sense and has rules and where everybody believes the same thing." That's why you have the Nicene Creed and the development of what we know as Western Christianity. But that's four hundred years after the time of Jesus and *that group rewrote history.* They rewrote everything so that now as most of us read the gospels we are always thinking with the creeds in mind: the Apostle's Creed, the Nicene Creed, all of these different things about the Trinity, none of which really appear in the gospels at all.

In Aramaic, what is the meaning of
"Son of Man?" "Son of God?"

When you work with the Aramaic, you start to see a lot of this theology falling away, because none of it makes sense either in the context of the Aramaic language or the Jewishness of Jesus at its time. For instance, there is only one word in Aramaic that means spirit and breath. Thus my breath is part of the Holy Spirit, it is not some thought-form or some person that is sitting up somewhere in heaven that is apart from my breathing life. *It is part of my breathing life.* The Aramaic language uses words for good and evil that really mean ripe and unripe. For instance, when Jesus talks about the good tree bearing good fruit and the evil tree bearing evil fruit, he is talking about something that has to do with ripeness and unripeness; that is, that which is appropriate for its time and for its place. Thus, wherever Jesus uses good or evil in the New Testament, we need to reevaluate the words in the sense of Aramaic language and its meaning of ripeness and unripeness.

To get back to your question about Son of Man and Son of God, to look at this we actually have to look at two different Aramaic expressions: *bar nasha* and *bar alaha*.

First of all, the original Aramaic Christians say, and this includes George Lamsa the famous Aramaic scholar, that when Jesus used the Hebrew-Aramaic term *bar nasha*, he simply meant "human being." To Jesus, it was another way to refer to himself without saying "I," and it may simply be like saying "this person" or "this human being" or "a human being" or "human beings" are like this. This is not a Messianic term, and according to most of the research I've looked at, "son of man" was never used as a Messianic title, or any title at all before the time of Jesus.

The term "son of God"—*bar alaha*—is slightly different. It appears only in the Gospel of John; Jesus never refers to himself in this way in Matthew, Mark, or Luke. You can also make the argument from an Aramaic point of view that *bar alaha* is not a title either, it is an expression of attunement with the divine consciousness. Any human being could become *bar alaha*; that is, one could become a ray or offspring (*bar*) from the Only Being, or Sacred Unity (*Alaha*). Each person has the potential to become a son or daughter of the divine in this sense. Many early Jesus Christians considered the title this way, as the Swiss theologian Hans Kung has pointed out. Jesus was a person who had fulfilled his divine potential as a ray of cosmic unity, and as he said in the Gospel of John, "those who come after me will do the things that I have done, and greater" (John 14:12).

> John's gospel is very different from the first three Gospels. That's where Jesus said, "I am the Way and the Truth and the Life. No one comes to the Father except through me."

The one question is, did Jesus really say "I am the Way and the Truth and the Life. No one comes to the Father except through me" (John 14:6,

NIV)? As an Aramaic scholar, the question I often ask is, *In the Aramaic, is there any wisdom there, a deeper meaning?*

In Aramaic and in Hebrew the name for God first means unity, so everything is included, nothing is excluded from *Alaha* or from *Elohim*.

From this standpoint, there is only one "I Am," only One Being. This is demonstrated in the old Hebrew tradition when the voice from the burning bush tells Moses that its name is "I Am that I Am" (or really "I Am Being what I was and will be Being," Exodus 3:14). My individuality and sense of self, my small "I am," is subsumed in that larger "I Am," which is the divine. When I become conscious of that link between "I am " and "I Am," then I reach the state of spiritual experience of which Jesus speaks. We can see this in the expression he uses in Aramaic, usually translated "I am." In Aramaic *ina-ina* expresses a doubled or intensified "I," a link of personal self to divine self (similar to the "I-I" expressed in the writing of Jewish theologian Martin Buber). When we find our own "I" within the heart of the divine "I," then we touch the place of what I call Simple Presence.

"Way" in Aramaic is *urha* and is related to light, and the illumination of a path in front of us, where to place our next steps. "Truth" is *shrara* and points toward the sense of right direction when we reach a crossroad in our path. "Life" in Aramaic is *hayye,* embodied life energy here and now, not something ineffable or far away. Where the Greek translations have the expression "eternal life," the Aramaic for this is *hayye d'alma,* life energy that renews itself at all levels of existence. The notion of heaven as a reward that one would get later for believing certain concepts would have been entirely unknown to Jesus and his listeners. It is a product of later theology.

So with this expression, Jesus is saying that unity with the Holy One is the way—the path where we place our feet. It is also the truth—the sense of right direction. Finally it is the life—the energy to travel the path. The second part of this saying in John (14:6) is also not exclusive: one does not touch the divine "I Am," except by going deeply into and through one's own. This process often gets ignited, at least in the Middle Eastern traditions, by following in the footsteps of one who has already realized this. In *The Hidden Gospel,* I translated the second part of the passage like this:

> *No one comes into rhythm with*
> *the Breathing Life of all,*

the sound and atmosphere
that created the cosmos,
except through the
breathing, sound and atmosphere
of another embodied "I"
connected to
the ultimate "I Am." (p. 66)

Virgin birth?

Aramaic Christians don't believe in the virgin birth. The Aramaic Christians split off before any of the creeds were written. They decided to opt out before they got involved with the Trinity, and with the virgin birth.

Abraham Rihbany, an early Aramaic Christian, wrote a book called *The Syrian Christ.* He said European Christianity has many different creeds and beliefs, but Aramaic Christianity has only one creed and one belief, and that is what Jesus said—"Love God with all your heart and love your neighbor as yourself." Within this, the virgin birth, the Trinity, and the Second Coming are all relatively unimportant.

Who killed Jesus and why?

The Romans killed Jesus because he was getting too dangerous. The Romans supported Jerusalem at that time by patronizing a certain sect of the Judean cult in order to keep people quiet. Jesus threatened the status quo in a number of different ways, so no matter what his claims may have been he was doomed because he threatened the status quo just by drawing people to him. It was like it was in the old Soviet Union; if you had a large group of people gathering around somebody, that person went to Siberia.

Resurrection?

Resurrection is good! What does it really mean to be resurrected? Early Aramaic Christians repeated Jesus' stories and words. They resurrected him in that way. They tried to heal like him and they invited people to eat with them, which again was a way of resurrecting him. This whole thing about the resurrection could be also seen as an inner experience that one has. If you pray with another person's words and atmosphere especially wholeheartedly, maybe you will have some inner experience of Jesus resurrecting in you.

Messiah?

Jesus never claimed to be the Messiah. The whole notion of the Messiah was unclear to the Jewish people at the time. If you look at the historical accounts, there were different people claiming to be "sons of Moses" or "sons of Abraham" or prophets or leaders and their different agendas usually included kicking the Romans out of Palestine and, therefore, most of them were crucified as Jesus was.

What made Jesus different was that he wasn't simply giving people social dogma, he wasn't just giving them rabble-rousing or revolutionary talk. He was giving them actual wisdom and his presence, including his healing presence, must have been extremely strong, much more than these other folks who were perhaps simply social-political revolutionaries. He was a genuine prophet.

But in Jesus' day, John the Baptist might have been more famous and there is still a cult that follows John the Baptist rather than Jesus in the Middle East, called the Mandaeans.

Second Coming?

That was not a concept that would have been understood by Jesus and his original listeners. Do I believe it is possible to have an experience of Jesus coming and speaking to one? Or of Jesus as acting as one's guide? Or acting as one's higher self in a certain way? Absolutely. That a person can feel a sense of guidance with a direct personal relationship with Yeshua? Absolutely. That's a good Middle Eastern tradition. But that he is going to come again in form or in body? No.

When Jesus said, "The kingdom of heaven is at
hand," was he saying the presence of heaven
is right here rather than it's coming
in an apocalyptic sense?

There are two ways of answering this question: the fundamentalist way and the historical Jesus way. The fundamentalists say, "No, it's apocalyptic, it's the Second Coming, it's going to be off in the future, the end of the world." The historical Jesus people say, "No, he was talking about the social conditions of the time, he was talking about kicking out the Romans." I fall between the two, but more on the historical side. Literally, *malkuta* (kingdom/queendom) could be translated as that in me which says "I can" to life, that is, the vision and empowerment that leads me to change my life and to do something in a new way, an entirely radical way. At the same time, for *malkuta* to be authentic, it has to come from an inner state and be expressed outwardly. When Jesus says, "The kingdom of heaven is within you or among you" the Greek versions have a preposition that can mean either *"within"* or *"among,"* which is a good expression of the Aramaic.

In addition, when you look at Matthew (and the other synoptic gospels), the Aramaic itself says, "the kingdom is *legau men,*" which means "it is from within you moving to outside of you." The kingdom starts deep in the belly, which is what *legau* means in Aramaic, and it unfolds itself outwardly in the way you live your life. Thus Jesus was saying that unless his listeners had a change of heart along with kicking out the Romans, whoever would take over would be just as bad as the Romans. The coming of the kingdom must be both a change of heart and conviction to change the external situation, otherwise it would end up being what we see happening in most political changes in the world—one set of bad politicians replacing another. But, he said, if we have a change of both group and individual consciousness to align with the divine "I Am or this I Can" then there will be a genuine revolution. You will have a wholesale change of heart and a change of culture, a change of society.

In his apocalyptic statement, Jesus warned what would happen if this wholesale change didn't occur—and it did happen. The Romans came in, and completely destroyed the indigenous people (early Christians and Jews) in two civil wars, largely because the people were not united. According to most historical accounts, there was as much violence among the indigenous people, with the different factions against each other, as there was against the Romans. The indigenous people were so divided that they had no hope against the Romans. Since they didn't have this *malkuta* or wholesale change of heart, the old culture was destroyed and everything had to start over again.

What spiritual techniques did Jesus teach?

Jesus taught three techniques: remembering and reliving the Jewish creation story, identifying with our original archetype as *adam,* and emulating Hokhmah (Holy Wisdom) by bringing together all the voices within us.

First, Jesus taught that you should go back and relive the Jewish creation story in your meditation—that's what it means to be "born again." You remember the creation story by going through that unknowing, that chaos, that darkness. In this way, we can reexperience the unity that occurs when we experience the Spirit in us that was before Abraham was—the "I Am." Then we come into the light, as in Genesis 1:3: "Let there be light and there was light." You reexperience some rebirth or connection with *aloha,* with the Divine. This is being born in beginningness (*bereshit*) from light and fire. According to many scholars, this was a Jewish meditation practice at the time of Jesus and maybe for a hundred years before.

Remembering the cosmic "before" could actually be compared to the Buddhist mediation on one's original face. You go back to the "before the before" and you go through the different stages of the Jewish creation story, you feel it, you embody it, you breathe with it, consciousness dawns—"let there be light"—and then you are in the place where Jesus said *"ina-ina"* or "I Am." Then the light is experienced as Simple Presence in all formed worlds. This is the saying that is translated as "I am the light of the world." I would translate this as "Simple Divine Presence illuminates all worlds of form." When you touch this "I Am" place by remembering the Jewish creation story, then all of the different levels of your life light up and are made clear. This is where translations become especially important because the usual translation has Jesus saying to Nicodemus, "You have to be born again," but the Aramaic says, "You have to be born from the first beginning," which means you have to be reborn from the "I Am" place. That is the place of God awareness that Jesus spoke about. And the words *men d'resh* (from the first beginning) points directly to the Hebrew *bereshit,* the "In the beginning" of Genesis.

The second technique has to do with fulfilling one's potential as *adam* and that is, as a fully human being. Many Jewish scholars researching the Jewish creation story see an all-encompassing archetype of the human being in Genesis as male and female, because it says in the first Genesis creation story, "Male and female, he/she/it created them." Therefore, we have to realize ourselves as both male and female, and some statements in the Gospel of Thomas point to this as well. Each of us has to fulfill our whole potential as *adam,* which means that we have to be, in a Hebrew/Aramaic sense, *dam* beings. *Dam* in Aramaic means blood or juice or wine or sap. This original archetype of being a human being shows that we are supposed to embody—as juice or wine or blood—the essence, the consciousness of the whole cosmos. We are supposed to be fulfilling this, not through dominating other beings but through realizing in ourselves the consciousness of the whole cosmos, the whole natural world, all the rocks, the plants, the trees, the galaxies, the stars, that's what we are supposed to be here doing, not dominating and destroying the planet.

The third technique Jesus taught was to bring in Holy Wisdom, Hokhmah of the Hebrew scripture, whose name in Greek is Sophia. Jesus emulated Hokhmah by bringing to his table all the different voices, the loved and unloved, the rich and the poor. Jesus ate with people he wasn't supposed to be eating with. He told stories of Holy Wisdom in the Jewish Bible and the essence of these stories is, "You try to unite the opposites within you." You bring to your inner table, both your loved voices and your unloved voices, your shamed voices and your honored voices, just like the Nag Hammadi scripture "Thunder-Perfect Mind" says. You bring all these paradoxes together in your inner awareness and you try to make sense of them. We might call this a psychological process, but at the time of Jesus, there was no separation of psychology and spirituality. Becoming a full human being meant then, and means now, to reconcile all of the opposites within us. His parables taught how to work with these different voices. For instance, the parable of the sower and the seed talks about receiving wisdom from a teacher. The seeds fall on the different soils within us, just as wisdom falls, and it's not necessarily that one is better than the other, but each becomes ripe in its own time. Some parts of us are not meant to receive things in a clear way, for instance, when we learn through our dreams, or a story or music or art. Other parts of us receive things in a very clear, direct, literal way; when we read something, we understand it.

It reminds me of when the Buddha just held
up a flower, and those who understood, did—
while others had no idea what he meant.

In Mark 4:10, Jesus said, "The secret of the kingdom of God has been given to you. But to those on the outside everything is said in parables."

Jesus is talking about different people; some who understand and some who don't. But as Jesus often does, his words point to a deeper meaning. The parables are given for the parts of our inner being that stand as though outside, that is, they are in the darkness or in a chaotic aspect of our being. Stories work like time-release wisdom, seeds in our inner being. For those parts of us that understand what Jesus says directly, Jesus tells us directly, and for the parts of us that don't understand, then Jesus tells us in stories indirectly. Again, this emulates the Jewish creation story—the darkness and the light both have equal places in the story. There is not a big split between darkness and light in this ancient Hebrew tradition, they both have to come together in Sacred Unity.

In the planting stories, when Jesus speaks of the *malkuta* or queendom as being like mustard seed or like leaven, it works slowly from inside out. You have to come to grips with the inner-ness of life, and as he told Nicodemus you have to go back through the darkness to go into that part of your being that is unknown before you are reborn with a new sense of self. It's almost like diving for pearls: You have to gather those parts of the self that were exiled and when you have gathered them—then the new "I Am" comes forth. That's a process that continues throughout our lives. We keep learning more and more about ourselves, so that we have a new "I Am" the next month, the next day, even the next moment.

✢ 48
THERE ARE MANY NAMES

It was raining and cold, and like an idiot, I got out of my motor home without a coat. I looked around before I went over to the gasoline pump because this was Detroit, and since I grew up in Chicago, I knew there were certain parts of any big city where you didn't want to be. I appeared safe—at least for the moment; I walked over to the pump and just as I grabbed the nozzle, I saw a paper sign taped to the pump.

PAY BEFORE PUMPING, the sign said. I rolled my eyes and sighed, then I trotted over to the gas station's convenience store. I pulled on the door, but it didn't budge. Then I saw a paper sign taped to the door.

PLEASE USE OTHER DOOR, the sign said, so I ran around the store to the other door, which was also locked. I continued to get rained on as I then ran to the front window and saw that it had one of those long bulletproof plastic arms that extended out. I rapped on the window to get the attendant's attention. He looked over and slowly walked to the window. Then he extended his long plastic arm, I tossed my credit card in and he retracted it. He looked at my credit card, and then back at me.

"I need ID," he said.

"ID?!" I asked, shivering. *"I need an ID to use my credit card?!"*

"ID," he replied. I ran back through the rain, grabbed my driver's license out of my motor home, returned to the giant plastic arm, and deposited both my credit card and ID into it. It slowly retracted. The attendant, an Indian man, stared intently at both plastic cards while the cold rain blew across my face.

"I cannot use—they are different names," he said.

Different names? What was he talking about? Then the plastic arm extended out to me, and I saw that my credit card said "Bill Elliott" while my driver's license said "William Elliott."

" 'Bill' " is short for " 'William,' " I told him.

"Sorry," he said, "they are different."

While the rain poured down and I shivered, I tried to think of a comparable Indian name—maybe "Babu" and "Bu" or "Rama" and "Ram" were forms of the same name like William and Bill.

"It's like Jonathan and Jon," I tried one last time. "They're the same name." But he just waved me away, turned his back, and began stacking packs of cigarettes in a rack above his head. I stood in the rain, angry.

Suddenly I was overcome by a realization, and then laughter, mad, cackling laughter. I ran back to my motor home with a skip and a jump, feeling like a loony leprechaun, amused at the fact that like God, I had many different names—and that there were people who didn't understand that.

✠ 49
MARIANNE WILLIAMSON

DETROIT, MICHIGAN

"Contempt prior to investigation," Marianne Williamson said (quoting Alcoholics Anonymous in her book *A Return to Love*). How perfectly this statement fit many of the people who heard Jesus' teaching two thousand years ago—and how perfectly it fits many of the people (both Christian and non-Christian) whom I have encountered while writing this book.

Jesus was both the Jerry Falwell and the Marianne Williamson, both the Billy Graham and the Matthew Fox, both the Marcus Borg and the N. T. Wright of his time—Jesus spoke the old and the new—and thus he was speaking in a way that many people could not comprehend and scoffed at. Thus it behooves us all not to have a knee-jerk reaction, not to scoff at the people in this book. Whether it's a Jerry Falwell, N. T. Wright, and Billy Graham or a Matthew Fox, Marcus Borg, or Marianne Williamson, be careful of whom you disregard in the way that many disregarded Jesus.

Marianne Williamson first burst upon the national spirituality scene when she appeared on the "Oprah Winfrey Show" and talked about her book *A Return to Love,* which was based on what she learned from *A Course in Miracles* (a three-volume curriculum of spiritual thought published in 1975 and written by a psychologist through a process of inner dictation she identified as coming from Jesus). When Marianne Williamson first read *A Course in Miracles* in 1980 she encountered Jesus "in a free and pure way" devoid of the Christian idea of hell and damnation.

I met Marianne Williamson at her home outside Detroit, Michigan. She's a petite, yet mighty soul—and Jesus would have loved Marianne Williamson because like Jesus, her relationship with God is the basis of her spiritual life, and because of that, like Jesus, she doesn't blindly follow the party or religious line.

"I see Jesus as a way-show-er," Marianne Williamson said. "I see him as an elder brother. I see him as someone who has achieved what we all can be."

Marianne Williamson is the senior minister of Church of Today in Warren, Michigan. She is an internationally acclaimed and beloved author and lecturer. Three of her books, *A Return to Love, A Woman's Worth,* and *Illuminata* have been number one on the *New York Times* best-seller list.

Who was/is Jesus?

Jesus was a human being who while on earth completely self-actualized, and fulfilled in all ways the potential glory that lies within us all. He became one with the Essence and Christ Spirit which is in all of us. In that sense, he is our evolutionary, elder brother. He demonstrated our destiny. He displayed for all to see the destination of this journey that we are on. The only thing lacking in any situation is our own awareness of love, and Jesus realized and taught that.

Jesus is a personal symbol of the Holy Spirit. Having been totally healed by the Holy Spirit, Jesus became one with him. Every thought, action, and deed of Jesus was guided by the Holy Spirit instead of ego. He's not the only face the Holy Spirit takes on—he is *a* face. To think about Jesus is to think about and bring forth the perfect love inside of us. Jesus actualized the Christ mind, and was then given the power to help the rest of us reach that place within ouselves.

He was sent down by God—as we all are. We are all extensions of the mind of God. We all contain nuggets of glory. Recently I was interviewed on a television program about miracles, and they talked about what constituted a miracle. They said the birth of a child was *not* a miracle. A miracle, they asserted, was this or that, but the birth of a child was not. My nine-year-old daughter was very bothered by that, and for good reason. The issue here is not that a miracle is something more extraordinary than the birth of a child. The issue here is that the birth of a child *is* a miracle. We are surrounded by the miraculous, but we don't yet have miracle-minded perception. We don't see the light that is all around us.

The greatest light is the light in our hearts. The point of Jesus' ministry wasn't to lessen or diminish our appreciation of each other, but to expand our appreciation by reminding us of the love in all of us. That is why Jesus is at the pinnacle of human evolution.

Was Jesus the only son of God?

No. I believe we are all sons of God, and it is our destiny to become like Jesus. He made manifest a state that is potential in all of us. The difference between us is that he was a son of God who fully remembered his divine essence, and he displayed that understanding. You might say the rest of us is still in process.

Secondly, there is only one soul. To say there is "only one begotten son" means that God created us as one. It doesn't mean that someone else wasn't the son of God. It means we're all it. There's only one of us here. In *A Course in Miracles* it says, "We are like sunbeams thinking we are separate from other sunbeams, or waves thinking they are separate from other waves. In fact, we have only one sun and only one ocean."

What spiritual techniques did Jesus teach?

There are two issues here. One is what he taughter, and few people of any religion would deny that he taught very good things indeed. The other is that, having taught them, *he then became the teaching* incarnate. He achieved within his personhood the living manifestation of the principles he taught. Having achieved that state, he now has the authority to help the rest of us get there. In *A Course in Miracles* it says that to say the name "Jesus" in any language is to be automatically reminded of the relationship between the Father and the Son. And that relationship is one of shared power.

To even think the name "Jesus" is to be reminded of one's essential nature and one's essential power. The Course does not teach, nor do I believe, that the word "Jesus" is the only word that can do that for us.

A Course in Miracles also says you do not have to personally invite Jesus into your thought system to aid you in your journey. But he can do more for you if you do.

Remember, I'm not a Christian. My conversion to Christ—and to me, conversion means a conversion of belief system—has in no way, at any point in my journey, included a serious consideration of a conversion to the Christian religion.

The argument that Christianity, or any religion for that matter, moves us closer to the heart of God, is preposterous. I believe all the great religious systems are doors to God's house. And I don't believe that Jesus can be contained by any religion. He is a force of nature. I don't feel I was born a Jew and I was meant to become a Christian. But I do feel I was born a Jew, I am a Jew, and I was meant to meet Jesus on my journey. I feel blessed to have met him, and to have met him as a Jew.

Jesus' religion?

Jesus was Jewish, as we know. I once heard a Christian woman say that Jesus had no religion. That particular piece of revisionism invalidates both Jesus and Christianity.

There are many people like myself these days—people relating to Christ who do not particularly relate to Christianity. There is a profound difference to many of us, between Jesus himself and the religion founded in his name. The world would be a beautiful thing indeed, if even a fraction of the people who claim to be Christian began to live what many of us would see as a Christ-centered existence.

Was Jesus married?

I'm fascinated by the life and story of Mary Magdalene, but I don't claim to know whether Jesus was married or not.

Virgin birth?

I'm not sure I believe in the virgin birth, but anything is possible with God. If that would have been the best way for Him to prepare a body to contain the impulses of total God consciousness, then it could have happened. I believe in miracles.

Accuracy of the gospels?

I'm no expert on the gospels, but in *A Course in Miracles* it says, "Some bitter idols have been made of him who came only to be brother to the world."

Why didn't all Jews believe Jesus
was the Messiah?

First of all, it is a historical inaccuracy to say the Jews rejected Jesus. Who were the early Christians? Almost all of them were Jews. But neither the Jews nor the Christians like to delve too deeply into the Judaism of Jesus and the disciples. It's the one area where Jews and Christians insidiously conspire. But the fact remains: the New Testament is a book about a bunch of Jews.

Regarding a Messiah, the Jews were looking for a political savior. They were occupied by the Romans and were living in virtual slavery. We realize now that a healing of one's heart is key to healing the world, and yet imagine if someone showed up in American politics today and said, "Instead of building more nuclear bombs and spending billions of dollars to destroy our enemies, let's throw out the whole defense budget and make our public policy that we love them!" That person would be laughed out of politics.

Yet that's what Jesus taught—love your enemies; *i.e.*, love the Romans. People don't buy that today, even though we live in a country that calls itself Christian. Jesus' message was radical two thousand years ago, and it is radical today.

I don't know where Jesus traveled, but I think he was in a lot of places. I don't know what he did, but I think he did a lot of things. Just because he had to learn things, doesn't make him less in my eyes; it makes him more. Given the spiritual immaturity of our species, it's probably best that Jesus' private life remains private.

So I don't know if he made mistakes. *I know more about who Jesus is, than who he was.*

Who do you think killed Jesus and why?

First of all, he had to die in order to teach us what he taught us. If there had been no crucifixion, there could not have been a resurrection. Had he not died, he could not have demonstrated that death does not exist. Had he not taken on the cruelty of the world and answer it with love and defenselessness, then he could not have demonstrated to us that love heals all things.

Resurrection?

I think the resurrection is a coded message to us, that God will always have the final say. That light will replace all darkness, love will replace all fear, and life will replace death. The extraordinary power of the resurrection of Jesus lies in the fact that, with his having overcome death, we are given the opportunity to share in the power of that act. His resurrection was a demonstration to us of what's possible, should we embrace God's love and extend it to the world.

I believe, along with the poet Rumi, that resurrection is the tendency of the universe. It's not just one event in someone else's life a long time ago. It is the energy of transcendence that is built into the cosmic order of things. All of us have been crucified, in our own ways. Life on earth, with all its meanness and fear, *is* a crucifixion of the spirit. Resurrection means we can align our hearts so deeply with God's love that we're lifted above the fears of the world.

242

Sin?

Sin is an archery term that means you've missed the mark. The mark is love; the only sin is when we deviate from love. To say that Jesus was without sin is to say that he lived in a space of total, unconditional love.

I've heard it said that we're not punished *for* our sins, but *by* our sins. God doesn't get angry and punish us for deviating from love. He sees such deviation as an error in perception that He wants to correct.

Such damage has been done on this planet by those who promulgate the notion that we're guilty sinners. We're mistaken, broken, wounded, all of that . . . but we're not guilty sinners. God Himself is all love, and we are created in His image. We remain eternally innocent, because God created us that way. Hell is what we create here on earth, through all our terrible lovelessness and fear. God doesn't strike at us for that; He weeps for us. And He sends help. That's what I believe.

Asking Jesus into your life?

If Picasso came in and said to an art class, "Would you like me to hang out with you for an hour or two?" would the students say, "No"? Of course not. You look to the master in any area to guide you. I see Jesus as a way show-er, an elder brother. I see him as someone who has achieved what it is my ultimate destiny to achieve. I see him as someone who has the power to help me achieve my own destiny.

There are situations in my life where I am unable to perceive without fear. I call on Jesus in those moments, saying, "I can't stop the fear and anger because I'm so mad at them at this moment and it's beyond my capacity to do that, but I want to see the innocence in this person, I want to unconditionally love them. Will you please lend me your heart and mind, so that I can see what you see? Deliver me to love."

That's the miracle. The miracle is a shift in perception. *A Course in Miracles* says, "We don't ask God for too much, we ask for too little." I often think of Jesus as someone sitting in a big office, behind a big desk, just twiddling his thumbs, wishing more people would ask for something! I don't think he wants to be idolized, I think he wants to be used!

You don't have to get youself perfect before you present yourself to

God. You just need to present yourself as you are and let Him perfect you. If we do our part, He will do His.

The Jews say the Messiah is coming, the Christians say the Messiah came, and Einstein said there is no time. *A Course in Miracles* says that the Second Coming is when he shall be perceived again, meaning that the Second Coming is our remembrance of who we really are. It's not like he was here, and someday he's coming again. He never left, but we have so many layers of illusion in front of our eyes that we can no longer see him. The Messiah is the consciousness of a divine self we all share.

Jesus' most important teaching?

Jesus' most important teaching was that we love each other. Period.

*What about being a mystic, and having
a relationship with God?*

I once saw mysticism described as a conviction of the heart. All the great religious systems have their mystical teachings. Mystical principles are universal, they are not unique to any one religious path. Mysticism is our inner journey to the heart of God.

A mystical relationship to God means a relationship to Him that is not based on a person or on any exoteric religious authority. It means we listen to God's voice within, and seek to live the life He wants us to live by seeking to love as He wants us to love.

✢ 50
MEETING JESUS

On my way to the Bible Belt, I parked at a rest stop and slept in the back of my motor home. My dreams came, and yet I was awake—lucid in my dream. I've learned that lucid dreams are magical and mysterious happenings. They are a window of opportunity and offer the dreamer a chance to ask a question and receive a vision. I asked to meet Jesus.

Instantly, I found myself walking down a dirt road. I saw two men. One man was sick; his body was contorted, and shaking from Parkinson's. The other man, a well-meaning healer, placed his hands on the sick man's head. Immediately, the sick man was healed, but the healer must have done something wrong, because he became sick.

I continued walking and I saw a man who was diabolical. He put one hand on the head of a healthy man, and the other on the man's groin. He proceeded to give the healthy man a Parkinson's-like illness.

Then, I walked a little farther and came upon a sick man. I placed my hands on his head and said loudly, "Jesus have mercy!" several times. The words "Jesus have mercy" created a stream of energy that flowed through me from head to toe and out my hands. I told the man to rise. He stood up and was healed. It was the energy that healed the man and not me.

I repeated the words "Jesus have mercy" over and over. As I did, I felt Jesus' presence around me, and he talked to me. He taught me the deeper meaning of the Jesus prayer, "Jesus Have Mercy." When I said "Jesus" I felt his presence and his understanding in my heart. When I said "Have" it actually meant "heart full" and I saw my own heart full of red lifeblood, bursting with love, excitement, and happiness. When I said the word "Mercy" Jesus told me "Mercy" actually meant understanding. An understanding of "the full heart" I had experienced. This understanding was so pervasive that it pierced every inch of my "full heart" with insight and complete understanding. Complete understanding caused my full heart to relax, and then it emptied and let go of the bright red blood, which spread to all corners of my being. Once emptied, my heart dissolved and what had originally only been Jesus' understanding was now my understanding *and* Jesus' understanding; it was *our* understanding and it was God's understanding *all* together. Then I heard the words "Complete understanding relieves the full heart and then dissolves it."

We then began the "Jesus Have Mercy" prayer again, and each time Jesus made sure I understood it. But I had questions about the prayer. For example, I personally didn't like invoking Jesus' name. I preferred God or Christ. As I said the Jesus prayer, I asked Jesus about this.

His answer was in words, but it was also answered in a way that *I felt* the answer in my very being. He showed me that many people have issues with or feelings about the word "Jesus," many of which are angry or resentful.

He said if the prayer is continued while being aware of these angry emotions, the emotions will eventually be cleansed. But, he said, it is important to feel what you feel when you say the word "Jesus." If you're angry, then be angry and say the prayer anyway. It's like saying the prayer in the midst of a dark cloud. Be aware of the cloud, realize the cloud's not all-encompassing or permanent, and know that by saying the prayer, the cloud will eventually disperse—not by wishing it away, or blowing it away, but in the way that the sun's warmth slowly burns away the cloudy mist.

Then Jesus had me play with the idea of whether it was really him talking to me or me talking to myself. I felt my presence together with his as I asked questions and yet I felt his presence with mine as he answered the questions. Then the words of John's gospel "You are in me and I am in you" suddenly took on a deeper meaning. As we shared this knowledge, it felt as though our sharing took place within God's limitless being.

"With the way you think now," he said, "you sometimes think it's me answering. But as your understanding deepens, our relationship will deepen and you will realize that the two of us have one root, or the way two wells that are far apart have one underground water source. It will sometimes seem to be me guiding you and sometimes it will seem to be you guiding yourself. At times, it will be us guiding you. Then there will be times when the whole idea of guidance will cease, and you will know what I meant when I said, 'The Father and I are one.' You will be so at one with the Spirit that you will not have to ask why. All will be just what it is."

I understood many things when I was with Jesus in that experience of "interbeing," some of which I have forgotten as one forgets a dream. But like some dreams, as the days pass, people I meet and experiences I have suddenly trigger the remembrance. Then the dream of Jesus' teaching slowly awakens in me and my life.

When we allow the teaching of Christ to become one with our life, this is called "picking up or bearing the cross." It creates a truly unique life in us, just as it did in Jesus, and is one in which the limited meets the limitless. Though Jesus made it clear that it was he who spoke with me in my heart, he also asked, "Can't you also hear your mother's voice? Your father's? Think of your friends; where it is that you experience them? We are all here in you."

He said this because he didn't want me to cling to him as the Only One. He wanted me to remember that these people are all in my heart, and that we're all in Christ together. Most of all, the point isn't to cling to Christ, but to experience Christ.

After I awoke from the dream of healing the man and speaking with Jesus, my hands vibrated as I lay in bed. My fingers felt longer, as though some unseen energy had extended them.

51
GAYLE AND HUGH PRATHER

"The Second Coming?" Hugh Prather asked. "The Second Coming will come in people."

"Like in Mr. Montoya," Gayle Prather said.

"Mr. Montoya?" I asked.

"He was a man who laid bricks in Sante Fe," Hugh said.

"Mr. Montoya left the Catholic Church," Gayle said, "because the priest said his daughter and his daughter's child had gone to hell because she had married outside the Church. But anyway this man, Mr. Montoya— just being in his presence was amazing. He didn't say anything, yet people stood in line just to get him to work on their house."

"They made up jobs," Hugh added, "just to have him around. I used to wonder, why is this man so peaceful? Why does he have this effect on people? It took me several days to get him to say something. Finally he said 'Well, I believe you should treat people well.' "

"And that's all he would say," Gayle added.

Hugh and Gayle Prather write books together such as *I Will Never Leave You* and *Notes to Each Other.* In 1972, during the time that Hugh wrote *Notes to Myself,* they worked on an Indian reservation. At that time, Hugh Prather had submitted a few manuscripts and books of poetry to publishers, but all were rejected. For the heck of it, he sent in his diary—it was accepted, became *Notes to Myself,* and sold five million copies. They are resident ministers of St. Francis United Methodist Church and their latest book is *The Little Book of Letting Go.* Hugh Prather is the host of *The Hugh Prather Show* on Wisdom Radio.

Who was/is Jesus?

HUGH: Jesus' teaching was very, very simple and its essence is just the two commandments; " 'Hear, O Israel, the Lord our God, the Lord is one. Love the Lord your God with all your heart and with all your soul and with all your mind and with all your strength.' The second is this: 'Love your neighbor as yourself.' "

The curious thing here is that Jesus said, "Love thy neighbor as yourself." He didn't say love all mankind as yourself, but *love your neighbor.* Jesus was devoted to the people around him. The big crowd stuff was a very small part of his three-year ministry. Take, for example the Last Supper. He takes his clothes off and wraps himself in what we would call a blanket or a towel—like a slave. He dresses himself as a slave, gets on his knees before his disciples, and washes their feet. In other words, he acknowledges their holiness. He washes their feet and then he prays to God this beautiful prayer of oneness, may they be one, in the way that we are one—which is basically an affirmation of their oneness. He tells his apostles that although they think they are going to abandon and betray him, they can't. They can't do that because he will never leave them. He will always be with them. His love for them even gets him killed and yet he comes back and continues to devote himself to them and all people.

What Gayle and I have found is that you have to start with the people around you, this is where your devotion starts. You must love your neighbor as yourself. Many people on the spiritual path talk in very beautiful terms about loving everyone but they don't treat the people in their family and people immediately around them well. Even though Jesus said, "My human mother and father are not my parents," on the cross he acknowledges his mother as his mother.

Jesus was very hands-on, very personal. The fact that he got on his knees and washed his disciples' feet and fed them says to them—who is the greater? The one who serves or the one who sits at the table? Of course, everyone says it is the one who sits at the table. But here I am among you as one who serves. And that's very much the way he lived his life, as one who served.

So, Jesus served in a very personal manner, and yet, here we are, two thousand years later and we have Jesus at a great distance. We've made Jesus into God, we sing these hymns about how unobtainable he is, how absolutely out of reach he is, he's the greatest, he's the all-knowing, he's the all-powerful, he's the one who will decide who goes to heaven and hell, and he's all these things. Although there is sort of lip service to a personal relationship with Jesus, the act of worship in most churches is to keep Jesus and God at a distance, not to embrace them. Whereas, the story that comes through to me in the gospels is almost the exact opposite. Here is someone who called himself our friend. He said in Luke 5:20: "Friend, your sins are forgiven" and in John 15:15: "I no longer call you servants, because a servant does not know his master's business. Instead, I have called you friends, for everything that I learned from my Father I have made known to you."

We tend to think of his miracles as public demonstrations of power but they were actually very private acts, acts for his friends. For example, the stilling of the sea was just for his friends who had gotten scared. It was a very private thing that he was doing, it was not a demonstration. Turning the water into wine, this is a very little thing. There was a party and they ran out of wine, so he did this nice thing.

The message of Jesus is that "oneness" is often experienced in the seemingly unimportant things that we do, not only in the important things. It's the little things that we do for our partner and for our children and for our friends, and the little errands and the little tasks, and so forth, as we go through the day, this is where the oneness of Christ, the oneness of God is seen and is exhibited.

Jesus' devotion to the two things which were/are his two commandments was absolute; he was devoted to God and he was devoted to the people around him. To me, those two things are the same thing. Love thy neighbor as thyself I think is a literal statement. You see yourself and those around you as God—Jesus even said, "The kingdom of heaven is within you." And obviously he thinks of God as in himself when he says, "The Father and I are One." Therefore, in a sense it's all one thing. He breaks it down into love God and love your neighbor but you can see that here is a man that really never did anything for himself. His whole life was devoted to doing things for other people and that's the way he worshiped God.

Many Christians get stuck thinking of Jesus as results oriented, so they believe if they say "in the name of Jesus" they will get great results. But Jesus' life did not get good results. He got very inconsistent results. There were people he healed and the Bible says there were many people he didn't heal. There were crowds that worshiped him and crowds who wanted to stone him. There was a very mixed bag of results.

But a saint is not necessarily someone who gets good results. The saint is someone who continues to bring a perfect effort in a sense, or a completely consistent effort to everything they do regardless of the results. And that to me is what is remarkable about Jesus' life . . . he left the results up to the results. He surrendered his results. The results were whatever they were. But his attempt was consistent.

Jesus the Only Way to God?

Some Christians would say, "Jesus is the Only Way," and for them that means Jesus expressed the Truth and there is only one truth.

GAYLE: I don't know where all the people, all the sons and daughters of God, come from, but they are in all religions, and no religions. They teach the same truth, although they may teach it in different ways and within their own cultures. Invariably, however, their message is misunderstood. It's used to separate "you" from "us" and make "us" special. What gets me is the people who say, "You could be a wonderful person, you could be loving, you could be kind, you could be generous, but if you don't accept Jesus as your personal Savior—you go to hell. On the other hand, if you are a horrible person, a murderer who accepts Jesus as your personal Savior right before you die, you are saved."

HUGH: What happened is that God's child, Adam, fell asleep and there is no record of Adam ever having awakened. And what happens to each of us when we sleep? Our mind fragments into all these other people—it forms all these different people with all their different emotions and minds and lives and dramas. But Jesus is a gentle reminder that "No, we are all one, there is only one child of God." You can look at that as a very divisive statement or you can look at it as a completely inclusive statement.

Did Jesus learn things?

GAYLE: I think the Buddha was right on that when he said, "Be a lamp unto yourself." You can't learn what Jesus knew from someone else. You can't be taught it, although you can certainly be led by another. Jesus may have been led at one time by someone, but the relationship he had with God can't be taught—it can only be experienced. Ultimately it was his willingness to keep turning to the God within him, to the truth within him, that made him different. It was his ability to continue trusting regardless of what was happening.

HUGH: Besides trust, you have to become acutely aware of your dark side, your murderous side, your hateful side, your petty side. You have to be acutely aware of it all times or else you are so mixed up that you don't know what you're hearing, or what you're consulting within you. The people who are most able to live consistently from the voice of God within are those who are acutely aware of their egos. People who admit throughout the day that their ego is saying this or that—are able to choose. Those who deny the ego's influence are blind to when the ego comes out, they don't really know what they are choosing, so they end up doing quite destructive things without even realizing it. For instance, look at the temptation of Christ. When I was a boy, I always wondered why Jesus didn't just cut the devil off during the temptation? It's because Jesus knew that you had to see all of what the ego offers you, otherwise part of it remains unconscious and controls you. Once Jesus listened to all the devil had to offer, then the devil (or ego) had no power over him, because its temptations were seen, not unseen: conscious not unconscious.

*Jesus often needed to know the name of the
demon before he made them leave.
Doesn't naming our selfishness, our darkness,
give us power over it?*

GAYLE: That's very much like Jesus hearing the devil out on the temptations, isn't it? And "name" comes from the root meaning nature. In a sense, he needs to see the nature of something before he can throw it out.

Did Jesus have human failings? Emotions?

Jesus did experience all the emotions that everyone else does. You can see, for example, when you look at all of his statements about the Pharisees and Sadducees, that he does seem judgmental there. When you look at the temple, you certainly could surmise that he may have been angry. He definitely seems to be frustrated with his disciples at times, quite frustrated with them. So he experienced frustration. He obviously experienced grief when Lazarus died. He experiences doubt on the cross, thinking that God has forsaken him. Now here is a man who taught and lived complete trust in God and yet, for a moment, he thinks God has forsaken him. We seem to have forgotten all this, to have separated ourselves from Jesus. And because we have got him at this distance, he can't touch our lives anymore. We like to think he experienced no human emotions, that he never felt lost or doubted. He did. But in the end, he always went back to his relationship with God. The real teaching of Jesus' life is not that he didn't make mistakes, but that he saw his mistakes and then went back to God.

Accuracy of the gospels?

HUGH: Politics took over, and then people took out and added things to the gospels. Did they destroy the essence of the teaching? No. But these are human beings who lived at a particular time in history and they had an agenda.

People sometimes get very frightened when they hear scholars report that different translations of the gospels changed words or passages because they want something that can be pointed at as absolutely right and the desire to be right is usually more overpowering than the desire to be free and possibly experience the truth. Because we want safety, because the world is so dangerous, so chaotic, absolute laws and rules appeal to many people.

GAYLE: I want to know (in an ego way) that everything is going to be okay. That's what rigidity promises and gives in many ways. There are no questions. You have these routines and these things you do and on Saturday night you all go play Bingo somewhere and there is lots of community. There is almost something frightening about not having the laws, rules, and absolutes—freedom from these can leave you floundering. But that's why Jesus went into the desert—in order to leave all the structures behind and wrestle with the essence of God—which is the Truth of Spirit. Structures and laws may in a sense keep out the devil—but they also may keep out the experience of God.

What spiritual techniques did Jesus teach?

HUGH: Jesus taught in the way that Gayle and I have tried to teach our children, by example. And Jesus even said, "I have set you an example." In our house, we just did our spiritual practices, our children saw us turning to God over and over. And then we noticed that often, if we said "no" about something—they would ask us to pray about it! In other words, they had seen that when we turned to God, God was much more easygoing than we were. God was much more likely to say, "Yeah, oh let 'em do it." Then they began to watch us pray and "let go of the struggles of the day" at the end of the day, and they wanted to join us. I prefer that style of teaching rather than teaching them any concepts.

Jesus urged people to turn to God, trust God, to love one another, and to forgive. He gave no specific practice on how to do that, instead he imbued them with his life and breath as if to say—this is your lifeblood and forgiveness is breath itself. Loving your neighbor is breath itself. Doing

253

unto others is breath itself, it's life itself. There is nothing wrong with having special periods set aside for special practices, but practice for what? Practice imbuing life with those attitudes.

Who killed Jesus and why?

GAYLE: Now it seems quite clear that Jesus could have avoided his death if he had wished to. Martin Luther King, Gandhi, and others who seem to foresee their death could have also—but a person has to relax into his or her destiny. You don't fight your destiny. You're going to die when you die and you don't get caught up in a struggle over that. Jesus, Gandhi, and Martin Luther King all could have gotten out of town. Instead of Jesus telling his disciples, "You're going to do this and you're going to do that tomorrow," he could have just taken them all out of town. But he saw the story unfolding—and changing the story was not part of his destiny. In that sense God did send Jesus to this destiny, did send Jesus to his death in order that people would come closer to God and be saved through his death. And we can learn from this. Accept the story, relax into your destiny, row your boat gently down the stream, don't try to start rowing up the stream. If you do that, the real story becomes how do you live your story—how does your mind, your heart, your spirit, and your soul—how do these things live out in your story?

Resurrection?

HUGH: When we worked with people in Sante Fe whose children had died, we found that just about everyone had experienced their children coming back.

GAYLE: Not visually, necessarily, but usually in the ways that were unique to the child. Well, the apostles didn't recognize him, did they? Why didn't they recognize him? My guess is he didn't come back as a physical body. He came back as a Spirit and began calling to them and they slowly began to recognize that.

HUGH: Jesus won't come back because *he's still here.* When someone wakes up to God's presence as Jesus did, then their wakefulness is merged with God's wakefulness—and they are always available to anyone who awakens. They don't go anywhere. It's illusion to think we go somewhere. Jesus was present then—and knew that he would always be present, waiting for those who awoke to his presence. So in a sense his eternal presence appears to be a Second Coming—even though he has never left.

✛ 52
MONTREAT

MONTREAT, NORTH CAROLINA

"Dad's at the Mayo Clinic in Florida," Gigi Graham said during dinner at her house, "because of his Parkinson's."

Through a strange turn of events, I found myself eating dinner with Gigi Graham, the daughter of Billy Graham, and a friend named Jane Alden. A few days before, I had met Jane Alden at a coffee shop in Black Mountain. Her family was somehow related to John Alden, the pilgrim, and her mother (also named Jane Alden) was a well-known Realtor in town. The senior Jane Alden was also known for the two toy poodles she carried in her backpack wherever she went. Jane Alden and I became friends, and after a few days, she told me she knew the Grahams, and that actually her family lived next door.

"The people in Montreat and Black Earth are very proud of them and very protective," Jane said. "People around here always talk about Billy's humility. Often when people ask him things about God or the Bible—he says, 'I don't know.' "

Later that day, Gigi Graham called Jane Alden, and when Jane mentioned me, Gigi invited us to dinner. Gigi Graham is the mother of seven children and married Stephan Tchividjian in 1963. She has the kind of bursting, volcanic energy that can handle seven children, a marriage, an occasional lecture tour, and still have energy left over. I'm the kind of guy who needs a rest after making a bank deposit.

The big energy that Gigi had must have made life difficult for her at times because there hasn't always been an outlet for, or acceptance of, powerful women like her—especially within Christianity.

"I tried to squash myself for a while," she told me. "You know, tried to make myself the quiet type. But then I realized God made me this way—and now I accept the way I am."

I must admit I felt awkward asking Gigi about her father because I liked her for who she was, and I didn't want to give her the impression that I was only interested in her father. But I felt the book would be incomplete without her father, so I had to ask about him.

"How's your father's health?" I asked. "Is he still at the Mayo Clinic in Florida?"

"He's fine," Gigi replied. "He just really likes the sun down there."

"I wanted to interview him . . ." I began.

"Just go down there," she said with a wave of her hand.

"But he's sick . . ." I ventured.

"He's fine," she assured me. "Just go down there and knock on his door and tell him Gigi sent you."

Later that night I visited Ruth Graham, Billy's wife, up at their home in Montreat. She designed their rambling country cabin—actually it's too big to be a cabin, but it isn't an estate either—which is a credit to the Grahams because they certainly could have had an estate if they wanted.

Ruth Graham, a petite woman with translucent skin, exudes a clear light that is at once both mischievous and kind. Although Billy is the well-known celebrity preacher, it is his wife, Ruth, who I have heard more than one person say "Is the saintliest person I've ever met." I had also heard that years ago she'd climbed through the second-story window of their house in order to wake up her young, rebellious son Franklin after he thought he had outfoxed his mother by locking his bedroom door. These qualities, together with the incredible life she must have led, made me extremely curious about her. I told Ruth that I wanted to visit her some time and talk about "anything and nothing."

"I'm very good at talking about nothing," she replied. Despite her protests, Ruth Graham does have something to say, and she's said it in her books *Legacy of a Pack Rat, One Wintry Night,* and *Mothers Together* (written with her daughter Gigi Tchividjian). She's also written a book of collected poems titled *Footprints of a Pilgrim.*

> *There will be less*
> *someday—*
> *much less, and there*
> *will be More:*
>
> *less to distract*
> *and amuse;*
> *More, to adore;*

As we sat by the fireplace, Ruth and I talked about everything and anything—and the more we talked, the more I couldn't help thinking that God had blessed Billy Graham with the best of all worlds.

"*That's the crux* of the disagreement," Brad Long said. He was the most out-of-the-closet mystic and evangelical minister I had ever met. Gigi Graham had suggested I give him a call, or maybe it was Claire, the wife of Tommy, one of Gigi Graham's childhood playmates, or maybe it was Jane Alden—anyway, in a town like Montreat/Black Mountain, there are only two kinds of people; those who are either friends or relatives of the Grahams and those who just "know of" the Grahams. Anyway, Gigi Graham told me to go down to Florida and knock on her father's door and say "Gigi sent me," but I didn't feel comfortable with barging in on Billy Graham at the Mayo Clinic, so I hung around Montreat for a few days. That's when I met with Brad Long, who was not ashamed of his mysticism. *Webster's* dictionary defines mysticism as "The experience of mystical union or direct communion with ultimate reality reported by mystics. The belief that direct knowledge of God, spiritual truth, or ultimate reality can be attained through subjective experience (as intuition or insight)."[1]

"How marvelous it was when I awakened to the presence of the Holy

---

1. *Merriam-Webster's Collegiate Dictionary,* Tenth Edition.

Spirit," Brad Long wrote in *Passage Through the Wilderness: A Journey of the Soul.* So we agreed on the importance of the mystical life and the experience of God's presence, but disagreed on what Jesus meant when he said, "I am the Way and the Truth and the Life. No one gets to the Father except through me." It was the "me" part of that statement that confused me and just about every Christian in one way or another. Was Jesus speaking from a place of deep Spirit? A Spirit that resided in all religions, but by other names? Or did he mean "me" as in Jesus who is "only" in Christianity? Whatever he meant, Jesus' words had caused some of the billion Christians to label the other three billion or two thirds of the world's non-Christian population as "them," or human beings who did not have *"the only right way."* They have led to a castigation of the Jews for not recognizing Jesus as their Messiah and the ostracizing of many Christians who were not convinced that other religions didn't also lead to God. Actually as Mother Tessa Bielecki pointed out to me, *the Catholic Church actually was open to a universal deep Spirit.* One of the conclusions reached at Vatican II was that "The Catholic Church rejects nothing of what is true and holy in these religions. She has a high regard for the manner of life and conduct, the precepts and doctrines which, although differing in many ways from her own teaching, nevertheless often reflect a ray of truth which enlightens all men . . . Let Christians, while witnessing to their own faith and way of life, acknowledge, preserve and encourage the spiritual and moral truths found among non-Christians, also their social life and culture."[2]

"Mystics can ground themselves in the scriptures," Brad Long said when I asked how a mystic guards against delusion.

"But," I asked, *"which interpretation* of the scriptures? Which translation of the scriptures? The prevalent attitude among scholars is that some of the words attributed to Jesus in the gospels are not his or that there are mistranslations—and even that some of the letters attributed to Paul are not Paul's."

Brad Long remained silent although a smile appeared in a face framed by curly hair and a beard. Was he silent because he agreed that there were questions about the Bible, but as a minister in a town as conservative as

2. Declaration on the Relation of the Church to Non-Christian Religions (*Nostra Aetate,* 1965) from the Documents of Vatican II.

Montreat he didn't want to comment? Or did he believe like me, that the Bible was an adviser in one's relationship with God—but it was our relationship with God that was the ultimate basis for our spiritual life? Or was he just allowing me to wrestle with the questions God had given me—just as he wrestled with his? Or was he just being too kind to openly disagree? Whatever the reason, Brad Long wasn't saying.

"I've met with scholars, mystics, and evangelists," I told John Seale. "Those three groups keep each other honest. Scholars seek Truth. Mystics seek the experience of God. Evangelists seek to understand, protect, and respect God's word. All of them together keep each other honest."

John Seale closed his eyes and thought deeply.

"They represent rationality, experience, and legalism," he said as he opened his eyes. John Seale was a friend of Brad Long's and another person recommended to me by Gigi Graham.

I relaxed and sighed deeply. Finally, someone who was not afraid to know God, to know Jesus in all ways. Many people know God in one way and they cling to that way until it begins to limit them *and God*. With all the mystics, evangelists, and scholars I've interviewed—very few go into all areas. They get stuck, they stop their journey, they go to *the end of themselves and stop*. But God is constantly asking us to go beyond what we know—to go beyond our pattern, our comfortable way of acting. To not hide behind personal experience as mystics do. To not hide behind the intellect as scholars do. To not hide behind the rules or blind belief as evangelists do. We often pick a spiritual path or way of relating to God that makes a virtue of our neurosis. The point is to go beyond our neurosis and know God in as many ways as possible. But fear keeps us in our safe little neurotic haven. Only love can break us out of our self-imposed jail because love drives out fear[3] and ultimately "God is love."[4]

3. 1 John 4:18.
4. 1 John 4:16.

53
AM I A CHRISTIAN

"No—you are not a Christian," the young minister said in response to my question about whether he thought I was a Christian. "You don't believe Jesus died for your sins."

I was on my way to Florida with the intention of visiting a friend and then possibly getting up enough chutzpah to bother Billy Graham at the Mayo Clinic—like I said, his daughter Gigi had said it was okay, which I had to keep telling myself because I didn't want to be known as the guy who barged in on Billy Graham while he was sick.

I had stopped at a small bookstore just outside Atlanta and begun talking with five seminary students and their teacher. We exchanged our thoughts, beliefs, and experiences along with the thoughts, beliefs, and experiences of others we had knowingly or unknowingly borrowed—*and I'm not sure anyone knew which were which.*

"Well," I said, "I believe he died because humanity was too ignorant to understand his message, and he may have also known that his death would change the trajectory of humanity . . ."

"But that's not it," he said. "Jesus was the sacrificial lamb and his death took away our sins."

"But there are many people who call themselves Christians," I said, "who don't believe that Jesus had to die as payment for our sins because it doesn't make sense. Why would God kill Jesus in order to forgive us? Jesus' life and death may have had to happen to help save human beings from the lives they were leading—but I don't believe God killed him in the way that the ancient Jews sacrificed animals in payment for sins or the way Aztecs sacrificed other humans to appease God.

"Jesus' disciples," I continued, "didn't understand him when he was alive, and I don't believe they fully understood him or his message after he died."

"*Do you believe* other religions get to God?" I asked the minister.

"Buddhists and Hindus believe in good works," the young minister said. "They believe if you meditate, you will get good karma and go to heaven."

This was a common Christian misunderstanding of another religion, and I had heard it before. But since I had immersed myself in other religions, I understood what their symbols and techniques meant. When you don't immerse yourself in another religion you project your own understanding onto their symbols. It's akin to a Hindu or Buddhist saying, "Christians are cannibals—they believe in eating the body and drinking the blood of their Savior."

"That's a misunderstanding," I said to the minister. "Buddhists and Hindus believe God's presence is already given and present, you can't earn that. What they are trying to do is experience that Presence, which is very similar to the Christian idea that salvation is grace, and that it can't be earned—only experienced. So Buddhists and Hindus meditate or pray in order to open themselves up and surrender to the fact of God's presence—they're not trying to do good works and earn heaven."

"But what about reincarnation and how they are trying to go up the ladder of rebirth?" he asked.

"Just like a lot of Christians who pray so that they won't go to hell," I said, "there are Hindus and Buddhists who do holy things just so they won't go to hell or be reborn as a bug. Same motivation as hell—but different concept."

Even though the minister and I disagreed on a few things, we agreed on many more. Especially on the most important—*the love of God*. I enjoyed talking with this man because it was a dialogue. He listened and I listened. We weren't trying to convince the other—we were expressing and sharing with respect. Most of all, we were so confident in God's love, and since "there is no fear in God's love" as 1 John said, we actually were open to what the other said.

God's love should set us free—not make us captives of and defenders of fear. Jesus said, "The Truth will set you free" (John 8:32, NIV), and the

Truth may come through someone who is seen as being outside our religion—as the parable of the Good Samaritan showed—or it may come from "one of the teachers of the law" who, "when Jesus saw that he had answered wisely, said to him, 'You are not far from the kingdom of God.' "[1]

I felt spiritually invigorated as I walked back out to my motor home. The warm Atlanta air mirrored the warmth I felt in my own heart. I had seen the effects of Jesus' teaching in the minister and his students, but it wasn't in what they said—*it was in how* they said what they said. Ultimately, the true test of a Christian is not found in their words or beliefs—it's found in their love.

✢ 54
SPILT MILK

Back in my motor home, I opened my backpack and found that some of my nondairy creamer had leaked out of a bottle and spilled onto my laptop. The laptop wouldn't boot up—it was dead!

Suddenly, I was depressed. A few days later, I sent the laptop to Dell computer. That night, I had a dream that it would only cost $150 to fix my laptop. Two days later Dell computer called, and they wanted $1,000 to fix it. I was worried because I couldn't afford $1,000. The worry quickly changed into stress and it filled my body.

I walked around my motor home throwing a sock here and a shirt there, asking God *"Why did this happen to me? Why did you do this to me?"* I guess these questions showed that it's hard to accept the stupid things I do. Sometimes it's easier to blame God, like in the Old Testament when the Israelites killed every man, woman, and child in the cities of Heshbon and Bashan[2] and said God told them to do it. I wondered *were those the commandments of God?* Or were they early man's attempt to explain away the stupid, vicious things they did?

1. 1 Mark 12:34.
2. Numbers 21:34.

I also wondered about my dream where the laptop only cost $150 to fix. Why did I have that dream? Obviously, it wasn't a prediction of the future. But I must admit, the dream comforted me until I found out the truth of what my actions had cost me.

When will human beings wake up to the truth of being responsible for what we do? That was why I ruthlessly pursued the truth of who Jesus was and is. To blindly accept the interpretations of Jesus by those who went before me is irresponsible. After Adam and Eve ate from the tree of knowledge of Good and Evil, the first man told God, "The woman you put here with me—she gave me some fruit from the tree." And when God turned to Eve, she said, "The serpent deceived me." I've always thought one thing in the serpent's favor is that he never denied what he did or blamed someone else. It's apparent that man's refusal to accept responsibility began at the beginning, and throughout the Bible this irresponsibility colors and perverts our loving God into a god of punishment and murder. In the Bible it said God put Adam to sleep in order to take out one of his ribs, but *the Bible never said God woke Adam up.* Maybe the human race has been asleep for thousands of years, and Jesus was someone who came in order to awaken us?

"Stay awake. Stay awake," Jesus told the apostles in the garden of Gethsemane. But they fell asleep anyway.

The next morning I woke up with an idea. Maybe my homeowner's insurance would cover my accident? I called their office, and sure enough, they'd pay to repair the laptop minus $250 for the deductible.

So often in my life, I complain to God about screwing me over. Sometimes I pray for something and don't get it, and then down the road it works out better. A week later, instead of repairing the old laptop, I decided to buy a new laptop with the insurance money. I sold the broken computer on ebay.com for $350. Together with the insurance payment, I got more than the computer was worth.

✤ 55
TALK WITH JESUS

While reading the New Testament in the bed at the rear of my motor home, I became aware of Jesus' presence. I started talking to him, and I cried because I was afraid, not of Jesus, but of the changes my spirit was going through.

"I'm joyful," I told Jesus. "I can feel tremendous joy in my chest, and yet, I'm afraid."

He just told me to stay with the joy, and to feel the fear. My attention went to the sensations in my chest, and as my joy increased, my fear did also. My tears continued to flow and this seemed to release even greater waves of joy and fear. Again and again I cried, and then always the joy came, followed by fear—while at other times they felt as though they were one and the same.

I told Jesus that I wanted to fulfill my life's purpose and God's will, but I didn't want to suffer as I once had. That I didn't want to go through those hellish years of despair that had followed my parents' death. Again, he told me to be aware of my fear and the experience around it.

"Be aware of how your life has taught you to expect suffering whenever you feel joy." He said, "Be aware of how at one time your joy depended on others and what they told or did to you. But now, the joy you feel is what is called 'the joy that depends on no-thing.' It just is. And it too, may pass—but *I will always be with you*—just as our Father is always with us."

56
BUMPY ROADS
AND KIND WORDS

After visiting a friend for a few days, I read in the newspaper that Billy Graham had been discharged from the Mayo Clinic and had returned to North Carolina—the place I had left a week before. Since there was no Billy Graham in Florida to interview, I waited for some kind of omen as to where to go next. I made a few phone calls about interviews, but nothing was definite. So while I waited in limbo, the doubts and "what if's" arose. *What if they said "no"? What if everyone said "no"? What if this whole book sucked?*

Instead of waiting any longer, I decided to try and make something happen. I jumped into my motor home and started driving to Texas. I already had an interview set with Josh McDowell, and there were three other evangelists—T.D. Jakes, Chuck Swindol, and Max Lucado who also lived in Texas. I figured I'd try the old Reverend Falwell strategy that had worked so well—just approach the other evangelists after their services and ask for an interview about Jesus. It was a long shot, but what the heck, it was for a good cause.

After a couple days of driving, I crossed into Arkansas. Immediately, my motor home started bouncing up and down like I was driving down a cobblestone street. At first I thought it was just a temporary problem with the roads, but it continued for hundreds of miles. Just past Little Rock, I stopped at Taste of D Light Oriental Cuisine. It was crowded. Jerry, the owner, a middle-aged black man, was at the counter ringing up and taking orders. I introduced myself and we talked for a few minutes.

"Your food must be good," I said as he handed me my takeout order.

"It's busy," he said, shaking his head. Then he looked at me with a big smile. "God bless Bill," he said.

I turned and walked away. Just as I reached for the door he called out.

"I appreciate you," he said.

I turned around and looked at him because the sincerity in his voice demanded one last look.

"I appreciate you," he repeated with his head bent over new orders and receipts. I continued out the door and into the night. As I walked through the parking lot, I listened to the sound of the crushed stones as they crunched beneath my feet. Then I stopped and looked up at the stars. Suddenly, I felt that I was part of creation—and I felt those stars throughout my body—as if they had been laid out on my heart and soul in the way that nightclothes are laid out upon the bed.

✢ 57
0 FOR 1: MAX LUCADO

SAN ANTONIO, TEXAS

On the back of one of Max Lucado's books (one of the fourteen million in print) it said that his church, the Oak Hills Church of Christ, was in San Antonio. I finally found the church phone number after I called information several times. When I called, a recording of a man's voice explained directions. I didn't know if that was Max Lucado's voice, but I immediately liked the person behind the voice. It was a warm, clear, and kind voice. The voice said I had lucked out because Max Lucado was preaching three times on February 6—*which was the next day.*

I pulled into the church parking lot sometime past midnight. I parked my motor home, pulled down the blinds, and went to sleep. Sometime the next morning I heard the sounds of one car after another pulling into the lot. I looked at my clock—the first service was starting in forty-five minutes.

Max Lucado's church was beautiful. At least that's how it felt, although if you looked carefully at the structure you saw basketball lines on the floor and realized that it was a renovated gym. But who cared? Max Lucado's sermon, together with the attitude of his support staff and congregation, showed what Christian worship can be when it's done with heart and soul. Besides, wasn't that the whole point of Jesus' teaching? That the structure or law or appearance weren't as important as the spirit.

People like Max Lucado are helping me heal the wound Christianity inflicted on me. Actually, the wound was not so much inflicted by Christianity as it was by life—but the suffering that surrounded the wound was made worse by the fact that I felt forsaken by Christianity while I suffered. But the Christianity of people like Max Lucado helped in that healing process.

"My conviction," he said in *Christianity Today*, "is to lead one congregation in one sizable city to the point where we lead such admirable, respectable, and contagious lives that we may never even verbalize that we are Christians, or put a fish sign on our car, or pick up a picket sign. We just live such attractive lives that people say, 'That's what I'd like to be.' "[1]

Not once during his sermon did I hear a divisive statement; there was no "us versus them" or "Jesus is the only one—and everyone else is lost" attitude. Afterward, I approached Max Lucado's assistant about an interview and told her that I was writing a book about Jesus.

"Sorry," she said in a nice, but firm way, "Max Lucado is too busy."

Then I saw Max Lucado coming out of the sanctuary, and I decided to ask him myself. Out of the corner of my eye, I could see the assistant watching me from a distance.

"Sorry," Max Lucado said in a nice, but firm way, "I'm too busy."

✦ 58
1 FOR 2: JOSH McDOWELL

DALLAS, TEXAS

Josh McDowell sat at a back table in a Texas barbecue restaurant named Sony Bryan's. He looked half football coach, half rancher. We talked about Jesus as ribs, sausage, fries, and pulled pork were eaten around us. How different the Last Supper and even the communion ritual would be if the Last Supper had been in Texas and not Jerusalem.

Josh McDowell has spoken to more than eight million people in eighty-four countries and is a traveling representative for Campus Crusade for

---

1. *Christianity Today* magazine, February 8, 1999, "Max's Maxims."

Christ. His whole life changed after becoming a Christian in college. Up until then he had hated his abusive father. But now he was able to tell his father that he loved him, and within months, his father had also accepted Christ into his life.

Josh McDowell has written more than forty-five books and his latest book, *The New Evidence That Demands a Verdict,* was written in part as a defense against the latest claims of modern scholarship.

"You can always find some scholars who will say almost anything," Josh McDowell said. "Some of the most absurd things have been said by scholars, philosophers, and theologians."

———————

Who is/was Jesus and what was his mission?

Jesus Christ was God incarnate. He was God taking on human flesh to identify with the very nature of man. He was just as much man as if he had never been God and just as much God as if he had never been man.

I don't know if one can narrow his mission down to one thing, but the gospel of John talks about Jesus as being the visible expression of the invisible God—that through seeing Christ we would know God the Father. This is difficult for us with our finite minds to understand. His ultimate mission was to bring us into a relationship with the Heavenly Father, which meant dealing with the sin problem, the self-centered problem, and offering a personal relationship with the Father through him.

Overcoming our self-centeredness.

My whole life was centered around politics and climbing the ladder. I had mapped out a plan to become governor of the state of Michigan and then go into the Senate. It was made up of fifty six-month segments of my life. I thought politics was using people and climbing the ladder of life. But when I came to know Christ personally, what amazed me was that without any conscious effort, I caught myself thinking of other people first. Not so much *what I could get* but *what I could give.* Not *what I could take,* but *what I could give.* Not *how I could use somebody* but *how I could be used.* Without any conscious effort, after I established this relationship with God through Christ, I found myself being other-person centered.

This ability that Christ has to turn a person outward rather than inward is what has led to the outpouring of humanitarian aid and ministries we have all over the world—to the hurting, to the poor, to the hungry, to the widows, and to the orphans. That's what Christ does through the Holy Spirit. When he comes to live within us, he starts to bring us into alignment with his nature.

That's different than being self-centered. I've come to know who I am as "self" through Christ. I don't believe that apart from Christ we can ever discover who we are. Our finite minds, apart from revelation (also meaning the scriptures), cannot know who God is, who we are. And without that, one can never have a healthy self-identity, which is totally different than being self-centered.

I was created in the image of God: He gave me the ability to will, to think, to love, to create, to make moral choices. In order to relate to God, we have been given the ability to relate to him as a person. Part of your personality is the image of God, and I found my identity in Christ. I dealt with self-centeredness by dealing with my identity in Christ, and only then did I come to know the identity of others—we're all created in the image of God. This is why I cannot understand racism and bigotry or anything like that, because we are all equal in the eyes of God. Now I believe some are saved and some are unsaved, but whether you are saved or unsaved does not affect the value of who you are as a person. What Christ did was revolutionary, because up until Christ you were loved because somebody thought you had value. But Christ loved us first—that gave us value. I believe the same thing today and I see in every individual the image of God, whether they are Christian or non-Christian, whether they are Buddhist, Muslim, whatever. The image of God is there! Regardless if I agree with them theologically or philosophically, I must treat all people with respect and dignity because they are of great worth and because Christ created them that way and died on the cross for them.

Now, I didn't say that Christ is in all people. I said the image of God is in all people. The ability to will, to think, to love, to make moral decisions, to relate to another person is the image of God. God is personal, and he created us with the ability to relate to him as a person. Now that's different than Christ being in everyone. Jesus said, "I stand at the door and knock. If anyone hears my voice and opens the door, I will come in . . ." (Revelations 3:20, NIV). So for Christ to be in us, that's a choice, it's not something we are born with, it's something we choose. But the image of God is in every person. You go to Psalm 8, Psalm 39, where it talks about how marvelous God's creation man is, and it doesn't say "believers" or "Christians." It says *everyone* is of great value. That's why I can't understand people hating one another. Because you are depreciating something that God created and *God don't create no junk!* People see someone in the gutter and say "he's worthless and makes no contribution to society!" But he's made in the image of God, and even if that person in the gutter was the only person alive, Jesus still would have died for him, there would still have been a Christmas and an Easter.

Is Jesus the only Son of God?

He was the only Son of God in the sense of a relationship with the Father and the Trinity. He was the only begotten Son of God, as Jesus said himself in John 3:16. I believe each one of us can become a child of God, but a believer is never referred to as the Son of God but is referred to as a child of God. I believe there is only one Son of God, only one redemptive Son of God—who is Jesus Christ.

Are other religions paths to God? Or are Christianity and Jesus the only way?

First of all I'm not the one saying it . . . Jesus did. It's pretty clear. He said, "I am the Way and the Truth and the Life. No one comes to the Father except through me" (John 14:6, NIV).

In today's concept of tolerance and rationale, however, we like to say "all is equal." But that's kind of dumb. I believe each one of us will be accountable to God on the appointed day for man to die, and then at the Judgment. If there was any other way for God to have saved man, why did his Son have to die? If salvation can be secured simply by being sincere or following your religious path or whatever, why did Jesus Christ have to die? Why did he have to go through the agony of being separated from the Father, which you and I can't even comprehend? You see a bit of the agony that Christ went through in the Garden of Gethsemane. So I would say there is no other way. But I'm not the one who said it first, Jesus did, so take it up with him!

Jesus' religion?

Jesus was Jewish and "Christian" basically means "Christ in you." So you can almost say that a Christian (I have to be careful saying this because some people would take it a different way) is a completed Jew.

Virgin birth?

I believe that Mary was a virgin in the sense that she had never had sexual intercourse or a sexual relationship, and that's what so surprised Joseph. He was like, "Come on, Mary, get real here! I'll help you hide him but don't give me this stuff about, God spoke to you through Elizabeth and the angel and all."

The virgin birth, which is predicted in the Old Testament, is the only way to understand the total life of Christ. To understand how he could take upon himself the sins of the world.

Why didn't all Jews accept Jesus as the Messiah?

It was predicted way ahead of time that Jesus would be rejected as the Messiah. If you go back before Christ's birth, there was a prediction that two Messiahs would come: one would be the "son of David," the reigning political Messiah; the other would be the "son of Joseph," the suffering Messiah.

These two predictions about two coming Messiahs—a political one and a suffering one—are interwoven in the Old Testament. When Jesus came onto the scene he said, "No, there are not two Messiahs coming; there is one Messiah coming twice. I have come, and I must suffer. Then I am coming back again and I'm going to reign." But you have to understand that historically, before the time of Christ, the Romans took Israel into bondage. When this happened the Jewish leaders needed to hold the people together. So they said, "We can't teach that the suffering Messiah is coming, because that won't keep people together under oppression." They also said, "We have suffered so much," and this is the belief of many Jewish people and scholars today who say that Israel fulfills Isaiah 52 and 53, that Israel has suffered for the sins of the world, through the Holocaust and other things. Since Israel is the Messiah of suffering, the Jewish leaders decided to teach that when the Messiah came, he would be a reigning-political Messiah who would throw the Romans out and set up the kingdom of God. This is why when you look at the disciples' conversations, the only way you can understand them is in a historical context. Remember they asked, "Lord, can we reign on your right hand?" Are they thinking of a suffering Messiah? No! A reigning-political Messiah! "Lord, is it now that you are going to set up your kingdom?" Were they thinking of a suffering Messiah? No! A reigning-political messiah! So when Jesus came onto the scene, all the disciples thought, "Man, we're going to reign! Jesus is going to come down, throw the Romans out, set up the kingdom, and we are going to reign with him!"

But Jesus said, "You don't understand—I've got to go to Jerusalem. I'm going to be crucified and buried, but I'm going to rise again on the third day."

Actually, I'm surprised that
the apostles were so dense!

What Jesus said was so contrary to everything his Jewish disciples had been taught from childhood up. They had learned that when a Messiah came, he would be a reigning-political Messiah. And they *did not* believe the Messiah could die. At that time, people believed in "good works" and salvation; the whole emphasis was on the human effort. But Jesus said,

"No, it is the Divine effort with a human response." That is contrary to the very ego and self-centeredness of man.

Mysticism—the emotion, the spiritual connection—are very critical to scripture. But it must always be tied to a stake that is driven down into and grounded in scripture. The problem is that today we don't have that stake driven down, so everybody is off to their own thing—a smorgasbord. Mystics can be dangerous because instead of using scripture to discern truth, they use their feelings, emotions, and spiritual aptitude at any given moment to decide what is true and what is not.

Is your faith based on beliefs or on an
experience of your relationship with God?

My faith is based upon the convicting Word of the Holy Spirit in my life. The Bible is a true, historically accurate and reliable message from God. It's infallible. Any experience must find its foundation in scripture. Many people today *read their experience into the scripture. We must read our experience out of the scripture.*

People come to me with phenomenal experiences like speaking in tongues, but that's contrary to scripture and totally outside the admonitions of scripture, so I question the validity of that experience. God knew we needed an ultimate focal point and that's the scripture. As the book of Hebrews says, "God revealed himself in multiple ways, but mainly through the scripture and the person of Jesus Christ." Today everybody likes to take any spiritual experience and call it "Christian." I can't! Satan can give spiritual experiences too. The Holy Word of God is the benchmark by which we can determine if a spiritual experience is a valid experience with the Living God.

Resurrection?

First of all, I believe in a point in time and history when Jesus Christ was raised from the dead. I believe there was a physical tomb, physical stone, physical grave wrappings—he was physically dead and on the third day he was physically alive. You better believe I believe that! But at one time I totally laughed at that and rejected it.

The disciples couldn't understand what Christ predicted. How could they understand the resurrection when they believed Jesus was the Messiah, who would be a reigning-political Messiah and couldn't die? So they couldn't believe in the resurrection, nor could they grasp the resurrection at that time.

Jesus' lost years from ages 12–29? Did Jesus learn things? Or make mistakes or sin?

During those years he probably had a lot of dates! Luke 2:52 says, "And Jesus grew in wisdom and stature, and in favor with God and men." In that period, Jesus matured in wisdom. In Philippians it says, "He came down and took on the form of man," and, therefore, he limited himself in many ways and limited the expression of his deity. So did his humanity have to learn anything? I don't know, but I don't think Jesus ever made a mistake morally. There is no indication in the scripture whatsoever that he fell morally. Even though he was tempted in every way, as you and I have been tempted.

Second Coming?

I believe in the Second Coming, and God believes in it too—that's why he sent Jesus. 1 Thessalonians 4 says, "as Christ was taken up, shall he come back . . ." I believe Jesus will come back and the dead in Christ will be raised and those who are alive will be taken up in heaven. Then he will come back to reign for a thousand years.

Some scholars believe that Jesus
thought the end would all take place
within that generation.

You can always find some "scholars" who will say almost anything. There is nothing that's been said that's so absurd that it couldn't be said by a scholar or a philosopher or a theologian.

I'm not sure Matthew has Jesus saying that the end of the world was going to be during that generation. First of all, the Jews had not yet returned from exile, so it couldn't have taken place in their lifetime according to Matthew.

Intimate relationship or married?

Jesus had relationships, but what do we mean by intimate? He had very close, intimate relationships. Intimate means "no barrier" between two individuals, but to me that doesn't mean sexual. There is no indication he had romantic relationships, and that probably isn't important. Jesus identified with us in all ways and what that shows me is that no matter what I go through, he has faced it emotionally—rejection, lack of trust, everything. But you don't have to have a sexual relationship to have that.

The most important teaching of Jesus?

I don't think you can say the things that Jesus said and be just a mere moral man and good teacher. I mean you'd have to be, as C. S. Lewis said, either "a liar, a lunatic or Lord" and there is no room for "legend"—that's been dispelled. The most important teaching of Jesus is that "God so loved the world he gave his only begotten son that whoever believeth in him should not perish but have everlasting life." John 3:16.

59
TALKING WITH JESUS

As I lay in bed that night, I asked Jesus why he was here in my midst; he looked around and raised his arms.

"Because of all this," he said.

"But why do I need you in order to relate to God?" I asked.

"You don't," he replied.

"Then why are you here?" I asked.

"Because you need me."

"*I don't understand . . .*" I began to say.

"Exactly," he replied.

60
1 FOR 3: CHUCK SWINDOL

Like many of the people whom I phoned or wrote for an interview, initially Chuck Swindol had said "no." But I felt inspired and persistent, and since I was in Texas anyway, I figured I'd just go to Chuck Swindol's church and after the service ask him face to face for an interview about Jesus.

Like many of the evangelists I've met, Chuck Swindol's church was a gymnasium turned temporarily into a church. As I walked across the grounds toward Stonebriar Community Church in Frisco, I was aware that all the people walking beside me had their Bibles.

"Bring your Bibles—*always*," Chuck Swindol said in a booming voice as I sat down on one of the hundreds of white plastic lawn chairs.

Chuck Swindol is a white-haired, sixty-ish preacher who was recently inducted into the Christian Radio Hall of Fame. I had heard Chuck Swindol many times on his "Insight for Living" radio program, and although I disagreed with him occasionally, his sermons were spiritually invigorating. Much of his power came from a voice that had a clear conviction together with the sound of authority. His voice seemed to echo off the walls of his church in the way that John the Baptist's voice must have echoed among the caves and cliffs of the Judean desert.

"I have an unpopular message today," Chuck Swindol warned the congregation, "but God's holy message is not PC."

"And you were dead . . ." Swindol said with an inflection that both echoed and dangled at the same time.

"Paul said people are lost in their desires," he continued. "They are dead, but you can't tell that by looking at them because they still talk . . . and think . . . and move."

I opened my notebook and scribbled *"spiritually asleep = death; while awake to God's presence = life."*

". . . but God!" Chuck Swindol said, punctuating the air. "Is that a great two words or what?!"

I nodded my head because that certainly was true of my life; if not for God, I'd be dead.

"I used to feel responsible for convincing people of God's love," he said. "But now I just tell the truth."

As I watched and listened to Chuck Swindol speak, I wondered if he knew where his truth ended and God's truth began. Often, they are the same thing—but often a person *just thinks they are the same thing.*

"This is a warning," Swindol said. "Those who are dead try to look good. But don't be fooled into thinking those who are dead are fulfilled. It's a ploy."

"Grace. Grace. Grace." He said. "Good works cannot save us, but good works follow and come after the acceptance of Grace."

"All I can do," Chuck Swindol said, "is accept Grace."

Once again I reached for my notebook and scribbled the questions: *Is the ability to accept Grace, also Grace? Is the true Grace found in realizing that there is Grace?*

"I can't," Charles Swindol said after his sermon when I told him about my Jesus book.

"I can't do an interview," he explained, "because I'm running three ministries and I don't even have five minutes for my grandchildren . . .

". . . *and they're more important to me than you!*" he said in a voice that was somehow intimate and booming at the same time.

He certainly was blunt—*but correct.* I turned, walked over to a chair, and sat down. It's a long ride back to Wisconsin, I thought, and it's even longer when you go back empty-handed. I geared myself up for another try. Sure this Chuck Swindol was a tough nut to crack—*but he'd never seen the likes of me.*

After a few minutes, I went up and asked him again.

"I've interviewed Jerry Falwell, Josh McDowell, many scholars—gotten to know the Grahams—and I think Billy might do it . . ."

"I can't do it," he said firmly. "It's nothing against you—I wouldn't care if you were Billy Graham himself asking for an interview—I'd still say 'no.' "

I rubbed my chin with my right hand as I looked at Chuck Swindol. He just stared back in a nice but firm way. I sighed after realizing there was nowhere to get a foothold with this guy—*his mind was made up.*

A made-up mindset is good because it holds to beliefs and gives clarity through a consistency of belief. This made-up mindset is also useful when you have to tell some pushy writer from Wisconsin "no" twice within the span of a couple minutes. The only danger is when this mindset becomes a habit, and unconsciously pushes away or keeps out any encounters that don't agree with the mindset. Whether it's an author with a purpose, a wife with a need to be heard by her husband, or God seeking to give us a newer and ever-expanding encounter with Grace—the walls of belief protect, but *also can imprison.* How do we balance our need for a strong conviction and belief, while remaining open and fluid enough to allow for God's ever changing, ever more intimate encounter? This is one of the meanings of the cross we (as human beings) must bear.

As I got into my motor home and drove away from Chuck Swindol's church, I sighed in disappointment. When I asked myself, Why? the answer was *because I wanted a perfect book!* Would Chuck Swindol's interview have made the book better? Made it more perfect? I had thought so, but that's where faith comes in. I had to trust in God, that while I worked my butt off, the book would be composed as it was meant to be. I suppose the New Testament authors must have believed the same thing. Thus, just as

I do, they must have prayed. While writing this book, often I prayed for the right motivation, right effort, and right surrender. It's been a struggle to balance "the right amount of pushy author seeking interviews" and the faith that the book will turn out the way it was meant to. In this world, the best we can do is to pray twice. First a prayer for what *we desire,* and second, a prayer for the acceptance of *God's desire.*

✣ 61
1 FOR 4: T. D. JAKES

DALLAS, TEXAS

Incredible. Dynamic. Inspired. That's T.D. Jakes. T.D. probably stood for touchdown, because he tossed one touchdown-inspired phrase after another into his congregation. They responded by clapping, arm waving, body swaying, and dancing.

"Praise God in the way David praised him," he said. "Dance till you lose your clothes—naked before the Lord."

This was a big change from Chuck Swindol's church. I had attended Chuck's service in the morning and not once did anyone stand up or clap or cry out in that service—but here, now—it was almost expected. The Sunday service began mildly enough: "I love the Lamb. I love the Lamb," the congregation sang over and over again. But then, as Bishop Jakes filled them up over and over with his inspired message, they became a community of ever-expanding and erupting volcanoes.

T.D. Jakes, a black bishop from Dallas, Texas, finally took off his suit coat halfway through the service—revealing a perspiration-soaked shirt underneath. Was his "drumming up of spirit" an egotistic and purely ecstatic energetic high? No, T.D. Jakes knew that a soul and body full of praise for God, is empty of self-centeredness. Now I've got to admit, since I grew up in a white, middle-class, Catholic Church, dancing and clapping to the Lord weren't a regular occurrence, and since I was one of the few white people in a predominantly black congregation—I was self-conscious and wondered if I was doing it right. But just then, T.D. Jakes said, "We've come here to praise the Lord—not watch each other."

What I'm trying to say is that Adam and Eve were naked and that wasn't their mistake. Their mistake was in assessing their nakedness as being bad, and, therefore, they had to hide. Since I didn't want to hide at the Potter's Church, I allowed myself to feel the eternal forgiveness and acceptance that was given before we discovered our self-criticism.

I needed that acceptance because after the service, Bishop Jakes' assistant told me that T.D. had just gotten back from California at 3 A.M. and he had done three services just like the one I was at, and he was exhausted. I was disappointed as I drove away from Potter's Church because I had gone one for four in Texas. I sought solace at an all-night gas station where I ate chocolate: one Musketeer bar and two chocolate cookies. It helped.

✛ 62
FALSE PROPHETS SPEAK
BUT DON'T LISTEN

"Can I challenge you?!" the woman asked rhetorically. She was studying to be a preacher and although she had fire in her eyes, they were at the same time strangely vacant.

"Sure," I said.

"I hope and pray that you develop a relationship in yourself with Jesus Christ instead of listening to everyone else . . ."

I immediately felt my anger rise because I had just talked with her and her friend for an hour about Jesus. They had shared their beliefs with me and I'd told them (in what I perceived to be an open-minded way) what I had learned so far while writing my Jesus book. I especially talked about mysticism and the experience of God's presence. But she was not giving me the same respect I gave her. She judged me heavily, basically saying I had no relationship with God while she did. By being open, I had made myself vulnerable—perhaps too vulnerable to her judgment. When was I going to learn? I had found out time and time again that there are religious people out there, especially some Christians, who do not discuss Jesus open-mindedly. Their minds are already made up, and the only reason they talk to you or me is to convince us to think like them. That's when it dawned on me.

"On the street," my brother, the Chicago cop, once said, "people mistake being nice for being weak."

That was it! As I have traveled these past years and spoken to people about Jesus some people have mistaken my open-mindedness for weakness. As though the fact that I wasn't clinging to thoughts about Jesus meant that I didn't know Jesus' heart. But that's what a relationship with God and with Jesus does—it sets you free—it doesn't hold you captive. It leaves you open, connected to God through love, not dogma.

I looked at the young preacher again, and what I saw this time was a scared child whose quick mind and intensity were being used to combat the fears of a confusing and disorienting life. At the bottom of every human being lies the fear that Jesus spoke on the cross: "My God, my God why have you forsaken me?" (Mark 15:34, NIV). And we all look for ways to deal with that fear. Jesus said, "I have come that they may have life, and have it to the full" (John 10:10, NIV), but some people choose dogma about Jesus and cling to that in order to hide from life's fear. But I believe Jesus meant, Let go into the love of God, the life of God with Jesus as guide.

"So you assume I have no relationship with God?" I asked with just a hint of anger.

"You're searching . . ." she began.

"I'll tell you something . . ." I said, still feeling my anger. For a moment, I thought about speaking from this anger, but then I took a deep breath and felt the presence of God in my heart. It was a unitive feeling, not divisive.

"There's a difference between searching and exploring," I continued. "A searcher is lost. An explorer explores what he or she has found. *God is explorable.* I think we've both discovered God's country. And maybe you want to settle in one city, but me, I love God so much—not more than you—but my love wants to know all of my Beloved. So I prefer to travel through the various parts of God's country. Exploring."

I don't think she heard what I said, because as soon as I had finished, she jumped on the chance to ask if she could pray with me.

"Sure," I replied. As I listened to her prayer, I realized she saw herself as a preacher praying for her flock—and unwittingly it was she who had judged the flock (although she told herself it was God's judgment), and now ironically, since she had judged them, she had to pray for them.

When she was done praying, I also said a short prayer. Then I went out to my motor home and retrieved a small bag of beads that Mother Teresa had blessed when I saw her in India. I offered one bead each to the two young women.

"Are these Indian things?" the aspiring preacher asked.

"Yes," I replied as she recoiled from touching them.

"But Mother Teresa blessed them," I said, trying to reassure her.

"No thanks," she replied.

I told them the story of how when I was in India one of Mother Teresa's nuns wouldn't take the beads to Mother Teresa.

"They're Hindu," the nun said. "Mother Teresa won't bless these."

"I think she will," I replied.

"No, she won't," the nun said. We repeated this exchange four to five times until the nun saw that I wasn't budging.

"Okay—I'll ask her," the nun said, taking the bag of beads. "But she won't bless them."

Ten minutes later the nun returned with a smile.

"She blessed them," she said.

"So you see," I told the two women, "that Mother Teresa blessed these, even though they're Hindu."

"No thanks," the young preacher replied, looking as though the beads might bite.

As I walked to my motor home, I wondered. Did she not want a Mother Teresa bead because Mother Teresa was Catholic and she was Baptist? Or was it because, even though the beads were blessed by Mother Teresa, they were still Hindu?

As I drove away, I rolled down the driver-side window. The air rushed by as I took in a deep breath and then exhaled a goodbye to God's town of Waco, Texas. I then focused on the road in front of me, and opened to that as of yet, next unknown place. The driving, the traveling, the journey, is often God's most Holy Place. It's between "this and that"—the place between places—perhaps even the space between thoughts. Ideally, God is seated upon the throne of our thoughts, and just as importantly, God moves mysteriously in that space between thoughts. Unknown, and vast, this space before form and even before void, is the place from which all "born again" experience is uncovered. Thoughts and beliefs about God may come from this renewing place, but *they are not the renewing place*. As the miles click away, I slowly let go of my thoughts until I am overcome by Presence.

✛ 63
THE LOVE OF GOD AND JACKED AROUND

While working on the Jesus book I'm continually up and down. I get hopeful when some people like Bill McCartney of "Promise Keepers" says he'll do an interview, then I get discouraged when he changes his mind. Others say "yes" and I'm excited, and then the next day their assistant acts as though they don't know who I am when I call, and put me off as though waiting for me to give up.

Isn't this the way of the world? It jacks you around? One moment it makes you high, and the next it brings you down. No wonder Jesus said, "I am in the world," but "not of the world."[1] I believe he meant don't base your life on the world of changing phenomena, base your world on the love of God because God's love is constant—and grows as we grow without ever abandoning us.

Often while struggling spiritually and financially to finish this book I want God to make it easier. To give me a different life—one that is easy and without worry. But, and it's a big "but"—*that isn't my life*. This is my life, and this is the cup I'm given.

When the cup of life is held or clung to, there is the agony of the Garden of Gethsemane. But when I offer up the cup of my life—to Him who gave it to me—there is peace. The journey of this book is one of continual clinging, surrender and renewal. Oh, how many times have I died while

1. John 17:14.

283

writing this book? Seven? Seven times seven? And seven times that? In some ways I am crucified upon this book. I want so badly to complete it, and yet I have to surrender my wants and longing. Some days I want it to be over—and yet, there are days when the grace and joy of my endeavor envelops me. Isn't this what it means to be human?

✣ 64
JESUS COMES AGAIN

I was reading Ephesians before I went to sleep. As I lay in bed, Jesus came to me.

"Look at me," he said. "Look at me—relax and breathe."

Several times I did that.

Then he said he would tell me a story. I immediately thought I would have to do the "thinking" for the story he would reveal to me. But I didn't want the story to be my creation only, so I relaxed and let the story unfold. He sent me the image of a sheep.

"There was a sheep . . ." he began.

"A sheep?" I asked.

"A sheep . . . and it was lost," he said. ". . . and the shepherd found it," he added.

Then he had me repeat it over and over again like a prayer.

"A sheep was lost," I said, "and the shepherd found it."

Each time I said "a sheep was lost . . ." I felt the words make their way from my head to my chest, into my heart and then all the way down into my feet. Then when I said, ". . . and the shepherd found it," I felt the energy begin above my head and move down into my heart. I said it over and over until the sheep and the shepherd were one in my body. I felt as though I were both sheep and shepherd.

"Aren't you the shepherd?" I asked Jesus.

"You can understand it that way if you want . . ." he said.

When I thought of it that way, I realized that Jesus taught me to find the parts of myself that were lost. *That's what a Savior does.* He reminds you that you're loved not hated. That you're found not lost—and *he sets an ex-*

ample. Jesus told me that I have a sheep inside me and a shepherd inside me, and that he was there to remind me of both.

Then Jesus took me to a place of understanding of Adam and Eve. He showed me why our first judgment is often "I am bad" instead of "I am good." He showed me that the moment we were born into this world, longing arose in our soul. *How we dealt with that longing decided how we experienced our life.* Jesus told me to rest in the longing of my heart and after I did, I understood that my longing is simultaneously God's longing for me. I relaxed into that longing even more deeply and it became a deep and powerful love.

"You can live from this longing and love if you want." He said. "Or you can live from the experience of Adam and Eve, which is one of longing *filled with fear and shame.* This kind of longing attempts to right itself by taking hold of judgment and the struggle between good and evil."

"But," he said, "*if the heart rests in love and God, then all judgment comes from that love . . . and then 'in this world we are like him.'*"

✢ 65
DOES JESUS SPEAK TO ME

Does Jesus *really* talk to me?

To answer "yes" sounds inflated and presumptuous, but to answer "no" would be a lie.

✢ 66
LUKE TIMOTHY JOHNSON

ATLANTA, GEORGIA

I'm embarrassed to say this, but one thing that stuck out about Luke Johnson is that he wore gym shorts. I think it had something to do with the fact that he's a professor, and an authority on Jesus—and somehow, he just appeared less authoritative wearing gym shorts.

I liked Luke Johnson because he was not afraid of being outspoken, whether it was about the Jesus Seminar or the immaturity of some Christians. Also he was one of the few people who had read my first book cover to cover and actually threw quotes back at me from the book. During our meeting, I occasionally disagreed with him (but if disagreements were automatic disqualifications for liking someone—I wouldn't like anybody) and he clarified many confused areas of understanding. One of which had to do with Christians or former Christians who reject their religion.

"Most Christians have a religious intelligence of less than eight years old," Luke Johnson said.

He told me about an English professor he knew who had had an awakening at thirteen and who said that after that "Everything I had been taught in Church suddenly seemed nonsensical, even preposterous."

"So this guy," Luke Johnson said, "decides at thirteen that Christianity doesn't make sense. Now he's a fifty-year-old English professor and he's still trying to work out why Christianity doesn't make sense. Of course he hasn't read any books about it in the meantime! He's still upset, angry, and operating with this, 'I thought Jesus knew everything from day one' third-grade belief. Well, it was Sister Mary of the Perpetual Suffering who told him that, and she was probably a seventeen-year-old Irish woman who had never read a book in her life!"

He helped me realize that part of what I was accomplishing by writing this book was that I was allowing my understanding of Jesus to mature. When I asked Luke Johnson why seemingly intelligent people held on to childish conceptions of Jesus he said, "An awful lot of that kind of religion is driven by fear. It is a culture of fear."

It was time for my Christianity to grow up. And if the Christianity of your youth doesn't make any sense, maybe it's because it was *the Christianity of your youth!* I've met many adults who fled the Christianity of their childhood and approached Buddhism, Hinduism, and Islam as adults. Consequently, they thought their new religion was more mature and made more sense, when often it was just that they were now adults learning new, adult things instead of being an adult who was trying to live with old, childish things. I realized I was an adult now, and I had to earn my beliefs by studying my beliefs and helping them to grow. Of course it was totally acceptable for me to change religions as an adult, but perhaps it was more profitable to just change my childish conception of Jesus into an adult one.

Timothy Luke Johnson was a former Benedictine monk and priest. He is now Robert W. Woodruf Professor of New Testament and Christian Origins at Candler School of Theology at Emory University in Atlanta, Georgia, and author of *The Real Jesus, Living Jesus: Learning the Heart of the Gospel* and *The First and Second Letters to Timothy.*

Who was/is Jesus?

The struggle within the Christian faith in its earliest centuries was precisely the struggle with the oxymoronic conviction that Jesus was both divine and human. On one side, here is Jesus, who is utterly human, born of a woman, born under the law. On the other side is the equal conviction that in him one is touched by and touches God! The way in which the paradox has been distorted has been through simplifying in one direction or another; by saying, "He is just a man," or "He is simply God." Classic Christian faith has declared both extremes wrong. One extreme leads to the ancient heresy called Arianism, which says that Jesus' humanity is all there is, together with a mystical unity he has accomplished. The other extreme leads to a Gnostic Jesus who is running around with a body but is not really human.

If one says, "He was God and he knew he was God," then he obviously cannot be human, for no human can simply be God and know with divine knowledge. If one makes it that simple, then one has lost the human Jesus. You have swallowed up his humanity in divinity. If, on the other hand, one says, "He was a good Jewish teacher who was really for compassion and wanted to invite sinners to his table, and that's pretty much it," then one has also lost something essential. I want to avoid those unhappy options. After two thousand years, Christianity retains the conviction that Jesus is truly human and died in the way that you and I die. Equally, we believe that in this human Jesus, God is truly and somatically revealed. Of course, this is preposterous. That's what makes Christianity both puzzling and attractive.

We can't get at a Jesus behind the gospels. What we have are literary representations of this figure. If you say, "It seems to me that the Jesus of Matthew's gospel is true," I would agree. But I would add that the Jesus of Mark's gospel is no less true, and that the Jesus of Luke's gospel is equally true, and that the Jesus of John's gospel is true as well. This is how I differ from those who are questing for the historical Jesus. I don't think we can get past the literary representations in any great detail. One could equally ask, whose is the real Julius Caesar? Is it Suetonius's Caesar or Plutarch's Caesar? Or, whose is the real Socrates? Is it Plato's, or Aristophanes', or Xenophon's? Likewise, whose is the real Jesus? Mark's, Matthew's, Luke's, or John's?

So when you say, "Jesus was X," I always insist on being a little bit persnickety and asking, "According to which gospel or (for that matter) other New Testament writing?"

Was Jesus the only son of God?

Christian belief says that Jesus is, by nature, what we become by adoption. He is meant to be the first-born of many children. Jesus is the cause of salvation, but also the pioneer and perfecter of a faith that we share. Jesus is the one who is called Amen and Son, *par excellence.* But others can come to share in his inheritance. Jesus is absolutely unique because in his being he represents what others can become. He is the first-born from the dead. He is the source of others' participation.

Is Jesus the only way?

The statement "I am the Way and the Truth and the Life" (John 14:6, NIV) appears in John's gospel. John is one witness to Jesus. And Christians believe that for them, Jesus is indeed the way to the Father, and the truth and their source of life. But John's witness must be heard with other voices in the New Testament. In Romans, Paul asks, "Is God the God of the Jews only? Is He not the God of the Gentiles also? Yes, of the Gentiles also, since God is One" (Rom 3:29). And in 1 Timothy, he says as well, "God wills all humans to be saved and to come to the knowledge of the truth" (1 Tim 2:4). These statements point to a wider vision of God's capacity to reach all people, even apart from Christian revelation. Even in the New Testament, Christianity is a complex conversation. One can prove anything one wants on the basis of Scripture. The real issue is how to think soundly on the basis of Scripture. There are some Christians who live in a mental village. There are others who want the world to be their village. The first sort are deeply uncomfortable with pluralism. They would like to have a government and culture that reflects their own narrow perception of what God is up to. That's an old temptation. It is called idolatry, the tendency to identify God with one's own understanding of God. I think the better vision is the larger one.

We are related to God by the fact that we exist. Everything that exists is related to God the creator. Every conscious creature has the capacity to assume and assert that relationship. It is possible for a Sri Lankan child and a Muslim child or an unbaptized child in Detroit to have a relationship with God that is utterly nondependent on anybody else's revelation. Jesus and the saints (whether inside Christianity or outside Christianity) show us the possibilities and potential for such a relationship.

Was Jesus perfect? Did he ever sin?

I want to be cautious. When you ask, "Do you think he ever sinned?" I need to ask in turn, "What do you mean by 'sin'?" Definitions matter. In my book *Faith's Freedom,* I distinguish between inadequacy, failure, and sin.

Every human being is inadequate in any number of ways. They are inadequate to do things they might like to do. I would like to be a major league baseball player. But that won't happen! I haven't failed. I am simply inadequate.

Failure happens when there is something one can do, but one doesn't do for a variety of reasons. The reasons may not have anything to do with malice, but may have something to do with sloth, laziness, inattention, and so forth.

Sin, however, is a conscious, deliberate, and knowing rebellion against what one perceives to be good, or the deliberate choice of what one perceives as evil. Was Jesus, like other humans, inadequate? Yes. Did Jesus, like other humans, fail? Yes. Did Jesus sin? Jesus did not. My faith is predicated on this truth about Jesus. And in the Letter to the Hebrews, it is stated that Jesus "in every respect has been tempted as we are, yet without sin" (Heb 4:9).

What religion was Jesus?

Jesus was Jewish. But what being Jewish meant in first-century Palestine was a very complex issue. Judaism was a tremendously diverse reality in the first century. There were many competing versions of Judaism. It is impossible to line up Jesus precisely with any one of those versions. And in some sense, Jesus lies at the jumping-off point of one of the most creative of all versions of Judaism, namely Christianity.

Virgin birth?

A way of rephrasing your question is, "Do I think that the virgin birth is a historical fact?" Then I would answer, "How could one possibly know that under any circumstances, since history has to do with verifiable events in time and space?" Whether or not anyone is a virgin at any point in life is something historians would find hard to verify under the best of circumstances. In other words, when Matthew and Luke talk about Mary as a virgin giving birth to Jesus, they are not concerned with the biology of reproduction. I don't think we (or they) could make a historical judgment on that. I think that the symbol of the virgin birth points to Jesus' origin as divine. That is to say, it is a deep Christian conviction that God's involvement in Jesus did not happen only after his death (in resurrection) but was active also during his human life. In that sense, yes, I affirm the virgin birth as a mythic, not a historical, statement. But remember that, for me, myth is often truer than history!

Accuracy of the gospels?

I believe the gospels are inspired. I don't think they are entirely accurate as historical records. The New Testament writings are irreducibly diverse. They do not speak with one voice. It is quite clear that they don't say the same thing on many points. This is certainly the case in the story of Jesus told by the gospels. But we do not have a referee who can say, "that one is correct and this one is wrong." We do know that the wording in Matthew's version says something different than the version in Mark, and that sometimes the gospels give quite different accounts. In John's gospel, for example, Jesus dies the day before the Passover, and in Matthew's gospel he dies on Passover. He can't do both, but we don't know which (if either) is correct.

Your question tries to get at the Christian tendency to justify positions on the basis of the New Testament. My bumper sticker on that point is that people claiming to live simply on the basis of what the New Testament says are liars. They either lie to themselves or to others. In fact, it is impossible to live simply by what the New Testament says, because the New Testament says too many contradictory things.

For example, what should be the Christian attitude toward the world? Should Christians regard the world in a neutral or positive sense, as Paul and Peter do, or in a negative way, as James and John do? These are opposite attitudes. They can't be harmonized.

What should Christian attitudes be toward Jews? Should we follow the gospel of Matthew, which says, "All the Jews cried out, 'His blood be upon us and upon our children'" (Matt 27:25), a passage that was used as the basis for a horrendous history of anti-Semitism in Western Europe, or should we follow the gospel of Luke, which in many small editorial touches tries to remove the populace from any responsibility for the death of Jesus?

What should we do or think about purity regulations? Are we reading Paul, or are we reading Revelation, which seems to be irritated at people holding positions much like Paul's? Different views, different voices.

On any number of points, the New Testament writings either don't talk about things we would like them to talk about, or talk about them inadequately, or talk about them contradictorily. This is why "Christian ethics" seems oxymoronic. Christianity is odd in its failure to provide clear and consistent guidance.

When I taught comparative religion at Indiana University to undergraduates, they understood Judaism instantly. God reveals God's rules, you do what God says, God rewards you. All is well. Likewise, Islam made perfectly good sense. Allah reveals Allah's will, you do what Allah has commanded, and Allah rewards you. All is well.

But in Christianity, we ask what we are to do! And it is not quite clear. How does God reveal God's will in Jesus? That's not so clear. Christianity is based on the experience of God in a human person. Nothing could be more paradoxical. Nothing could be more difficult to understand.

This is one reason why Christianity, together with Buddhism, remains a powerfully attractive tradition for many throughout the world. Christianity and Buddhism both begin with the tragic character of human existence and the reality of suffering. By comparison, Judaism and Islam are cheerily optimistic. If you know what is good, you can do it. Knowledge assumes the power to perform. But Christians and Buddhists share a strong sense of human entrapment in illusion. This sense is as powerful in Christianity as in Buddhism. It is called idolatry. How do we break the chain of suffering? How do we reach fullness of being? Buddhism shares with Christianity the centrality of suffering and (in the concept of the Bodhisattva), the compassionate one who participates in the suffering of others. In Christianity, however, human suffering is not removed but it is transfigured through God's participation in suffering through Christ.

Who killed Jesus and why?

For all their inadequacy as historical records, the gospels hit on two probable historical elements in the death of Jesus. Jesus was executed by Roman authorities, and there was some involvement by some Jewish leaders. Not many serious scholars would disagree with these two propositions. This is partly because under Roman rule in the first century, the Prefect had the right to execute under a wide range of circumstances. If there was a riot in the city, for example, he could—for the sake of order—say, "Take the first four suspects and hang them." That's the way to quell a riot. Was there a formal Sanhedrin hearing? Was there a religious issue? Or did some Jewish leaders who did not like Jesus say to the nearest Centurion, "He's the one who's causing this riot. Hang Him!"? There might have been a quick kangaroo court, and as a result Jesus is crucified. We can't really historically reconstruct the exact reasons for Jesus' execution or the sequence of events. It could have been either the combination of elements that the gospels report, or something quite different. The gospels portray it as a religious dispute, shaped into a political challenge. Thus, an intra-Jewish debate becomes projected by the Jewish leaders to the Roman official as something politically volatile, and then we have Pilate, who is nobody's idea of an ideal governor. He takes it from there, perhaps along the lines I have suggested.

Resurrection?

I believe in the resurrection of Jesus as his full entry into the life and power of God. I also believe in a bodily resurrection. But I don't believe in a bodily resuscitation. It's an important distinction. The difficulty in talking about the resurrection is that we assume we know what bodies are, but we don't. We especially don't know what living bodies are. We don't know where our bodies begin and where they end. We don't know how much our body is simply us. What is essentially us and what is only accidentally us? The phenomenology of body is a very difficult subject. Do you *have* a body, or *are* you a body? Well, both! And that's the problem. The body is the symbol of the self, yet the body also is the self. If we take the body as the symbol of the self, then if Jesus is not raised bodily, it is not Jesus who is raised, and that is at the heart of the Christian confession.

What would Jesus think of Christianity today?

Some people think that, beginning already with Paul, Christianity has basically misunderstood Jesus. I prefer to say that Christianity has been a tragically inadequate body of the resurrected Jesus. But Jesus still has found a way, through the saints, to constantly vivify Christianity. The necessity of saints is that they speak the truth about God's work, and through them God's work is done.

Second Coming?

I agree with early Christian belief and the constant creedal conviction that Jesus will share in God's future triumph. There are two elements, here. One is that Jesus' story is not finished. The other is a profoundly optimistic sense that somehow history is moving toward God's victory, and that Jesus will be part of that victory.

Do scholars, mystics, and evangelists see Jesus,
or do they see their own reflections?

I am by no means a despiser of historical scholarship. In fact, I wrote *The Real Jesus* as a defense of proper historical method. My argument is that good historiography must respect its own limits. Using the most critical historical methods, the same we would apply to Cicero or Caesar, historians can make a number of very important and highly probable statements about Jesus: that he was a Jew who lived in Galilee, that he spoke in parables, that he was a wonder-worker, that he had followers, that he associated with the marginal, that he proclaimed God's rule, that he was baptized by John, that he performed a prophetic action in the temple, that he was executed by the Romans.

The difficulty is that the nature of our sources puts up intractable barriers to going further by means of history alone. And when we try to push past those barriers, that's when we create a Jesus in our own image.

In other words, because the gospels don't speak with one voice, because they are written from the perspective of faith in Jesus as the resurrected one, because they cover at most three years of his activity, the efforts either to harmonize them or to pick one version to trump the others, or— as John Dominic Crossan and the Jesus Seminar do—to run all the pieces through a sieve to determine the authentic ones and then reassemble them, all of these efforts end up as modes of projection.

It's not that the historical task is unworthy. It is simply that the number one requirement of a good historian is modesty. There is a limit to what we can say historically. In the case of Jesus, what is most important to know can't be known by historical means.

My tack, therefore, has been to insist that history is not the only legitimate mode of knowing. History becomes a problem only when we insist that it is the only way to know.

The process of learning Jesus is not a process of reconstituting a historical figure from the records of the past. It is, rather, engaging in a complex conversation involving those who know and encounter Jesus both in the past and the present. Our ongoing experience of Jesus and these ancient texts come together in a living conversation. Jesus can be known and is known through multiple bodies: in the body that is the community, in the bodies of the saints, in the body of the sacrament, in the bodies of strangers and the little ones of the earth. The New Testament itself suggests an intense unity between the Jesus who was and the Jesus who is: whoever receives a child in his name receives him; those who visit the sick and welcome the stranger and feed the poor and clothe the naked do so for and to him. Knowing Jesus really, it seems to me, involves these multiple modes of knowing.

Faith itself is a way of knowing. Not simply as an intellectual assent to a proposition, but as a living response to a living presence.

✢ 67
I'VE CHANGED

MADISON, WISCONSIN

"Bill," Marge, a friend and wife of a minister, said, "You look and sound different. A year ago you seemed angry as though you were trying to disprove something about Jesus."

I told her that my relationship with Jesus had deepened. With that, a broad smile spread across her face.

"Oh, Bill," she said, genuinely happy for me, "it sounds like you've had a conversion."

She was right, I had changed, but there was something in the way she spoke that alarmed me. It was the sense that somehow I was now part of her group—*that I had joined them.* While my experience was that the sense of separation or difference between me and other people became less as I came closer to Jesus and God. Jesus always said, "I am the son of man," which was his way of saying, "I am a human being." *That was it*—as I came closer to Jesus and God, I became more of a human being. I became more alive and communed more with God's creation. It wasn't a matter of us and them, because *there is only us.*

✢ 68
IT'S TOO BIG

"It's too big!" my mind shouted to itself. "It's too big!"

I was overwhelmed by the magnitude of what I was doing and the fear that it wouldn't work. Lately, whenever I called people for interviews, it seemed they were either not home, or out of town. This led to a constant battle with my doubts and fears of rejection.

I persisted and when I finally reached them, most of them said an interview wasn't possible now.

"How about in a few months?" I asked. Their replies all seemed to be vague. My anxiety didn't want to wait—but what choice did I have? What could I do? Where do I go now? How do I finish on time?

Finally, all I could do was take a deep breath, and let the answer come. *Be thorough. Do your best and let God do the rest.*

✢ 69
NEALE DONALD WALSCH

MADISON, WISCONSIN
In 1992, Neale Donald Walsch's life changed when, in a moment of extreme frustration, he wrote an "angry letter to God." His best-selling book, *Conversations with God,* is an account of the answers he received in his dialogue with God. Of course, any intelligent person would have to ask: how do I know that was really God talking to Neale Donald Walsch? The obvious answer is, *Ask God yourself.*

Neale Donald Walsch's books inspire while exposing the state of our own relationship with God. Do we have conversations with God? If so, how often? How do we know it's God speaking to us? I suspect conversing with God is like being in love. Actually I suspect *they are the exactly same thing.* 1 John says, "God is love" (1 John 4:16, NIV) and no one can tell you if you are in love. Somehow *you just know*. And no one can tell you if you are talking to God, *you just know*. Now, of course, just like love, often we have to learn to discern God from our own concepts or projections of God—but isn't that the whole point of spiritual practice? To learn to love the real God, and not our concept or idol. Jesus said (quoting Jewish scriptures), "Love the Lord your God with all your heart and with all your soul and with all your strength and with all your mind." Jesus didn't say, "Love the God you were told about," he said, "Love *your* God . . ." (Mark 12:30, NIV) That's why a lover of God never just accepts what people tell him/her about God. A lover of God goes beyond the false idols of words, concepts, and beliefs about God—*and goes to God.* Sometimes one can merge and disappear in God. But more often than not, being human means conversing with God. We may ask God, "Father, if you are willing, take this cup from me," or say to God, "not my will, but yours," or perhaps even go into the desert for forty days in order to silence the devil and more easily hear and speak with God. But it's all done within a relationship of loving conversation, and even when it is not so loving on our part—*it is always loving on God's part.*

Is finding God easy? No, but finding God *is simple.* We do it by having *conversations with God, conversations with love.*

Neale Donald Walsch is the author of the best-selling *Conversations with God* books and he is the founder of ReCreation, a nonprofit organization that sponsors lectures, programs, seminars, workshops, and retreats across the country for persons interested in spiritual and personal growth. He lives with his wife, Nancy, and his dog, Lady, in Oregon.

Who was/is Jesus?

Jesus was all the things we think he was. First of all, Jesus *was God* coming down.

Second he was a wise man who was deeply connected to the highest spiritual truths and the deepest understandings of life. He held his understanding of ultimate realty deep in his heart and lived it in every moment of his life. He was enormously compassionate and very wise. He was no more nor less than any or all of us could be and are, and his greatest teaching was John 14:12: "Anyone who has faith in me will do what I have been doing. He will do even greater things than these." He realized himself, *made himself real,* which is the process of realization. The greatest difference between Jesus and most people on the planet isn't that he was different, but that he was more aware of who he was.

Was Jesus the only Son of God?

Jesus wasn't the only Son of God—God isn't that stingy. The generosity and love of God are unlimited. God didn't just send only one Son to earth. On the contrary, God has populated the earth with nothing else but sons and daughters of God. But there are people who do not believe that and do not experience that and, in fact, there are people who need not to believe that. They have a deep need not to experience their sonship of God, because they have the need to deify another at a higher level than they would deify themselves. Indeed, to even think of deifying themselves would be the greatest blasphemy. But in order to honor God at the highest level, we must declare ourselves one with her. The greatest and truest messages of Jesus have been lost: "Even as I am, so too can you also be" and "God and I are one and you and I are brothers." He tried to teach a message he lived and experienced in his heart, which was "the eternal oneness of all things."

We experience each other as separate from each other and separate from everything else. We imagine all things to be separate from all other things—trees to be separate from earth, to be separate from fish, to be separate from humans, and humans to be separate from each other. This doctrine of separation is one of the ten illusions that cause human beings to live their lives in the way that they do. Jesus and other great saints and avatars and sons and daughters of Gods came here on a mission to remind us, in powerful and memorable ways, of our oneness with each other and with God, and that the concept of oneness is not merely a theological construction but a practical tool with which to express and experience our daily lives. They remind us of what oneness can and will produce. They told us that we will never really make any major improvements in our daily lives until we make the concept of "the understanding of oneness" experiential. Unless we shift our experience into oneness, we will continue living the same sorrows and repeating the same mistakes from generation to generation, from century to century, and millennia to millennia. Because, despite all of our technical advances, we still face many of the same dilemmas and difficulties. Greed, avarice, and violence run as rampant today as they did thousands of years ago, and they will continue to do so until we get to a place where we can take the Jesus-teaching of oneness and apply that teaching as a practical matter in our everyday life and express the truth of that teaching through our everyday life in our politics, in our economics, in our education, in our religions, and in our every expression of life.

What spiritual techniques did Jesus teach?

Jesus spent forty days and forty nights in the desert. He was saying unless you spend time alone with yourself you cannot understand that *there is no way to be alone.* Ironically, the only way not to be alone is to be alone. In the silence of being alone, you will discover that it is impossible not to be united. But you cannot experience your unity with all things until you (temporarily and on a regular basis) physically separate yourself from the frenzies of everyday life. Then you experience and deeply understand the one truth of all life, which is that all life is one truth. Everything is a circle.

The first spiritual technique of Jesus was singular contemplation of ultimate reality or what we would call meditation. Another tool that he encouraged us to use was the tool of knowingness, which some religions have called faith. Jesus' version of knowingness or faith was much greater than the word faith could hold. Because faith is a belief that something is true or will occur, whereas knowingness is an absolute knowing that it will. The faith of Jesus went beyond faith and was an absolute clarity from knowing that is beyond any experience that the word "faith" can convey.

When human beings experience that knowingness, then it's not a question of faith because faith is the art of deluding yourself and scholars and evangelists don't understand that. Faith is looking at the appearance of things and refusing to believe the appearance of things: "Judge not by appearances." All people of true faith are in fact involved in the art of self-delusion. They see one thing and imagine another. They see a person who is deathly ill and imagine that person can be healed through the power of prayer. Through a miracle! Faith is a process of deluding yourself or refus-

299

ing to believe in the reality of the world as it presents itself to you and choosing instead a higher reality that your faith announces to you as what is truly so. That is how Jesus performed miracles.

Virgin birth?

I don't believe in anything. Beliefs are what destroy human spiritual experience. Beliefs are dangerous because they are simply frames of mind that we adopt and accept because someone has invited or encouraged us to. Or in the case of some religions, demanded that we do. The sad irony is that organized religion has done more to separate people from each other and from God than any other institution. Organized religion didn't mean to do that but in my view they simply misunderstood the essential teaching of Jesus and of all mystics and masters. They required people to believe a certain thing in order to have everlasting union with God or what religionists call heaven. Churches and various religions teach what they call truths, but they are actually doctrines. For some, the virgin birth is a theological doctrine and you cannot enter into the kingdom of heaven unless you believe it. The danger with beliefs is that they require a human being to set aside his or her own instinctual understanding of things and to accept what someone else has told them is the truth.

The way religions justify their teachings is by deifying the human beings through which the teachings came. Whether it's Mohammed or Krishna or Christ, while these people walked on the earth, they were really God-people and the rest of us are not. And furthermore, there will never be anyone else again. Not only are the rest of us not God-people but there will never, ever, ever, ever, ever be another one again, so just forget about it. Just accept the words that have been brought through by Mohammed or Jesus or Krishna because there will never be another one, another instance where God confers upon a human, divinity itself. But this is the antithesis of what is so. God has conferred upon all people divinity itself, and it's just that these extraordinary humans were among the few of us who realized it, who understood it deeply, who experienced it and expressed it in a way that was so astonishing to people around them that, indeed, people around them called them divine. I don't *believe* in the virgin birth, or in any particular theological doctrine of any organized religion. My spirituality is not based on beliefs, it is based on my direct experience and what it is that I know to be so.

Gospel accuracy?

It's important to understand that from the point of view of those who wrote them, they are one hundred percent accurate. That is to say they are one hundred percent reflections of the truths expressed, experienced, understood, and shared by those people who wrote them.

People ask me how accurate do I think my book *Conversations with God* is? I tell them it's a hundred percent accurate if you're asking me "Is this a reflection of your experience?" Nothing's been shaded, nothing's been changed in order to sell more books or somehow appeal to the masses; there's been no compromise in that material, nor is there any compromise in the gospels. On the other hand, if you asked me, "Given that it is a one hundred percent representation of your truth and your experience, is it one hundred percent true in terms of what is objectively so?" I would say probably not. I'm not aware of any scripture or any writing or any experience of human beings that would be one hundred percent in accordance with what you and I would call for the purposes of this discussion—absolute reality. That is because the information that is brought through the human soul is brought through the filter and the screen of our own minimized experience. I say minimized experience in that to the degree that we are housed in our bodies and captured by the devices called our minds, we are to that degree experiencing minimal understanding of ultimate reality. In order to understand ultimate reality, you must be literally "out of your mind" and aligned with the mind of God.

Because in the moment I am out of my mind, in that moment I really do begin to understand, in an unlimited way, alternate reality. People who have had these flashes or "born-again" experiences are sometimes forevermore changed by just a moment, a nanosecond, walking along a stream or flying through the air in an airplane or meditating in the middle of the night or making love or singing a song or just cooking dinner and washing dishes. At these times, somehow or another, a flash of awareness comes to them. They are literally "out of their minds" and move to another place of awareness where it all becomes clear to them. A one one-thousandth of a second is all it takes and that window shatters of all their beliefs about things and moves them to a place of what they really know. You see, I don't *believe* we are all one, I *know* it. I've had a cellular, knowing experience of that. I've *seen* the oneness of humanity, I've seen the oneness of all reality. I've experienced it at the level of my cells. This is a cellular knowing. It has nothing to do with belief.

Who killed Jesus and why?

He was killed for the same reason we kill all avatars, teachers, and masters—because they are dangerous. They threaten the then-current social order. They unravel the threads and pull the bricks out from under all the constructions on which we have based our entire society, and the largest and most threatening of those constructions is "we are all one." Right now there are several million people who have read my books, but if it ever got to the point of fifty or a hundred million, then I would be a very, very dangerous individual. Because the message of *Conversations with God* is antithetical to everything that our society is now doing in its economics, in its education, in its politics, in its social structures, and perhaps most profoundly in its religions. If I get to the point where I'm considered dangerous by some people, first they will try to kill the message by minimizing and ridiculing it. If they are unsuccessful in minimizing the message, they will try to minimize the messenger and that's why Jesus was killed.

The key theological question is not why do you think they killed Jesus, but why do you think Jesus allowed them to? The answer behind that question provides the truth that opens the door to the richest understanding available to the human soul. That's the question you should be asking of every one of your subjects: "Why do you think Jesus allowed them to kill him?"

Christianity says "Jesus died for your sins."
What does that mean?

That's true if we define sin as any action, thought, or deed taken against one's self. For instance, if I think that I'm less than I am, that's a

302

sin, in the sense that my thinking opposes the truth or image of God that resides in the depth of my soul.

If we say Jesus died in order to demonstrate that our lowest and worst thoughts about ourselves were not true, then it would be true that he died for our sins. But he did not die to save us from our sins in the sense that some insane deity in heaven required the most extraordinary kind of death in order to render everyone else on the planet worthy of reentry into his kingdom. And if they happened to be Jewish or Buddhist or Islamic or belong to some other belief system, then this insane deity would say "I'm sorry, you've led a wonderful life, you've been a deeply compassionate and glorious person, your gifts were marvelously shared with everyone whose life you touched but you're outta here because you didn't accept the doctrine of Jesus' sacrificial/salvational act on the cross at Calvary."

Jesus died to save us from our sins if we define sin as a thought about ourselves that simply is not so. Jesus died on the cross to demonstrate to the entire human race who we really are. Since we couldn't believe who we are, Jesus said, "Then believe on me. If you can't believe in yourself, then watch what I'm doing and understand who I am. Perhaps in understanding who I am, you will one day experience who you are. If nothing else, have faith in the miracles you are witnessing. Watch the miracle of me and one day you will be in touch with the miracle of you." Jesus offered himself as an example, not as a sacrifice to the human race. John 13:15: "I have set you an example that you should do as I have done for you."

Resurrection?

There is no doubt in my mind that he resurrected physically in order to show us who we really are—that we are larger than death itself and that we are, in fact, divine beings able to do extraordinary miracles including come alive again. He was able to demonstrate that death itself does not exist, that it's an illusion, and his resurrection was the grandest demonstration of that. The Christ-teaching and the Christ-experience changed human reality forever. He was probably the single, most impact-full personage ever to walk upon the face of the earth. There were others like Mohammed, Krishna, the Buddha, and these are a handful of people, a handful of beings who walked this planet and whose movement through life changed life and our understanding of life forever.

Was Jesus ever married or
in an intimate relationship?

A sexual relationship? He was in an intimate relationship with the whole human race, which continues to this very day, so let's not flinch and use words that are much larger than we want to use. The words "intimate relationship" are much larger than the words "sexual relationship." I am in an intimate relationship with all of life and with many, many aspects of life. Every moment that I express my authentic truth, share it with others, and visibly demonstrate and live it my life is intimate. That is to say—in-to-me-see. But if you're asking whether I thought Jesus ever had sex with anyone, which is an entirely different and much smaller question, it's such a tiny question it's almost irrelevant but I would say I don't know. I don't even limit my definition of sex to a physical intimacy—my book *Conversations with God* defines sex as a synergistic energy exchange. Given that, I have sex with my personal assistant, Lisette here, probably twelve times a day. We're having sex all over the place because we have a synergistic energy exchange. That's true between me and many, many people on this planet. Hopefully, one day it will be true between me and all people that I meet as I grow to a level of mastery and understand that it is safe to do so. But right now I hold a belief system that even this conversation I am having with you might not be safe. A part of me is saying, "Why are you saying these crazy things to this man who is going to put them into a book?" And another part of me is saying when these insane thoughts of mine become widely distributed, the insanity itself on the planet will disappear. See, we will be healed by the dog that bit us. The hair of the dog that bit you. So it is going to take a bit of this so-called insanity in order to heal the insanity of the world. In truth, these thoughts are not insane at all.

Second Coming?

The Second Coming occurs every time a child is born. God returns to earth in human form every time a newborn baby cries. If we would understand that, everything would change: the way we treat each other, the way we construct our society, the way we interact together. Everything would shift; it would shift overnight if we would simply accept the truth that the Second Coming occurs every time a child is born. That teaching of Christ is the teaching of all true spiritual masters.

Jesus' religion?

Jesus didn't belong to any religion. Nor did he belong to any (in the larger sense) race or ethnic group. He was, as are all true spiritual masters, without boundary. The moment we try to ascribe to Jesus or to any human being or to God certain characteristics, or slap labels on each other like Catholic or Jew or liberal or conservative or even male or female for that matter—as soon as we do that, we limit our understanding and experience and even our ability to interact with another person in a fully authentic way.

Jesus, like all spiritual masters, observed the social and religious traditions of the community into which he was born and from which he emerged. He was obedient, to a point, to the spiritual and political dictates of his time and place, until he returned from his forty days and forty nights in the desert. In the desert he realized he was larger than all of it. Yet he still counseled people to remain true to their secular routes and not to divorce themselves completely from some of the organizing principles which allowed them to experience life and society in some kind of functional way. Thus, he would say things like "render unto Caesar that which is Caesar's" and "render unto God that which is God's" (Mark 12:17, American Standard Version). He said we should obey civil authorities and allow ourselves to submit to the decisions of the largest number of people in the organizing structure that is current to our present experience.

Jesus' lost years?

He was remembering, not learning, and he was engaged in interactions with others. He devoted that time in his life to esoteric study and to the nourishment of his soul that he might emerge from that process purified of all of his old thoughts about things and reconnected again to the highest realities and the deepest understanding of his soul.

If he came back, he would say, "You've got me all wrong."

To the degree that you allow your belief in what you call Christianity to separate you from others of the human race and to cause other members of this human race to feel separate from you, to the degree that you would actually announce and declare as a theological doctrine that only people who are Christian have a gateway to God and those who are not, no matter how they act or behave, no matter who they are or how they choose to grow and what they become, have no access to a return to the divine or to an experience of the divine in this present moment, to the degree that these are your teachings and your doctrines—to that degree you have deeply misunderstood every teaching and every message I sought to bring you. It is profoundly sad that human beings of every stripe and color, of every political persuasion, of every philosophical underpinning, have found one way or another to use the very doctrines that have aroused their heart, to close the heart.

✣ 70
I AM YOUR FRIEND

My morning prayer was painful and difficult. I spontaneously said, "Jesus Have Mercy" three times, and immediately I felt my chest crack and open. At the end of the meditation, I bowed and said with great love, "Lord Jesus have mercy on me."

Then a voice came back and said, "Bill, what are you doing?"

It was Jesus.

"I'm bowing to you," I said.

"Bill—friend," Jesus said, "get up and look at me."

I sat up.

"I am not your master and you're not my servant," Jesus said lovingly, echoing John 15:15. "You're my friend. And remember—*I am your guide and we're going to God together.*"

✣ 71
IN MONTREAT AGAIN

I drove into Montreat, North Carolina, for the third or fourth time in the last year and a half. That's close to eight thousand miles of driving in a motor home at eight mpg and $1.50 per gallon of gas. That's a lot of money for a guy who lives in a trailer.

I kept returning to Montreat because I had made friends there and maybe, just maybe during one of my visits—I would get to interview Billy Graham. Without him, my book would be—at least it would feel—incomplete. Right away, I ran into Brad Long and John Seale at the coffee shop. That's the way it should be I guess. I like John Seale and Brad. We have a lot in common even though they are more conservative than I am. In a way, even though we barely know each other, I consider them brothers, because like me, they always are trying to know God more deeply. We are honest truth seekers, willing to explore Jesus/God with open minds—*we are not afraid*. Rather *we are not afraid of our fear*—because we have faith in God. The temptation in any religion can be to make up one's mind about God and thus leave no way for the Living Presence of God to enter our minds or to grow. Jesus called Peter "Satan"[1] because Peter had his mind made up about God. Close-minded thinking about God is man's way—*who among us can think in God's way?*

The phone rang.

"Hello?" I said, picking up the phone.

"The parade starts in a half an hour," the voice said. I knew it was Jane Alden. I had met her on my first trip to Montreat. It was through her that I first met Gigi Graham (Billy's daughter) and then Ruth Graham. It turned

---

1. Matthew 16:23, NIV.

out that Billy Graham had left town unexpectedly—which was temporarily frustrating, but it worked out because the people I met in Montreat—the Grahams, Jane Alden and her relatives/friends—were helping me to heal a wound that my past experience with hollow, judgmental Christians had sliced open. They weren't doing it by talking about God or Jesus, but by opening their hearts to me and calling me friend.

Besides, I salvaged the trip by attending the Annual Montreat Fourth of July Parade! Since Montreat was a small town, the parade was small and over in a matter of minutes, and I was still chuckling to myself over how the town's new sanitation truck had proudly brought up the rear when I noticed that no one was leaving.

"Why isn't anyone leaving?" I asked Jane Alden.

"Because," she said, "the parade is so small that it usually goes around the block and comes back a second time."

Sure enough, a few minutes later, the parade turned the corner with the sanitation truck once again bringing up the rear. Among the parade participants was a man on a horse who was dressed as the evangelizing minister of the Old West. There were various third, fourth, and fifth graders dressed as aliens with green face paint and antennas made out of pipe cleaners. The local high school girls and boys were dressed up as cavemen and cave women. They were covered with mud and wore animal skins, grunting loudly as they banged wooden tree branches and oversized clubs on the ground. The highlight was the Scottish band dressed in kilts and playing bagpipes.

Later that night I watched the fireworks show over the lake with Jane Alden and her friends. Though I had missed Billy Graham again, the town was starting to feel like a second home. Actually this was making things difficult and confusing because I initially went to Montreat to interview Billy Graham, and now that I had met many of his friends and family who were becoming my friends, I didn't want them to think I liked them only to get to him.

After I confessed my fear to Calvin Theilman, whom I had met on my first trip to Montreat and who was a friend of Billy Graham's, he said "Bill, you're a writer and that's your job—besides I also know you're a kind and sincere man. And," Calvin added, "I will help you anyway I can."

"*When Satan is* brought into the light," the smiling woman said, "he feels uncomfortable."

I would have smiled also, except *she was talking about me.* She was surrounded by eight of her students and she referred to my objections at being judged and attacked harshly by her and her protégées. They had come to Montreat for a Christian retreat weekend, and I had befriended two of her students at the coffee shop twenty minutes before she showed up. It all started when she asked me an innocent question about who I thought Jesus was. I had said that "Jesus was in communion with God and that's why he said, 'The Father and I are One,' but that he wasn't the creator God because he said, 'Why call me good?—there is no one good but the Father' and that when Jesus said he was returning to 'My Father and your Father'—he didn't say he was returning to himself."

It was then the attacks began. First from the teacher, and then from her students. They were the usual attacks: "You're unsaved," "Jesus is the only way," "You're not a real Christian," and then there was the "Satan" comment—one, which I admit, I hadn't heard before. They sat in a semicircle around me and as they spoke, it felt as if the circle closed tighter, like a noose around my neck.

"You're judging me and attacking me," I said. "You basically called me Satan, and assumed that I don't have a relationship with Christ, and that only you do."

"I'm only talking to you like this because I love and care about you," the teacher said, smiling (she was always smiling whenever she attacked me). "I used to be where you're at."

"There you go again," I said. "You're sitting in judgment of me, and you believe you know Christ and I don't."

"Well," she said, "I know where you're coming from . . ."

"What you're saying is that you're evolved to where you are—and one day I'll reach the place you're at."

Then her students started in on me. The two who had talked to me as friends only moments before had now changed. The friendliness and warmth were gone from their eyes, and now they were blank and dark—

and this blankness seemed to allow them to attack me without conscience. Suddenly, I understood how the crowd in Jerusalem could turn against Jesus two thousand years ago.

Their teacher looked on, smiling, proud of her students and proud that they attacked me with the words and concepts she had armed them with. It slowly dawned on me that no matter what I said, they would keep attacking because they fed off each other's attacks; a mob of disciples; blindly following the lead of their teacher.

How do I get out of this? I asked myself. I said, "Jesus have mercy" three times silently. Then the presence of Jesus arose in my being, and I asked him for help.

"Speak truthfully," Jesus said, "and with a sensitive feeling."

"You know," I said to the teacher and her students, "I considered you friends as we shared our understanding of Jesus—but now do you see what's happened? You're sitting in judgment and your emotional energy toward me doesn't feel like love. There's something else going on here."

"Well," the teacher said, "if you're strong in your faith, it shouldn't bother you! Because it wouldn't bother me!"

And then it hit me. She was really saying, *"Nothing can touch me because I have Jesus."* She was using her beliefs about Jesus to keep her safe, and, consequently, *she did not have the heart of Jesus.* I saw in her how easily "smug belief" became a hardened heart. How easily she—*and I*—go from an open yearning for a deeper truth in God to a fear-based, iron-clad righteous assurance that won't let anyone in—especially God. But isn't that what Jesus railed against? The bulletproof smugness of "the keepers of the law" who kept faithful to laws and concepts of God, while being blind to the living spirit?

"On the outside," Jesus said, "you appear to people as righteous but on the inside you are full of hypocrisy and wickedness . . . like whitewashed tombs which look beautiful on the outside but on the inside are full of dead men's bones and everything unclean."

I reflected back to them their Sadducee-like stance.

Then I found myself saying ". . . and I suppose in some ways *I'm no better.* We each have an idea of who Jesus was or is—and we each believe it to be the right one. But at least we probably agree that Jesus taught love . . . and what I've felt from you was anything but loving."

Immediately, I sensed a shift in the group, and their eyes were no longer hardened against me—instead they looked away as though ashamed.

"I'm sorry," the teacher said. But she wasn't really apologizing, if you know what I mean. She was only saying what was called for—like a politician who apologizes for his words because it's the only way to maintain his position in the eyes of his constituents after the tide has turned against him.

She wasn't done though, and she was sly I must say. Because she had read about my parents' death in the author bio of my book *Tying Rocks to Clouds,* her new attack came couched in sheep's clothing.

"Your eyes are . . ." she said, then paused. She looked at me in a way that made me think she was going to say "loving," but she hesitated, perhaps because that word would have given me too much credit.

". . . warm," she said. Her students nodded their heads in agreement. I opened to her compliment, and as I did she spoke.

"I can see . . ." she began. "Actually some people have told me I'm psychic—perhaps intuitive—but I can see you have had deep hurt and sadness in your life . . ." Then she smiled and looked at me. I could not believe what I had just witnessed. She gave me a compliment, expecting me to lower my guard, and then she thought she could sneak in the back door by manipulating my vulnerability. A "trap," albeit a compassionate appearing trap, had been set.

"Well," I said, "it's through our pain and suffering that we open to God's presence in our life."

All her students nodded—they heard and felt what I said. But she didn't immediately acknowledge it. She stared at me blankly. Finally, she nodded and smiled while looking a bit disappointed because I hadn't taken the bait.

"And you can see the sadness and pain of my past," I continued, "because you've been through it also. That's why *I can see it in you.*"

She stopped in her tracks and smiled stiffly.

The feeding frenzy was over, but not without one last judgment on her part.

"I will pray that you will come to know Christ . . ." she said.

"There you go again," I said. "Assuming I don't have a relationship with Christ."

Then a young, innocent-looking girl, who had sat quietly in her chair while all this had transpired, leaned forward.

"Well," she asked without judgment, "do you have a relationship with Christ?"

"Yes I do," I replied, while looking directly into her eyes.

"Okay," she said with a warm, relaxed smile. Then she sat back in her chair and looked at me, satisfied that the only question worth asking had been answered.

✛ 72
RELAX INTO LOVE

While lying in bed, I became aware of Jesus' presence. Then he said, "Look at me."

When Jesus says, "Look at me"—I do not see a face, and I do not see with my eyes, rather I see with a gaze that begins somewhere deep in my soul.

I see, and sense a presence that is his—and it always asks only one thing of me.

"Relax into me," it says and as I do my own heart opens—for that is the only way to really know Jesus—and by knowing him in this way, I know myself as never before—*in ways that I had forgotten.*

✛ 73
MARION WOODMAN

MADISON, WISCONSIN

I was bummed because *I really* wanted to meet Marion Woodman, but she had just gotten over a major illness and she wanted to do an interview by phone.

"Bill," she said in low, raspy voice, "I'm afraid you might come all the way to Canada and I'd be too ill to meet with you."

For a moment I considered pursuing what I wanted to do because you don't write a book that contains meetings with some of the world's top mystics, scholars, and evangelists without being somewhat pushy. And like the woman who fought her way through the crowd just so she could touch Jesus' robe—I had to fight through my fears, doubts, and even the fear and doubts of others—in order to make this book happen. But often in life acceptance is called for, and this was obviously one of those situations. So at 10 A.M. with a tape recorder and Radio Shack recording device attached to the phone I called Marion Woodman.

I must admit I couldn't have felt closer to Marion Woodman if I had been there. "For where two or three come together in my name, there am I with them"[1] is all I can say. It was the kind of conversation that gives a heartened assuredness of God's existence not because of what is said, but because *it happens within God's presence* and there is no denying it.

An hour and a half later, I hung up the phone and cried. Was it a weeping that comes from being seen and understood by another? No that wasn't it—it was more of a weeping that came from being one's deeper self with another—from aligning with another and finding you were "being" together as one being—and the result was a joy that made me want to cry.

Marion Woodman is an internationally renowned Jungian analyst and lecturer. She first came upon the works of Carl Jung "mostly by accident" after seeking medical help with her autoimmune disease. She realized that while she was successful at making herself "as efficient as a woman could be in an organized, patriarchal system," she had ignored her feminine side and consequently her spirit and body were dying. With this understanding, Marion Woodman became a major voice in the growing awareness of the need to reestablish a balance between the feminine and masculine principles existing in God and alive in all human beings.

She is author of *Addiction to Perfection, The Pregnant Virgin, The Ravaged Bridegroom, Conscious Femininity, Leaving My Father's House, Dancing in the Flames* (with Elinor Dickson), *The Maiden King* (with Robert Bly), and *Bone: Dying into Life*.

1. Luke 9:48.

For me, there is a difference between Jesus and Christ. Jesus for me is a historical being and Christ is the God Consciousness within. People of other faiths call it by other names. It took Jesus some time to come to that God Consciousness. It was after the baptism that God said, "You are my Son, whom I love; with you I am well pleased." Then Jesus spent forty days in the wilderness to refine his relationship with that God Consciousness.

We have also to look at his mother Mary. Not many people are able to sustain intercourse with the Holy Spirit. They are not a container strong enough to relieve that impact. We are talking about a femininity that is not unique to Christianity. It is found in Greek mythology, in Egyptian mythology, where "mater" is permeated by spirit and a new child is born. The divine child is born from a femininity strong enough, mature enough, to surrender to the creative power of the Holy Spirit. From that union, new consciousness is born. This happens in individuals and, in times past, in cultures. Out of the stable that is the repressed, rejected side of a culture or an individual comes Jesus. He came from Nazareth: "Nazareth! Can anything good come from there?" was what Nathaniel said. From the filth of a cowshed because there is no room in the Holiday Inn for this kind of activity—the Holiday Inn accepts what is acceptable, nonthreatening and expected. But Jesus brought something new—he brought something unexpected, something threatening, and thus unacceptable.

Virgin birth?

I don't honestly care whether he was the son of Joseph and Mary or whether he was a miracle child born of the Holy Spirit permeating human flesh. Jesus was so in touch with the Divine that he was able to bring about a whole new consciousness on this planet. A human virgin was confident enough in her own Being that she was able to surrender to the Holy Spirit and able to allow that intercourse to come into her to such an extent that she could carry that seed to birth, and bring that divine child into the world. Mary embodied the true meaning of the word "virgin." She had a feminine consciousness authentically grounded in her own Being and had the courage to act from that reality.

The same mythological story can go on in all of us whether we honor it or whether we don't. Without an understanding of myth or religion, without an understanding of the relationship between destruction and creation, death and rebirth, the individual suffers the mysteries of life as meaningless mayhem.

How does the Jesus story manifest in our lives?

Often in dreams. Dreams have always been an important part of Christianity. Look in Genesis 28:11, God talked to Jacob in a dream. Daniel interpreted dreams for the King in the Book of Daniel. And there's the angel that appeared to Joseph in a dream in Matthew 1:20. People often have a dream similar to the Jesus story, but they often don't recognize it. They just know that there was a magnificent child born to them last night, golden skin, often golden hair. Sometimes he can speak. He has the eyes of an old man. Dreams like this are an immense gift because they are a sign that something radical has happened in the unconsciousness of that person. If the dreamer doesn't respond, it's all too easy just to forget. Then it's a great treasure lost.

I work with many addicts. Eventually that's the question they hit, "Do I want to live or do I want to die? Is there any meaning in living?" Then a dream may come. It may take a while, but if they—addicts and non-addicts—take time each day to honor their own inner being, and patiently wait—dreams begin to come almost nightly and in progression. There is a dream process that goes on all the time throughout our lives, whether we honor it or not.

Jesus embodied a new consciousness?

The Old Testament is about Jehovah, a very jealous, very patriarchal Being. His are the ten Commandments: "thou shalt not—thou shalt not— thou shalt not." It was a tribal culture and rule was by power. Then comes the Book of Job. Job is obeying the laws to the letter; suddenly he starts to

315

lose everything. He cries out, "I have done everything the law requires. This is not just!" A new consciousness is born in the Book of Job, a consciousness that prefigures the birth of Jesus. After many trials, God asks questions of Job that Job cannot answer, questions about the mysteries of life, Job surrenders. He can have faith while leaving the questions unanswered. That's breaking from a masculine way of thinking into a feminine way. His soul surrenders, becomes receptive and open, and pushes Job's ego out of the channel that needs to be open to God. The individual "I am" surrenders to the divine "I am." That's what I see with the coming of Christianity.

Second Coming?

This is how I understand Christ Consciousness. It is the experiencing of the shudder and shimmer of God within. The individual soul is confident enough to surrender to the unknown. Tragically, in our culture, many people are not sufficiently grounded in their body to dare to surrender. Letting go would feel like death. They are living in their heads and consequently don't understand the experience of living in their body. Thus they live with a lot of words, but never feel the spirit actually going through the heart or through the kidney or through the bowels—they don't embody it. They are body-numb.

Christ works with outcasts, because that's where the hope of change is. He himself was born in a cowshed. He's that part of us that we try to keep locked up, that part that cries out (often in our dreams), "I do exist, I am a human being, I do have rights, I do feel, I *do* have compassion. You don't care whether you cut down the whole forest, but I care whether you cut down this one tree." "I recognize the unity of every living thing on this planet and I am willing to fight for what I *know*. Not believe, *know*. There is the only hope for this planet." If we can hold that Christ Consciousness—that inner "I am," what I call the soul, the God within each one of us—then we can go on no matter how depressing the planetary situation is.

Often hear that voice, "My God, my God, why hast thou forsaken me?" But if I connect with "I am," what I'm calling "Being," the soul of every human being, I can be as depressed as it is possible to be from watching television or whatever . . . but I can go out into the garden and see the glory of a sunflower. I see the order, the color, the precision, and there is God manifest. I see God the Spirit as the masculine side of God and God manifest in form as the Mother (mater), the feminine side of God.

Patriarchy?

Patriarchy is a parody of masculinity. It is an immature masculinity that has been channeled into power on our planet. It is a wounded masculinity that would destroy others in order to master them. A dangerous energy on this tiny planet that will not be able to sustain its growing population with polluted air, water, and earth. It is *not* a manifestation of the Holy Spirit that would bring all things into their full beauty. For me, the real masculine can be seen in a sunflower. I look at that sunflower. The ring around the outside is yellow, perfect order, then another ring of red, perfect order, and then the brown. The symmetry in nature is awesome. What makes me bow down with awe is the fact that I can see the sunflower. Spirit is manifest through the feminine mother. I can relate to it through my eyes, my ears, my nose, all my senses.

Momentarily, I feel the mystery shuddering within me. I am quickened. The "I am-ness" connects me to the sunflower, to the tree, to you, to the smile of a stranger, the glory of the giraffe, or the glory of the little sparrow family outside my window.

Jesus the only Son of God?

I'm not a theologian, so I can't answer those questions. He brought us a vision of God. He was manifest God. He was carrying a frequency in his body that made him shine in a way that nobody else was shining. He attracted people to him to such a degree that it upset the Roman Empire and changed the planet.

The resurrection is made possible through the crucifixion?

I believe in the evolution of consciousness and I believe that God manifests on the earth when the earth is at a place where it needs to have a new vision. The patriarchal world of the Roman Empire had to break open into a much wider and deeper understanding of the feminine in order to find a new balance. The feminine is again breaking down patriarchy which is why people are so terrified of it. *If you look at an ordinary human life, most people stay in an old order until something happens that blasts them out of it. In fact, they will cling to an old order long after it's dead, rather than break into something new.* It often takes horrific chaos before they can give up their addiction to old ways and say, "Not my will, but thine be done," and "I can't do this alone, you've got to help me, God." This "new order" or new life is a resurrection coming out of crucifixion.

Jesus' spiritual technique and teachings?

Meditate on the paradoxical things he said and those simple stories he told. Jesus taught that God was in our very midst, both inside and outside.

For example, the gospels say, "The Word became flesh." They were not referring to the fact that a word became creation, they meant Divinity had entered creation. God is entering matter in a new consciousness. When Einstein recognized that matter is energy, we were catapulted into the atomic age. The human being at this moment in our evolution is carrying a very different energy than s/he was five hundred years ago, or even two hundred years ago. If you are working with the energy in our electromagnetic body then you know the frequency of your body can change. I believe this is one reason people break down—as, for example, autoimmune breakdown the psyche is trying to bring a new consciousness to matter, and matter is slower than the psyche to grasp the shift.

Original sin?

That comes out of a rejection of the body. In the Old Testament Satan was Lucifer, who was the brightest star. But then, of course, he got into greed and the defiance of the patriarchal god. At that point Eve, in other words the feminine, became connected with Lucifer or Satan because people are so terrified of the feminine—because *the feminine does not obey the old order.* Therefore, the feminine had to be punished!

The patriarchal world loves to have things either black or white because that's easy. We can think easily if we say, "This is good and this is bad." It's a lot harder to differentiate—this is good—this is better—this is best. In the patriarchal world, Mary Magdalene (she's the black) is the prostitute carrying all the lust and being the outcast, while the "Virgin Mary" (she's the white) is put up on a pedestal; we can't touch her because she's perfect! She's the perfect mother. And if she is perfect, we don't really have to deal with her because perfection is inhuman. If we idealize something, the polar opposite is to demonize it. This is where Christ comes in to smash the either/or. Christ loved Mary Magdalene. She was the one who was at the open tomb on Easter morning when he was resurrected.

In the same way we have to honor the outcast part of ourselves and bring lust and love together. In other words, get the mother and idealized feminine off the pedestal and raise Mary Magdalene, the outcast body, and bring those two together. In this union the new feminine lives. And that new feminine requires a new masculine as partner. We can't run around having a wife and a mistress and a husband and a lover, but that's what's happening in so many relationships. The psychic splitting is manifested in the outer situation. This is where the soul, the "I am," the Christ Consciousness, will say, "I will not dishonor my own body by having intercourse with someone I do not love." It's an integration principle on a new level of consciousness.

My hope is that the new millennium will bring in a new map of wholeness, a new mandala. Since we have no sense of spirit at the center right now, many people are left with nothing because the "concept" of the great God in the sky is dead. For many people all that is associated with that is dead. Now they have nothing to project their immense energy onto. Perhaps they can project it onto the Church and be held at the center by the law and order of the Church. At present, even that authority is being called into question. When the Church as the center is taken out, then we have to find the God within. Of course, you have to watch the danger of grandiosity. We have to remember we are human beings, not gods or goddesses. We have to find the axis within whose "I am" as individual meets "I am" as God.

Is cyclical crucifixion necessary? It almost
seems that after a spiritual realization,
something in us has to solidify in that space
for a while and then after that—we have to
grow again—and then that solidified place has
to go through a crucifixion—so that we can
grow spiritually.

William Blake said, "He who binds to himself a joy, /Doth the winged life destroy/ He who kisses the joy as it flies, /Lives in Eternity's sunrise." In other words, if you nail a butterfly down, you kill it. If you kiss it as it flies, it will be always alive. This is the way our soul works. It is always changing. I see life as a series of birth canals. We go through a birth canal, all the pain and anguish of the near death, and we go through into a new life. We're on a plateau for a while, getting used to that and learning who we are on that plateau. Then the masculine side of us starts to consolidate that consciousness, and often it starts to stagnate or solidify. That's when you get fundamentalism—whether it's Muslim, Christian, Buddhist, or Jewish fundamentalism—it comes from the wish to control, which in turn comes from the feeling of fear and chaos. This is when the feminine begins to question the stagnation of the masculine and change occurs—when patriarchy or the masculine is left without the feminine, it turns things into concrete.

When an addict hasn't got anything to project onto, hasn't got anything to project God onto, they will concretize spirit and alcohol, or concretize mother in food, and then they worship it. We are called to a continual death and rebirth—and death is the greatest of all births. But most people are terrified of change. Despite the fact that the world of the soul is in continual change. We are always being asked to mature, to be responsible for ourselves, to open, open, open, to new possibilities.

Was Jesus' resurrection a
spiritual and bodily one?

There is a marvelous old saying by a rabbi: "Spirit without body is ghost, body without spirit is corpse." We can't see God as spirit, it's so far outside our comprehension. Yet to resurrect without spirit is not possible.

The great thing about the Christian dispensation is that "matter" is sacred, and we must learn it or we're gonna destroy it! We have to learn as Jesus said that the body is a temple of God, and that the earth is the manifestation of God.

The earth is just a larger body?

That is right, and once you experience, really experience, your own body, you walk on the earth and you feel that energy. That's what the Indians and the aborigines have to teach us and we have to learn it. The body has a wisdom that comes right out of the earth, but is so often ignored or covered up. Even as we speak, I'm watching a huge machine claw out the earth from underneath the pavement outside. It's heartbreaking to think of the earth underneath that cement all the time. It's like putting a corset on and saying, "Breathe!"

I learned a Buddhist meditation called
Vipassana, where you watch the unconscious
by observing body sensation.

When you are working with symptoms and trying to heal, the manifestation of the unconscious will come right through the body. As we are growing up, even in utero, all that is not bearable, we push down into the unconscious, into the body. The body carries the unconscious. A trauma that we cannot allow ourselves to think about consciously is automatically pushed into the cells of the body and the body carries it. This is the work of the therapist who works with someone and their rejected aspect—the stable of the rejected Virgin Mary and Jesus. I try to create a safe space where we can go into meditation, go into the depths of the body, take the armoring off and let what is in the very depths come out. That's where the real energy and the real life are. That's where the "I-am" is.

Christ is the feminine side of God and he provides that safe container. We had the Jehovah-masculine God in the Old Testament and then we have the feminine side of God in Christ. At the same time, he is the new masculine, a spirit that fires the energy. I mean, literally sets it on fire! Baptism by fire! Because I've seen people who could hardly walk because they were so burdened down with grief and depression—but once they contacted this, they were suddenly alive. They want to sing, they want to dance, they want to paint or make sculptures. Their whole creative life came alive with the creative force of God the Creator. Mind you, that can be quite painful because often they have to deal with quite a bit of repressed pain coming up and, as Jung said, "a conflict too painful to be dealt with is carried in the body until the psyche is strong enough to face it." So this creative life of Christ is not all joy by any means, but Christ Consciousness; that "I-am" gives people a sense of reality and support.

✛ 74
TRAVELING

FROM MADISON, WISCONSIN,
TO DENVER, COLORADO

I complained all day because traveling to Snowmass, Colorado was an expensive hassle. I was going there because Father Thomas Keating lived at St. Benedict's Monastery in the Rocky Mountains. He was one of the few Christians who stressed not just talking intellectually about God but being in God's presence.

Of course, I knew that once I got to St. Benedict's I'd be happy, but I wasn't there. I was here, at the beginning, and like many beginnings, I was in no mood to start. I'd rather stay home, eat a bowl of ice cream, and watch television.

"The root of all prayer is interior silence," Thomas Keating wrote. "Deep prayer is the laying aside of thoughts. Contemplative Prayer is the opening of mind and heart—our whole being—to God, the Ultimate Mystery, beyond thoughts, words and emotions. We open our awareness to God whom we know by faith is within us, closer than breathing, closer than thinking, closer than choosing—closer than consciousness itself. Contemplative Prayer is a process of interior purification leading, if we consent, to divine union."

Divine union or not, it was a long trip to St. Benedict's and I had gotten up early, so I was crabby. The trip started with a two-hour bus ride to the airport in Milwaukee, followed by a flight that went backward to Cincinnati (I lost four hundred miles!). Then a connecting flight to Denver, which arrived at 10 P.M. and then . . . I don't know what?! Because I hadn't made a reservation at a motel in Denver. Why? Because the Greyhound bus I needed to catch for Snowmass left Denver airport at 6 A.M. (eight hours after my flight arrived) and I didn't think it was worth the time and money to get a hotel for six hours only to have to be back at that same airport by 6 A.M.! Therefore, I'd decided I'd stay in the airport and sleep. But I already had misgivings because I was crabby—and combine that with the crappy sleep I'd get in the airport—by the time I got to the monastery in Snowmass I'd be ready to tell the monks what they could do with their prayers and Gregorian chants. Of course, it was my own fault because I always left everything for the last minute, including this trip, and when it came time for me to die, I'd probably do that at the last minute too.

The first leg of the trip, the two-hour bus ride from Madison, ended when the bus driver yelled, "Mitchell Field Airport!" I awoke abruptly from a deep sleep and stumbled off the bus. Since the retreat in Snowmass is ten days with no washer/dryer facilities, I'd brought two big duffel bags of summer and winter clothes (it's mountainous in Colorado after all), together with all my meditation cushions. After years of meditation retreats, I've learned a few things. One of which is that one's butt, legs, and back often get sore from sitting in one position for five to ten hours a day. Therefore, just like a pair of well-worn shoes—it's best to bring a meditation pillow that fits one in a very intimate way.

I carried the two large bags up escalators and eventually to the ticket counter. I was sweaty, tired—and, of course—still crabby. Once on the plane, I questioned the trip.

"I don't really need to go," I thought while stowing my carry-on bag in the overhead compartment. "I can turn around in Cincinnati and go back home. Then I'll have ten days to finish my book at home."

"Besides," I continued to think as the attendant passed out the peanuts, "there's nothing in Colorado for me to learn. God's not any more present in Colorado than in Wisconsin. I've already done a lot of silent ten-day retreats, and I've even had decent experiences of God's presence. I probably even know more than those people at the monastery. Maybe I will go home."

While I waited for my connecting flight in Cincinnati, I planned my stay in the Denver airport. I imagined sleeping in a corner of the airport with my head against one duffel bag, and my lower legs plopped on top of the other duffel bag.

"Is Denver a nice, spacious airport?" I asked an older couple while waiting for the plane to board.

"Very spacious," they replied.

"Good," I said. "I have to take a short nap there."

Just then, a woman standing beside me, who held an assortment of papers, purses, and other objects—dropped a few of them. I bent over and picked up her cigarettes while a tall athletic-looking black man dressed in a warm-up suit picked up her purse.

"Yep," I said sarcastically as we handed the items to her, "us men are always picking up after the women."

The other man winked at me, and we all enjoyed a momentary chuckle. Though the whole exchange was over in a few seconds, I swear there was a connection that spoke lifetimes. A sort of glance that we all shared together, and it said "We're all on a trip together—it's called *humanity.*"

"The flight is delayed for thirty minutes," the overhead announcement said. Secretly, I hoped they'd cancel the whole flight and put us all up for free at a hotel for the night. I sat down next to a very conservative-looking man and asked him about the spaciousness of the Denver airport. Eventually, we talked about Jesus, and my Jesus book. Since I wasn't sure where he stood on Jesus or how conservative his religious beliefs were, I told him I had interviewed everyone from Jerry Falwell to Deepak Chopra. Then I told him I intended sleeping in the Denver airport.

"Stay at my house," he said. "My son's gone. You can stay in his room and I'll bring you back to the airport at 5 A.M."

After I said a few "No, I can't put you out" throwaway lines that I didn't really mean, we agreed that I would sleep at his house. His name was Phil Hopkins and on the flight to Denver, we sat together. As we talked, I noticed that the woman seated next to us was reading a book about death and what happens after.

Her name was Patty, and the three of us proceeded to talk about spirituality, and how through a series of unfortunate events we were brought together on this particular flight.

"I was in Cincinnati to be with my mother while she died of cancer," Patty said as tears welled up in her eyes.

"Your mother was lucky to have someone like you with her," I said. "I bet you were *real* with her—and didn't try to avoid what was happening by talking about the weather or other things . . ."

"It was really a very deep spiritual experience," Patty said, her voice cracking. "We were really connected—and we talked about everything."

"Sounds like it was beautiful and sad at the same time," I said.

"It was," Patty said with a bright smile and tearful eyes. "It really was."

The three of us just sat silently for a moment, a moment we neither wanted to push away or cling to.

"I got into an argument with a friend while visiting him," Phil said. "He was my law school roommate thirty-five years ago, and now he's this big millionaire who, two days into my visit, said he had to get back to work. *Can you believe that?* I flew all the way out to Michigan to see him and after two days he tells me that! So I left early."

"I was kind of crabby," I said, bringing up the rear. "And didn't want to come on this trip, but now I'm glad I did."

We were amazed at how our less than perfect situations had led to a perfect meeting. We were three human beings who talked intimately and truthfully—and consequently that formula led to its unavoidable conclusion—a love which slowly materialized somewhere over St. Louis.

Patty talked more about her grief. Phil talked about his divorce. And me, well, my crabbiness had been transformed into a chuckle, a realization that everything was unfolding as planned. I was humbled—not into the ground—but humbled into an alignment with Spirit that is not attainable through deed, or building up of self, but only through humility. After all, what is humility? Humility is the naked realization that our spiritual cartwheels and assorted psychological tricks are all unnecessary—*they're extra.* God's kingdom does not allow extra. Humility is the state of dropping all that is extra. Even the sense of feeling good or bad about oneself is extra— and that is why a rich man or a poor man or a camel cannot get through the eye of a needle into God's kingdom. *Those are all extra things added onto the Spirit.*

After we landed in Denver, and while walking through "the" airport, Phil bumped into a woman he hadn't seen for years.

"What a surprise to see you here," she said. "I'm waiting for my boyfriend—he's flying in from England."

"This is a really strange night," Phil said. "It feels like there's destiny everywhere I turn. First meeting Bill and Patty on the plane. Now seeing you again after all these years."

"There he is," the woman said, pointing to her boyfriend as he got off the plane.

I turned and smiled warmly. It was the black man who had picked up the lady's purse in the airport while I had picked up her cigarettes. Sometimes it's just funny how things come together.

"*Make yourself at* home," Phil said at his apartment. "I'm going to bed."

Just as he was shutting his bedroom door, he poked his head out and said, "In the freezer are burritos, TV dinners, and Italian calzones. Eat anything you want."

I told him I wasn't hungry, but later, as I watched the over two hundred channels on his satellite television, I ate a calzone and two, maybe three hot dogs . . . before finally going to bed at 2 A.M.

✤ 75
DAY ONE

The next morning Philip decided to take the day off from work and drive me the four hours to the monastery.

"It will be a beautiful drive," he said. "Besides, I can tell that our meeting was predestined."

On the way to Snowmass we passed a sign that said, EXIT 134: NO NAME. That figured. Before I went forward into a retreat and a deeper experience of communion with God, I had to leave behind all names and concepts of God—even the idea of *no name* had to be left behind.

Philip and I arrived at St. Benedict's Monastery at 4:30 P.M.—thirty hours after I'd left Madison. After saying good-bye to Philip, I checked into my hermitage. I must admit the hermitage (a small one-room structure) was much more "cushy" than I expected. It was carpeted, with two beds, a stove, microwave, and full bathroom. I had expected something more along the lines of what I'd stayed in while on a ten-day retreat in India in 1986. Then, I stayed in a "real" grass hut with a bed whose mattress was more grass. At the time I enjoyed the sparseness, but now that I was fifteen years older the real mattress and hot shower added a "kindness" to my subtle thoughts of God. As Jesus said, "My yoke is easy" (Matthew 11:30, NIV), and so, in these wall-to-wall carpeted times, his words became even truer.

My roommate was a twenty-five-year-old man named Peter. We hit it off right away despite the fact that on the first night, he borrowed some of my dental floss without asking.

"I took some of your dental floss," he said as he came out of the bathroom, showing me a modest twelve-inch piece. "I hope it's okay."

Of course it was okay, but for a while it was less okay because when I went to floss the next day, the plastic floss box dispensed a two-inch piece of floss before suddenly revealing its end. The rest of the retreat I had only a two-inch strip of my floss while my roommate had a good *twelve inches of my floss.* The floss incident was such a little thing, but it's the kind of little thing that on a partially silent retreat can drive a person crazy.

The next day, life seemed to play with my sense of possessiveness even more. I had brought a carton of rice milk with me and when I placed it in front of me at the table after using it the first time an older woman came over, grabbed it, and used it. I wanted to say, "Hey, that's mine," or at least have her know it was "mine," and *I let* her use it and get kudos for my generosity. Instead, I said nothing although I contemplated getting a black marker and writing my name in big letters across the carton. Each day as she grabbed *my* rice milk from the territory surrounding *my* breakfast bowl, I wanted to let her know that it was *my rice milk,* and that I was being nice for letting her use it. But all thoughts of *my* dental floss and *my* rice milk disappeared after *I looked into the eyes of God.*

✢ 76
JAMES I. PACKER

"James I. Packer is a legend among evangelicals," Tullian, Gigi Graham's son, and Billy Graham's grandson, had told me. That's why I flew to Vancouver, British Columbia, because James I. Packer taught at Regent College and his book, *Knowing God,* had been called "a spiritual classic" by John Stott. Published in more than fourteen languages, it has sold nearly two million copies.

In the fall of 1944 while attending a sermon at Corpus Christi College at Oxford, James I. Packer saw a mental image of a home where a party was in progress and he understood that symbolically, "They were inside and I was outside." He realized that one got into the party by accepting Jesus Christ as his Savior. After singing "Just as I Am" with the congregation he converted and left the church knowing, "I was a Christian."

Since then he has written close to forty books including *Fundamentalism* and *The Word of God.* I was impressed with his biblical knowledge, but what stayed with me, even after all the insightful words and concepts faded away, was his kindness and warmth—and that is knowing God.

Translation is a human venture and it's not guaranteed that any translator will be infallible, so the work of translation has to go on; we've had any number of translations in the last half century. My favorite is the old Revised Standard Version. If it's going to be an award of stars, I give the Revised Standard Version four stars out of five, the NIV is three stars out of five—the reason being that the sort of light, bright, skipping, English style that they use all the way through doesn't work well for the New Testament. I don't think there is another version to which I would give more than three. I hope that the English Standard Version, which is a full-scale opening up of the Revised Standard that I myself helped to produce, might perhaps merit five stars, but that is something others must decide. The King James is like Shakespeare, you have to learn a good deal before you can properly appreciate the King James and since we've got these modern translations, it's not the best use of people's time and energy.

We test our lives and spiritual experience through the Bible. As 1 Thessalonians says "test all things." The Bible is the Word of God and one way of bringing it to life is to *get to know Paul, John, and Peter just from their writings,* and then to imagine one of them or all three of them looking over your shoulder and checking your ideas as you do your own reading, studying, and thinking and writing. Ask yourself—what would Paul say of this idea of mine? Would he agree or wouldn't he? I do a lot of that in my own study and in my teaching.

When is the Bible symbolic and when is it literal?

Whether a particular sentence is literal or symbolic usually becomes clear if you read the sentence in context. It's only by pulling sentences out of context that you really find yourself mystified as to whether this should be understood as a parable or analogy or illustration or a literal statement in the sense similar to that in which newspaper reports of things are literal statements. When I'm teaching and this word "literal" comes up I always say, well now I take it by literal you mean "factual and unimaginative" the way that newspaper reports or journalistic accounts of things are factual and unimaginative. They are brisk but they're not imaginative, they simply train your attention on what you would have seen if you had been there and they try to tell you that as clearly as they can.

At one point, so John 16 tell us, Jesus said that up till then he had been speaking "figuratively," but the word that he uses in Greek simply means "by the use of illustrations, pictures, parables, analogies." Every sentence is to be understood as part of the whole. Therefore, if you want to understand the thrust of something that is said in chapter 16 of John, you have to read the first fifteen chapters, looking for the symbolic, illustrative, analogical, dimensions of Jesus' teaching all through.

Jesus the only Son of God?

I believe that Jesus was, as John's account in his gospel tells us, the second person of the godhead; that he is called "Son" and he calls himself "Son of God" because it is his nature, within the mystery of the triune Divine life, not to operate independently but always to do the Father's will and seek to please his Father, which is the model of Sonship that is taught throughout the Bible. Sons ought to honor their fathers, and this Son does.

The parallel between Jesus and us who believe is that we are sons or children of the Father in the sense that we are accepted, are loved, are the objects of God's good will and generosity, and it is his delight to exalt us. Jesus said, in effect, over and over, "You, my disciples, as sons of God, you have to learn to live as I live," that is, making it our business to love, honor, serve, exalt, and glorify the Father—which is the way Jesus lived. If we do that, then God the Father will bless and enrich us, just as he exalts the Divine Son.

But this parallel is very different from the liberal idea that human beings are all sons of God by creation. This idea that we are all sons of God did not exist prior to the nineteenth century, and it was popularized a hundred years ago by a top German scholar named Adolf von Harnack. He said, "Christianity is the essential teaching of Jesus, forget about Paul, forget about the rest of the New Testament. It's Jesus' teaching that we go for and Jesus' teaching is essentially three principles which belong together; the universal fatherhood of God, the universal brotherhood of man, and the universal obligation of neighbor-love, which becomes good will to everybody because everybody is within the family." I believe Jesus did indeed teach "love your neighbor" universally, but he didn't teach the universal fatherhood of God, nor the universal brotherhood of man yet. Jesus taught that our neighbor is certainly the person we must love—and who is our neighbor? Absolutely everybody.

But the New Testament teaches that it is by redemption that we are made children of God. Without Christ, we are not children and heirs of God at all, we are rational, human creatures who have gone wrong and are guilty before God—and having failed to love him with all our heart and mind and soul and strength *all we can expect is that he will decline to love us. He will deal with us as we deserve* in judgment rather than salvation. That sounds brutal, I know, but if you have read C. S. Lewis, you know Lewis said, "God gives you the life that you've chosen. If you choose to live without him, so you shall."

Virgin birth?

I believe in the virgin birth. It's much more difficult not to believe in the virgin birth than to believe in it. If you are going to deny it, a priori, then you have to explain how the story started and that's not easy to do. In the same way, if you don't believe in the resurrection of Jesus from the tomb, you have to face the question, how did the story of his resurrection start? No one would have invented the virgin birth story, just as no one would have invented the resurrection story if it hadn't actually happened.

Some people have said the virgin birth is an idea that comes from Greek mythology, but it doesn't. What comes from Greek mythology is the idea of a god mating with a virgin, producing a hero, for example Hercules. But the virginal conception and birth is the miraculous entry into this world of the eternally existing Son of God.

Did Jesus have to learn anything?
His lost years?

Jesus had to learn. He was, as he still is, God incarnate and what that means is that he, the Son of God came to live within the dimensions of full-scale humanity with a human body, human mind, human thought processes: in other words, came to live a fully human life. The negative of that is that at no point did he act simply as God and leave his humanness behind. Beginning with the moment of conception in Mary's womb, he had to go through the trauma of birth the way all children do, then learn what the newborn, toddler, child, and then teenager has to learn. The unique thing about Jesus' consciousness was his awareness that at all times he was uniquely the Son of the Father. At the Father's will he was limiting himself to learning through human experience the way that all children, all growing people, all young folk do, as I said. So you see he really became a model for all of us right from the word go.

During his lost years, as some call them, that is, the years of his life that we are not told about, and so are lost to us, he was working for Joseph doing what a good Jewish lad growing up would have been doing. He lived a perfect human life. He took his place in the family business because that's what Jewish boys were expected to do. Various people have fantasized about Jesus doing other things or traveling to the East, but that started with D. H. Lawrence and then, you know, came *The Last Temptation of Jesus* and much more of that kind of thing.

Did Jesus ever sin or make a mistake?

I don't believe Jesus ever sinned because it isn't in the nature of God to sin and make mistakes. But at the same time, he didn't actualize his omniscience and omnipotence beyond ordinary human limits, because he knew the Father did not will this. That's a way of saying Jesus knew every moment what the Father wanted him to be doing or not doing, and always he did accordingly. To be God the second divine person, living a fully obedient life, was the name of the game for Jesus.

Jesus' religion?

He was a Jew, but his version of the Jewish religion involved the entire historical fulfillment the Old Testament had hoped for and looked forward to. When Jesus told the Samaritan woman, "We know whom we worship, for salvation is of the Jews," he was saying, "I am a Jew and one of the things that all non-Jews must do is to humble yourselves to the point of admitting that what you need to know for salvation you must receive from us." Gentile Christians (of which I am one) ought to be rather humble about this and acknowledge that what God did was to involve us in the fulfilled hope of Israel. It isn't that Christianity was de-Judaized, as if God's turned his back on the Jews and is now only interested in gentiles. What we ought to say, rather, is that God in his grace involved us gentiles in the plan of grace and mercy that he had for the Jews. When Paul talked in Romans 11 about an olive tree that is the covenant community which was the seed of Abraham to start with, he says, "Now for unbelief, a lot of the natural branches in the olive tree have been broken off. And branches from a wild, *olive,* tree that originally had nothing to do with this—that's you gentiles, you've been grafted into this olive tree." Jewishness for the world was Jesus' religion, and he saw this as the plan of God.

Was Jesus married?

Marriage is an honorable condition, but the Father gave Jesus his ministry to fulfill and marriage couldn't have come into it because of what he had to do. He had first to model a perfect human life in a way that resonates with everybody—with women as well as men, with widows and bachelors, with elderly folk like me who are more than twice the age at which he died, and with young people too. He had to do that and then he had to die the death of the cross, which was a sacrifice for the sin of the world, then to rise from the dead and ascend to the Father's throne. That kind of agenda really leaves no place for marriage, family, and settling down to rear children. We should note that in the Bible, marriage, children, and child rearing are aspects of a single ball of wax, the marriage package as God designed it. We today don't always appreciate that. Catholics have been right on this one and we evangelical Protestants need to catch up again with their rightness at this point.

Jesus said, "When he, the Spirit of truth,
comes, he will guide you into all truth" (John
16:13, NIV) he meant further revelation
would come in the future through the Holy
Spirit. How do we prevent ourselves from
becoming a modern Pharisee who doesn't
believe the new truth the Holy Spirit
reveals now?

I take the "new truth" to be the deepening insight into the meaning of what Jesus and the apostles taught that comes as we use scripture to assess all that goes on around us. Paul leads us to do this when he says in his first letter to the Thessalonians, right at the end of the letter, "test all things, hold fast what's good." The fault of Pharisees, ancient and modern, is to limit their perception of scriptural teaching by reading the Bible through a grid of externalism. I try to never forget Jesus' emphasis that true godliness begins in the heart, with the motivation that's driving us: Are we driven by the spirit of love, which seeks to honor and glorify God, and serve other people? Love is a purpose of making loved the ones great in the sight of God. That doesn't mean indulging them, giving them everything they want just because they want it badly. It means you've got to be responsible and clear in your own mind that what you are giving them is something that if they accept it will help to make them great in the sight of God. Jesus rebuked the Pharisees because of their externalism and because they offended God by failing to realize the self-righteousness, pride, and vainglory in their hearts. They thought they were God's special favorites.

Some Christians today clearly think the same. I know that in saying that I put my head on the block. I can only say before the Lord that I am tempted to be as prideful as anybody. So I ask that he show me when I'm lapsing into arrogance and help me know it. I think all Christians need to do this. The problem with the Pharisees at the time of Jesus was that their arrogance and pride never became an issue for them. We must learn to be wiser, or we shall never grasp what God via scripture is really saying to us.

Jesus said, "Up until now I've been speaking
figuratively and I haven't told you everything
because you couldn't bear it all and the Holy
Spirit will come and teach you all things."

Jesus knows that what he's been saying to the disciples through parables is something that they haven't fully caught up with. When he says he's spoken figuratively, he means he has been using parables, that is, symbolic stories and illustrations. This reveals his profound wisdom about human nature. Since his day we've learned that the brain has two lobes, the left brain is for logic, the right brain is for pictures, imagination, and drama. The best communication involves both lobes of the brain. Logical expression without imagination is monochrome, while fancy or letting the imagination run free without logic is fun but it doesn't tune you into fact. Real communication occurs when the logic and solidity of reasoning are blended with the vividness of images and pictures. Jesus did it better than anyone. The New Testament is far more pictorial in its style and, therefore, is involving the right lobe of the brain far more fully than a lot of the professional students of the New Testament recognize. I see that the writers of the New Testament letters and the Book of Revelation very obviously understood this balance, and they deliberately communicated in that way. What they shared was, I believe, Spirit-taught, and so was their method of sharing it; and it is the same Holy Spirit who, by involving both lobes of our brains, enables us to understand it.

Is your faith based on beliefs or your
experience of God's presence?

My faith is not based on, but is confirmed by the experience of God's presence. All that I believe comes from the Bible, which I receive as the Word of God, just as Jesus received our Old Testament as the Word of God. In effect, he promised that there would be a New Testament to complete it. Jesus said "the Holy Spirit is going to come to you disciples to enable you to bear true witness." Bearing witness comes from faith confirmed by experience; apostolic witness is the heart of the New Testament. Christianity isn't my invention, Christianity isn't anybody's invention. Christianity is a Divine revelation, given to the world through Christ and his apostles.

Is Divine revelation happening now?

What is happening now is that the Holy Spirit is at work doing what Jesus told the disciples he would do for them. The Holy Spirit is enabling humble Bible readers to understand and apply all that the Bible says. The Holy Spirit gives understanding in the Church.

So I don't want everybody to go off into a corner, ask for the help of the Spirit, and then read the Bible on their own and never compare notes. I believe that each of us as individuals is called to learn in the fellowship of the Church. No Roman Catholic could say that more emphatically than I say it, although I don't define the fellowship of the church the way that they do. They believe that Jesus has given the church the grace of infallibility in its teaching. I don't believe that, but I maintain that it is as we explore the Bible together that wisdom and truth become ours.

Why do some Christians consider mysticism a bad word?

Different people use the word mysticism in different ways and for some it isn't a bad word at all. I believe in personal conversion and in my preaching and teaching ministry I try to induce experience of the Holy Spirit—which some may call mystical—but I prefer not to use the word myself. Evangelicals like me are gospel people and we believe the gospel is about turning to the living Christ in personal repentance and faith. In the discussion of world religions that has been going on for a century and a half, ever since other religions began to be studied in their own terms, mysticism is a word that has come to mean unmediated awareness of God, unmediated contact and fellowship with the divine reality, "the flight of the alone to the alone," as it has been called. But "unmediated" is the key idea. I believe fellowship with God is certainly a personal reality, but it is not unmediated. Jesus is the mediator, my Savior and my Lord, and it is Jesus who brings me to the Father by virtue of his atoning death. In Hinduism, there is the idea of "the adept," a person who accepts the discipline of devotion so that he will be able to make direct contact with God—that's pure mysticism. For example, Thomas Merton was a gifted student of spiritual life who ended his days trying to map parallels between Christian communion with God and Hindu communion with God. With great respect, I think he was on a false trail. The significant thing here is the difference rather than the similarity.

Who killed Jesus and why?

The Jewish leaders manipulated Pilate, the Roman governor, in order to make Jesus' execution happen. They knew very well that they, as Jews in Roman-occupied country, had no authority to execute a person whom they found guilty of breaking their law. Pilate clearly thought he was giving them the brush-off when he says, "Well, you take him and deal with him according to your law." But they said, "Look, you know very well, sir, we are not allowed to execute people and execution is what this man deserves." Then Pilate, who appears in the story as a peace-at-any-price man, asks himself, "In the Roman penal system, what then can I put him to death for?" In order to gratify the Jews, he executed Jesus as a political pretender, a subversive and a revolutionary. When a person was crucified there was always a notice nailed to the cross saying what his crime was. Above Jesus the notice said *Jesus of Nazareth, King of the Jews*—as if to say this execution really is a preemptive strike against insurrection. Jesus is claiming to be King of the Jews and we know that will mean a rebellion, so we are eliminating him. Pilate then could write a perfectly respectable report to his superiors on how in this instance he kept the peace. But the leading Jews wanted him out of the way because they had recognized that he was getting so much support that he was a threat to them and their position.

Resurrection?

I believe that Jesus rose from the dead as the New Testament says he did, and that this was an event of momentous meaning for everyone everywhere.

First of all, Jesus' resurrection guarantees his continuing life, which is of enormous important to all of us because we can now come literally to the living Christ as the gospel invites us to do. Jesus is not just a potent historical memory, like Socrates or Winston Churchill, but a living person, Savior, Master and Friend, in whose company believers will spend eternity.

Second, it guarantees his sacrifice has been triumphantly completed. If ever we wondered whether he'd succeeded in putting away our sins by his death on the cross, well, now we know he did, because he rose from the dead. If he hadn't risen, we could never have been sure. The cross succeeded in its purpose and Jesus is alive today.

Third, the resurrection has another significance in that Christians look forward to the resurrection of our body and Jesus was a model of that. If Jesus did not rise from the dead in a transformed body, well, then my Christian hope is weakened. Bodies are for experience and expression; human life is lived, and its riches are enjoyed, through the body; if there's no hope of a resurrection body then a great deal of what I look forward to will never happen.

Second Coming?

The Second Coming will be a personal confrontation for everybody with the person of the Savior. I don't find that hard to believe, because after all he is Divine and already he is giving his undivided attention to millions of us! God can do that now and will continue to do it. So there will come a moment when suddenly everything around us falls away and each individual is aware of being confronted by Jesus and the final decision about his or her destiny will be announced.

What spiritual techniques did Jesus teach?

Jesus taught faith in himself, which is a matter in the first place of acknowledging that he's there. For his disciples he was physically there, but now we who are his disciples have to reckon with the fact that by the Spirit he is present with us personally, even if not physically. It's in that personal relationship with him that the Spirit will work and the light will come. Then Jesus taught his followers to pray—that is, give thanks, make requests, and listen—to his Father as their Father, and to practice self-denial in serving him by obeying his commands. This in a church. You don't please

Christ by going off into a corner on your own with the Bible; instead you learn with God's people in a fellowship, which is what a church is. These spiritual techniques, or disciplines as most Christians call them, are the true way of life.

✣ 77
DAY TWO

According to Thomas Keating, Contemplative Prayer was the goal of Christian spirituality during the first sixteen centuries of church history. But after the Reformation, Contemplative Prayer as a living tradition was lost. In the 1970s, together with Fathers Basil Pennington and William Menninger, this group of Trappist monks resurrected a way of being in God's presence called "the Centering Prayer," which was based on the fourteenth-century classic *The Cloud of Unknowing*. Christianity had lost many people to the Eastern religions over that last fifty years because the experience of God's presence was no longer stressed in the Church. As one joke says, "If a Christian is given a choice between hearing a lecture about God or having the experience of God's presence—most pick the lecture."

The retreat schedule included three prayer/mediation sessions a day. One before breakfast, one before lunch and one before dinner. Each lasted an hour and fifteen minutes.

After the second prayer session on the second day, I walked into the dining room, and to my left, out of the corner of my eye I saw a smiling face. The joy from that face was so bright that before I had fully turned to look at the source I was already laughing. On the kitchen counter lay a woman, and she took such great delight in lying there, that I laughed again.

Then slowly, as the whole situation came into focus, I realized something was askew. It was her body—it didn't seem to go with her countenance because her body was crippled—like a rag doll whose legs and arms were confused and tangled, and yet when I looked at her face—*oh . . . my . . . God!* She radiated a profound joy. Our eyes locked onto each other in such a way that everything else receded into the background. She looked at me with a gaze so crystal clear and true, that as deep as I looked her gaze was always deeper, and it went on for, seemingly, an eternity. There was no fear or self-consciousness in her eyes. And when self-consciousness did cloud our interaction it was because of me, not her. Her blue eyes were as vast and clear as the sky. When she smiled, it was as if the whole sky smiled. I could not fathom the love or the joy. *They were the eyes of God . . .*

. . . and I kept walking, because as amazing as her eyes were—they scared me.

Before the retreat began, I expected the Trappist monks who lived at St. Benedict's to be kind of quiet and reserved. I also anticipated a peaceful, slow letting go into God's presence.

"Why don't you shave your head?" the old monk said. This was my first meeting with Monk Theophane, and actually it began when I walked into the bookstore and he yelled, "Hey, baldy!" Since I'm kind of bald, I turned—but he was talking to my young roommate, who in his youthful experimentation had shaved his head. Then Monk Theophane, who was on the plus side of seventy, turned to me and said, "Why don't you shave your head?!" The question was in part a "hello," and in part, his way of teasing.

"My name is Theophane," he said. "They gave me that name when I first got to the monastery. It means 'gift of God'—but once they got to know me they tried to take it back!"

Now I've got to tell you, I came to a monastery to forget about my self-judgments, so when this monk called attention to one of the things I've judged myself about—especially when I was a young man—it bugged me. Over the years, I've learned that hiding from the things that bugged me only led to enslavement by them. So whenever something did bug me, I looked within myself to the root of that pain and made sure I felt it and didn't deny it. When Monk Theophane mentioned shaving my head, I began my usual pattern of feeling that ancient pain—but then something in me said, "You don't have to do things that way anymore." Instead of walking down that red carpet of past pain, I stopped, acknowledged it, and looked back at the old monk. He seemed to have quite a bit of hair—and he was even combing some over a receding hairline.

"Why don't you shave your head?" I replied. After all, I thought, you're the one who's a monk.

The old monk just looked at me, and then without replying, he walked away.

For a moment, I felt a pang of guilt. Did I do something wrong? Did I react to him out of anger? I searched my conscience and came away convinced that for the most part I acted—not reacted. Later I spent much of the retreat trying to get to know Monk Theophane partly because I wanted to make sure there weren't any hard feelings, and partly because I wanted to know, Did he intentionally press on one of my insecurities? Or was it just spiritual coincidence?

As I learned more about Monk Theophane, I realized he was *trouble* in the nicest sense of the word. Teasing was his modus operandi, and if his teasing didn't unfold as planned—*he bolted*. Actually, he was the kind of guy who liked to tease and bolt *before* a comeback was possible. An example of that was later on in the retreat when I asked to meet with him for a short talk.

"Talk to my secretary," he said as he disappeared behind one of the many mysterious doors of the monastery. Of course, I knew he didn't have a secretary, but I wasn't going to let him get away so easily. I quickly opened the door and poked my head through.

"Let me know who your secretary is," I said.

The monk was already scurrying down the hall when I spoke. He raised his hand to acknowledge he heard me, but he kept walking. I shut the door and stood there for a few moments. Suddenly, the door opened again and Monk Theophane poked his head out.

"I don't really have a secretary," he said.

"I know . . ." I said as the monk disappeared and the door shut once more.

"I just wanted to talk . . ." I said, my voice trailing off as I realized I was speaking to the door.

A few seconds passed—then the door opened again.

"Maybe later," Monk Theophane said with a mercurial elusiveness, "during the week—sometime."

Then before I knew it, the door shut as quickly as it had opened.

⊹ 78
DAY THREE

Over the next few days, whenever I walked through the dining room, Sarah was there lying on the kitchen counter. Her mother, Pat Johnson, worked as a cook in the kitchen and as a retreat guide. She later told me that Sarah had developed spinal meningitis when she was a year old, and now, thirty years later, Sarah weighed about seventy pounds and was four feet tall. While the illness had affected the use of her body (her mother carried her everywhere), and her speech—it had not affected Sarah's brain in any way.

I usually watched Sarah from a distance because I felt safer. Every so often she looked my way and we would smile, but I never held her gaze for too long because after a few seconds of staring into her eyes I felt naked and seen to the extent that everything false in me was also seen. Yet, as fearful as it was, something in me wanted to be seen—*totally seen.*

During the evening meditation, I became aware of God's love in a very powerful way. I bowed my head down to the ground because I felt unworthy in God's presence.

"I'm unworthy," I said softly, despite the fact I was in the presence of unconditional love. The fact that it was unconditional only seemed to magnify my unworthiness.

"I'm unworthy," I said again.

"You're not unworthy," God said.

"I'm unworthy," I said.

"You're not unworthy," God replied.

"I'm unworthy," I said again.

"You're not unworthy," God said. "And who are you going to believe— you or me?!"

As I let go of my "unworthiness" and resistance, the love of God flooded into my being. I felt worthiness all throughout my being—but it was more than that *or less,* because *the me* that had resisted—was now dissolved in the light of this love.

"Earlier today I was thinking," Monk Theophane said. *"Are we seen, more than we see?"*

It was after the evening vespers and as I looked through the various spiritual books in the bookstore, Monk Theophane had approached me. I quickly recognized his question as some sort of Christian Koan.

"I think we see as much as we're seen," I said, referring to my experience that human beings really do see everything—it's just that we blunt our ability to be conscious of how much we *really* see.

"Well . . ." Theophane said, hesitating—as though he didn't want to appear as though he were trying to correct me. "I think we're seen much more than we see."

✛ 79
JOHN MEIER

John Meier is a professor at Notre Dame and the most famous Catholic scholar in the world. His first book on Jesus was 484 pages, the second 1,118 pages. *I had never met anyone who had written a 1,000-page book before.*

I drove five hundred miles to see him, and our first meeting lasted exactly ninety seconds—give or take a minute.

"Notre Dame's the first right, then the next left," the attendant said after I paid a buck seventy-five at the South Bend exit tollbooth. After a few blocks, I glimpsed the Golden Dome of Notre Dame and drove through the front gate without asking for directions to John Meier's office. It was a typical Bill mistake. I just wanted to see if I could find his building on my own, but after a few minutes of driving around aimlessly, my initial interest in such a challenge turned to growing frustration. I pulled over and asked a coed for directions.

"It's back a few miles," she said, "by the front gate."

A few miles and minutes later, the elevator stopped at the seventh floor. I got out and followed the office numbers. . . . *702, 704, 706 . . .*

Motivation? That question ran through my mind as I walked toward John Meier's office. *What was my motivation for writing this book?* I breathed deeply and asked for a *spiritual* motivation and guidance in my dialogue with John Meier. I silently prayed that our meeting would inform and heal the people who would eventually read this book.

The office door to John Meier's office was cracked open. I knocked and poked my head in.

"What happened?" John Meier asked. He was a thin man with close-cropped brown hair and he had his winter parka on because he was ready to leave. My mind raced.

"Wasn't our meeting at three-thirty?" I asked.

"It's four-thirty now," John Meier said.

"Is Indiana a different time zone?" I asked, standing before a professor and feeling very stupid.

"This part is," he replied.

"Can you still do . . ."

"Not till Monday."

Back in the elevator, I giggled to myself over the confusion. Before I got back into my car, I told everyone from a woman in the elevator to the next tollbooth attendant about my stupidity regarding time zones.

Three days later I returned, driving another five hundred miles to see John Meier, and he conveyed the same sense of integrity, clarity, and carefulness I had come across in many of the scholars I met. And courage—they all had that, at least the best of them did whenever they faced their fears (and the fears of others) as they peeled back beliefs in order to find truth.

John Meier's three books on Jesus are all titled *A Marginal Jew* and are considered classics in the field of Christian scholarship. He was born a Catholic and found that biblical research "was very enlightening" and pushed him "towards a maturation of faith."

One has to be very careful when comparing Jesus with the Eastern religion's concept of avatar. With comparative religion, everybody is big on the similarities, people tend to forget the dissimilarities. With the avatars, the one and the same deity can keep coming down and appearing in various avatars in various periods of history. Why? Because, in the Eastern idea there is no true incarnation in the sense of what the fourth gospel of the Christian faith proclaims about incarnation. Namely, that once and for all, the second person of the Trinity became totally, exhaustively identified with this one human being. He didn't simply appear as this human being. He didn't just seem to become human, he became totally, fully human. The constant refrain throughout the New Testament then is once and once for all and never again, because this is not just an appearing in the flesh, this is a becoming flesh. Therefore, Eastern avatars are not examples of incarnation in the way that Catholics understand incarnation. What you have in those avatars is something much closer to Gnostic myth, where various Divine figures keep appearing in human form—but it's only in appearance. Hence the Christians heresy known as docetism, that the Son of God only seemed to become human. He appeared in human form but, of course, the Divine couldn't really become human, it was just an appearance, it was just a show, just making an appearance.

Jesus' mission?

Historically, it certainly seems that Jesus took on the role of the eschatological prophet, the prophet of the last days sent to Israel to more or less perform the function of Elijah. After all, in the Old Testament, Jesus most resembled Elijah, who was a miracle-working, itinerant prophet, active especially in northern Israel, in conflict with the authorities, and after his being taken up to heaven was expected (by at least some Israelites) to return and gather the scattered, fragmented Israel back together again, preparing it for God's coming-again time. To a great degree, that does seem to be what Jesus is all about . . . itinerant, miracle-working prophet, especially in northern Israel, proclaiming the coming of God's kingdom definitively, symbolically beginning the gathering of the twelve tribes of Israel by creating a group of twelve disciples whom he sends out as missionaries to Israel.

What is the ultimate purpose of Jesus' mission? We can say a certain amount simply from the viewpoint of historical research. But the fuller vision of faith is had only through faith.

Gospel authorship and accuracy?

We don't know who wrote the gospels. The only things we can really put names, a face, and a person on, are Paul's authentic epistles. Everything else in the New Testament is indeed either anonymous or pseudonymous—originally it bore no name. The so-called Epistle to the Hebrews, probably things like the pastoral epistles, Ephesians, etc., were probably written by a disciple of Paul in the name of Paul, which was quite respectable and acceptable at the time—nothing immoral or illegal about doing that. You took on the mantle of your revered teacher and wrote in his name.

I suppose, hilariously, one of the few writings that would not be anonymous or pseudonymous would be the Revelation of John, where somebody, this seer or prophet apocalyptisist who happens to be called John, is writing this apocalypse. He makes no claim to be John the son the Zebedee. But he would be, along with Paul, I suppose, about the only direct voice with the direct name we have in the New Testament.

So, unlike these pseudonymous Epistles of Paul, which claim to be by Paul but are by a disciple, the gospels never claimed to be written by anybody in particular. Matthew, Mark, Luke, and John are precisely not meant to be the individual voice and individual message of one person. They're meant to be a proclamation of the whole gospel as it was taught, preached, lived, in this whole church.

It's a fact the various gospels disagree with one another on some points regarding details of both history, chronology, geography. When Jairus comes to Jesus asking for healing of his daughter, in Mark's version she is very ill, but it is only on their way there that they get the message that she has died. In Matthew's version, to heighten the element of faith and prayer, Jairus comes, saying, "my daughter has just died but come lay hands on her, she will come back to life" (Matthew 9:18, NIV). Now either she was dead or she was not dead at the beginning of the story. With Matthew, it is very interesting because he has Mark's story in front of him and knows that Mark's story says she's at death's door. Matthew's community apparently had heard Mark's gospel proclaimed for some time, yet Matthew decides he is going to change the beginning of the story by having her dying at the beginning rather than dying later. His community, no doubt, knows the Mark version of the story, and apparently it doesn't bother either Matthew or his community that he changes the story. Obviously, the point is, as far as they are concerned, in either case Jesus winds up raising somebody from the dead, whether she was dead at the beginning or died later on in the story is a minor detail which is of no great concern. Notice, they don't care themselves. It's not that we have discovered that there is discrepancy here! Matthew knew what Mark was saying and he blithely changes it to make a different theological point. Luke ends his gospel with Jesus ascending into heaven on Easter Sunday evening. Luke then opens the Acts of the Apostles by having Jesus ascend forty days later. It doesn't bother Luke in the least but it drives us up the wall.

One of the problems here is that the modern, mainly low-church, fundamentalistic Protestant (it infects Catholics also), views the gospels, not as first-century writings, but rather as modern German history, which the gospel writers never claimed to be writing. It would never enter their minds.

Up until now I have been treating this simply as a historical question. If we then raise the theological question—What does this have to say about inspiration and the nature of inspiration?—I believe God inspired first-century people and these inspired first-century people wrote like first-century people, with the mindset of first-century people. Does that have anything to say, one way or the other, about inspiration? Only if we think, as some moderns do, that somehow the first primary object of inspiration is to guarantee historical accuracy, but that is *not* the purpose of inspiration. The purpose of inspiration is to make certain statements by human beings the vehicle of God's Word to human beings. That can be done through fanciful poetry, through myth, through historical narration, through epistles, through any and every literary form imaginable. Within the Bible, you have just about every literary form imaginable: sober history, myth, epistles, and fanciful poetry. All of it is the vehicle of God's Word and self-disclosure. The idea that only historical narrative can be the proper object of inspiration is a rather curious and modern idea.

I certainly think the New Testament is true. The question is what does one mean by that proposition? That every verse in the New Testament is a videotape? A Dan Rather reporting live from Calvary? I mean, that is so bizarre and inadequate in understanding of both the literature of the New Testament on a historical level and a mature, theological understanding of inspiration, that one can only be sort of astounded at the very idea. The important thing in inspiration is that God uses these human words to speak his word of love to humanity. The whole point of revelation is God's self-disclosure.

John's gospel and anti-Semitism?

That's an interesting question, the origins and the history of the fourth Gospel are endlessly fascinating. One of the problems is that of all the gospels, John probably has the longest history and, indeed, may have gone through a number of stages of writing—not only stages of oral tradition, perhaps even written additions. So which author of John do we talk about? The main author? Or the final author? At any rate, there is a good chance the main author of the gospel was Jewish. Certainly the Johanian community seems to have been mainly Jewish. So although you do have this heavy negative use of the term "Jews," for the most part it is restricted to the hostile authorities in Jerusalem. It is quite common in that context and indeed goes throughout the whole gospel. But it doesn't refer to every and any Jew indiscriminately, it refers to the hostile authorities in Jerusalem. Jesus himself is affirmed quite pointedly as a Jew, and Jesus even says, "Salvation is from the Jews" (John 4:22, NIV).

Why didn't all Jews accept Jesus as the Messiah?

This may sound like an attempt at comedy, but the fact is you'd have to ask them. There seemed to have been plenty of Jews who were quite happy not expecting a Messiah. Those who did expect a Messiah had many different ideas about what a Messiah would be because there were many different ideas about Messiahs at the time. No doubt Jesus fit the conceptions of some people but didn't fit the conceptions of other people. How do we know why some Jews accepted Jesus? Obviously, every single Jew who met Jesus would have his or her own personal reason for accepting/not accepting, believing/not believing.

Paul certainly thinks we are all sons of God. In Romans he says "and this is the proof that you are sons of God, the God has sent the spirit of son into your heart crying of the father." Obviously, later theologians make the distinction that Jesus is Son of God by nature, we become sons of God by grace. Namely, we participate in that one-son-ship that he has. Or the way John's gospel puts it is that Jesus is the *monogenes huios theou,* that he is the *only Son of God,* we are *tekna theou,* we are children of God, which is his way of making the same distinction, son by nature/son by grace. He uses different words, two things.

Virgin birth?

As a believing Christian I believe in the virgin birth, but not precisely in my capacity as a scholar. Do I think it can be proved by historical, critical research? No. Just as I don't think the Trinity can, although I believe in the Trinity.

One has to be careful—are you asking a question about the person's scholarship and the person's scholarly position or are you asking a question about the person's belief system? One might also ask a further question then—what is the relationship between the two?

Jesus' religion?

Jesus was a Jew, but being a Jew doesn't only apply to the religion. It as an ethnic designation. Jew originally meant a person from Judea. In the time of the Maccabees that particular label came to have very strong religious connotations as opposed to other religions. Therefore when we say, "Oh, he was Jewish," as opposed to being Catholic or Protestant that isn't the way people thought about it at the time. And even if we understand *Jewish* to be an ethnic/religious designation of the time, perhaps even a geographical/ethnic/religious designation of the time, it still opens up as many questions as it answers because today we appreciate much more the plurality of expressions of Judaism.

Now some scholars speak of *Judaisms* in the plural at the time of Jesus, but today we have incredible differentiations within Judaism whether reformed, Conservative, Orthodox, Secular, Progressive, or Reconstructionist. Despite this, however, we speak of one Judaism and we end up speaking of one Christianity, even though we have Protestants, Catholics, and Greek Orthodox. At the same time I don't think that prevents us from seeing a sort of basic, if vague, mainstream of Judaism within Palestine at the time with all its, no doubt, variations. So when you say Jesus was a Jew, both ethnically, geographically, and religiously, in first-century Palestine it both answers a question and poses a question. What sort of Jew was he? Where does he lie on the map, a very variegated map, of first-century Palestinian Judaism? There has been every attempt under the sun to make him a Pharisee, to make him Hellite, to make him Shemite, no he was a Sadducee, no he was an Essene, no he studied at Qumran, no he was the enemy of the state, no he was a zealot, etc., etc., every label imaginable has been used . . . Even mutually exclusive labels have been applied to him at various times, which makes you suspicious of the labeling process.

The vast majority of Palestinian Jews at the time were none of those things; they were Jews, and it was sort of the meat-and-potatoes, mainstream, vague Judaism where you were circumcised if you were male and kept a basically kosher household, at least according to the basic rules of the Torah. If possible, you went up to the temple of Jerusalem for the major feast days, observed Yom Kippur, and had a Passover meal. You would observe the Sabbath some way, but rules, as we can see from the Essene material, Jesus' statements, and the mission of the Babylonian Talmud, rules about observing the Sabbath were debated among various Jewish groups. So there was sort of this generic Judaism Jesus no doubt belonged to. What more specifically he was by way of being a Jew, how he defined his Jewishness, that is part of the problem that scholars have tried to work through.

The New Testament affirms quite specifically that Jesus did not know certain things. In Mark 13, even as Jesus is in the process of prophesying his coming in glory, etc., etc., he says, speaking of the day of judgment, that that day no one knows, neither the angels nor the son, but the Father only—right there in Mark!

Then Matthew takes it over when the woman with the hemorrhage sneaks up behind Jesus in the crowd and touches his garment, saying, "If I can just touch the garment I'll be cured" and he feels power going forth and asks, "Who touched me?" The disciples say, "What do you mean who touched you? Everyone is pressing in on you." But he keeps insisting "somebody touched me" until the woman comes forward trembling and confesses it (Mark 5:31, NIV). So you have a number of cases in the New Testament that say that Jesus didn't know something.

In Luke it says, "He grew in grace and knowledge." If he grew in wisdom and knowledge, that meant he learned things. So, the problem once again is the finite is not commensurable with the infinite. The problem and mystery of the incarnation is that the infinite, Divine one became truly human and Jesus' intellect (since he was human) was by definition finite, subject to growth and subject to limitations. That would seem to be the natural corollary of the traditional, Catholic doctrine of the incarnation and to use big words, the hypostatic union, the union of two natures in one person.

Was Jesus married or in an intimate relationship?

On the first, could he have been married? Of course, all things are possible and, indeed, that was a quite natural thing among Jews of the day. Therefore, some people have written books trying to show Jesus must have been married or certainly was married and trying to know the unknowable. The simple fact is the New Testament says absolutely nothing about the marital status of Jesus one way or the other, which of course is not the same question as—did Jesus have sex or not? Which is a more unknowable thing.

Those who argue that he could have been married say it was just natural that all Jewish males at the time got married so it is taken for granted even though the New Testament doesn't mention it. But the problem is that we know that there were various Jews of the time or around the period who did not marry. Josephus indicates that most of the Essenes were celibates, so there were Jewish celibates at the time. And judging by the lifestyle of John the Baptist, one would presume he was not married. Mrs. Baptist would have had a very hard time with his hanging out in the desert. Similarly, we hear of other solitary Jewish ascetics in the desert. Josephus spent some years with a person by the Jordan who simply clothed himself in tree leaves and drank water. There were all sorts of interesting and strange people from whose lifestyles we can either presume that they were not married or had long since left marriage. Therefore, it's not impossible that Jesus would have chosen celibacy, however rare and unusual, but of course, he made a lot of rare and unusual choices. All we can say definitely then is that there is an intriguing argument either way. Granted, the silence about any wife or children whatsoever by the people around him (including all sorts of family members who are mentioned or specifically named) does begin to look curious. But from a purely historical point of view there is no way of deciding the matter one way or the other.

Who killed Jesus?

Josephus says Pilate condemned him to death. It's a stark, short statement. John does not have a full Jewish trial at all. Rather, there is just this quick, night hearing before the high priest, after which Jesus is given over to Pilate for a more lengthy Roman trial. As far as we can tell, some of the aristocratic, chief priests in Jerusalem, along with the high priest at the head, finally decided that this lay teacher and prophetic figure was attracting so many people and creating such upset, especially during the time of Jerusalem's great feast, that he was a threat to public order. This made the Romans nervous, and neither Caiaphas the head priest or Pontius Pilate would have profited from a blowup. Caiaphas seemed to have been quite adept in cooperating with the Roman authorities. If you take a look at the list of high priests in the first century, it's a revolving door most of the time. Caiaphas has the single, longest tenure of any high priest in the first century, from 18–36, and perhaps, not coincidentally, that overlaps for the most part the tenure of Pontius Pilate, 26–36. This leads us to believe they worked well together and when Pilate got deposed in 36 so did Caiaphas.

John is right there. Jesus had been to Jerusalem any number of times for various feasts (we aren't to take the synoptic view that this just happened once suddenly out of the blue), preaching to the people, and this was stirring up more and more expectation and fervor and the priests decided, "This town just ain't big enough for both of us anymore and somebody has to go and it is going to be him rather than us." But John claims that while the priests might theoretically be able to pass the death sentence, they could not carry it out. Only the Roman prefect had the power of the sword of practice. Therefore, he had to be handed over to the Roman authorities. Why Judas handed Jesus over, with what intentions he did it, we don't know. John Dominic Crossan is correct to that extent that obviously the bare bones of the narrative of the passion get filled out very quickly with also some references to the Old Testament. But his mistake is thinking that the Old Testament created and gave the narrative its purpose. It's rather that there was a very bare skeletal narrative that needed to be filled out, and the Old Testament provided the prophesies that allowed the author to do so.

Resurrection: Spirit and body?

Again, one must be very careful here. In the New Testament Paul himself speaks paradoxically of the spiritual body, which seems a contradiction in terms. His whole point is (and it's the basic Catholic view of the nature of resurrection) is that there is both continuity and discontinuity in the risen body. It is the same person. The same Jesus of Nazareth who lived, suffered, died, is the same Jesus of Nazareth who rises from the dead. It's not somebody else, it's not a poltergeist. Nevertheless, when Jesus dies he undergoes a true, full, human death. The resurrection is not to be thought of as his coming back from the dead, in that phrase we usually use. That would be true of the people that Jesus raised from the dead during his earthly life, the daughter of Jairus, Lazarus. Namely, they come back from the dead in the sense that they come back into that earthly life they had before, which means they are going to have to die again at some future date. It's not a total release from death, it's a reprieve. They come back to that old body, with its built-in death warrant, so their being raised from the dead was purely a sign. It was not the ultimate rescue from death at all, but simply a reprieve.

But Jesus' resurrection is not to be thought of as that type. Rather, Jesus dies fully, really, definitively, once and for all, and he does not come back from death into this earthly life. He goes through death into the fullness of life in God's presence. He goes beyond death into the fullness. He rises, completely transformed and glorified. His whole being is radically transformed by this experience of true death. His true resurrection, however, in no way nullifies or reverses his true death. He truly died once and for all, just as surely as we all do, and that *resurrection is, therefore, not a coming back from that death but rather a going through that death forward into the fullness*—into a totally new mode of existence that involves his entire human being, body, soul. But this glorified body is inconceivable, as spiritual realities often are. Namely, it is the full human person, body and soul, but in a totally, radically, transformed existence. Therefore, if we talk about Jesus rising from the dead, it must be understood that it is not like a Renaissance picture of his walking out of the tomb with the body he went into the tomb with. It is a radically new human existence. The whole point of the New Testament is that this is true of every believing Christian. We indeed truly die, but by God's grace and mercy and union with Jesus, we, like Jesus, pass through this experience of death into eternal life. To use the metaphor, we come out on the other side of death. But to stress the idea that Jesus came back from the dead in some sort of storybook fashion, both trivializes and misconceives what is being talked about.

Second Coming?

The New Testament never used that exact phrase "Second Coming." For what we call the Second Coming it uses the word *parousia*. It's in that sense of triumphant, glorious arrival and power of the emperor that Parousia is used when speaking of Jesus coming at the end of time. But it's only Justin Martyr in the middle of the second century, who for the first time uses Parousia both of the first and Second Coming. So again, as always, we must be a little bit careful with our terms lest we start importing into the New Testament precise concepts that the New Testament doesn't work with.

In the New Testament, the Second Coming is often painted with the colors of Jewish apocalyptic, which was the mindset of the time: all history is moving toward a consummation in Christ and in the end God will be all in all. But that doesn't mean you have to take literally all the symbolism of Jewish apocalyptic. These were the colors on the palette to paint the picture at the time, and one affirms the basic picture without necessarily taking literally all the colors on the palette.

Barabbas meets "Son of the Father?"

That rests on understanding the proper etymological derivation of Barabbas and it certainly looks like it could be bar abba or son of the father. Not everybody agrees, though, that that is the proper etymological derivation of that name, so that depends somewhat on how you judge the original meaning of that name. Much of our confusion about the Bible is due to our spiritual immaturity and as Paul said, "The problem is you are like children right now and you have to grow up." Faith is not something we can ever produce, create, or manufacture on our own. As the whole Bible keeps proclaiming—faith is a gift of God that we can receive but we cannot give ourselves. Then the whole point is, once one receives that gift of faith, what does one do with it?

✢ 80
DAY FOUR

After I sat on my cushion before each meditation/prayer session, I immediately said, "Jesus have mercy" silently three times to myself. Then I opened myself to God's presence. If a thought, emotion, or body sensation pulled my attention away from God's presence, I acknowledged that distraction and rested once again in God's presence. Or when using the Centering Prayer technique, I acknowledged my distraction by saying sacred words like "Abba," "Christ," "letting go" or "Jesus" before returning to God's presence.

What was the point of this silent prayer?

Intimacy with God. Because the days of *just* going to church on Sunday and keeping the commandments during the week while keeping God at a distance are over. God is asking more from us, just as we are asking more from God. Why? Because love tends to do that, and eventually one hopes for moments of union with the focus of our love.

The Bible supports this deep, silent resting in God's presence. "Be still, and know that I am God," Psalm 46:10 says, and "Be still before the LORD and wait patiently for him" says Psalm 37:7. That is also why Jesus went into the desert for forty days, and is why "very early in the morning, while it was still dark, Jesus got up, left the house and went off to a solitary place, where he prayed." (Mark 1:35, NIV) Or why "Jesus often withdrew to lonely places and prayed." (Luke 5:16, NIV).

In Matthew 6:6, Jesus also directed us to pray in solitary and silent ways "When you pray, go into your room, close the door and pray to your Father, who is unseen." Jesus is using metaphor here because in Jesus' time, very few families had more than one room in their house, and the Greek word used is *tameion,* which means secret chamber, closet, or storehouse. So the room Jesus spoke about was the inner room, a secret room in which we meet with God.

But some people resist this stillness—as though they were afraid of it. As Thomas Keating wrote "Some people think that if you quiet your mind, you open yourselves up to diabolical forces. But according to St. John of the Cross, you are never safer than when you are absorbed in God's presence. We do not have to be afraid of opening ourselves to unknown dangers by practicing Contemplative Prayer. No one can join us at that level except he who is deeper than that level, the God who dwells within us and out of whose creative love we emerge at every moment."[1]

Perhaps much of the fear associated with stillness before God comes from the fact that in Western society we are addicted to movement and speed. Silent prayer opposes this addiction and breaks the habit of filling the silence with a restless movement or inflated sense of self.

"The saint's duty is to be still and listen,"[2] Oswald Chambers wrote in

1. Thomas Keating, *Open Mind Open Heart.*
2. Oswald Chambers, *My Utmost for His Highest,* January 19 entry on vision and darkness.

his spiritual classic *My Utmost for His Highest*. "*Abraham went through thirteen years of silence, but in those years all of his self-sufficiency was destroyed. He grew past the point of relying on his own common sense. Those years of silence were a time of discipline, not a period of God's displeasure. There is never any need to pretend that your life is filled with joy and confidence; just wait upon God and be grounded in Him.*"[3]

Some people fear this opening, and it is their fear that they associate with dark forces. But if a person is unsure, then a short prayer to God or Jesus before the meditation will invoke God's presence—and then whatever fearful, dark and judgmental places come up in the meditation will come up in order to be healed in the presence of God.

"*Bill,*" *my young* roommate Peter asked, "are we bad people?"

"I know what you're saying," I said. "I've been feeling and thinking that I'm a controlling, power-hungry, efforting bastard—*and I think everyone else is too!*"

It was close to midnight, and we had shut off the light an hour ago, but instead of sleeping we continued to talk in the darkness. Over the past few days, the demons of projection had slowly arisen in Peter, me, and our fellow retreatants. The afternoon group discussions were getting heated. I was also thinking things about people that disturbed me, and when I told Peter, he said he had been thinking the same things.

"That guy over there is a rigid, controlling Christian," I thought during our group discussion. "He's just repeating church doctrine like a robot."

"Look at that woman over there—all she does is monopolize all the groups. She's a controlling power monger who thinks she knows everything."

"And that monk over there—he's trying so hard to experience God! Don't try so hard . . ." I wanted to shout.

I also knew from past retreat experience that during a retreat, unconscious habits became conscious so that they can be healed—and the criticism and judgment of others and oneself were certainly habits of mind. As Jesus said, "Why do you look at the speck of sawdust in your brother's eye

3. See Isaiah 50:10–11.

and pay no attention to the plank in your own eye? How can you say to your brother, 'Let me take the speck out of your eye,' when all the time there is a plank in your own eye? You hypocrite, first take the plank out of your own eye, and then you will see clearly to remove the speck from your brother's eye."[4]

That was one of the reasons I did a retreat every year—because I wanted to become aware of my projections, my judgment, and my planks. Usually during every retreat I've done over the last fifteen years, I've unconsciously picked out another retreatant or two and projected my dislikes onto them. During one seven-day retreat ten years ago, I continually thought negative thoughts about a guy who sat on the cushion next to me. He couldn't do anything right in my mind. It was a silent retreat, so it wasn't anything he said—*it was what he did.* He always made little noises during the meditations or distracted me on my walks outside by doing Tai Chi on the grounds. My criticism of him got so crazy that I criticized him for *what I thought he was thinking.* For example, whenever I opened my eyes during a meditation/prayer session and looked over at him, I imagined that he thought he was better than me. At the end of the retreat he approached me.

"I want to thank you," he said with a smile. "You really helped me."

"I did?" I asked.

"Yeah," he said. "It was a hard retreat for me. But whenever it got too hard I just looked over at you. You looked so joyful and loving during meditation that it gave me the strength to go on."

✢ 81
MOTHER TESSA BIELECKI

MADISON, WISCONSIN

The word Catholic originally meant "universal," and Mother Tessa Bielecki, a Catholic nun, pointed out to me that this spirit of universality was still present in the Catholic Church's official stance.

4. Matthew 7:3, NIV.

"I believe the essence of Christ is in other religions," Mother Tessa Bielecki said, "and it's actually official Church teaching since the Second Vatican council."

"The Catholic Church rejects nothing of what is true and holy in these religions. She has a high regard for the manner of life and conduct, the precepts and doctrines which, although differing in many ways from her own teaching, nevertheless often reflect a ray of that truth which enlightens all men. . . .

"Let Christians, while witnessing to their own faith and way of life, acknowledge, preserve and encourage the spiritual and moral truths found among non-Christians, also their social life and culture." Declaration on the Relation of the Church to Non-Christian Religions (Nostra Aetate, 1965) from the Documents of Vatican II.

"Be careful," Mother Tess Bielecki said when I told her about my search for a place to spend forty days in the desert.

"There's a lot of crazies out there," she said. "When I went to St. George's Monastery in Israel, I was warned by another woman to watch out for a particular dirty-old-man-monk in his eighties. First, he will ask you if you want to go see some religious relics, then he will grab and fondle you."

Later when we talked about the quality of prayer she said, "The biggest problem isn't prayer, it's what I would call 'unlived life' or 'life failure.' People simply aren't alive enough, so they don't come to know Jesus who is *life in full*."

"And when I'm talking about being alive," she continued, "I'm not talking about those enthusiastic zombies who sell their tapes on TV at three o'clock in the morning. Spirituality has taken a little turn in this country because now you can remain a zombie, as long as you are an enthusiastic zombie!"

Tessa Bielecki became a Carmelite[1] nun after meeting her spiritual teacher and best friend, Father William McNamara, OCD, when she was

---

1. The Carmelite tradition takes its name not from an inspired individual but from a mountain in the Holy Land. In Mother Tessa's words, "We see our path as a joyous, adventurous, arduous climb up Mount Carmel."

a junior in college. Up to that time, she had thought that vitality and holiness were mutually exclusive.

"But Father McNamara embodied both at once," Mother Tessa said. "He was passionate, earthy, hilarious, and holy. After that meeting my heart said, 'This is the man, and this is your life.'"

Mother Tessa Bielecki is cofoundress and Mother Abbess of the Spiritual Life Institute, with retreat centers in Colorado and Ireland. She is the author of *Teresa of Avila: Mystical Writings* and *Teresa of Avila: Ecstasy and Common Sense;* editor of the quarterly magazine *Desert Call;* and in her words, "most important, a hermit and avid gardener."

Who was/is Jesus?

The question is as vast as the universe, because Christ is cosmic. I do not believe that Jesus was just another avatar. In the Eastern-Western religious dialogues that I've been engaged in since 1981 I've tried that sort of thing on for size, but I kept experiencing Jesus, as the Son of God, coming up again and again. My focus is that of Jesus as spouse or bridegroom; as a Carmelite, we grow into our relationship with Jesus through what we call a spousal relationship or spiritual matrimony.

I am not very good at speaking theologically or very abstractly. I'm extremely experiential and very concrete; however, theology does *inform* my experience. As a Roman Catholic, my whole understanding of God is Trinitarian. Jesus is not the creator. There is Father, Son, and Holy Spirit. I cannot speak very experientially about the Father because my own personal life is much more Christo-centric. But there's that wonderful passage from the Book of Proverbs which refers to Jesus—I believe it's somewhere in Proverbs 9—which says, "And before the earth was even made, I was there with him playing in his presence, playing before the face of God and the face of the earth." So there's the sense of Jesus as really the child Christ or the boy Christ, playing before the face of the Father in the act of creation; he's a part of it. But he certainly isn't the creator God.

I'm interested in what you said about "Lord"; the idea of "Lord" versus that of friend. I notice as I read and talk to people, the number of people who speak of "The Lord" in a kind of distant, separate way. Whereas, someone like St. Teresa or John of the Cross or myself speaks much more personally of "My Lord." You reach a point where that distance is bridged and not only does "The Lord" become "My Lord" but also, because of the intimacy, "My Lord" becomes "My Spouse." He is always "Lord," and you never lose that sense of majesty, but it's extremely intimate.

First of all, in mystical experience "The Lord" becomes "My Lord," so the relationship is extremely personal. At the same time it's very appropriate to speak in terms of Jesus having said, "I no longer call you servants, but friends" (John 15:15, NIV). For the mystics, and this would definitely be true for me, yes you are Lord but you're also a friend and there is equality. This is because God elevates you to such a height. Yet, at the same time, I have no problem in thinking of myself as a servant of God or even as a slave of God. St. Teresa is my favorite mystic and she has this *marvelous* passage that reflects my own experience; "We are the SLAVES of Christ, and our foreheads are branded with his brand which is the sign of the cross." I know people who are repelled by that, but I have *absolutely* no problem with that at all, because when you love, you are prepared to serve to the extent of being a slave. I'm ready to be God's slave, but God is ready to elevate me to the role of spouse. I'm not being held down. An earthly king or an earthly lord will keep the slave, the servant, or the serf in its place, but that isn't how God loves. It is perfectly fine to use that kind of language. It's extremely out of fashion, but in my whole community, a community of twenty men and women, we are extremely at ease with this kind of language.

"Sin" is an extremely important word, and I see it as "missing the mark." Sin is extremely mysterious. We are capable of profound misdirection and misorientation and need to come to terms with that. It's too simplistic and certainly not profound enough to just think in terms of isolated bad deeds, most of which have to do with sex. That's not the point. The greater sin is actually the sin of omission, a failure to love, or a lack of charity; these are far worse sins than some sort of sexual lapse. The worst sins are sins of pride, apathy, disregard for one's neighbor and for the rest of the world. Some of the corporate sins in the name of globalization—those are really heinous.

I know from profound human experience that we are misdirected. For me, the story of Genesis is as good a way as any other to account for what happened, but I don't believe it literally. If I were talking about my whole community (because we are a whole), we would say the Bible is on the mythic level, which means it's truer than fact. Even if the whole Genesis story is a myth, it doesn't mean it's not true. It means it's truer than if it were literal and factual. The Bible is very accurate mythically.

As a contemplative community, our whole outreach is to bring the riches of the Christian contemplative tradition out of the monasteries and into the marketplace. One way of looking at the Genesis story is that it was a fall from contemplation, in the sense that instead of merely contemplating this tree, and understanding its depth, Adam and Eve used it. The sin was utilitarianism, taking what was too good to be used, and using it, instead of simply letting it be, contemplating and enjoying it.

What religion!? (laugh) Jesus was a Jew! Absolutely! My favorite images are the paintings by William Holman Hunt, where Jesus is very, very

Jewish looking. The more Jewish looking he is the better. He was very dark and very swarthy; he did not have blue eyes and blond hair.

Jesus intended to start Christianity?

Initially Christians were known as "People of the Way." Jesus didn't intend something very institutionalized, it was more of a spontaneous path. But we haven't been free enough for that, so we have taken that freedom and that wildness, and basically tamed it. This doesn't mean that I'm anti-institutional, because institutions are important, but they need to be very, very light and very transparent. They are tools and not ends in themselves.

*Why didn't all Jews accept
Jesus as the Messiah?*

I really don't know enough historically, but my sense is that they had another expectation and that possibly it involved, as the disciples indicated, some kind of earthly glory. But because Jesus came as a suffering servant and the outcome was something quite different from the realization of earthly glory, there might have been a confusion which we still see today.

Only Son of God?

Jesus is unique and I am not exactly like Jesus. Jesus is by nature what we are by grace. We are all sons and daughters of God by virtue of Jesus, who is by nature the Son of God. That would be the theology of it, and my experience of it.

Virgin birth?

Jesus was conceived in Mary's womb, virginally? Yes, I do believe that. Can I prove that? No! I believe in mystery and miracles, and that the mystery of God is so unfathomable that incredible things happen.

The physicality of the resurrection makes all the difference in the world! Basically we are called to live forever. But in another modality, Jesus came, and did it all, and showed it to us so we could really understand. It was *not* simply continued aliveness in the mind of the disciples. My favorite gospel of all the gospels is the resurrection appearance where Jesus cooked fish on the beach. The physicality there is important, because it was important to Jesus. He kept demonstrating over and over again, that this was his body. He ate bread, he ate fish, he had people touch him. He wanted everybody to know, "Look, this is my body, this is a resurrected, glorified body!" What gets me in that gospel of fish on the beach is—here he is! Resurrected from the dead! He's back from the tomb after this incredible ordeal—you'd think he would do something spectacular and flashy, and what does he do? He cooks fish on the beach! Over and over again, this miracle of the ordinary, the ordinary, the ordinary.

*Holy images and concepts of
Christ keep us from Christ?*

Christianity isn't mystical enough and one of the most important dimensions of mysticism is precisely that, to get beyond images and ideas and concepts to the reality behind them. If you aren't taught that that is where you are supposed to go, then of course you get attached to the concepts, and you get stuck.

A lot of American Buddhists are what I would call disaffected or disenchanted Christians or Jews. They have left Judaism or Christianity at the level of Sunday school and then they are very sophisticatedly educated in Buddhist meditation and contemplation, but they don't even know that such a thing as Christian mysticism exists. I run into this over and over again, Christianity is often dismissed as being nonmystical, and this is just ignorance.

For the last ten years we have taught a course on Christian mysticism at Colorado College in Colorado Springs, and it's *amazing* to expose college students to texts from the actual mystics. They may know a little bit about Buddhism or Sufism or Hinduism but they are kind of shocked to find out that there is something very, very similar in Christianity. It's definitely a weakness in Christianity that mysticism is not more mainstream, but that's why communities such as ours.

Second Coming?

I don't know what that means, (laugh) but I do. Part of the trouble with the Bible and a lot of Christian teachings *is* that conceptualization: What did Jesus mean when he talked about that? And what is that all about? I can imagine if you asked an evangelical about the Second Coming, there would be a very clear answer. But from my more mystical perspective, I don't know how to talk about that. I can talk very, very concretely about what my experience of Jesus is, but as soon as you get on that other level, who knows? The kind of tightness you find with fundamentalists is not peculiar to Christianity or even to religion. It's a human problem, a narrowing of focus and reification where we really think we have a handle on something and the way we see it is the way it is. I certainly used to think I had quite a handle on things but I see things quite differently now than I did when I was younger; I'm fifty-eight next month. I'm much more fluid than I was. That's part of maturation.

My basic principle for dealing with any person now is that we need to meet people where they are. I try to understand—to use the colloquial expression—where a person is coming from, with compassion and understanding.

What is Love?

Often we settle in on a certain level of being or "perceived" love, which is inadequate. We think we know what love is but until we have gone through the process of loving out of will and not feeling we don't really know what it is because love is not a feeling. Love is a gospel command and whether it feels good or not is completely irrelevant. Love is not about how I feel; love is for the sake of the other. It is the other that is the focus, not myself or my feelings, or even my understanding. You can still be loving, even when your heart's feeling absolutely tight and constricted, or feeling nothing at all because love is an act. It isn't a feeling.

My favorite definition of love is, and every one of these words is important, "an efficacious desire for the well-being of the other." The word "efficacious" is very important because it doesn't just mean desire: efficacious desire means that you have to do something for the well-being of the other. It's not just a feeling that you'd *like* the other to be in a situation of well-being, but that the other's state of well-being is *your* responsibility. It has nothing to do with feeling, and it's exhausting! Ultimately, it will kill us. That's what crucifixion is all about. You give everything until you have nothing left to give.

Is the ego what gets in the
way of experiencing God's presence?

I believe that whatever circumstances we are in, our day-to-day life gives us plenty of opportunity to die to ourselves and to live for the sake of the other. Whether it is a family, a community, or a workplace, wherever, our life provides those opportunities. We can forget about ourselves and think, act, and make decisions in terms of the other. That's how we die to self. In Christian mysticism they teach certain things to help that along, but I don't think that *any* of that is anywhere near as important as being awake and alert to the existential circumstances of your life, watching for the opportunities. And they are all there; life gives us these opportunities.

One of the ways I notice it especially is in commercial exchanges. When standing in a line, are you going to push and shove and try to get ahead? You go through a checkout—how does the checkout person relate to you and how do you relate to the checkout person?

"What is a Christian?"

There is the nominal Christian who simply goes through the motions and calls himself or herself Christian. For example, people talk about the United States as a Christian country. This is *not* a Christian country. This is *nominally* a Christian country! There is nominal Christianity and then there is *real* Christianity, which is when someone has put on the mind of Christ and is thinking, loving, living, like Christ. That's a Christian.

Jesus had a sense that he had very little time and that he had a lot to cram in. One of my favorite and most consoling lines from Jesus' life is from the cross, when he says as he's dying (in Latin it's *consummatum est*)—"it is consummated." By that he doesn't mean, as some translations say, "It is finished." I don't believe that he meant merely that his life was finished and he was about to die, but instead that he had completed what he had come to do. It was consummated. It was finished. That has to be seen in relationship to another line, "You will do even greater things than I." He knew that he had done his part, and now it was up to the rest of us to pick up where he left off.

Did Jesus have a spiritual teacher?

If I believe that Jesus is the Son of God, then what I believe he was doing in those hidden years was listening to the Father. I do not believe that he had a human teacher, which does not mean that on the human level, as a gracious human being, he was not learning. His mother was teaching him something and his father was teaching him something and his friends and his family and nature and animals were teaching him something. But, no, I don't believe he had a spiritual teacher and I *certainly* don't believe that he went to India, to get really specific about it! That is part of the kind of the craziness of our age. Jesus was born and raised a Jew; he came out of that whole culture, and he was enlightened by the Father in his way, not in the Eastern way, but in his way.

What spiritual techniques did Jesus teach?

Jesus didn't teach techniques; that is part of the freedom of the children of God. Jesus didn't even come to teach us to pray, he came to teach us how to live. He was sure that if we were really living, we would inevitably pray. He wasn't teaching techniques, apart from the Lord's Prayer, which was requested by his disciples. He was teaching us how to live; whether in agony or ecstasy, throughout every rhythm of our life, even during the most ordinary rhythms. He taught us that prayer was a cry from the heart.

Mystics follow teachings that are an amplification of what Jesus did, but you don't need any of that. You don't need any techniques whatsoever. You simply need to live your life. That's what Jesus came to teach. You do not need to go to the temple, you do not need to pray a certain way, you do not need to go through these rituals. You simply need to live your life attuned to that sacred dimension. That's why Christianity is different. It is *not* a spiritual technology and in a sense it's not even a religion—it's a path. We get to know Jesus through the whole of life, through nature, through our work, through all our personal relationships, through our play, through liturgy, through worship, through prayer, through study. All of it is important because your whole life is your spiritual life.

✢ 82
DAY FIVE

ST. BENEDICT'S MONASTERY

Mass was held in the chapel three times a day—at 3 A.M. and 9 A.M. and 7 P.M. During the service, the monks wore white robes and sat in a circle at the center of the room while the retreatants sat along the walls.

At the beginning of the retreat, the monks had all looked alike to me—solemn. Even Monk Theophane looked passive and formal when in the circle of praying monks. But after a few days, their differences revealed themselves. At least two of the twelve monks were over six foot seven. A couple others were six foot two, and so of course whenever I was bored during the religious services—I imagined them playing basketball. Their flowing robes would give them an air of majesty as they ran the full length of the chapel on a fastbreak. I pictured one monk, who was short, head-shaven and stocky, as the playmaker who tossed "alley-oop" passes to the tallest monks. They'd then throw down ferocious dunks, which relieved them of any pent-up emotions and brought them to life.

Usually their Gregorian chants snapped me out of any creative absorptions, but then again, my imagination wasn't really all that crazy because several of the monks actually wore high-top gym shoes. Their shoes were one of the few ways they expressed their individuality: a couple monks had Birkenstock sandals, three had orthopedic shoes, two wore tennis shoes (besides the ones with high tops) and three wore dress shoes.

I also noticed that their faces, which all looked expressionless when I first arrived, became quite distinct and animated as the days went by. One monk, named Brother Bill, had a shaved head. He was one of the cantors and always looked to be in religious ecstasy. Another monk had an eternally furrowed brow, as though he was *willing* God to appear. Three or four others looked confused and sad, as though they were still trying to figure out why and how they got there, while the abbot always appeared controlled in a calm sort of way. Even his voice, which conveyed peace and wisdom—seemed to hold something back through its levity. Perhaps that's because he was the abbot, the one who kept the other monks in line. Then there was Monk Theophane, the tall, very thin, gray-haired, bearded monk who—until I got to know him—appeared stern and serious.

Now, don't get me wrong, I respected every monk, and their devotion was an inspiration. But that's the point; none of us gets through life without a trial or two . . . a disappointment or two. And while on a partial silent retreat, there's plenty of time to make up a story or two for each monk . . . what they left behind, what they've found, and also what they've missed. Who knows what aspects of God they've encountered through cloistering themselves away, and what aspects of God they've missed through that same cloister. I imagined among the monks there must have been at least one or two broken hearts. Perhaps those hearts were later healed in godly ways, but still, there are some wounds that only another human being can heal. So in the shadows of early-morning vespers, as the monks prayed for me—I also prayed for them.

I finally approached Sarah on the afternoon of the fifth day. No one else was around, and as I walked toward her, I was afraid. What if she didn't like me? What if she rejected me?

As I stood before her, all judgment by me immediately fell by the wayside. It wasn't my judgment of her that fell away (because there was never a judgment about her)—but my judgment of me. It was healed by her glance—just as one look from Jesus must have healed whoever had the eyes and heart to look back.

Our eyes engaged each other, and she glowed with a fiery clarity that became a sort of "burning bush" radiating God's presence. I took her hand and Sarah slowly smiled a smile so large that it engulfed us. My attempts to put words, rhyme, or reason to what I experienced, seemed pitiful—any words at all, whether of philosophers, theologians, or saints and even scriptures fell short in the face of such wonder.

"Dear God," I silently prayed, "teach me to see with those eyes. Teach me to see with that heart."

I melted before her gaze, and as I did, I fell into my heart, and then into our heart—and then into God's heart of being. As I looked into her eyes, there was something in me that welled up from so deep that every muscle in my body tightened. It was the beginning of an earthquake, and my chest wanted to explode. I was afraid of her, and yet I saw in her *everything I had ever wanted to be.* She was a pure, naked expression of love, and she looked on all with nothing but acceptance.

Then she gurgled because she couldn't speak. A sound that started softly like a whisper and then rose quickly, until it mushroomed into an expression of total delight. I was in awe—both "in love" and afraid. I couldn't get my mind, my words, even my emotions around what I saw and felt. But I never detected any interruption of our meeting in her eyes, whether through fear or haphazard thought. *She was just happy to meet me!*

Then, I finally got the message that her being conveyed. *Just let go.* When I finally let go of every thought, judgment, emotion, and body sensation, I swear no lama, swami, or saint has ever been more at peace or in love or unshackled. I finally looked up at the clock, and realized that *a half hour had passed since I first took her hand.*

Later that day, as I wrote about our meeting, my hands trembled and tears flowed. The Red Sea of my heart parted, and a force so powerful came through that I sought refuge and solitude in the chapel. There, seated and alone, I sobbed until I wept so deeply that my body took on a posture long forgotten. My hands clenched in prayer—torqued and twisted against my chest. My heart broke again and again as I heard the words that my *deepest depth* had prayed long ago.

"Please, God!" I had begged almost thirty years ago. "Please. Please. Please. Don't let my mother die. Please . . . Please. . . ."

Suddenly, I lay crumpled at my mother's feet as I pleaded again and again for her not to die. I prayed as I pleaded. A plea and prayer so deep that it was my very life that begged. My body twisted, and my heart wrenched as tears fell from my face into the cracks and crevices of my balled-up hands.

"Oh, God, don't let her die . . ." I prayed again and again.

I sobbed this way for a thousand eternities—each one outside of time, and gradually my moistened hands unclenched. Soft, open, and pink—they were like baby hands, and they were the hands of a prayer that was never answered, as my mother had died that day. Yet, they were also the hands of a prayer never prayed—but answered—because I now had a life of Spirit that I could never have imagined.

"Please, God," I prayed anew, "lead and accompany me to the places in my heart and soul where I have not dared to go. In my depths is your original prayer—it is a prayer so deep in me that I cannot touch it, and prayed so long ago that I cannot remember it. Yet it is the prayer I have always yearned to pray."

Afterward, as I sat by the open monastery window with my pen in hand. I was left with no prayer of my own, instead as I looked outside at the brown- and green-covered Rocky Mountains, *I saw God's prayer*. Then the wind blew lightly, and the tall grass swayed, and *I heard God's prayer*. The sun's rays came through the window and rested upon my face and shoulder, and *I felt God's prayer*.

I remained still and eternally paused as it arose from within . . .

. . . *I am God's prayer*.

✣ 83
DAY SIX

"Should I call you Monk Theophane or Father Theophane or just Theophane?" I asked the old monk. He just looked at me with a rascally grin.

Whenever he smiled like that, I wanted to call him Theophane. But whenever I looked at his robes, I wanted to call him Monk Theophane. And whenever he conducted mass, or I watched him walk—shaking with Parkinson's and looking every bit his seventy plus years—I wanted to call him Father Theophane. But over the past week, our relationship had evolved (or perhaps disintegrated) to the point of honest informality—and there were no names for that.

"I can always tell when I'm talking to a Protestant," Monk Theophane said with eyes smiling, "because they call me 'sir' instead of 'Father.' "

He referred to Matthew 23:8 where Jesus told his apostles to not to call anyone rabbi, teacher, or father. Then Monk Theophane got that look on his face, a look that I came to recognize. First he would grab his jaw lightly with his right thumb and forefinger, then he would lean close so that no one else could hear. Then he would speak with a sort of intimate hesitancy, as though he didn't want to be too forward, and yet had to share a little spiritual secret with you.

"My name used to be *me* . . ." he said, pausing, ". . . and now it's *you.*"

"Yeah," he repeated to himself as he rubbed his chin lightly with his fingers, "my name used to be *me,* but now it's *you.*"

✣ 84
DAY SEVEN

During the morning prayer session, my body stiffened in resistance, my chest became as impenetrable as cement, and my jaw tightened as teeth gnashed against themselves. I fought to maintain control of myself. Control against what? Here I sat, supposedly in God's presence, and yet I resisted something. Could it be God's heartfelt presence that I resisted? Was I opposing "the life in full" that Jesus had promised?

At that moment I realized, I was *efforting and willing my goodness,* like that monk with the scrunched-up face. I had hated that about him, and now I saw that I hated this about myself—this muscular effort to realize the good God. Then I heard the words *just let go,* and I saw Sarah's laughing face— she laughed at the fact that I held to things that didn't mean anything. As I let go, my jaw softened, my body opened, and my chest shuddered like a newly emerged butterfly. I cried softly till the fear turned to joy.

Dear God, I prayed. Forgive me, for in my ignorance I made your angels into demons, your joys into fears, a full life into a partial death. Also, help to rid me of my judgment, which quickly turns heaven into hell.

"So?! This is it—isn't it?" I said to you, as you smiled wider than the prodigal son's father upon his return. "The last barrier between me and myself, and me and you—was *my judgment* of the mistakes I had made. It was the enemies within me who made your kingdom into a hell, and now that I have seen that *they are me*—I wept at what I have done to this world. But instead of allowing me to wallow in my self-judgment, you gave me the look of love, and said, 'Let's kill the fatted calf. Judgment is only more death! My son who was dead—is now alive.'"

As I stood and walked from the prayer room, I walked into your open arms. One arm was joy, the other, forgiveness. Whatever direction I turned, I was embraced—until *I became your embrace.* As I looked out at the mountains, I felt a joy that was simultaneously your joy and mine. *There was no difference.* The love I felt was your love and mine. *There was no difference.*

✤ 85
N. T. WRIGHT

"Marcus Borg and I recognize each other as Christians," N. T. Wright said, "but we each think the other is a bit of a muddled Christian."

Time and time again, whenever I asked scholars: "Who is the most respected Evangelical New Testament scholar in the world?" N. T. Wright was the reply. *Christianity Today* wrote that "no evangelical has shown more *courage* in this contested field than N. T. Wright."

I would add wisdom and compassion to that assessment of N. T. Wright because he (like Jesus) invited all to the table. N. T. Wright even wrote a book, *The Meaning of Jesus: Two Visions,* with Marcus Borg, a prominent member of the Jesus Seminar.

"Marcus came to visit me when I was dean of Lichfield," N. T. Wright said, "and we began the book by sharing in the Eucharist together. Then we went to my house, made a cup of coffee, and sat down to begin work. We consciously did our work within a framework of Christian fellowship.

"There is always a danger with any dialogue," he said, "that it simply becomes personal and defensive. One of the key insights of the Enlightenment is that reason and discourse matter, that we can learn from one another and we can think something through and arrive at a different judgment."

N. T. Wright is Canon Theologian of Westminster Abbey. He taught New Testament studies for twenty years at Cambridge, McGill, and Oxford Universities. He is author of *The New Testament and the People of God* and *Jesus and the Victory of God,* which are the first two volumes of his projected six-volume series entitled *Christian Origins and the Question of God.*

Who is/was Jesus?

First, Jesus was perceived as, and saw himself as, a prophet announcing the kingdom of God. To understand that you have to put him into the first-century Jewish context. At that time he was a prophet announcing the kingdom of God, and it gradually became apparent that he thought he was more than simply somebody talking about the kingdom of God, he thought he was in some significant way bringing it himself, even embodying it himself, and this fitted his own spin on the expectation of a Messiah. At that time, there was no one template for what a Messiah might look like—there were different possibilities, but it seems Jesus took those existing possibilities and expectations and molded them to his own agenda. But it was definitely a Messiah profile that he was putting across. Ultimately, as I have argued in great detail, Jesus believed, and I think he believed this long before the start of his ministry, but I think it was only when his public career was in full swing that everyone could appreciate what it meant, that he was not just talking about God, that he was in some significant way embodying the one true God. Now, this is quite unlike the avatar idea (which is found in Eastern or Hindu religion) because what you have in the New Testament is much more a picture of somebody saying this within first-century Judaism, where the temple was the place where God was supposed to live—Jesus ultimately challenged the temple. He went about doing and saying things that really make it look as if he believed he was embodying Israel's God in himself, which is, of course, and was, a very scary notion, and he knew that. This was not a cheap, let's-try-it-and-see-if-it-works thing—Jesus staked his life on it.

Jesus was a prophet, Jesus believed he was a prophet, believed he was the Messiah, believed he was the embodiment of Israel's God. Of course, lots of people at the time disagreed with that assessment and lots of people subsequently have disagreed with that assessment. The reason that I accept it is substantially because of the resurrection, which again, as a historian as well as a believer, I accept in its full, normal sense. The resurrection vindicated Jesus' claims. But I fully understand that people who don't believe in the resurrection can look back at Jesus and say, "Well, maybe he did think some of those things, but I disagree."

Virgin birth?

In Matthew and Luke, you have a family tree through Joseph, which then raises another question: Why do we have two different family trees, the Lukan one and Matthaean one? Let's deal with that question first. Maoris, who have been in New Zealand much longer than the white people, still delight in tracing their ancestry back. Many of them can give you the full genealogy back to one of the original eight canoes that arrived in New Zealand. They have a lovely name for it, "whakapapa," a Maori word that means genealogy: knowing who your ancestor was. The same Maori can often give you two or three different genealogies because, of course, there has been a lot of intermarriage among the small tribes. So the same person can have easily two or three genealogies, which all end up back at the same point, because of all sorts of different vagaries that happened along the way. I think the differing genealogies in Mathew and Luke happened in much the same way.

The point is that the virgin birth is not a very important New Testament doctrine. In the New Testament, the death and resurrection of Jesus is absolutely front and center.

It's very interesting that in post-Enlightenment Western thought the virgin birth and the empty tomb have occupied sort of parallel niches in people's understanding as two things where you really have to shut one eye and stand on your head to believe them. We live in a culture that has enormously elevated Christmas and has rather downplayed Easter so the birth narratives have been made to bear a weight which in the New Testament they don't bear. At Christmas, some journalist almost always rings me up to ask if there were really oxen and asses in the crib and was the manger in the stable at the time, and the answer is, Why should we worry about that? This is not the main Christian question. What is central is that both Matthew and Luke are sketching out a Jewish theology about Jesus over and against a pagan world that knew perfectly well that there were Roman emperors who claimed to have been born without human intercourse. So both Matthew and Luke must have known that any claim to virginal conception would appear to be a cover for an illegitimate birth, and why would they then expose themselves and expose Jesus to that unless they really believed it?

What about the controversy surrounding the
mistranslated word "virgin" in Isaiah and how
that prophecy seemed to refer to the immediate
future in the Old Testament and not
Jesus' birth?

Matthew used a Greek Old Testament version of Isaiah 7:14 to refer to a prophecy about the virgin birth,[1] but there is now some disagreement about mistranslation because the word that was translated as virgin from the Hebrew Old Testament into Greek was *almah,* and some scholars insist this does not mean virgin, and that the better word is *betulah.* But in the Hebrew Bible whenever the word *almah* is used it refers to a young woman who is presumed to be a virgin, while *betulah* actually means more biological virgin. But *almah* does not simply mean a young woman. People have often said, "It just means young woman, not virgin, therefore it is not a problem." It's not actually that easy.

Prophecies often seem to have a double meaning or a triple or quadruple meaning and people find fresh meaning in it over and over again. You see that process going on within the Old Testament itself. For instance, in Jeremiah the Jews are told the exile is going to last seventy years and then the angel tells Daniel that actually the exile is going to last seven times seventy, which is 490 years. There's a sense of an initial fulfillment and then a further fulfillment. That's the way that prophecy works, and it's not a problem.

This is the problem with an imitation model. The New Testament does talk about us imitating Christ. But the reason it can do that is because we

---

1. Isaiah 7:14 says, "Therefore the Lord himself will give you a sign: The *virgin* will be with child and will give birth to a son, and will call him Immanuel." The Old Testament was originally written in Hebrew, then translated into Greek, and Matthew used a Greek translation of the Old Testament when alluding to Jesus as being the "Immanuel" referred to in this prophecy. A problem arose because the word translated as virgin in this prophecy is "almah," which is usually taken to mean "young woman" and not virgin. "Betulah" is usually the Hebrew word for virgin.

are given the spirit of Christ and those two go together. In the New Testament you are never simply told as a human being, "Hey, here's a model you can imitate." That's not the way in, as it were. The imitation comes once the indwelling of the spirit of Christ is there.

He really studied the scriptures for himself. I know there are those like Crossan and others who constantly suggest that Jesus may have been illiterate, but I find that totally absurd and unnecessary. Jewish boys were taught to read because they were to be bar mitzvahed and be sons of commandments. Judaism always was an educating religion, at least for its young males, and Jesus had a rich sense of the whole story of scripture and how the prophecies worked. From his early days, he was aware that he had a particular, unique role to play. Among other things, from very early on he had a unique prayer relationship with the one he called "abba—father." He must have been aware that most of his friends and family growing up didn't seem to have the same sort of thing. He did know that he had a vocation and a vocation shaped by scripture and thus he must have been soaking himself in scripture from an early age.

The category "religion" that we have didn't exist in Jesus' day. For them, life was a single complex whole in which what we call politics, culture, society, and religion, were all tied up together so tightly that it was "one body." Just as I can distinguish among my skin and my bones and my flesh and my muscles, and yet, I normally just think of my body, they had things that they could have distinguished but they didn't. It was all part of the same thing. Jesus was a first-century Palestinian Jew who practiced Judaism and believed in the God of Israel and discovered within that a vocation to a specific and decisive role within the purposes of the God of Israel. Jesus believed he was a fulfilled Jew, or *the* fulfilled Jew perhaps.

Because the agenda that Jesus came with, his kingdom picture, his kingdom announcement, was so deeply challenging to the ideology of the time, which involved particularly a sense of huge national security, of tightening of the boundaries of law and land and so on. This, together with the fact that Jesus was embodying God's call to Israel to be the light of the world—not the judgment of the world—made it impossible for them to accept him. He says again and again, "You've got to turn back from this confrontation with the pagan world and learn to be God's light to the world," but Israel refused because she was a beleaguered country. It's like trying to make peace in the Middle East today; try to tell somebody they've got to give up land for peace. So Jesus was saying, "This is God's way of peace and you are going the wrong way." Jesus was opposing things that they were fixed on, injustice within society and a confrontational agenda for the outside world. He was saying that these things do not embody God's vocation, but unfortunately they embodied what most Jews of his day seemed to want.

Roman soldiers killed Jesus. Why did they do it? Because the Roman authorities decided it was an easier way of dealing with the problem that Jesus' sudden appearance and activity in Jerusalem posed. But they probably wouldn't have done it if they hadn't been pushed to it by the chief priests, who were angry about what he had done in the temple, because that was the center of their power base. The Jewish elite, the Jewish hierarchy, and Roman justice put Jesus on the cross together. Whether or not, and to what extent, Pharisees—the ordinary mob—were involved is very difficult to discern.

Jesus died for our sins?

What does it mean that I love my wife? Does it mean that I wash the dishes every night? The answer is no. That is one of the things I do because I love my wife, but that is not what love consists of. Now, in the same way, the early Christians made this little formula, very, very early on: Christ died for our sins according to the scriptures. It is probably the earliest Christian confession of faith we've got. It's there in 1 Corinthians, chapter 15. And it seems to be saying this, that the whole of the Bible from Genesis onward is about God's rescue operation for the human race, and Israel was the bearer of this rescue operation and Israel's destiny was fulfilled in Jesus, who took the hatred and the anger and the bitterness of the whole human race, which was somehow concentrated and focused on that little part of the Middle East. This is, of course, completely countercultural to Enlightenment ideas.

The word "resurrection" in the first century in Judaism definitely has to do with bodies, it's not about a spiritual survival of death and leaving the body to rot somewhere. If somebody believed that's what happened, they wouldn't have used resurrection language about it. Resurrection language was around in Judaism at the time because, of course, it was what God was going to do to all the great saints and heroes of old . . . they would all be raised to new life. This did not refer to something like "John Brown's body lies moldering in the grave but his soul goes marching on."

So we can certainly say as historians that all Christians believed Jesus really was bodily raised from the dead. Why did they come to that view? The most obvious and easiest explanation why they came to that view is that something really did happen to Jesus' body. It was not a resuscitation, as Marcus Borg and I debate about endlessly. It was not resuscitation in the sense of simply coming back into exactly the same kind of existence as before. Indeed, one of the fascinating things about the whole concept of resurrection in the early Church is the way in which it sharpens up the Jewish expectation by speaking of resurrection also as transformation, but not as transformation into a nonbodily existence. The disciples really did experience Jesus after his death in a bodily sense and the tomb really was empty. How we move beyond that is a matter of stumbling forward, trying to find some way to make sense of it, and somewhere down that line lies Christian faith.

If Jesus resurrected bodily,
why didn't his disciples recognize him?

You have to ask, "Why would anyone writing fictitious stories, a generation later, that were designed to prove the resurrection, leave that issue so extraordinarily open?" It seems much more likely in John 21 that the reason none of the disciples dared asked him his identity is because they knew the figure was the Lord. Then again on the Emmaus road in Luke 24, there is a sort of scary awareness about Jesus; they know it's him but they also know that there is something different, something that is transformed, and yet the same. It's like seeing somebody who has been through an extraordinary operation and you can hardly believe it is the same person. And yet, when you are with that individual you think—yes, this really is the same person! Now, the nature of that transformation is (at this point in history) unique. That's built into the structure of early Christian belief from Paul at least, onward; that nobody else has had this happen to them. And, frankly, it's extremely difficult to explain the rise of Christianity without having the bodily resurrection. Dominic Crossan's own big book is witness to that, because although he has this phenomenal imaginative construct, all really designed to explain the rise of Christianity without the resurrection, frankly it just doesn't work. It's a wonderfully ingenious system but it's much, much easier historically to say that Christianity began because something really happened to the body of Jesus.

Second Coming?

In the New Testament, many of the texts that refer to it talk about Jesus "appearing" rather than "coming." The danger with talking about "coming" is that it always sounds as though Jesus is a very long way off and might one day pay us a visit; whereas, the force of "appearing" for instance in the first letter of John, chapter 3—when he appears we shall be like him, we shall see him like he is—much stronger. The point is that Jesus is always present, though hidden, and one day will appear.

But if you choose to use the word "coming" then there are three "comings": The first coming of Jesus is Christmas, in his conception and birth.

The second is a secret, private coming as when Christ is always appearing secretly, in people, in movements, in church, in the world, in all sorts of things that are happening. We need to learn to recognize it.

The third you need to put into a larger framework. We have talked about the Second Coming in the church but we have often forgotten that in the New Testament what God promised is a total renewal of the cosmos, a world in which justice and peace will thrive and triumph, and not just a little better than we've got at the moment. We're not talking about a little

more hard work and a few more Nobel prizes for peace and we'll be there—
we are talking about a major renewal. About something happening to the
world that is like what happened to Jesus at Easter. In the middle of that,
will be the reappearance of Jesus in person. Now I find it very difficult to
envisage that, but then, you know, there are lots of things I can't envisage
but that are, in fact, true.

Gospel authorship and accuracy?

No one knows who wrote the gospels and anyone who says that they
firmly do know is deceiving themselves. At the same time, I do believe the
gospels we've got in the New Testament were written by people with access to very good sources about Jesus. Whether they were, in fact,
Matthew, Mark, Luke, and John, we have no absolute means of knowing
and we don't actually know when they were written, either. Lots of people
will tell you exactly when they think the gospels were written but I have to
say as a historian, it is all ultimately maybe this and possibly that. But the
test of accuracy is not who wrote them and is not when they were written
but whether the story they tell really makes sense and dovetails with first-
century Palestinian-Jewish history. I have spent most of my life arguing that
it does.

Are the gospels true? Anyone who tells *any* story edits it and all editing
is done according to a principle. That may be a literary or aesthetic principle but it is quite likely to be a content and argument principle as well. It
doesn't mean the conversation didn't happen, merely that you are then going to choose—as every television editor, radio editor, book editor, newspaper journalist chooses—to highlight certain things and omit others. Every
story in the gospels carries meaning beyond what is obvious and the stories
encourage us to find deeper and more profound meaning. The gospel writers are all very well aware that Jesus told stories that had profound meaning but which didn't happen; there never was a prodigal son, there never
was a Good Samaritan, etc., etc. But those stories, though fictitious, carried meaning because it was in a culture where people understood how stories like that worked. So, the question then is, were the evangelists also
writing parables when they said one day Jesus came into a village and
healed somebody and the Pharisee said this and Jesus said that? The an-

swer has to be—no, they didn't think those were parables. They thought those were selected, edited, highlighted stories but that they were stories that actually happened. Now, the further question that the historian asks—can we be sure that we agree that these things actually happened? Of course, then you're back with the old ancient historian's problem, that in ancient history we have so few sources that it is very difficult to come up with a clear positive or negative verdict. Concerning the early Roman Empire, we only have Tacitus, Suetonius, and one or two other little fragments here and there. Therefore, if Tacitus says it and we don't have any other evidence, what do we do? Often, we are in that situation with the material in the gospels.

Who is a Christian?

A human being who follows Jesus of Nazareth as Savior and lord and trusts what he has done in his death and resurrection as the means of ultimate salvation.

> *I've talked to scholars, mystics, and*
> *evangelists, and some people cross the lines*
> *and are a combination of those three,*
> *but most people are stuck in one aspect and*
> *they refuse to go into another.*

Christians tend to fall into one of four categories. First, those for whom personal spirituality is the center of everything. Second, those for whom the theology and the biblical study that goes with it are everything. Third, those for whom the political and social engagement and the desire to change and heal the world is the main thing. Fourth, those for whom the wonders of charismatic phenomena, body healing, and other signs are the main thing.

The really interesting people are the people who pull two, three, or even four of those things together because, for goodness' sake, they are all there in the New Testament. They are all there in Christian tradition and it seems to me if we want to grow up and be mature, we need all four in the right balance and in the right measure, to be operative.

I've found that when people talk about Jesus—
it's really the part of themselves
that they see in Jesus.

Wouldn't that be nice! When my dear friend Walter Wink runs classes, he gets people to write about what they aspire to for themselves and then a little later in the class he gets them to write about their picture of Jesus and then he invites them to compare the two and they are often very similar! I would certainly say that I aspire to be like Jesus in all appropriate ways. Of course, there are lots of ways in which I am not and I cannot be. I don't intend to die for the sins of the world and indeed, if I did that it would show I was not honoring Jesus because I believe he did that uniquely and that I don't have to do it. But as a historian, I have to say the Jesus I discover is very unlike me in all sorts of ways, and I did not find that Jesus by projecting my own view—or my own alter ego, as it were—on to the screen of hypothetical history. I discovered that Jesus by immersing myself in the world of the first century, particularly its Jewish documents and so on. I tried to understand what sense the gospels make within that context. I've spent most of my life doing that and the Jesus I come up with then is very, very challenging, and he certainly isn't a self-portrait.

Do you consider yourself a mystic?

A mystic? It's not a word I normally use about myself, but one of the reasons for that is that it's so imprecise. In our culture, the word mystic often carries something of a sort of New Age flavor about it, as though one has a special inside track on access to God. I see myself as a praying Christian. Prayer is pretty important to me and pretty central to my life. My life is structured in a rhythm of both more formal prayer and of private prayer. That's just part of who I am. I've occasionally wondered what would happen if I didn't pray for a week or a month—but it's like wondering what would happen if I didn't eat for a week or a month? It's not an experiment I'm prepared to make!

Marcus Borg, who is a close friend of mine, says that there are mystics in every religious tradition and no doubt there's a sense in which that's true.

But if the Christian claim is true, namely that we discover who the true God is in and through Jesus Christ, then to think of somebody in a Buddhist framework or whatever, having a mystical experience—and no doubt they do have experiences that one might call mystical experiences—makes me ask, "Well, is it actually an experience of the true God and if it is, why isn't it Jesus' shape?" But ever since the Enlightenment, modern Western culture has desperately wanted to say that all religions are basically the same. In America, that is enshrined in the Constitution, and out of that comes this extraordinarily powerful agenda (which I meet in some parts of Britain and Europe but it's much more strong in America) which says that any claim to specialness, or uniqueness is just about the most politically incorrect thing you can do because we *must* say that basically everyone is just the same and on the same footing. Now if you want to go down that road you'd better kiss Judaism and Islam good-bye because they make specific and exclusive claims. If you read through the Old Testament from cover to cover as well as classic Jewish writings, they are celebrating the fact that the God of Israel is not like the gods of other nations. He is different, he is the superior God and they are inferior, he is the god of justice and they encourage injustice, etc., etc. Christianity picks up that essential Jewish emphasis and says, "Yes and the God of Israel has made himself known, fully and finally, in and as Jesus of Nazareth." That is a very Jewish thing that Christianity does. The attempt to say that actually Jesus is just one way to God or one of many sons of God, or whatever, is a way of being nice to everybody, but it's also a way of going back on basic central Christian claims. Early Christians lived in a world where there were many gods and many lords and they said—for us there is one God and one Lord.

Through grace that we are saved?

If human beings are to be true children of God and if they yearn to be saved in the full sense, both here and hereafter, then they must depend on the gracious activity of God. In other words, it cannot be a matter of human beings pulling themselves up by their bootstraps or of human beings claiming the privilege of birth—that because they were born to a particular parent or in a particular place or in a particular time or whatever, therefore they are automatically all right. The point of grace is to stress that it isn't our moral effort that gets us in and that it isn't our ancestry or geography that gets us in.

It's when somebody comes into a living experience of God and starts to live out of the love of God that the battle really starts. Up until then, you are just going with the flow and it's quite easy to go with the flow of whatever is going on in the world and in life. But when you say, "I'm going to live out the love of God," then you discover that you are swimming upstream and the current is against you. I know this for myself; when I'm writing, when I'm preaching, when I'm working, doing specifically Christian work, often it's a real struggle, it's a real battle. There are distractions and there are temptations and there are all sorts of things to blow you off course. It's not just a matter of basking in God's love and hence floating along easily as though there was no problem, far from it! God's presence is demanding. It's like going to an exercise class; there are some spiritual and emotional and intellectual muscles to be exercised and that is demanding.

✠ 86
DAY EIGHT

ST. BENEDICT'S MONASTERY

"I read some of your book," Theophane said after morning vespers. "I guess I shouldn't joke about your bald head."

He referred to a chapter in my first book, *Tying Rocks to Clouds*, where I had written about the shame I felt when I started going bald at eighteen years old.

"That really bothered me when I was young," I said. "It still bothers me once in a while—you'd think after all the retreats and spiritual experiences I've had that that would be completely gone. But I guess that shame really pointed to a deeper shame. *The shame of being seen—of being naked.* It's that old Adam and Eve thing—we human beings hide our true selves because we're ashamed."

"So," I continued, "the big question then is, *How is it we know we're seen?* There must be something in us that sees—even as we act ashamed and blind."

After everyone went to the chapel for the afternoon prayer session, I held Sarah's hand for a few minutes.

"I have to go to the meditation room," I found myself saying to her, "and do some . . . some stupid things."

And *stupid* is how it seemed. After being in "this loving acceptance" with Sarah—it seemed utterly ridiculous to go sit on a cushion so that I could be . . . what? What could be greater than this?

When I let go of her hand, we laughed together at the predicament of all human beings. *A manipulation of ourselves in order to experience the un-manipulated.* Whether it was my retreat group praying and meditating on God's presence or the Trappist monks wearing robes and taking vows— why? What is it we seek to experience? It is nothing but *an intimacy long forgotten—that's all.*

Back in my room, I laughed out loud! You can attend a ten-day re-treat. Pray five hours a day. Attend mass three times a day. Be silent. Do all the right things. But they won't get you there! They won't. Because words or actions cannot pierce it. Just stop. Look. And relax that which is doing the looking. That's all . . . and if you're blessed, what already is, will be ex-perienced.

✢ 87
DAY NINE

"The kingdom of heaven is at hand," Jesus said. As I recalled those words in my prayer meditation, their powerful and simple directness melted my heart. What blind people we are. We yearn to hold in our hand what is already in our hand—whether we open or close, let go or grasp.

"Please, God," I began to pray, "teach my blind heart to see again. Help me to feel love for the pain that caused me to blind myself. Help me to see with a heart of love—to see life as it is—born of love. My nightmare was caused by blindness. A blindness that changed your angels into demons, your touch into pain, your teaching into trials and torture.

"I now see only love can cure the ills that I have cast upon the world. Asleep in Christ, only love can awaken me. And not to me, but awaken me to you living in me. Slowly, the world takes on a color and shape that reminds me of your garden. What was once dead is now golden and alive. It speaks to me, and says only one thing—your name. It is not the name that my ancestors called you—but the name you call yourself. Unspeakable, yet clear. Unknown, yet known. Seen from that place before eyes, and heard in that place before ears. I shudder as I realized that my breath is your breath, and that my name is your name. Now that my ears have fallen away—I hear. Now that my eyes have dropped away—I see. It has always been you—not me."

✥ 88
THOMAS KEATING

S N O W M A S S ,   C O L O R A D O
I met with Thomas Keating on the final night of the retreat. He was a tall man with a quiet and cavernous soul.

"You can actually make a living as an author?" he asked while paging through my first book, *Tying Rocks to Clouds*.

"Not yet," I said. "But I'm getting close."

Thomas Keating is a Cistercian priest, monk, and former abbot of St. Joseph's Abbey in Spencer, Massachusetts. He is author of *Open Mind, Open Heart, The Mystery of Christ, Invitation to Love, Intimacies with God,* and others.

St. John, in the Prologue to his Gospel, says that the eternal Word or Son of God became flesh. Christ is the great enlightened being sent into the world to manifest God in a special way. Because of his Divine dignity and power, *Christ became the man Jesus.* Paul calls Jesus the second Adam, the new head of the human family.

The doctrine of the Council of Chalcedon said that Jesus was fully human and fully Divine at the same time. How could he be fully human when he didn't come into the world the same way as everybody else does? I don't know. *All I know is that we are asked to believe as Christians that was the case.*

We are all sons and daughters of God, in Christ. Some theologians think Jesus became fully aware of his Divine personhood at the time he was baptized by John the Baptist and the Spirit descended upon him and the voice from heaven cried out, "This is my beloved son in whom I am well pleased" (Matthew 3:17, KJV). But we are all the sons and daughters of God, as well as part of the human family, just by virtue of being born. God created us, so he's the Father in the fullest sense of the term, and when Christ took the whole human family to himself, this loving father relationship became much more intimate, because we share with Jesus (at least potentially) his experience of God as Father, Abba. The loving Father is precisely at the heart of the Christian religion. That's what is communicated through all the Christian symbols, sacraments, rituals.

Is Jesus the only way?

Other religions are ways to God, too. God has given many revelations. No one religion exhausts the whole of God. People who say Jesus is the only way are mistaking and confusing Christ, the Son of God, with Jesus the historical Christ, who is limited by his historical circumstances. But the radical potentiality to become sharers in the Divine nature is the fact that God, in becoming a human being, has taken the whole human family to himself. That's what Paul means by "the mystery that has been hidden from the beginning of the world and is now revealed in Christ" (Col. 1:26,

NIV). Christ is the eternal Son of God and the whole of creation is the body of Christ.

Jesus died on the cross for our sins?

Theologically, one view of the crucifixion of Jesus is redemption, which was very strong in the Middle Ages. But a number of theologians think that God's Son, the Word of God, would have become a human being even if there wasn't any sin. In this view, redemption isn't so much the primary purpose of the incarnation, as it is a manifesting of the infinite goodness of God and a sharing of that goodness with creatures who are capable of enjoying it through the gifts of intelligence and free will.

The fact that human nature has fallen also manifests things about God that otherwise wouldn't be manifested—such as God's humility, his forgiveness, his mercy. The disintegration and dying of our false self is our participation in the passion and death of Jesus.

Original sin?

Original sin is not a result of wrongdoing on our part. Original sin is a way of describing the human condition, the experience of coming to full reflective consciousness minus the certitude of personal union with God. This gives rise to our intimate sense of incompletion, dividedness, isolation, and guilt—hence the false self. At baptism the false self is ritually put to death and the new self is born. Though we are not God, God and our true self are virtually the same thing.

Hell?

Hell is a psychological state rather than a place, and it's going on right now in some people. Hell is a psychological state of alienation from God—there are various aspects of it. According to the creed, Jesus descended into hell when, after his death, he entered into complete identification with the human condition, alienated from God. It is out of that state that he rose from the dead. Since God wills all people to be saved, according to Paul, it would seem that the full power of the resurrection may be manifested in the eventual redemption or salvation of everyone, even those who appear lost. However, since free will exists, one could choose to be separated from God forever.

Only a deluded person would choose hell?

It's hard to conceive of choosing hell but I suppose if freedom is absolute then it's possible. But there are many reasons why people's choices are not really fully free. Maybe it's only when we are brain-dead that we actually experience complete freedom for the first time and can make a choice that is really free. Theologian Karl Rahner said "As Christians we have to believe that hell exists, but we don't have to believe that anyone is there." That leaves open the opinion of a few of the early fathers of the Church and others, that ultimately God's mercy will triumph over every obstacle, including human freedom.

Origen was a theologian who believed that everyone will ultimately be saved. He was considered heretical in his day for various reasons, so a lot of his original works were destroyed. Therefore, we are not absolutely certain we have reconstructed all his opinions. But he's not the only one. Evidently, Karl Rahner believed in the final redemption of everyone. I know people who are advanced in mystical life, and having experienced God's goodness, they don't believe in a permanent hell. Perhaps hell is a threat aimed at people who require severe treatment (or the threat of it) in order to deter them from courses of action that are destructive of humanity as well as themselves.

Jesus' religion?

Obviously Jesus was a Jew! He followed the rituals of the Temple. Anyone who says he was a "Christian" shows they know very little about the history of religion.

Gospel authorship and accuracy?

We don't know who wrote them. St. John's gospel comes out of a certain milieu and probably from the Church of Ephesus. The gospel was never intended to be a purely historical document. Obviously, parts of it are somewhat mythologized. Myth was not a bad word in those times. It was simply a poetic way of trying to express a truth that was beyond rational expression. For example, the infancy narratives have elements of truth and elements of myth, usually based on scriptural images, to show how the life of Jesus fulfilled certain prophetic sayings in the Old Testament. That doesn't mean that every one of them is true, but the idea is that Jesus is the fulfillment of the prophecies of the Old Testament; that's the point that is trying to be manifested. Obviously a document that is written forty or fifty years after the fact is not going to be a literal historical document; reporting the same incident, the evangelists don't all agree, so it's obvious they are sometimes using the incidents in a pastoral way to speak to the needs of their congregation. They sometimes disagree in the reporting of particular incidents.

Virgin birth?

The doctrine of the Council of Chalcedon said that Jesus was fully human and fully Divine at the same time. How could he be fully human when he didn't come into the world the same way everybody else does? I don't know. The virgin birth of Jesus is strongly affirmed in the gospel narratives. But if it should prove not to be true, and if in actual fact Joseph was the father, there would be no reason to change any fundamental truth of faith.

> Jesus said, "I am the Way and the Truth and the Life. No one comes to the Father except through me."

No one can come to the Father except through the Son. If the Father dwells in the Son, that's the only place he is, in the sense of locus; otherwise, he's everywhere. To come to the full knowledge of the Father, we need to go through that person in whom the Father dwells, consubstantially—in the fullness of his being. Christ is the consubstantial Son of God, in whom all that the Father is, is present. Therefore, to come to the Father, you have to go through the Son. There is no other choice. It's not a limitation. It's the ultimate fullness, because the Son is the creator of all that exists and sustains it in being.

Christ is our leader, our paradigm, our teacher, the enlightened one, the master. But these are not just titles; he actually is all these things in reality. He affects in us what these titles symbolize, so we are really incorporated into Christ's spiritual body or mystical body. We share Christ's destiny, power and mission, as well as his glorification. According to Paul, since we are in the body of Christ, we all have the same Spirit; it dwells in the whole body, hence we have, so to speak, the Divine DNA in us. We have all we need to carry out the divine plan of salvation, for ourselves and others, that was carried out in Christ as in a paradigm. We are united in Christ. That's why the Church always prays *through* Christ because Christ does not separate us from the Father but rather joins us to the Father. The Father lives in the Son more than in himself. Hence, there's no place else to go to find him. There are others who know Christ, but not by that name. Instead, they know Christ as the ground of being, the Ultimate Reality or the Absolute, Allah, Brahman, or Great Spirit.

Second Coming?

Depends what level of consciousness one is on. A human being understands these words differently as his/her life and penetration of the scriptures advances through the experience of a growing relationship with Christ (which we call divine union). Christ is risen, but at the same time, Christ is coming, and yet he's already here. What "comes" is really us. We come to Christ.

The idea of the Second Coming is sometimes confused with certain other comings that have historical significance, namely the fact that when the sun runs out this universe as we understand it will end. But the main "coming" occurs when we die; that's our judgment. For us, that's our individual final coming of Christ, who will render to each of us what the love of God has done in us, in spite of us.

Jesus did not teach a specific method of meditation, at least not one that is recorded. Read the four gospels, and get acquainted with Jesus by talking to him about things that are of interest to you; your troubles or your joys. *Lectio Divina* has been a way for hundreds of years of reading and listening to the texts of scripture as if we were in conversation with Christ and Christ was suggesting the topics of conversation. This conversation simplifies and eventually gives way to communing, or "resting in God," as Gregory the Great said in the sixth century when summarizing the Christian contemplative tradition.

Contemplative Prayer is the normal development of the regular practice of *Lectio Divina,* and is an opening of mind and heart to God. The Centering Prayer, which is taught around the world and here at St. Benedict's, is a method designed to facilitate the development of Contemplative Prayer by preparing our faculties to cooperate with this gift. We should choose a spiritual practice that takes us to God. Later we may leave the spiritual practice behind when called by the Spirit to surrender to the Spirit's direct guidance.

I believe in also trying to see God in all things: in nature and art, friendship, love, service of others. And then to see all things in God.

How do I love when I don't feel the love?

St. Francis of Assisi said, "Where there is no love, put love." When we don't feel pleasant toward people, love makes an effort to be pleasant. It is an act of our spiritual will and spiritual love. Granted you can't always "turn love on," it depends on how advanced your own relationship with God is. But the fact is that in those times God is available to give us his own love. Jesus said *love one another as I have loved you,* so this statement presupposes that we have that potential to love as he does. Thus, we must have been given the gift of Divine love that would enable us to do what is beyond the usual scope of human relationship. It's pretty hard to love someone who is beating you up or has done you in, but love might manifest itself in forgiveness and in trying to be reconciled if possible.

In our language, we have only one word for love, whereas other languages have five or six: there is a different kind of "love" between friends, spouses, or parents. In Greek scripture it's *eros:* self-seeking love, love seeking the reward of love, and *agape:* pure love, self-giving love, self-forgetful love. This is what is translated into Latin as *caritas.* St. Paul, in 1 Corinthians 13, sings the praises of that kind of love: love is kind, love always lasts, love is ultimately all there is.

Who is a Christian?

Christianity is a living tradition. A Christian is someone who has faith in Jesus Christ as the Son of God, and who is beginning to share in Christ's experience of the Father as Abba, the God of infinite goodness and tenderness. Whatever Jesus meant by Abba as an experience, that is the heart of the Christian religion and this is what is to be transmitted down through the ages.

✢ 89
THE FINAL JOURNEY

MADISON, WISCONSIN

I didn't want to get out of bed, and the thought of going on another trip only filled me with dread. First there was the fear of the fact that I would run out of money again in a few months. Then what?

Second, there were a couple ways of getting to North Carolina in order to see Billy Graham. I had already been there four times and this would be the fifth. Should I fly? Or should I drive again, which meant that I would have driven over ten thousand miles in my attempts to meet with Billy Graham.

Perhaps my biggest fear—which I didn't want to think about—was that something in me thought this might be my last trip to North Carolina for a while. If I didn't meet him this time then well . . . my book—as I envisioned it—would have to change. For days, ever since I'd gotten the latest letter from Billy Graham's assistant saying "no," I had worried about it. I prayed, talked to God, and then prayed some more. Then I called Gigi Graham, Billy's daughter—and she said she would call her father and ask him to meet with me if I came to North Carolina.

"But I can't guarantee he will be here," Gigi said. "He's feeling sick again and might go back to the Mayo Clinic."

Since there were no guarantees, I had to let go and trust that the book was unfolding as God planned. It had been years since I began this book and developed it. I had called and written countless people about interviews. I had found the money to complete it by working at different jobs, getting a grant from Mort, and borrowing money from relatives and friends. I had agonized over the right word here or there. I had learned about the positive and negative attributes of scholars, mystics, and evangelists. I had gotten up again and again after being knocked down. I had done all these things and more.

Yet, if this book had only been about me and what I could do I wouldn't have gotten very far. Obviously, I had felt called and inspired by something larger than myself. And during its creation, there had been countless interchanges between *me and the God* who inspired it. This collaboration had led to numerous agonies because at times it felt like "me" doing the book, while at other times, it was "me" in God's presence—and then there were the times it was just God—with *me* barely, if at all, doing anything.

Jesus also oscillated between three ways of being. At times he expressed his oneness with God when he said, "I and the Father are One" (John 10:30, NIV). At other times, he expressed the difference and subtle separation between himself and God: "Why do you call me good, no one is good—except God alone" (Mark 10:18, NIV). Then, when Jesus was in the Garden of Gethsemane he had said, "Take this cup from me" (Mark 14:36, NIV), and his separation from God was not so subtle—instead it was a momentary expression of his wish not to do God's will. This was the genius of Jesus—as filled as he was by God, he still struggled with the relationship at times, and this fact allowed me not to be so hard on myself for struggling with my own relationship with God.

As I lay in bed, so afraid of the future, I prayed and told God of my fear. I then rolled out of bed and bowed down to the floor. As I emptied out my fear through words, I felt God's love and presence reassert itself. I felt Jesus' hand and the hands of the apostles on my back and shoulders comforting me. I cried out my fear as I opened to their support.

In the next few hours I found the courage and inspiration to start again. I packed, bought a new motor home battery, and changed the oil. I was on the road by 9 P.M., and Billy Graham was a thousand miles away.

✥ 90
AN INNOCENT MAN

I drove until almost 3 A.M., and then pulled over at a rest stop near Indianapolis. I awoke a little after eleven A.M., and began driving again. I was suddenly awakened from my daydreams somewhere near Knoxville, Tennessee, by the whirl of flashing lights in my mirror. Since I knew I hadn't been speeding, I wondered why I had been pulled over.

"Can I see your license?" the trooper asked without really asking. He looked to be about thirty, with a short military-looking haircut.

"Sure," I said, handing it to him. "Why am I being stopped?" I asked.

"You're not *being stopped,*" the trooper said, correcting me. *"You are stopped!"*

I immediately felt my stomach tighten.

"The light over your license plate is burned out," he said. "I'm writing you out a citation."

"I wasn't aware of that," I said. "This motor home was parked for three months. I just got it out of storage. Can't you give me a break? I really didn't know. Now that I know, I'll get it fixed tomorrow."

"Everybody says that," the trooper said. Then he asked me to follow him back to his car where we waited while another trooper walked a drug-sniffing dog around the RV. Then to my amazement—*the dog barked!*

"We're gonna have to go farther with this," the trooper said. "Our dog gave a positive indication to the presence of drugs in your RV. We're going to have to search your motor home."

I sat in the back of the squad car for the next hour and a half while my motor home was searched. Every fifteen minutes a trooper came back and asked me the same questions.

"Do you have any drugs in the motor home?"

"No," I replied.

"Guns?"

"No," I said again.

Finally a heavyset trooper came back to the car and said, "Where are the drugs? Our dog just about passed out by your gas tank. When we knocked on it—it sounded hollow!"

"I don't have any drugs," I said, "but I understand you have to do your job—my brother is a Chicago cop, and so was my dad and my niece. I come from a family of cops . . ."

"That don't mean anything," he said. "Half the cops I know have family members in the penitentiary. You can still wind up in the penitentiary, you know."

After about another thirty minutes, the heavyset trooper returned.

"Is that a photo of you with the Dalai Lama on your refrigerator?" the other trooper asked.

"Yeah," I said. "It is."

"Are you one of them Buddhists or something?" he asked.

"Well," I said, "I stayed in a Buddhist monastery fifteen years ago, but over the last few years, I've been getting back to my Christian roots because of the Jesus book I'm writing. Maybe you saw the painting of *The Last Supper* I have in the back . . ."

"And you don't have any drugs in your motor home?" he asked, interrupting me.

"No I don't," I assured him.

"We got a trooper with a stick that has a camera on the end of it. He can put that in your tank and see if there have been some welded seams in there . . . what do you think of that?"

"Go ahead." I said. "I don't care."

Then the trooper shut the door, and stood behind the squad car with two other troopers. They talked and laughed loud enough for me to hear.

"I almost tried the religious angle on him," the one heavyset cop said. "I was going to say 'Okay, if the Dalai Lama were standing right in front of you and asked you where the drugs and guns were, what would you say?' "

After a few minutes the door opened.

"Okay. You can get out of the car," the trooper who originally pulled me over said. "We're going to let you go. But we don't feel good about it. No, siree, we don't feel good about it at all."

I got back into my motor home and just before I drove away, the trooper leaned against my door and repeated, "I don't feel good about letting you go—not one bit."

I woke up late the next morning feeling crummy and kind of down. I think being called a liar and a criminal for an hour and half by people who were supposedly authority figures took its toll—and even though I was innocent—it tore at my soul.

While driving the last few hours to Montreat, I thought about Jesus and sensed his presence. My familiarity with him and the depth of our relationship had definitely deepened over the past few years. My heart now understood Jesus in ways my mind could never express. *How is it that a human being can understand more, and yet know less at the same time?*

"But I don't want to get into debates about who you were," I said.

"Then don't," Jesus replied.

"But . . ."

"When someone makes a point," Jesus said, "don't debate, just smile and say 'thank you for sharing.'"

⁘ 91
BILLY GRAHAM

MONTREAT, NORTH CAROLINA

"I've got some good news and some bad news," Jane Alden said as we sat down with our coffee. Here we go again, I thought, I bet Billy Graham has left town . . .

"Billy's not feeling well," Jane said. "He saw his doctor this morning and his doctor told him to go to the Mayo Clinic tomorrow morning. He's feeling tired and down."

"But," Jane continued, "Gigi said she would take you up to the house for a while—and maybe if he hears us talking, he might come out and join us."

I drove up to the Graham house with Jane and her mother. When we got there, I saw Billy Graham walking up the stairs to his house. He wore a plaid cap and used a cane. The house was located on a hilly hundred and fifty acres of land that was purchased for $13.50 an acre—which "sounded exorbitant" to Billy and Ruth Graham almost fifty years ago.

Gigi pulled up in her car, got out, and motioned for us to follow her. I followed everyone into the house, which is a very large, homey, Appalachian log and frame house. The house looked much older than it was because when it was built they used salvaged logs from old abandoned log houses that Ruth Graham had found by scouring the countryside.

I walked down a short hall into a dining room that was connected to the kitchen. Billy Graham sat in a black-and-white plaid wing-back chair. To his left was a large fireplace, and on his right was a matching plaid chair separated from his by a small table on which sat a bowl of caramel corn (with nuts). On the wall near the kitchen was a telephone, beneath it was a desk, and on it were assorted pads of scratch paper and a bowl that had the word *mistakes* written on it—but the word *mistakes* was upside down.

"Hi, Billy," Jane said as we walked in. I sat in the chair next to Billy Graham, which had been strategically left unoccupied by the others. Then Gigi introduced me and Billy Graham looked over in my direction for a moment.

"Daddy," Gigi asked, handing him a stack of Time-Life books that had his picture on the cover and was titled *Billy Graham: God's Ambassador*, "will you sign these books for me?"

Since Gigi called him "Daddy," and Jane had called him "Billy," I wasn't sure what to call Billy Graham.

"Should I call you Mr. Graham or Reverend Graham . . . ?" I said, leaning over toward him.

But he just ignored me . . .

I sat back in my chair and gathered my thoughts. Was I too forward?

Had I broken some kind of rule of Southern etiquette? Should I have remained silent till he acknowledged me? Then I remembered that Gigi had said his hearing wasn't so good, and when I looked back at him, I saw his hearing aid.

"Bill Elliott wrote a book," Gigi said, speaking quickly. "He traveled around the world and talked with the Dalai Lama, Mother Teresa, Norman Vincent Peale, and other people and wrote about it and his spiritual search."

"He published it himself," she added. "And it sold a hundred thousand copies."

I was surprised how much Gigi had remembered about my book, although she was wrong about it being self-published. Billy Graham turned to me and I started talking, but he still had a blank look on his face as if he didn't understand anything I said.

"Sit over on this side," Gigi said.

"My hearing is bad on that side," Billy added.

I grabbed a kitchen chair and sat down a few feet away from Billy Graham and told him about the people I met.

"Mom's outside playing croquet," Gigi said, looking out the back window. Then Jane Alden, her mother, and Gigi stood up in unison and went outside, leaving me alone with Billy. We sat silently for a few moments; and since Billy Graham was looking content and as though he wasn't going to say anything in the near future, I searched my mind for something to talk about.

"You're a big golfer, aren't you?" I asked.

"I love golf," he replied. "I played it almost every day of my life."

"Ever play Augusta?" I asked because I had always wanted to play Augusta National, which was the site of the Master's Tournament—perhaps the most famous golf tournament in the world.

"Many times," he said. "I have many friends there."

"I heard the greens are fast," I said.

"Yes they are," he replied.

"Ever had any eagles?" I asked.

"Two or three," he replied. I paused for a moment hoping he'd ask me the same question because I've had a bunch of eagles—but he didn't.

"Any holes-in-one?" I asked.

"Two," he said, smiling for the first time. "So where do you work?" he asked.

"I used to work on a psychiatric unit," I said. "But now I write books. In my first book I traveled around and met with Mother Teresa, the Dalai Lama, Robert Schuller, Norman Vincent Peale . . . and people like that. Now for the last four years I've been working on a book about Jesus. I've met with Luis Palau, Jerry Falwell, J. I. Packer and Josh McDowell . . ."

"So who do you think Jesus is?" Billy Graham asked.

I was taken aback. Did William Franklin Graham, Jr., who was born November 7, 1918, in Charlotte, North Carolina, who grew up on a dairy farm, and at the age of sixteen was converted by a well-known Southern evangelist named Mordecai Ham, who married Ruth McCue Bell in 1943, who had gained national attention in 1949 through his revival meetings in Los Angeles, which attracted the attention of media giant William Randolph Hearst, who—even though he had never met Billy Graham sent a message to his editors that said "Puff Graham"—did this Billy Graham who then became a household name and has preached for over sixty years in over eighty countries and to over 110 million people, who, since 1951, the annual Gallup poll has listed among the ten most admired men in America, who has received over fifty major awards, including the Templeton Prize for Progress in Religion (1982) and the Presidential Medal of Freedom (1983), America's highest nonmilitary honor,[1] did this Billy Graham *just ask me* who I thought Jesus is?

He did. Oh God, I thought, this wasn't what I had intended, and if I could have, I would have stood up like one of those movie directors and yelled "cut." But this wasn't a movie, and Billy Graham was seated a few feet away from me—peering at me through his glasses.

"Well, I was brought up by my mother to always talk to God . . ." I said as I searched Billy Graham's eyes and manner, looking for any sign of disapproval, ". . . to talk to God directly. Jesus was there, but he was more on the side as a consultant."

"Jesus is God." Billy said abruptly. For a moment I got even more anxious. What if I said the wrong thing and he got mad and told me to leave?

---

1. *Who's Who in Christian History,* Quickverse 6.0.

I became very aware that we were looking into each other's eyes in the way that two people who were speaking honestly do. We watched each other closely and since the eyes really are the mirrors of the soul, if I said something I didn't believe, Billy Graham would see that "blip" or "glitch" in my eye as I fibbed or glazed over my conscience with a semiconscious ignorance as I said words I really didn't believe. Conversely, if Billy Graham disliked what I said, I'd also see that reflected in his eyes. Either way, Billy Graham would see—and so would I.

"Well," I began, without breaking his gaze, "that's what I've been understanding more deeply. As I've worked on this book, Jesus has come more into my heart and vision."

"I also talk with Jesus . . ." I continued while paying especially close attention to any disapproving signs in his eyes—but I saw none. "Usually Jesus just looks at me, and when I look directly at him, he tells me to relax—and then as I relax I feel his love—God's love, in my heart."

"You believe Jesus resurrected?" Billy asked. "Do you believe he resurrected bodily?"

"Yes," I said, and again I became very aware of how our souls were connected in such a way that it seemed if there was a flinch in him or in me, that we would be aware of it.

"The crucifixion?" he asked. "What do you think? Do you believe Jesus died for your sins? That you're forgiven and loved?"

"I believe we're forgiven and loved," I replied. "When I was twenty-one years old, I was so depressed that I wanted to die. Then I had an experience of God's unconditional love and forgiveness. That changed my life. But it was God directly who had saved me. What that experience taught me was that God had never held anything against me, therefore, he didn't need to forgive me. But I needed to forgive myself. Jesus teaches me that, but I'm not sure about the idea that Jesus died for our sins—as though it was some kind of business transaction with God. Like we got into an automobile wreck, and we had to pay for the damage, otherwise God would send us to hell. As though God demanded a payment in the form of Jesus' death . . ."

"Maury," Billy Graham said, looking over at a man whom I hadn't noticed and who stood in the kitchen. "Come over here, I want you to hear this."

For a moment, I wondered why Billy had called this man over—was I saying something interesting? Or something that in Billy Graham's eyes was crazy? I quickly let go of the need to know why, and just started explaining to Maury. Then after I was done explaining, for some reason, I heard myself saying, "It's not bad to question that, is it?"

"It's not bad to ask any question," Billy Graham replied with a kind acceptance that made any anxiety immediately evaporate.

"Don't get caught up in all that theological stuff," he said. "Just accept that Jesus forgave your sins and loves you. We can't forget our sins, but Jesus took on our sins and *he can forget them.*"

"You know as I travel around writing this book on Jesus," I said, "I get caught up in those debates with people . . ."

"That's all theological stuff," Billy Graham said. "I don't get into that. I'm just a simple farm boy. You don't have to know what it means that 'Jesus died for your sins'—*I don't,*" Billy Graham said. "Just accept that it's true."

I liked Billy Graham the more he talked, and the more he talked the more I relaxed. His voice had a calmness in it—its tone conveyed forgiveness and the deep relaxation that comes from knowing that no amount of doing will achieve the grace of forgiveness. It was almost as though his vocal cords had relaxed, that the strident preaching and effort of the old days was no longer needed. He seemed relaxed in his chair and relaxed in his relationship with God. He had boiled it down to the essence.

"Forgiveness and love," he said. "That's who Jesus was. And that he died for your sins."

"I agree with you," I said. "When I met Luis Palau, we talked about C. S. Lewis and how C. S. Lewis said, 'Jesus was either a liar, lunatic or lord.' I mentioned to Luis that more than any of those Jesus was a 'lover.' "

"Luis Palau is a good man," Billy replied. Then we sat in each other's presence, and we were just being. I guess "just being" is easy when you feel forgiven. It allows for a deep soul relaxation that goes all the way through the body because you realize you don't have to do anything in order to be loved—you just are.

I still had a list of Jesus questions in my backpack, and I thought about asking them, but the questions seemed less important than just sitting with

Billy Graham and feeling God's presence. We had been truthful with each other, and because of that, Christ's presence seemed palpable.

"So when I travel around and people want to debate who Jesus was . . ." I asked again.

"Just smile," Billy said—and then he smiled at me, showing me how to do it. Then after a few moments of silence he said, "Were you teaching the Dalai Lama and Mother Teresa when you met and talked with them?" Billy Graham asked.

"Teaching?" I asked. "No—I just listened. Unless they talked to me like you—I just listened."

Again there were a few moments of silence as I wondered why he asked me if I was teaching the Dalai Lama and Mother Teresa when I met them.

"Should we pray?" Billy asked.

"What?" I asked. Because I thought he'd said *pray,* but I wasn't sure . . .

"Do you want to pray?" he repeated.

"Yes," I replied.

"Dear Father," Billy said as we bowed our heads, "help us to know your will. Teach us . . ."

Then I started thinking *I have to try and remember all of what he's saying so I can write about it.* But as I tried to remember with my mind what he was saying I could feel that I was losing the heart of what he said, so I quickly decided that it was more important to be present with the prayer than to commit it to memory.

". . . Jesus went to a lot of places and did a lot of things . . ." Billy said, and as I let those words find their place, I felt a kinship and similarity between Jesus' life and mine. We had both traveled a lot, sought a deeper relationship with God, and met lots of people.

"Bless this man with your companionship and bless me . . ." Billy said ending the prayer, ". . . because I need it also."

Billy and I looked at each other as the fireplace blazed in the background. We were in a deeply spiritual and yet simple place together.

"I almost didn't make it," I said while looking into Billy Graham's eyes. He looked back and smiled—the flames, a dancing combination of light and dark, reflected in his glasses. I thought he knew what I was talking about without me having to explain. How years ago, I had been caught in a hell of a life; fashioned out of the deaths of those I loved, together with the loss, the depression, the despair, and eventual desperate agony of my soul wanting to die one way or another. I had died all right, but not in a way I had ever imagined . . .

I searched his eyes—did he know what I was *really* saying?

He just smiled, as if to say, "I told you *I'm just a simple farm boy.*" Then Gigi came back into the house with Ruth, Jane, and Jane's mother.

"I'm tired," Billy said. "I'm going to bed."

He struggled to get up from his chair. Gigi went over and lifted him up by his right arm. I followed her and grabbed his left arm.

"I can do it," he insisted. I let go, and he slowly pushed himself up. I returned to my chair and sat down. As Billy Graham walked toward his room, he turned toward me and said, "Thank you for sharing your story."

✣ 92
BEYOND WORDS

ST. BENEDICT'S MONASTERY

The retreat was over, but before I left, I stopped in the monastery bookstore and looked for a few gifts. Monk Theophane was there, and I noticed that, as always, he ran the bookstore without keeping track of what books or how many were sold. He never handled the money either, because over on a corner table was a cigar box with a note that read *Drop Money Here.*

"Here's the best book in the bookstore," he said, taking me to a stack of books. "And this book over here is a brilliant book about economics. And this book over here . . ." he said enthusiastically.

"I can't afford all these books," I said. "I'm a poor author."

"Well," he said, "if you can't afford a book—*just steal it!*"

I looked at him and rolled my eyes.

"*Really!*" he said, "*I'm not kidding—steal it! One book isn't going to break the monastery.*"

Suddenly, Monk Theophane's body stiffened, and a pained look appeared on his face.

"Are you okay?" I asked.

"It's just my sciatica," he said, as he leaned gingerly against a table of books. Suddenly, I was reminded that he wasn't young—at least his body wasn't; *he was an old man.* But I swear there was part of him that only yesterday had been playing stickball in the street, and even now was no older than the day he was born.

"You know," he said, still cringing from the pain, "I'm a poor author too."

"You are?" I asked.

"You haven't seen my book!?" Monk Theophane said with mock astonishment. "Come this way."

We walked over to a table, and sure enough there was a stack of books titled *Tales of the Magic Monastery* by Theophane the Monk.

"If you read my book," he said, waving a copy in my face, "you won't need to read the Bible!"

I caught a ride to the Denver airport with a Baptist minister named Cindy. Women ministers are rare among Baptists and nonexistent among Catholics. Just a few days earlier, President Jimmy Carter had severed his ties to the Southern Baptist convention due to their new creed, which said that women should not be ministers and that ministers are to be the main interpreters of the Bible.

Cindy and I took the long route to Denver, through the Rocky Mountains and Independence Pass. It was a perfect ending to our retreat, and as we spoke about the importance of our spiritual lives, the mountains continually reminded us of our insignificance—not our insignificance before God, but the insignificance of our "self-importance." Jesus said, "Whoever loses his life for me will save it" (Luke 9:24, NIV), and now that there was less of "me," the meaning of Monk Theophane's words "my name used to be 'me' but now it is 'you'" became even clearer.

As I looked at the mountains and trees with eyes born again, I saw only mountain, only tree. There seemed to be no "me" between the mountain and my experience. There was less of "I'm thinking of that mountain," and more of *just mountain.* Although I knew the mountains were outside me, in some way they were now inside. Is it possible for my heart to be big enough to accommodate the mountains of Colorado? The monks, the land, the retreat guides, and my fellow retreat brothers and sisters, and of course Sarah, have all become part of me now. In some strange way my spiritual wound had been "that they hadn't been part of me," that they were "outside" me. But now I had developed a relationship with each of them—a relationship that began "inside" with no outside.

When Jesus was crucified, it was so he could open his heart to everything until nothing remained without. Open to the tax collector, prostitute, priest, and Pharisee. Encompassing the heavens and the earth, the desert and the city, the waters and the land—and even our soul's alienation from itself. Jesus' separateness was crucified upon a heart that knew a deeper truth. Finally, the day came when the whole world collapsed into his heart and uttering a final cry, his heart fell into humanity—touching each of us— past, present, and future—in ways beyond words.

INDEX

✢

Einstein, Albert, 244
Elliott, W. J.
  attitudes of, toward Catholic Church,
    158–59
  deaths of parents of, 1–2, 8, 371
  despair, depression, and doubts of, 4–5,
    95, 120–21, 296, 395–97
  dialogue of, with others on his status as
    Christian, 260–62, 280–83, 309–12
  dreams of, 3–4, 245–47
  encounter of, with police, 397–99
  experiences of, of God and Jesus, 5–7,
    49–50, 265, 276, 284–85, 306, 312,
    342–43, 370–73, 387–88, 395–97,
    399, 408
  financial problems of, 9–10, 120–21,
    219–21
  maturing relationship of, with Jesus,
    286, 295
  Mort's grant for, 219–21
Enlightenment, 179
Evangelists, 9, 259
  J. Falwell, 95–105
  T. D. Jakes, 279–80
  M. Lucado, 266–67
  J. McDowell, 267–74
  J. I. Packer, 328–39
  L. Palau, 146–57
  C. Swindol, 276–79
  R. Zacharias, 24–32
Evil, 69

Fables, 18–19
Failure, 289
Faith, 299
  author's, 87, 278–79
  beliefs versus, 155–56, 273, 335–36
  particularity of, 15
Falwell, Jerry, 66, 95–105
  author's meeting with, 95–96, 97
  author's search for, 81–84
  author's waiting for, 86–87
  on Christianity, 99–100, 101
  M. Fox on, 166, 167
  on God, 103–5
  on gospels, 100–101
  on Jesus, 97–100, 101, 102–3
  on prayer, 102
  prayer with, 105–8
  on sin and pride, 103
  Thomas Road Baptist Church of,
    84–86, 96

Fear, 5, 39, 356–57
  love versus, 147
  M. Williamson on sin and, 243
Feminine, 179–80
  M. Woodman on Jesus and the, 314,
    317, 318, 319
Forgiveness, 7, 45
Fox, Matthew, 158–70
  on Christianity today, 169
  on God, 165
  on gospels, 162–63
  on Jesus, 159–62, 166–70
  on religious beliefs, 165–66
Francis of Assisi, 169–70
Fundamentalist Christians, 58, 65, 194,
    365
  M. Fox on, 161
  N. D. Klotz on, 232
Funk, Robert, 127

Galileans, 74
Gandhi, Mahatma, 22, 28, 60, 162, 168,
    254
Garden of Gethsemane, 141, 185–87, 396
Genesis, Book of, 63
  as myth or literal truth, 362
Gnostics, 177, 202, 226, 287, 345
God. See also Holy Spirit; Kingdom of
    God/Kingdom of Heaven
  T. Bielecki on, 366
  M. Borg on, 128–30, 137–38
  D. Chopra on human projections and
    concepts of, 62–64
  as explorable, 218, 281
  J. Falwell on, 103–5
  focus on Jesus versus on, 42
  Jesus on humans as, 151–52
  N. D. Klotz on unity with, 228–29
  love and, 218, 219, 261–62, 296–97,
    366, 388
  many names of, 236–37
  respect for, 79–80
  Shekinah, 63 n.
  Son of (see Son of God, Jesus as)
  Spirit of, 56–57
  word of (see Word of God)
God's presence, author's experience of,
    5–7, 49–50, 370–73, 387–88
Good Samaritan, parable of, 77, 164, 262
Gospels, accuracy and authorship of. See
    also names of individual gospels, e.g.
    Matthew, Gospel of

M. Williamson on Jesus' teaching of, 244

Lucado, Max, 265, 266–67

Luke, Gospel of, 18, 19, 23, 68, 125, 130–31, 199, 200, 201, 208, 214, 375

McCartney, Bill, 283–84

McDowell, Josh, 267–74
on beliefs versus relationship with God, 273
on Jesus, 268, 270–75
on mysticism, 273
on other religions, 270–71
on overcoming human self-centeredness, 268–69

Mack, Burton, 127

McNamara, William, Father, 359

Mandaeans, 231

Mark, Gospel of, 18, 19, 23, 68, 123, 125–26, 199, 200, 205, 214

Marriage of Jesus. See Intimate relations/marriage of Jesus

Mar Saba monastery, 144–46

Mary, mother of Jesus, 59, 73, 123. See also Virgin birth

Mary Magdalene, 44, 61, 123, 191, 240
as wife of Jesus, 72–73

Masculine and masculinity, 317

Matthew, Gospel of, 18, 19, 23, 68, 125, 130–31, 199, 200, 208, 214, 275, 291, 375, 377, 389

Meal practice, Jesus', 139

Meditation, 299, 394

Meier, John, 343–55
on gospels, 346–48
on Jesus, 345–46, 348–55

Menninger, William, 339

Merton, Thomas, 337

Messiah, Jesus as, 39, 123–24
N. D. Klotz on, 231

Messiah, Jews' rejection of Jesus as
T. Bielecki on, 363
M. Borg on, 135–36
D. Chopra on, 60
D. Crossan on, 24
J. Falwell on, 100
H. Kushner on, 92
J. McDowell on, 271–72
J. Meier on, 348–49
J. Packer on, 337
L. Palau on, 153

E. P. Sanders on, 208–9

Z. Schachter-Shalomi on, 192–93

M. Williamson on, 241

N. T. Wright on, 378–79

Midrash, 67, 76

Miracles, 2

Mission of Jesus
M. Borg on, 131–32
J. McDowell on, 268
J. Meier on, 345–46
E. P. Sanders on, 209–10

Montreat, North Carolina, author's visits to, 48–54, 255–59, 307–12, 395–97, 399–406

Morrissey, Mary, 38–48
on Christianity, 41–42
on forgiveness, 45
on gospels, 43–44, 46
on Jesus, 39–40, 41–46, 48
on learning to love, 40–41
on original sin, 46–48
work of, 38–39

Moses, 191–92

Moses, Book of, 62, 63

Mother Teresa, seeking and meeting, 33–37

Mount of Olives, visit to, 141

Muslims, 27–28

Mystic, 9, 257–58, 259
T. Bielecki as, 359–68
A. Harvey as, 173–84
Jesus as, 123
T. Keating as, 388–95
N. D. Klotz as, 222–35
M. Williamson as, 237–44

Mysticism
beliefs and, A. Harvey on, 176
Christian, T. Bielecki on, 364–65
defined, 257
B. Long on, 258–59
J. McDowell on, 273
M. Morrissey on, 43
J. Packer on, 336–37
J. S. Spong on, 78–79
N. T. Wright on, 384–85
R. Zacharias on, 30–31

Myth, 75, 290, 362

Nature and experience of the Sacred, 137–38

Nicene Creed, 160, 227

Nicodemus, 222